VARSHA PANDYA

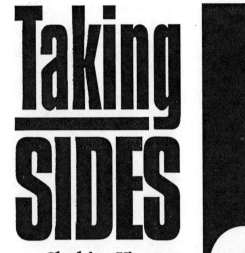

Taking SIDES

Clashing Views on Controversial Issues in Family and Personal Relationships

Third Edition

Edited, Selected, and with Introductions by

Gloria W. Bird
Virginia Polytechnic Institute and State University

and

Michael J. Sporakowski
Virginia Polytechnic Institute and State University

Dushkin Publishing Group/Brown & Benchmark Publishers
A Times Mirror Higher Education Group Company

To my parents, Vincent B. and Marjorie J. Wanager, whose acceptance of four children with decidedly clashing views has always amazed and inspired me (G. W. B.)
To Walter A. Garrett, the consummate facilitator of clashing views on controversial issues (M. J. S.)

Photo Acknowledgments

Part 1   NYT Pictures/Sara Krulwich
Part 2   Marcuss Oslander
Part 3   UN Photo 140732/L. Barnes
Part 4   DPG/B&B

Cover Art Acknowledgment

Charles Vitelli

Manufactured in the United States of America

Third Edition

10 9 8 7 6 5 4 3 2 1

Library of Congress Cataloging-in-Publication Data

Main entry under title:
  Taking sides: clashing views on controversial issues in family and personal relationships/edited, selected, and with introductions by Gloria W. Bird and Michael J. Sporakowski.—3rd ed.
    Includes bibliographical references and index.
    1. Family—United States. 2. Interpersonal relations. I. Bird, Gloria W., *comp.* II. Sporakowski, Michael J., *comp.*

306.85'973
96-85806

0-697-35715-5

 Printed on Recycled Paper

PREFACE

This text contains 34 selections, arranged in *pro* and *con* pairs, that address 17 controversial issues relating to family and personal relationships. Each of the issues is expressed in terms of a single question in order to draw the lines of debate more clearly. The articles selected for inclusion in this volume introduce recent empirical research in the field of marriage and family studies, and in many cases the authors of the selections are well known for making contributions to research, theory, or critical thinking in the area of focus.

Today, approximately 90 percent of individuals in the United States either are married or will eventually marry. Most of them, as well as those who do not marry, will interact daily for much of their lives with the members of their families of origin. It is within the family that people gain many of their insights into the nature and context of personal relationships—what a relationship is, how it works, and the range of appropriate and inappropriate behavior. But family and personal relationships are inevitably influenced by the larger social context in which they occur. The social context impinges on individual and family choices and the freedom to exercise such choices. Throughout this book you will find essays and reports that will challenge you to think about personal and family issues.

Plan of the book   This book is primarily designed for courses in marriage and the family, and the issues are such that they can be easily incorporated into any marriage and family course regardless of organization or emphasis. The selections were gathered from a variety of sources—books, journals, magazines—and were chosen for their usefulness in defending a position and for their accessibility to students.

The issues in this volume are self-contained: Each issue has an issue *introduction* that sets the stage for the debate as it is argued in the YES and NO selections. And each issue concludes with a *postscript* that makes some final observations about the selections, points the way to other questions related to the issue, and offers suggestions for further reading on the issue. For many issues, we have provided Internet site addresses (URLs) that should prove useful and informative. The introductions and postscripts do not preempt what is the reader's own task: to achieve a critical and informed view of the issues at stake.

As you read an issue and form your own opinion, you should not feel confined to adopt one or the other of the positions presented. Some readers may see important points on both sides of an issue and may construct for themselves a new and creative approach. Such an approach might incorporate the best of both sides, or it might provide an entirely new vantage point for understanding.

At the back of the book is a listing of all the *contributors to this volume*, which will give you additional information on the scholars, practitioners, and social critics whose views are debated here.

Changes to this edition   This edition represents a considerable revision. Part 2, Challenges to Successful Relationships, and Part 4, Relational Conflict and Dissolution, are new. There are 7 completely new issues: *Are American Families in Decline?* (Issue 1); *Are Stepfamilies Inherently Problematic?* (Issue 3); *Is Intimate Attachment the Key to Successful Relationships?* (Issue 5); *Do Men and Women Speak Different Languages?* (Issue 6); *Are Women's Lives More Stressful Than Men's?* (Issue 7); *Have Men Lost Their Sense of Fatherhood?* (Issue 9); and *Is There a Double Standard for Marital Violence?* (Issue 15). In addition, for Issue 8 on the division of family work, the question has been recast and a new reading has been added to provide a new focus for the issue. In all, there are 15 new selections.

A word to the instructor   An *Instructor's Manual With Test Questions* (multiple-choice and essay) is available through the publisher for the instructor using *Taking Sides* in the classroom. A general guidebook, *Using Taking Sides in the Classroom*, which discusses methods and techniques for integrating the pro-con approach into any classroom setting, is also available.

Acknowledgments   In working on this revision, we received helpful comments and suggestions from the many users of *Taking Sides* across the United States and Canada. We particularly wish to thank those who responded with specific suggestions for the third edition:

Ann M. Beutel
University of Minnesota

Susan Coady
Ohio State University

Roberta Coles
Marquette University

Katherine Covell
University College of Cape
   Breton

Mary Kirby Diaz
State University of New York
   at Farmingdale

Kenneth Hardy
Syracuse University

Clarence Hibbs
Pepperdine University

Nan Hornberger
Modesto Junior College

Diane W. Lindley
University of Mississippi

Joan Metz
St. Joseph's College

Richard Millikin
Mississippi University for
   Women

Robert Penton
McMurry University

Edward J. Steffes
Salisbury State University

Cynthia L. Sutton
Thiel College

Edward Stevens
Regis College

We are grateful as well to David Dean, list manager for the Taking Sides series, whose gentle reminders kept this project on task and on target, and to David Brackley, developmental editor, for keeping mistakes to a minimum. And finally, to our families we extend a special thanks for their patience and support.

Gloria W. Bird
Virginia Polytechnic Institute and State University

Michael J. Sporakowski
Virginia Polytechnic Institute and State University

CONTENTS IN BRIEF

CONTENTS

David Popenoe, dean of the College of Arts and Sciences at Rutgers University, argues that the American family has been in a serious decline for the past three decades. He claims that an inward focus on individualism has put children in families at risk. Arlene S. Skolnick, research psychologist in the Institute of Human Development at the University of California, Berkeley, counters that family bashing serves no good purpose. She faults pronouncers of family decline for ignoring recent trends, offering few solutions, and placing blame on families for what she believes are really societal problems.

Freelance writer Barbara Dafoe Whitehead concludes that former vice president Dan Quayle was correct in advocating the two-parent family as best for children. Psychologist June Stephenson argues that a variety of family forms, including single-parent families, can produce children who are as well-adjusted as or better adjusted than those who are reared by two parents.

David Popenoe, dean of the College of Arts and Sciences at Rutgers University, argues that stepfamilies are biologically and culturally inferior to intact and single-parent families for raising children, and he recommends that every effort be made to halt their growth. Psychologist Lawrence A. Kurdek characterizes stepfamilies as a natural outgrowth of societal change and states that most stepparents and stepchildren are coping successfully.

Andrew Sullivan, former editor of *The New Republic,* proposes that allowing gay couples to marry would give them many social and legal advantages. Gay rights activist Paula L. Ettelbrick argues that marriage would further constrain lesbians and gay men and make it more difficult for them to validate relationships that do not include marriage.

Susan Johnson, director of the Marital and Family Clinic at Ottawa Civic Hospital, and Hara Estroff Marano, editor of *Psychology Today,* argue that couples often break up because they fail to form an emotionally intimate and secure attachment to each other. Clinical psychologist Geraldine K. Piorkowski maintains that couples in satisfying relationships need to maintain some distance from each other.

Robert Bly, a leader of workshops on men's issues, and professor of sociolinguistics Deborah Tannen team up for a dialogue in which they propose that conversational differences exist between men and women. Professor of psychology Mary Crawford argues that gendered talking styles are media hype, the result of flawed scholarship and popular opinion.

Jeff Grabmeier, managing editor of research news at Ohio State University, makes the case that in comparison to men, women experience more distress, less happiness, and, as a result, a poorer quality of life. Warren Farrell, a leader of workshops on men's issues, argues that men suffer greater life stress and, as a consequence, have a significantly shorter life expectancy than women.

Bickley Townsend and Kathleen O'Neil, both with the Roper Organization, argue that the division of family work is inequitable and that women are becoming increasingly vocal about the need for change. Joseph H. Pleck, the Luce Professor of Families, Change, and Society at Wheaton College in Norton, Massachusetts, states that significant numbers of men have substantially increased their involvement in family roles but are given neither credit nor respect for their efforts.

David Blankenhorn, chair of the National Fatherhood Initiative, argues that America is becoming a fatherless society because increasing numbers of men are refusing to face the responsibility of caring for their own children. Sociologists Haya Stier and Marta Tienda maintain that fathers are not irresponsible scoundrels who have retreated from their family ties.

Denise Schipani, a writer who publishes frequently on women's and family issues, portrays mothers as the primary roadblock to fathers' active participation in childrearing. Brent A. McBride, professor of human development and family studies, argues that fathers' parental involvement is strongly linked to their own lack of knowledge and experience.

Felice N. Schwartz, president and founder of Catalyst, an organization that consults with corporations on the career and leadership development of women, argues that corporations would be wise to create two career paths within the organization, one for "career-primary" women and the other for "career-and-family" women. Journalists Barbara Ehrenreich and Deirdre English maintain that the "mommy track" notion ignores the real issue of why corporations continue to promote work policies that are incompatible with family life.

Sociology professor Monica B. Morris maintains that surrogate mothering represents a positive advance in reproductive technology. Richard John Neuhaus, director of the Rockford Institute Center on Religion and Society, denounces surrogate mothering as "a new form of trade in human beings."

P. Lindsay Chase-Lansdale, a fellow of developmental and family research at the Chapin Hall Center for Children, and professor of history Maris A. Vinovskis accuse public policy proponents of overlooking the benefits of marriage for pregnant adolescents. Human services educator and family researcher Naomi Farber argues that adolescent mothers express legitimate concerns about rushing into marriage solely because they are pregnant.

Freelance journalist Robin Warshaw argues that date rape is a real problem experienced by many women but reported by few. Author Katie Roiphe asserts that declarations of a date rape crisis are overblown.

Armin A. Brott, a freelance writer and lecturer on fatherhood and parenting
issues, argues that there is a double standard for domestic violence, with
men being ignored as real victims of spousal battering. Professor Russell P.
Dobash and his colleagues protest that the notion that women and men are
equally victimized by marital violence is greatly exaggerated.

Clinician and researcher Judith S. Wallerstein contends that children whose
parents divorce are at greater risk of health problems than are children whose
families are intact. Sociologists David H. Demo and Alan C. Acock argue that
much of the research showing children of divorce to be at greater risk is
theoretically or methodologically flawed.

Assistant professor Joyce A. Arditti makes the case that there are legitimate
reasons for some noncustodial fathers to refuse to provide financial support
for their children after divorce. Journalist Steven Waldman argues that fathers
should not desert their financial responsibilities to their children following
divorce.

INTRODUCTION

The Study of Marriage and the Family

Gloria W. Bird
Michael J. Sporakowski

Most of us were raised in families and have had the chance to observe a variety of marriages and families throughout our lives—kin, friends, neighbors, and so on. This is valuable life experience that generally serves us well as we relate to others. Attempts to take this personal life experience, however, and apply it to all families distorts the reality of what *most* marriages and families are like. Some of our own memories and hopes of "the way things ought to be" mesh with what we actually see around us, creating assumptions that are selective and generally inaccurate.

HISTORY OF FAMILY STUDIES

Serious study of marriage and family life began only relatively recently, although commentaries about marriage and family life can be found throughout much of recorded history in religious and historical literature. Family scientists now rely on a multitude of research methods, including mailed surveys, personal interviews, observational studies, and content analyses of historical documents, to produce accurate information about what families are like today and were like in the past. One of the more recent trends is the study of family history through the examination of personal journals and diaries, census reports, and other artifacts of earlier times. By studying these items, scientists have gained valuable insights into American family life from the early 1600s through the 1800s. These attempts to reconstruct an accurate historical record have resulted in a greater understanding of how American families have been living over the past three centuries.

In addition to family sociologists, psychologists, economists, lawyers, and physicians also have groups within their larger professional organizations that specialize in family research and counseling and other work with families. The contributions to the field by this varied group of professionals continue to be useful in theory development and practical application, as evidenced by some of the articles offered in such journals as *Journal of Marriage and the Family, American Journal of Family Therapy, Journal of Divorce and Remarriage, Family Law Quarterly,* and *Marriage and Family Review.*

Books addressing different aspects of marriage and family development both within the United States and internationally have been written by anthropologists, psychologists, sociologists, and historians alike. Examples of some early works include Edward Westermarck's *A History of Human Marriage* (1896) and G. E. Howard's *A History of Matrimonial Institutions* (1904). Both of these books looked at marriage from a longitudinal perspective; that is, they examine marital relations over a long period of time. Works by Bronislaw Malinowski and Margaret Mead provided insight into the cultural variations of marriages and families around the world. Havelock Ellis and Sigmund Freud provided not only cross-cultural but also intrapersonal perspectives on how families function.

Family-focused literature published during the 1920s, 1930s, and 1940s in the United States explored such topics as intermarriage, the effects of the Great Depression on families, and factors that promote marital success and failure. More recently, family demography, marriage and family therapy, family life education, and family research have been prominent topics in the literature.

FAMILY STUDIES AS A FORMAL DISCIPLINE

Since the beginning of the 1960s there has been a concerted effort to organize and synthesize each decade of research on marriage and family life. In 1964 Harold Christensen edited the *Handbook of Marriage and the Family*, which provided, among other things, a historical perspective on the evolution of the marriage and family field. More recently, the *Journal of Marriage and the Family* published three decade reviews (briefly discussed below) that examine what has occurred in the marriage and family field during the periods of 1960–1969, 1970–1979, and 1980–1989. And in 1987 Marvin Sussman and Suzanne Steinmetz edited the second edition of the *Handbook on Marriage and the Family*. All the chapters in this book were written by prominent scholars on their specialized areas of family studies.

Decade Reviews: 1970–1990

In the first decade review (1970), edited by Carl Broderick, the authors provided an overview of preselected, family-relevant topics. In the 1980 review, sociologist Felix Berardo introduced the volume by discussing Clark Vincent's 1966 opinion that the family acts as a sponge, adapting to what is going on in the larger society for the benefit of its members and mediating between individual family members and the larger society. Many of the topics covered in this second review, such as family violence, sex roles, family stress and coping, and nontraditional family forms, were relatively new to the family field but had been researched often in the 1970s. The third decade review (1990), edited by Alan Booth, begins with Berardo's commentary on trends in family research during the 1980s and suggestions for future research directions.

Notable Changes Since 1960

In the latest decade review the following changes should be noted: sex roles are now referred to as gender roles, reflecting recent changes in thinking and language; domestic violence, which had previously focused primarily on wife abuse, has been expanded to include the specific topic of child sexual abuse; racial and cultural family variations concentrate more specifically on black and Hispanic families; articles on divorce and remarriage are more numerous; and issues such as kinship, cross-societal research, family power, and family stress and coping have been integrated into other topic areas and are not presented separately. Topical additions to the 1990 review include religion and families, feminism, parental and nonparental child care, family policy, family economic stress, and family relationships in later life.

FAMILY STUDIES—AN EVOLVING DISCIPLINE

The National Council on Family Relations (NCFR) is the primary professional organization for researchers, educators, therapists, and others who study and provide services to families. It was organized in 1938 as an interdisciplinary professional association interested in family research, education, counseling, and social action. The NCFR continues to be vital today, providing a number of integrative programs, publications, and public policy actions for the benefit of families.

Sociologist Wesley R. Burr, in his 1982 NCFR presidential address, discussed the evolution of the study of the family as a profession, from the contributions of Ernest Groves, who was credited with teaching the first college-level course on marriage and the family in Boston in the 1930s, through the development and proliferation of graduate programs related to family, and, most recently, through the professional identity struggles the NCFR and related organizations have been experiencing. In his presentation, Burr defended the maturity of the field of study and suggested that it had met all of the criteria that would make it distinctive in the larger world of disciplines and professions. Although there is general agreement that the study of marriage and the family is indeed a discipline, the issue of what to call this discipline has not been resolved. Burr pushed very hard for the use of *famology* to describe the study of the family. Various groups within the NCFR have promoted various other names, including family studies and family science.

RECENT TRENDS IN AMERICAN FAMILY LIFE

Living Arrangements
Recent data attesting to the continuing demographic changes in American family life can be found in "The Future of Households," *American Demographics* (December 1993). The data show, for example, that more individuals are now postponing marriage until later in life, but cohabitation has increased among adults aged 21 to 35. There seems to be a need among these individuals for intimate relationships, but not necessarily within the bounds of marriage.

Also, more young adults aged 18 to 24 are choosing to live with their parents—an increase of over 25 percent since 1960. Some young people are finding that their jobs do not pay well enough to allow independent living arrangements and that parents may actually make good housemates. With the rising costs of higher education, some young adults are living with their parents and attending colleges and universities close to home.

Furthermore, census figures show an increase in the number of adults aged 25 to 34 who live with their parents. Some move in with their parents out of economic necessity after going through a divorce—sometimes accompanied by young children. Others are single people who, like younger adults, find that their paychecks are inadequate to meet their living expenses.

At the other end of the spectrum are couples who choose not to have children at all. According to the data, the number of childless couples has grown and will continue to grow into the next century. The majority of these couples will consist of aging baby boomers, although the growth will be partially offset by a smaller population of younger, childbearing couples.

Marriage and Divorce

The median age of marriage is now 26 years for men and 24 years for women. Postponement of marriage is related to other trends, such as the increasing number of people who are seeking advanced education and higher annual incomes. Many highly educated women are postponing marriage and, when they do marry, are becoming part of dual-career families. Many of these women are also delaying childbearing and having fewer children than other women. The average family today is smaller than ever before—less than two children per family.

Another trend that affects marriage and family life is the growing divorce rate, which remains high despite a recent leveling off in the late 1980s. Sociologists project that one-half to two-thirds of today's marriages will eventually end in divorce. One result of divorce is more single-parent families. This family type has increased by 36 percent since 1980, and women and children make up the vast majority of such families. Because women often have less education than their husbands and earn less money than men do, and because divorced fathers pay child support for an average of about two years before discontinuing payment, most single-parent families are at greater risk of economic hardship than are other families.

Single and Working Mothers

Today, unwed mothers are less disposed than were their counterparts in the 1970s to wed the fathers of their children. Many say that they would rather live as single parents than risk marriage and later divorce to men they describe as unprepared for marriage and family life. In single-parent households, where 26 percent of children under age 18 now reside, 39 percent live with a divorced parent (usually the mother) and 31 percent live with a parent who has never married (also usually the mother). Families headed by women who have never married increased 1,000 percent during the past two decades. The causes for this, and the consequences for individuals and for the entire social fabric, are areas of current inquiry and debate. (See several issues in this volume, for example!)

The majority of mothers today are employed outside the home. In fact, the largest increases in employed mothers have been among those families with preschool children. In addition to the increasing numbers of single-parent and dual-worker families, the high rate of divorce has led some social commentators to express special concern for the children in today's families and to question whether or not we as a society are doing enough to help families with children.

IMPLICATIONS OF CHANGE IN AMERICAN FAMILIES

Though it has become increasingly popular to discuss the "traditional" American family as being an endangered entity, the truth is that American families have been changing since the first settlers arrived on the shores of the New World. Unlike today, however, there used to be laws that clearly defined and enforced the roles of family members. Family matters were actually seen as community matters—the greater good outweighed individual needs and desires.

In the book *Habits of the Heart: Individualism and Commitment in American Life* (1985), sociologist Robert N. Bellah and his colleagues describe individuals today as caring less about community and family matters and as being more concerned with personal autonomy. The authors assert that because marriage and family life are now typically viewed as sources of emotional fulfillment rather than of instrumental need and moral obligation, marriages, families, and communities are in danger of becoming increasingly unstable. Bellah and his colleagues interviewed a number of people for their book and found that the interviewees tended to discuss their marriages in the context of how they were different from those of their parents. Those interviewed found that expressing intimacy, sharing feelings, and solving marital problems was much easier for them than they perceived it was for their parents. Yet, the overall assessment of the authors was one of caution about individual autonomy, fragile and vulnerable relationships, and a waning commitment to community.

An opposing view is offered by sociologist Francesca Cancian in *Love in America: Gender and Self-Development* (1987). Cancian traces the changing definitions of love across time in America and concludes that the current conception of love involves a "weness"—the expectation that individuals must be connected to others for maximum well-being. She also discusses ways that couples are bonded, providing research findings to support her thesis. Cancian contends that individualism and autonomy were ideals of the late 1970s and early 1980s that were never really reached. More recently, she has seen a movement toward commitment to relationships through marriage, kinship, friendship, and community.

Recent polls evidence the changes in how Americans view marriage and family life. They indicate that men are more committed than in the past to family roles and to women's needs in the workplace and that women are more willing to negotiate gender roles within the family. However, women report that they still feel stress because husbands do not share as much of the housework and child care as is needed (Virginia Slims/Roper, 1990). Polls also provide evidence of some stability in American family life. For example, most American families make major efforts to eat their evening meals together, and community volunteerism in the United States has become prominent (*The New York Times*/CBS News, 1991).

The two books and the polls we have mentioned are only a few examples of the many informational sources on the topic of American families that are published each year. Changing trends in marriage and family life have become points of contention among various private and public organizations and among the major political groups, and the ensuing debates are becoming increasingly bitter.

Those who seek a return to "true family values," for example, often characterize today's families as rootless, troubled, and dysfunctional. This group sometimes describes the parents within what they term "broken" or "unhealthy" families as selfish, undisciplined, and lacking in commitment, and sometimes even portray such family members as bereft of spiritual values. Others deplore this labeling of individuals and families as biased and unscientific and as based on nostalgic views of the stereotypical "traditional" family rather than on what family life was really like in the past. This camp argues for the importance of acknowledging the adaptive strengths of today's diverse family forms and for helping such families find the resources to cope with contemporary life.

CONTEMPORARY ISSUES IN MARRIAGE AND THE FAMILY

Sociologists, psychologists, historians, and other professionally trained students of family studies are becoming increasingly concerned with providing accurate accounts of what marriage and family life is like today as well as with giving accurate descriptions of families from a historical perspective. Each group necessarily proceeds from its own unique view of the world, and different groups provide different and sometimes contradictory answers to the same questions. In professional circles, as well as among the larger public audience, books, research studies, speeches, and other informational presentations are more often being debated.

The self-appointed family authority, typically with little or no formal training, who "tells it like it is," will find it increasingly difficult to find a believing audience. The family field is composed of individuals with various kinds of expertise and training; however, the vast majority of these diverse groups is interested in research-based conclusions that have application to "real-life families."

The issues in this book are now being discussed and debated among people considering the current state of marriage and the family. Some of the questions you may not have previously seen as having multiple sides. Part of your task is to critically examine your thinking about these issues in light of contemporary knowledge. Sometimes the readings will reinforce what you believe; other times you may find yourself rethinking your position; and sometimes you may wish to read more about a particular topic before you form your final opinion.

PART 1

Marriage and Family Life: Rethinking Traditional Assumptions

Traditional views of the family, as well as attitudes toward marriage itself, are changing. Many people, for example, consider the American family to be in decline. Others, such as gay men and lesbians, protest that the very institution of marriage detracts from the validity of alternative cohabitational lifestyles and that it cheats single individuals out of certain legal benefits. Now that marriage is no longer considered a prerequisite to childbearing, the structure of families is changing too. As the number of single-parent families has increased, the notion that the two-parent family is the best for children has come into question. Another increasingly common family form is the stepfamily, the benefits and drawbacks of which are also under debate. Many of the traditional assumptions concerning marriage and family life are challenged in this section.

- Are American Families in Decline?

- Is the Two-Parent Family Best?

- Are Stepfamilies Inherently Problematic?

- Should Gays and Lesbians Fight for
  the Right to Marry?

ISSUE 1

Are American Families in Decline?

YES: David Popenoe, from "American Family Decline, 1960–1990: A Review and Appraisal," *Journal of Marriage and the Family* (August 1993)

NO: Arlene S. Skolnick, from *Embattled Paradise: The American Family in an Age of Uncertainty* (Basic Books, 1991)

ISSUE SUMMARY

YES: David Popenoe, dean of the College of Arts and Sciences at Rutgers University, argues that the American family has been in a serious decline for the past three decades. He claims that an inward focus on individualism has put children in families at risk.

NO: Arlene S. Skolnick, research psychologist in the Institute of Human Development at the University of California, Berkeley, counters that family bashing serves no good purpose. She faults pronouncers of family decline for ignoring recent trends, offering few solutions, and placing blame on families for what she believes are really societal problems.

In the first chapter of her book *The Way We Never Were: American Families and the Nostalgia Trap* (Basic Books, 1992), family historian Stephanie Coontz tells of asking students in her course on family history to write down their ideas about the "traditional family." Many of the resulting descriptions are infused with nostalgic images of comforting extended families; responsible, available parents; respectful, helpful children; and loving, intimate marital partners. These visions are understandable, given the emphasis Americans place on close family relationships. But, Coontz warns, they are ideological images of perfect families that never really existed.

In her book, Coontz explores the realities of family life from colonial days through the 1990s. She notes that social analysts, religious leaders, and elected officials throughout history (in almost every decade) have fretted about "the American family." They typically declare the family an endangered institution, identify villains, and attempt to enact legislation to punish families that deviate from the ideologically "normal" American family.

In the following selection, David Popenoe acknowledges that we cannot recapture the stereotypical family of the 1950s, but he maintains that since 1960 American families have experienced a decline that can best be described as steep and serious. He reviews three decades of information collected by the U.S. Census Bureau and uses it to buttress his argument that American families have relinquished all but two essential societal functions—childrearing and the provision of companionship and affection to its members. The reason for the decline, Popenoe believes, is that people are less willing to invest time, money, and energy into developing and maintaining family relationships. Instead, people have chosen to invest in themselves. Popenoe claims that this individualistic approach to life has resulted in an American culture that places less value on family relationships and has eroded children's right to a protective, stable home life.

Arlene S. Skolnick does not agree with Popenoe's assessment. Although she admits that families are having some difficulty meeting their own as well as others' expectations for marriage and parenthood, Skolnick says that most people continue to believe in the benefits of family life. She cites research indicating that men and women confess increased anxiety over the many changes in families over the past three decades but still view families as the bedrock of America. Women and men also report investing much time and effort into establishing and maintaining family connections. Skolnik contends that people are aware of complexities of life in families today, and she advocates getting beyond the myths that constrain people's thinking about family well-being. The answer, she says, is in finding ways of coping with life in the present.

Is it true that some serious problems are confronting families in the 1990s? Should some recent family changes worry us? If the answer is yes, then which problems are the most pressing and what are the sources of those problems? Is the individual who fails to get an education, won't work, or neglects children at fault? Or are current concerns about American families really larger societal issues, such as the employment situation (e.g., more jobs require training beyond high school, fewer jobs pay enough to support a family, and jobs consume so much time and energy that there's little left for family)?

If problems in families originate with individuals, does that mean that efforts should be made to resocialize people? Should society educate people in family values such as educational attainment, community responsibility, and parental commitment? On the other hand, if family problems originate within the economic and social structures surrounding families, should government and business leaders be resocialized? If we value families and the individuals within families, should we be concerned if an employee's monthly paycheck is not enough to support a family, if health care benefits do not cover family medical needs, or if child care and elder care are not affordable?

As you read the following two selections, think about the opposing views presented. Which evidence do you find most compelling? Is one side more reflective of your views than the other? Does either selection cause you to rethink any of your ideas about families?

YES   David Popenoe

AMERICAN FAMILY DECLINE, 1960–1990: A REVIEW AND APPRAISAL

Family decline in America continues to be a debatable issue, especially in academia. Several scholars have recently written widely-distributed trade books reinforcing what has become the establishment position of many family researchers—that family decline is a "myth," and that "the family is not declining, it is just changing" (Coontz, 1992; Skolnick, 1991; Stacey, 1990)....

My view is just the opposite. Like the majority of Americans, I see the family as an institution in decline and believe that this should be a cause for alarm—especially as regards the consequences for children. ...

Families have lost functions, social power, and authority over their members. They have grown smaller in size, less stable, and shorter in life span. People have become less willing to invest time, money, and energy in family life, turning instead to investments in themselves.

Moreover, there has been a weakening of child-centeredness in American society and culture. Familism as a cultural value has diminished....

WHAT IS A "FAMILY"?

... I define the family as a relatively small domestic group of kin (or people in a kin-like relationship) consisting of at least one adult and one dependent person. This definition is meant to refer particularly to an intergenerational unit that includes (or once included) children, but handicapped and infirm adults, the elderly, and other dependents also qualify. And it is meant to include single-parent families, stepfamilies, nonmarried and homosexual couples, and all other family types in which dependents are involved....

Turning from the question of what a family is to what a family does, the domestic kin groups should be thought as of carrying out certain functions(or meeting certain needs) for society. These functions or needs, as spelled out in almost every textbook of marriage and the family, have traditionally included the following: procreation (reproduction) and the socialization of children; the provision to its members of care, affection, and companionship; economic cooperation (the sharing of economic resources, especially shelter, food, and clothing); and sexual regulation (so that sexual activity in a society is not completely permissive and people are made responsible for the consequences of their sexuality.)

Saying that the institution of the family is declining is to say that the domestic kin groups are weakening in carrying out these functions or meeting these societal needs....

AMERICAN FAMILY CHANGE, 1960–1990...

The Number of Children
... Since the late 1950s, childbearing among American women, both as an ideal and a practice, has rapidly lost popularity.... Because child postponement has become so extensive,... some demographers have predicted that between 20% and 25% of the most recent cohorts will remain completely childless, and that nearly 50% will either be childless or have only one child.... Although the childless estimate of 20% to 25% has recently been lowered to around 15% to 20%, it is clear that a substantial portion of young women today will reach the end of their childbearing years never having given birth (Bianchi, 1990; Ryder, 1990).

This change is connected with a dramatic, and probably historically unprecedented, decrease in positive feelings toward parenthood and motherhood.... In less than 2 decades, from 1962 to 1980, the proportion of American mothers who stated that "all couples should have children" declined by nearly half, from 84% to 43% (Sweet & Bumpass, 1987; Thornton, 1989).

...[C]hildren today make up a much smaller proportion of the American population than ever before (a situation that is accentuated by increased longevity).... [T]he continuing decline in the number of children has significant ramifications for the priority our society gives to children, and for the cultural attitudes we hold concerning the importance of children in the overall scheme of life.

Marital Roles
... Major elements of the traditional nuclear family have almost become a thing of the past. First, and in some ways foremost, the marital roles associated with the traditional nuclear family have altered. As a cultural ideal, the doctrine of separate spheres, in which adult women were expected to be full-time housewife-mothers while their husbands were the breadwinners, has virtually ended.... A recent survey found that some 79% of adult Americans agreed that "it takes two paychecks to support a family today." And only 27% favored a return to "at least one parent raising children full-time" (Mass Mutual American Family Values Study, 1989).

Today, mothers are in the labor market to almost the same extent as nonmothers, with the fastest increases occurring for mothers of young children....

Family Structure and Marital Dissolution
At the same time that our society has disclaimed the role of wives in the traditional nuclear family, it has also heavily discarded the basic structure of that family type—two natural parents who stay together for life....

One family type that has replaced the intact family of biological parents, and currently is the focus of much social research and public discussion, is the stepparent family. But the fastest growing new family type in recent years has been the single-parent family (almost 90% of which are headed by women)....

One of the main factors accounting for the increase in single-parent families is the growing incidence and acceptance of divorce, especially divorce involving children....

[T]he probability of dissolution of a first marriage contracted today [is] about 60% (Bumpass, 1990; Martin & Bumpass, 1989)....

The causes of the rising divorce rate in modern societies are, of course, multiple (Furstenberg, 1990; Kitson, Babri, & Roach, 1985; Phillips, 1988; White, 1990). They include growing affluence that weakens the family's traditional economic bond, higher psychological expectations for marriage today, secularization, and the stress of changing gender roles. To some extent, divorce feeds upon itself. With more divorce occurring, the more normal it becomes, with fewer negative sanctions to oppose it and more potential partners available. One of the significant changes of recent years is the rising acceptance of divorce, especially when children are involved. Divorces in which children are involved used to be in the category of the unthinkable. Today, children are only a minor inhibitor of divorce, although more so when the children are male than female (Heaton, 1990; Morgan, Lye, & Condran, 1988; Waite & Lillard, 1991)....

Another reason for the increase in single-parent families is that many more of today's families start out with just one parent; the children are born out-of-wedlock and the father is absent....

Clearly, then, family instability has come to be a dominant characteristic of our time. If childhood experiences and adult risks of marital disruption are taken into account, only a minority of children born today are likely to grow up in an intact, two-parent family, and also, as adults, to form and maintain such a family. And because the children of broken homes, compared to the children of intact families, have a much higher chance as adults of having unstable marriages of their own, the future in this regard does not look bright (McLanahan & Bumpass, 1988).

Marriage

A widespread retreat from marriage is another of the major family changes of our time (Espenshade, 1985a, 1985b)....
For females born in 1983,... the chances of ever marrying are calculated to be slightly less than 90% (Schoen, 1987; Schoen, Urton, Woodrow, & Baj, 1985). For certain segments of the population, the proportion expected eventually to marry is even lower: only about 80% for women with a college education, for example, and 75% for black women (Glick, 1984)....

The marriage rate is expected to drop further in the future....

The psychological character of the marital relationship has changed substantially over the years (Davis, 1985). Traditionally, marriage has been understood as a social obligation—an institution designed mainly for economic security and procreation. Today, marriage is understood mainly as a path toward self-fulfillment. One's own self-development is seen to require a significant other, and marital partners are picked primarily to be personal companions.... No longer comprising a set of norms and social obligations that are widely enforced, marriage today is a voluntary relationship that individuals can make and break at will. As one indicator of this shift, laws regulating marriage and divorce have become increasingly more lax (Glendon, 1989; Jacob, 1988; Sugarman & Kay, 1990).

Apart from the high rate of marital dissolution, there is growing evidence that the quality of married life in America has taken a turn for the worse. There has always been a strong relationship between being married and being relatively happy in life. But an analysis of survey data over the years between 1972 and 1989 indicates that this relationship is weakening. There is an increasing proportion of reportedly happy never-married men and younger never-married women, and a decreasing proportion of reportedly happy married women (Glenn, 1991; Glenn & Weaver, 1988; Lee, Seccombe, & Shehan, 1991). Thus to be happy, men may not need marriage as much as they once did, and fewer women are finding happiness through marriage.

Nonfamily Living
... Along with the high divorce rate and the residential independence of the elderly, early home-leaving is a major factor that lies behind the tremendous increase in nonfamily households and nonfamily living. . . .

Also on the rise has been nonmarital cohabitation, or unmarried couples of the opposite sex living together. In part, the declining marriage rate has been offset by the increasing cohabitation rate (Bumpass, Sweet, & Cherlin, 1991). While nonmarital couples still make up only a small proportion of all households (3.1% in 1990), their numbers are growing. . . .

There is evidence that life for young adults in a nonfamily household may become a self-fulfilling prophecy; not only does it reflect a flight from family life but it may actually promote such a flight. Especially for young women,

it has been found that living away from home prior to marriage changes attitudes and plans away from family and toward individual concerns (Waite, Goldscheider, & Witsberger, 1986). Also, living independently may make it more difficult, when marriage finally does take place, to shift from purely individual concerns to a concern for the needs and desires of other family members, especially children (Rossi, 1980). . . .

There is also a growing body of evidence that premarital cohabitation is associated with proneness for divorce (Booth & Johnson, 1988; DeMaris & Rao, 1992; Thompson & Colella, 1992), although the effect may be declining with time (Schoen, 1992). Cohabitation does not seem to serve very well the function of a trial marriage, or of a system that leads to stronger marriages through weeding out those who find that, after living together, they are unsuitable for each other. More likely, a lack of commitment at the beginning may signal a lack of commitment at the end. . . .

FAMILY CHANGE AS FAMILY DECLINE

To the average American, [many of] the family trends of the last 30 years, summarized above, clearly signal the widespread decline of the institution of the family. . . .

Despite such seemingly inexorable trends, it has taken a while for many family scholars to comprehend both the magnitude and the negative consequences of the changes that have occurred. At first, there was widespread resistance to the suggestion that the family was weakening or in any kind of trouble. . . .

With the full realization of what has actually happened to the family over the past 30 years now becoming clear, ... a change of mind among family scholars has become commonplace. ...

In 1987, Norval Glenn, then editor of the influential *Journal of Family Issues,* asked a group of 18 prominent family sociologists to put in writing how they felt about what was happening to the family in America (Glenn, 1987). Most were scholars who for years had sought to withhold their personal values and beliefs in the interest of scholarly objectivity. Nine of the scholars were "concerned" about family change in America, while only three were "sanguine." ... The main focus of their concern, incidentally, was children.

As noted at the outset of the present article, however, there is still a reluctance among many scholars of the family to admit that the family is declining. The preferred term is *change,* leading to *diversity.* This may seem to be a mere terminological quibble, but it reflects deep ideological differences.

The problem is not only that the family as an institution has declined, but also that a specific family form —the traditional nuclear family—has declined. And therein lies the basis for much ideological conflict. ... Today, those who believe in less male dominance and greater equality for women—and that includes most academics and other intellectuals, including myself—share the views of the women's movement in favoring an egalitarian family form, with substantial economic independence for wives. From this perspective, the movement away from the traditional nuclear family is regarded as progress, not decline.

Speaking of family decline under these ideological circumstances, therefore, is seen to be implicitly favoring a dis-credited family form, one that oppresses women. Indeed, the term *decline* has been used most forcefully by those conservatives who tend to view all recent family change as negative, and who have issued a clarion call for a return to the traditional nuclear family (Dobson & Bauer, 1990). But properly used, the term *decline* should not carry such ideological baggage. ...

For me, the term decline is important because it provides a "best fit" for many of the changes that have taken place. These changes, in my view, clearly indicate that the family as an institution has weakened. A main cause of this weakening may or may not be the shift of the family away from its traditional nuclear form; that is something requiring further investigation. Those who believe that the family has not declined, on the other hand, must logically hold one of two positions—either that the family has strengthened, or that its institutional power within society has remained unchanged. I believe that one is very hard put, indeed, to find supporting evidence for either of these two positions.

Let us review the evidence supporting the idea of family decline, or weakening. The evidence can be amassed in three broad areas—demographic, institutional, and cultural. In the course of this review I hope that the reader will suspend, for the moment, the automatic reaction of associating decline only with that which is negative. Some of the following aspects of family decline, as discussed below, certainly can be considered beneficial, or positive.

Demographic
Family groups have declined as a demographic reality. They have decreased in size and become a smaller percentage of all households; they survive as groups for

a shorter period of time and they incorporate a smaller percentage of the average person's life course. Family groups are being replaced in people's lives by nonfamily groups—people living alone, without children, with an unrelated individual, in an institution, and so forth....

Institutional

There are three key dimensions to the strength of an institution: the institution's cohesion or the hold which it has over its members, how well it performs its functions, and the power it has in society relative to other institutions. The evidence suggests that the family as an institution has weakened in each of these respects.

First, individual family members have become more autonomous and less bound by the group; the group as a whole, therefore, has become less cohesive....

With more women in the labor market, for example, the economic interdependence between husbands and wives has been declining. Wives are less dependent on husbands for economic support; more are able, if they so desire, to go it alone. This means that wives are less likely to stay in bad marriages for economic reasons.... By the same token, if a wife has economic independence (for example, through state welfare support), it is easier for a husband to abandon her if he so chooses. However one looks at it, and unfortunate though it may be, the decline of economic interdependence between husband and wife (primarily the economic dependence of the wife) appears to have led, in the aggregate, to weaker marital units as measured by higher rates of divorce and separation (for a contradictory view, see Greenstein, 1990.)

As the marital tie has weakened in many families, so also has the tie between parents and children. A large part of the history of childhood and adolescence in the twentieth century is the decline of parental influence and authority, and the growth in importance of both the peer group and the mass media (Hawes & Hiner, 1985; Modell, 1989).... Similarly, there is much less influence today of the elderly over their own children....

The second dimension of family institutional decline is that the family is less able—and/or less willing—to carry out its traditional social functions. This is, in part, because it has become a less cohesive unit. The main family functions in recent times have been the procreation and socialization of children, the provision to its members of affection and companionship, sexual regulation, and economic cooperation. With a birthrate that is below the replacement level, it is demonstrably the case that the family has weakened in carrying out the function of procreation. A strong case can also be made that the family has weakened in conducting the function of child socialization....

By almost everyone's reckoning, marriage today is a more fragile institution than ever before precisely because it is based mainly on the provision of affection and companionship. When these attributes are not provided, the marriage often dissolves. The chances of that happening today are near a record high.

A decline of the family regulation of sexual behavior is one of the hallmarks of the past 30 years (D'Emilio & Freedman, 1988). Against most parents' wishes, young people have increasingly engaged in premarital sex, at ever younger ages. And against virtually all spousal wishes, the amount of sexual infidelity among married couples has seemingly increased....

Finally, the function of the family in economic cooperation has diminished substantially.... The family is less a pooled bundle of economic resources, and more a business partnership between two adults (and one which, in most states, can unilaterally be broken at any time.) Witness, for example, the decline of joint checking accounts and the rise of prenuptial agreements....

The third dimension of family institutional decline is the loss of power to other institutional groups. In recent centuries, with the decline of agriculture and the rise of industry, the family has lost power to the workplace and, with the rise of mandatory formal education, it has lost power to the school. the largest beneficiary of the transfer of power out of the family in recent years has been the state. State agencies increasingly have the family under surveillance, seeking compliance for increasingly restrictive state laws covering such issues as child abuse and neglect, wife abuse, tax payments, and property maintenance (Lasch, 1977; Peden & Glahe, 1986)....

Cultural

Family decline has also occurred in the sense that familism as a cultural value has weakened in favor of such values as self-fulfillment and egalitarianism (Bellah, Madsen, Sullivan, Swidler, & Tipton, 1985; Lasch, 1978; Veroff et al., 1981)....
Familism refers to the belief in a strong sense of family identification and loyalty, mutual assistance among family members, a concern for the perpetuation of the family unit, and the subordination of the interests and personality of individual family members to the interests and welfare of the family group.

It is true that most Americans still loudly proclaim family values, and there is no reason to question their sincerity about this. The family ideal is still out there. Yet apart from the ideal, the value of family has steadily been chipped away. The percentage of Americans who believe that "the family should stay together for the sake of the children" has declined precipitously, for example, as noted above. And fewer Americans believe that it is important to have children, to be married if you do, or even to be married, period....

EVALUATING FAMILY DECLINE

The net result—or bottom line—of each of these trends is, I submit, that Americans today are less willing than ever before to invest time, money, and energy in family life (Goode, 1984). Most still want to marry and most still want children, but they are turning more to other groups and activities, and are investing much more in themselves....

The increase in individual rights and opportunities is, of course, one of the great achievements of the modern era. No one wants to go back to the days of the stronger family when the husband owned his wife and could do virtually anything he wanted to her short of murder, when the parents were the sole custodians of their children and could treat them as they wished, when the social status of the family you were born into heavily determined your social status for life, and when the psychosocial interior of the family was often so intense that it was like living in a cocoon....

Many scholars have noted that the institution of the family could be said to have been in decline since the beginning of mankind. And people of almost every era seem to have bemoaned the loss of the family, even suggesting its imminent demise (Popenoe, 1988). Yet we, as human beings, have made some progress over the centuries. Why, therefore, should we be unduly alarmed about the family decline of our generation? This question is a good one and demands an answer.

... Once the only social institution in existence, the family over time has lost functions to such institutions as organized religion, education, work, and government (Lenski & Lenski, 1987).... Education and work are the latest functions to be split off from the family unit, the split having occurred for the most part over the past two centuries.... From its earliest incarnation as a multifunctional unit, the streamlined family of today is left with just two principal functions: childrearing, and the provision to its members of affection and companionship. Both family functions have become greatly magnified over the years....

[W]hat kind of family decline is underway today that we should be concerned about? There are two dimensions of today's family decline that make it both unique and alarming. The first is that it is not the extended family that is breaking up but the nuclear family. The nuclear family can be thought of as the last vestige of the traditional family unit; all other adult members have been stripped away, leaving but two—the husband and wife. The nuclear unit—man, woman, and child—is called that for good reason: It is the fundamental and most basic unit of the family. Breaking up the nucleus of anything is a serious matter.

The second dimension of real concern regards what has been happening to the two principal functions—childrearing, and the provision to its members of af-

fection and companionship—with which the family has been left. It is not difficult to argue that the functions that have already been taken from the family—government, formal education, and so on—can in fact be better performed by other institutions. It is far more debatable, however, whether the same applies to child-rearing and the provision of affection and companionship. there is strong reason to believe, in fact, that the family is by far the best institution to carry out these functions, and that insofar as these functions are shifted to other institutions, they will not be carried out as well....

CONCLUSION

My argument, in summary, is that the family decline of the past three decades is something special—very special. It is "end-of-the-line" family decline. Historically, the family has been stripped down to its bare essentials—just two adults and two main functions. The weakening of this unit is much more problematic than any prior family change. People today, most of all children, dearly want families in their lives. They long for that special, and hopefully life-long, social and emotional bond that family membership brings. Adults can perhaps live much of their lives, with some success, apart from families. The problem is that children, if we wish them to become successful adults, cannot.

REFERENCES

Bellah, R. N., Madsen, R., Sullivan, W. M., Swidler, A., & Tipton, S. M. (1985). *Habits of the heart: Individualism and commitment in American life.* Berkeley: University of California Press.

Bianchi, S. M. (1990). America's children: Mixed prospects. *Population Bulletin, 45,* 1–43.

Booth, A., & Johnson, D. (1988). Premarital cohabitation and marital success. *Journal of Family Issues, 9*, 255–272.

Bumpass, L. L. (1990). What's happening to the family? Interactions between demographic and institutional change. *Demography, 27*, 483–498.

Bumpass, L. L., Sweet, J. A., & Cherlin, A. (1991). The role of cohabitation in declining marriage rates. *Journal of Marriage and the Family, 53*, 913–927.

Coontz, S. (1992). *The way we never were.* New York: Basic Books.

Davis, K. (Ed.) (1985). *Contemporary marriage: Comparative perspectives on a changing institution.* New York: Russell Sage Foundation.

D'Emilio, J., & Freedman, E. B. (1988). *Intimate matters: A history of sexuality in America.* New York: Harper & Row.

DeMaris, A. J., & Rao, K. V. (1992). Premarital cohabitation and subsequent marital stability in the United States: A reassessment. *Journal of Marriage and the Family, 54*, 178–190.

Dobson, J., & Bauer, G. L. (1990). *Children at risk.* Dallas: Word Publishing.

Espenshade, T. J. (1985a). Marriage trends in America: Estimates, implications, and underlying causes. *Population and Development Review, 11*, 193–245.

Espenshade, T. J. (1985b). The recent decline of American marriage. In K. Davis, (Ed.), *Contemporary marriage: Comparative perspectives on a changing institution* (pp. 53–90). New York: Russell Sage Foundation.

Furstenberg, F. F., Jr. (1990). Divorce and the American family. *Annual Review of Sociology, 16*, 379–403.

Glendon, M. A. (1989). *The transformation of family law.* Chicago: University of Chicago Press.

Glenn, N. (Ed.). (1987). The state of the American family. [Special issue]. *Journal of Family Issues, 8*(4).

Glenn, N. (1991). The recent trend in marital success in the United States. *Journal of Marriage and the Family, 53*, 261–270.

Glenn, N. D., & Weaver, C. N. (1988). The changing relationship of marital status to reported happiness. *Journal of Marriage and the Family, 50*, 317–324.

Glick, P. C. (1984). Marriage, divorce, and living arrangements: Prospective changes. *Journal of Family Issues, 5*, 7–26.

Goode, W. J. (1984). Individual investments in family relationships over the coming decades. *The Tocqueville Review, 6*, 51–83.

Greenstein, T. N. (1990). Marital disruption and the employment of married women. *Journal of Marriage and the Family, 52*, 657–676.

Hawes, J. M., & Hiner, N. R. (Eds.) (1985). *American Childhood.* Westport, CT: Greenwood Press.

Heaton, T.B. (1990). Marital stability throughout the child-rearing years. *Demography, 27*, 55–63.

Jacob, H. (1988). *Silent revolution: The transformation of divorce law in the United States.* Chicago: University of Chicago Press.

Kitson, G. C., Babri, K. B., & Roach, M. J. (1985). Who divorces and why: A review. *Journal of Family Issues, 6*, 255–293.

Lasch, C. (1977). *Haven in a heartless world: The family besieged.* New York: Basic Books.

Lasch, C. (1978). *The culture of narcissism.* New York: W. W. Norton.

Lee, G. R., Seccombe, K., & Shehan, C. L. (1991). Marital status and personal happiness: An analysis of trend data. *Journal of Marriage and the Family, 53*, 839–844.

Lenski, G., & Lenski, J. (1987). *Human societies.* New York: McGraw Hill.

Martin, T. C., & Bumpass, L. L. (1989). Recent trends in marital disruption. *Demography, 26*, 37–51.

Mass Mutual American Family Values Study. (1989). Washington, DC: Mellman & Lazarus.

McLanahan, S., & Bumpass, L. (1988). Intergenerational consequences of family disruption. *American Journal of Sociology, 94*, 130–152.

Modell, J. (1989). *Into one's own: From youth to adulthood in the United States. 1920–1975.* Berkeley, CA: University of California Press.

Morgan, S. P., Lye, D., & Condran, G. (1988). Sons, daughters, and the risk of marital disruption. *American Journal of Sociology, 94*, 110–129.

Peden, J. R., & Glahe, F. R. (Eds.). (1986). *The American family and the state.* San Francisco: Pacific Research Institute for Public Policy.

Phillips, R. (1988). *Putting asunder: A history of divorce in western society.* New York: Cambridge University Press.

Popenoe, D. (1988). *Disturbing the nest: Family change and decline in modern societies.* New York: Aldine de Gruyter.

Rossi, A. S. (1980). Life span theories and women's lives. *Signs: Journal of Women in Culture and Society, 6*, 4–32.

Ryder, N. B. (1990). What is going to happen to American fertility? *Population and Development Review, 16*, 433–454.

Schoen, R. (1987). The continuing retreat from marriage: Figures from the 1983 U.S. marital status life tables. *Social Science Research, 71*, 108–9.

Schoen, R. (1992). First unions and the stability of first marriages. *Journal of Marriage and the Family, 54*, 281–284.

Schoen, R., Urton, W., Woodrow, K., & Baj, J. (1985). Marriage and divorce in twentieth century American cohorts. *Demography, 22*, 101–114.

Skolnick, A. (1991). *Embattled paradise: The American family in an age of uncertainty.* New York, Basic Books.

Stacey, J. (1990). *Brave new families.* New York: Basic Books.

Sugarman, S. D., & Kay, H. H. (Eds.). (1990). *Divorce reform at the crossroads.* New Haven: Yale University Press.

Sweet, J. A., & Bumpass, L. L. (1987). *American families and households.* New York: Russell Sage Foundation.

Thomson, E., & Colella, U. (1992). Cohabitation and marital stability. *Journal of Marriage and the Family, 54,* 259–267.

Thornton, A. (1989). Changing attitudes toward family issues in the United States. *Journal of Marriage and the Family, 51,* 873–893.

Veroff, J., Douvan, E., & Kulka, R. A. (1981). *The inner American: A self-portrait from 1957 to 1976.* New York: Basic Books.

Waite, L. J., Goldscheider, F. K., & Witsberger, C. (1986). Nonfamily living and the erosion of traditional family orientations among young adults. *American Sociological Review, 51,* 541–554.

Waite, L., & Lillard, L. A. (1991). Children and marital disruption. *American Journal of Sociology, 96,* 930–953.

White, L. K. (1990). Determinants of divorce: A review of research in the eighties. *Journal of Marriage and the Family, 52,* 904–912.

NO

Arlene S. Skolnick

THE STATE OF THE AMERICAN FAMILY

The debate about whether the family in America is falling apart, here to stay, or better than ever has continued unabated since the 1970s.... There is of course no way of resolving the issue. "Most of us," observes Joseph Featherstone, "debate these matters from our general instinct of where history is tending, from our own lives and those of our friends.... One of the difficult things about the family as a topic is that everyone in the discussion feels obliged to defend a particular set of choices."

While the argument shows no signs of reaching a resolution, some of the debaters have wandered away. Others have switched sides. Most of the radical voices who celebrated the death of the family have disappeared. Those who denounced the family as an oppressive institution and lamented its persistence have also passed from the scene, although continuing critical attacks have granted them a kind of immortality....

There is no doubt that the family transformations of recent times have left a great deal of disruption in their wake. But those who lament "the decline of the family" lump together an array of serious problems, as well as changes that are not necessarily problems at all: divorce, the sexual revolution, working mothers, the rising age of marriage, teenage pregnancy, abortion, childhood poverty, child abuse, domestic violence, the economic effects of no-fault divorce for women and children, the failure of many divorced fathers to pay child support and maintain contact with their children, an increase in the percentage of people living alone, young people "postponing" adulthood and refusing to leave home, latchkey children, the "dysfunctional family," drug use in the ghettos and suburbs, problems of minority families.

Wrapping these issues in one big package labeled "decline of the family" muddles rather than clarifies our understanding of family change. Some of these problems arise out of the old plague of poverty, which has grown worse over the past decade; others are by-products of an American economy afflicted by recession, inflation, and industrial decline and dislocation....

Moralistic cries about declining families and eroding values hinder public discussion about the kinds of modifications that can be made in other social institutions to alleviate current strains in family life. Framing the issue in terms of "the declining family" also leads to an overemphasis on personal and moral failings as the source of family and social problems, and draws attention away from the social sources of family change . . . : the economic and demographic factors that have drawn women into the workplace, the life-course revolutions that have reshaped families as well as the processes of growing up and growing old, and so on. The popularity of recent critiques of individualism reflects a strong American tradition of blaming serious social problems on individual moral character rather than on institutions and economic structures. . . .

INDIVIDUALISM VERSUS ATTACHMENT

It is not clear why social scientists have become so much more pessimistic than they used to be. The deepening gloom does not correspond to marked shifts in demographic trends. In the 1980s, for example, such vital indicators of family life as divorce rates and birthrates, which had changed sharply in the 1970s, leveled off. Toward the end of the 1980s, new births reached baby-boom levels, confounding the expectations of demographers. As a 1990 review of trends in family life put it, "Predictions of childlessness and large-scale abandonment of family life for this generation, a generation supposedly obsessed with individual fulfillment and achievement, will not be realized."

Some family scholars may have been reacting against their overly optimistic assessments of family change in the 1970s. Responding to alarm about the impending "death of the family," many researchers, pointing to demographic and survey evidence of persisting commitments to family life, argued that the family was "here to stay." Emphasizing the benefits of recent trends—more freedom from the constraints of sex roles, greater opportunities for women, closer and more satisfying marriages—they tended to downplay the costs and hardships that come with changes. As if to compensate for that optimism, in the 1980s they stressed the negative.

But family scholars in recent years also seem to have been influenced by the pessimistic views of American character and culture that began to dominate intellectual discourse in the mid-1970s. The landmark work in this genre during the 1980s was the widely acclaimed, widely discussed, best-selling book *Habits of the Heart*, by Robert Bellah and his colleagues. . . .

Bellah and his colleagues criticize both "utilitarian individualism"—the pursuit of self-interest and success—and "expressive individualism"—the pursuit of happiness, the belief in each person's "unique core of feeling and intuition." The book argues that the two kinds of individualism have perniciously combined to form the therapeutic ethos, which forms the model for many relationships. Yet the authors portray Americans not as asocial loners, devoid of family ties and community spirit, but merely as lacking a moral language to justify the commitments they do have. . . .

Yet, as a number of critics have pointed out, the book's analyses are variations on older themes in the critique of modernity, such as the decline of community, the isolation of the self, the loss of religious certitude. . . . Like those earlier critiques, it contrasts a romantic vision of the past with a jaundiced vision of the present. . . .

The fact that these recent attacks on individualism strike such responsive chords in the American public suggests that moral and communitarian values are alive and well. American culture has always been marked by an ambivalent yearning for autonomy on the one hand and attachment to family and community on the other. It is not simply that Americans are individualistic or communitarian, but that the tension between these impulses is a central theme in American culture. Yet most writings on American character ignore this duality and the psychological and social tensions it creates. And aiming criticism at personal and moral failings not only is in keeping with American religiosity—we are the most religious of Western countries, in both belief and churchgoing—but promises that we can solve our problems through changes of heart rather than through the difficult and divisive route of political and social change. But the problems of family life are located less in the realm of personal defects and declining values and more in the difficulties of making and maintaining families in a time of sweeping social change, in a society that is neglectful of families and their needs.

The most recent extended argument for the decline of the family from a family scholar has been put forth by David Popenoe. Popenoe is precise about what he means by "family decline." Since the 1960s, he argues, four major trends have signaled a "flight" from the traditional nuclear family as both ideal and reality: declining birthrates, the sexual revolution, the movement of mothers into the workplace, and the divorce revolution. Citing *Habits of the Heart*, Popenoe suggests that the trends toward expressive individualism and the therapeutic attitude have contributed to family decline. He is also precise about what he means by "traditional nuclear family": it is "fo-

cused on the procreation of children" and consists of "a legal, lifelong, sexually exclusive, heterosexual, monogamous marriage, based on affection and companionship, in which there is a sharp division of labor (separate spheres) *with the female as full-time housewife and the male as primary provider and ultimate authority*" (italics added).

Popenoe's argument illustrates that the debate over the declining family is often not so much about the decline of family life as about preference for a particular pattern of family and gender arrangements. He is certainly correct in claiming that what he defines as the traditional nuclear family is no longer dominant. Yet his definition is an essentially nineteenth-century portrait of family and gender roles, today favored by conservatives and the New Right but no longer shared by a majority of Americans. Clearly, the two-worker nuclear family is becoming the new cultural norm, and, while most people describe themselves as strongly pro-family, they favor a more symmetrical version of marriage.

Traditionalists like Popenoe place too much emphasis on family structure and not enough on the emotional quality of family life. Structural characteristics like divorce or maternal employment, as another researcher observes, "are weak predictors of the consequences most of us really care about: personal and family well-being, economic mobility, educational attainment, children's health." ...

THE STATE OF THE CHILDREN

Anxiety about the state of the family often focuses most intensely on the young. Children are not only profoundly vulnerable to any trouble in the family; they also embody the future for both their parents and the society. Thus people worry about their own children as well as other people's children. Today the vast majority of people—nearly three out of four in one survey, both parents and nonparents—believe that the quality of life for America's children has declined since their own childhood.

Yet this worry, like worries about the declining family in general, is often built on a muddled mixture of issues. With the huge increase in working mothers, divorce, and single-parent families, today's children certainly grow up in very different circumstances than did children only a few decades ago. Most have working mothers, fewer brothers and sisters, and a good chance of spending time in group care. By the time they reach adulthood, at least half of American children, according to current estimates, will spend some time living in a single-parent family. How children are faring under these circumstances is an issue with profound implications for the future of our society....

Alarming stories about the state of children and young people have become a media staple in recent years....

To put today's anxieties into perspective, it is useful to recall that the supposed golden age of family life, the 1950s, was beset by a number of crises concerning children and youth. Shocking reports of juvenile delinquency, gang fights, all-night drinking parties, and sex clubs in teenage suburbia appeared in the mass media. In the professional literature, sociologists and psychologists analyzed the problems of alienated youth and the decline of parental authority. Congress held hearings on the corrupting influence of comic books on the nation's children.... A 1955 best-seller, Rudolph Flesch's *Why Johnny Can't Read*, described America as a nation of illiterates.

To point to the hysteria of an earlier time is not to minimize the difficulties facing today's children and young people. But cries of alarm and doom need to be subjected to serious scrutiny. Making sense of the changes in children's lives in recent years is more complicated than most people assume. Several family researchers have recently published comprehensive assessments of the state of children and young people in America. In general, these reports show that, while the well-being of children has worsened in some ways, not all of the news concerning America's children is bad—in fact, some of it is good.

... As Nicholas Zill and Carolyn Rogers point out, children's well-being is a "multifaceted phenomenon." Analyzing trends in indicators of children's economic, physical, and psychological well-being since the 1960s, Zill and Rogers challenge the widespread assumptions that the overall condition of children is deteriorating.

Taken together, these studies present a mixed picture of children's prospects. On the plus side, the average American child's physical health has improved dramatically since the 1960s. Although our infant mortality rates are higher than those of most other industrial societies, both our infant and child mortality rates have dropped considerably. Declining family size has increased most children's share of the family's material resources, even though overall family income has declined since the 1970s. The educational level of most parents has risen since the 1950s, a gain that has been most striking among black women.

On the other side of the ledger, troubling social behavior on the part of young people—delinquency, drug use, early sexual activity—has increased over the past several decades. But many of these trends leveled off or declined in the 1980s....

Now, as in the past, many of the difficulties facing children arise out of economic factors. During the 1980s overall poverty rates increased, and children became the poorest segment of the population; since 1988, one out of five children has lived below the poverty line. Several factors have led to the large increase in child poverty in recent years. One is the general decline in wages, especially for younger men in their peak child-rearing years. The enormous growth of poverty among working people *not* living in inner-city underclass communities is one of the untold stories of the 1980s. A second source of child poverty is the rise of single-parent families due to divorce and out-of-wedlock births. The impact on children of both of these trends has been worsened by shortsighted government policies—cutbacks or inadequate investments in housing, health care, child care, and other social supports.

Other stresses arise out of the time pressures parents experience and other dilemmas of balancing work and family. Although there is little that government or business can do directly to reverse trends in family structure, policy choices such as child care, parental leave opportunities for both parents to work part-time while children are young, and measures to fight poverty and joblessness can alleviate some of the current strains on families.

Surprisingly, the evidence linking family changes such as divorce and maternal employment to declines in children's well-being is weaker than most people think.... For example, many negative indicators leveled off in the late 1970s and 1980s, at a time when the family dis-

integration hypotheses would have predicted increases....

Much public concern and recent research has focused on the effects of maternal employment on young children. But despite the widespread belief to the contrary, the research literature shows that children whose mothers work are no more likely to suffer from developmental problems or behavioral difficulties than are children of stay-at-home mothers. Maternal employment alone reveals little about the well-being of a child. A working mother's attitudes, the amount of emotional and practical support she receives, and the quality of available child care play a tremendous role in her morale and the functioning of the family. The most depressed mothers are those who want to work and can't, and those who would like to be full-time homemakers but must work....

The evidence on divorce is more mixed. Few would deny that it is often a stressful experience for children or that children are best off with two parents in a good marriage. Even most children whose parents have a bad marriage would probably prefer to have them stay together. Yet we know surprisingly little about the long-term effects of divorce on children. Is it uniformly devastating to all children who go through it? Does it create deep psychological wounds that never heal?

A relatively small number of largely middle-class white children has served as the basis for much current research about the impact of divorce on children. ...

There can be little doubt, though, that the time around the breakup of a marriage is a crisis for all concerned. The experiences associated with divorce and remarriage often increase a child's risk of developing problems of various kinds

—psychological, social, and academic. But clearly not all children whose parents divorce develop such problems. Researchers in recent years have begun to focus on differences in children's responses to divorce and the conditions that influence whether they do well or poorly....

The major factor influencing a child's long- and short-term well-being after divorce is the relationship with the parents, especially with the custodial parent, usually the mother. A child who can maintain a warm, supportive relationship with one or both parents, or with a grandparent or other adult, has a much better chance of dealing successfully with the stresses of divorce....

There is increasing evidence that parental conflict, whether in the form of shouting or hitting or cold hostility, which may exist in both intact and divorcing families, is a key factor in children's psychological well-being....

If we care about children, we need to focus less on the form of the families they live in and more on ways of supporting their well-being in all kinds of families. We need to accept the fact that while the family is here to stay, so are divorce, working mothers, and single-parent families. As the anthropologist Paul Bohannon suggests, we need cultural models of the successful divorce and the successful postdivorce family—one that does the least harm to children and leaves them with good relationships with both parents....

American society is prepared to deplore the plight of children and to exhort parents to fix it. It is less willing to make the kinds of investments in children's well-being that other advanced nations do....

"A HIGH RISK AND HIGH STRESS SOCIETY"

... In the 1970s and 1980s two kinds of economic changes had profound effects on families—the structural shifts that came with the move to a postindustrial society, and a downturn in the economy that ushered in a prolonged period of low growth; one economist labeled it a "quiet depression." The cyclical change exacerbated the dislocations resulting from the decline of manufacturing and the loss of blue-collar jobs. In the 1980s, government policies and social program cuts made them even worse....

Conservatives blamed increasing poverty rates on changes in family structure. Yet the widening gap between rich and poor could not be attributed solely to the increase in single-parent families —unmarried women and their children. Moreover, recent research supports the view that among the persistently poor, family breakups and teenage childbearing are largely a response to, rather than a cause of, persistent poverty.... Throughout most of the postwar era, poverty was almost synonymous with being unemployed. The 1980s saw the rise of the working poor; by mid-decade the salary offered by nearly one-third of full-time jobs could not keep a family of four above the poverty line.

The 1980s were particularly hard on young people, women, minorities, blue-collar workers, the unskilled, and those without a college education. Young adults across the range of social classes devised a number of strategies to cope with declining real earnings. According to one study, "they postponed marriage, both spouses entered the labor market, they had fewer children, and they went into debt." ...

The most malignant effects of the declining fortunes of the young have fallen on those who are both poor and members of minorities....

RECONSTRUCTING THE DREAM

... The New American Dream mixes the new cultural freedoms with many of the old wishes—marital and family happiness, economic security, home ownership, education of children. But the new dream is more demanding than the old, and even the basics—a secure job, a home, health care, education—are becoming more difficult to achieve. The new life course has more twists and turns than it did in the past; it offers greater opportunities for autonomy, but greater risks of loneliness. Further, even the middle class faces more travails than in the past: divorce, time pressures, and the dilemmas of raising children in a world that has grown more dangerous, competitive, and uncertain.

... For better or worse, family life, and an idealized image of what the family should be, remain at the source of our greatest joys, our deepest worries, our most painful hurts.

It is possible to build a convincing case for either the optimistic or the pessimistic view of recent changes. Pessimists point to high divorce rates as evidence that the family is falling apart and that people are no longer capable of deep and lasting commitments. Optimists argue that getting divorced is not the same thing as rejecting marriage. Besides, they point out, three-quarters of divorced people remarry, and higher rates of divorce only indicate that marriage has become so important that people are no longer willing to put up with the kinds of unsatisfying, conflicted, or "empty-shell" marriages earlier generations tolerated.

When people are polled about the most important elements in a good life, they place family values—"a happy marriage," love, and emotional support—at the top of the list. Through all the years of dramatic changes in the leading family indicators, surveys have shown that about 90 to 95 percent of young men and women—the alleged Me generation—have planned to marry. National surveys also show that, once married, the vast majority of people report being "very satisfied" or "very happy" with their marriages. But the pollster Lou Harris recently reported that while 87 percent of men say they would remarry their wives, only 76 percent of women say they would remarry their husbands. And contrary to notions of a male "flight from commitment," a greater proportion of men than women marry and remarry.

Not only have young people continued to value marriage but they expect to have children.... [S]urveys of both sexes during the 1980s revealed that young adults felt a near-universal urge to have children. In one study of parents and children, 88 percent of the parents said they would choose to have children again, and 71 percent described their families as "close and intimate."...

Further, numerous surveys show that despite talk about the disappearance of the extended family, family ties beyond the nuclear family persist. Regardless of mobility, most Americans had ready access to members of their family, nearly 90 percent having at least one household of relatives living nearby. Sixty percent of these people saw nearby relatives at least once a week.... It seems likely that most of these people were in touch with their families by mail and phone, visited on holidays, and mobilized to help one another during emergencies. Clearly, the image of contemporary Americans as isolated, rootless loners is far from reality....

During the 1980s,... family and children came to be reinvested with deep-seated values, in an almost religious revitalization easily exploited by politicians and advertisers.... "The new consensus," observed one feminist critic, "is that the family is our last refuge, our only defense against universal predatory selfishness, loneliness, and rootlessness; the idea that there could be a desirable alternative to the family is no longer taken seriously."...

Yet if the past has any lesson to teach, it is that inflated expectations for family life are a recipe for personal disenchantment and social neglect. The emphasis on the home as the source of both personal happiness and social order has been responsible for the recurring sense of crisis concerning children and the family that has afflicted American culture since the 1820s. For almost two centuries, social critics have been both singing the praises of the family and decrying its failures....

Rather than yearning for an elusive perfected family, we would be wiser to consider new social arrangements that fit the kinds of families we now have and the kinds of lives we now lead. We need both political will and social creativity in order to devise ways, for example, of living with divorce and of coming to grips with the implications of living in history's first mass-longevity society. Our traditions have not prepared us for the long and fluid lives we live today. The current celebration of marriage and family does not take into account that most of us will spend parts of our lives

living apart from family. We need to think of how to supply substitutes for the comforts and companionship of home.

We also need to think of how to encourage a broader sociability. Middle-class Americans have substituted a vision of the ideal home for a vision of the ideal city. As a result, our lives are divided between home and work, leaving us yearning for a broader sense of community. Yet what we may be missing is not the idealized small town of our imagined past, but that "third realm" of sociability and social cohesion beyond the home and the workplace—public spaces and informal meeting places—that our European counterparts take for granted as part of the good life.

There are no quick, easy, or cheap fixes for the problems of family life today. And there is good reason to believe that we may never solve some of the dilemmas of family—our paradoxical needs for autonomy and attachment, for privacy and community, the ambivalence built into deep emotional bonds, the tensions stirred by intense intimacy, conflicts between genders and generations. But there is much that could be done to alleviate some of the major, outer sources of stress and strains; sooner or later, policy makers will translate rhetoric and genuine public concern about children and families into ways of addressing the new realities of family life.

Without minimizing our current troubles or our attempts to resolve them, we need to remember that many of the most vexing issues that confront us derive from the very benefits of modernization, benefits too easily forgotten in our yearnings for a lost past. There was no problem of elder care when most people died before they grew old; the problems of adolescence were unknown when work began in childhood; education was a privilege for the well-to-do; and a person's place in society was determined at birth. And when most people were illiterate and living on the margins of survival, only aristocrats could worry about sexual satisfaction and self-fulfillment.

However great the difficulties of the present appear, there is no point in giving in to the lure of nostalgia. There is no golden age of family life to long for, no past pattern that, if only we had the moral will to return to, would guarantee us happiness and security. Family life is always bound up with the economic, demographic, and cultural predicaments of specific times and places. We are no longer a nation of pioneers, Puritans, farmers, or postwar suburbanites. We must shatter the myths that blind us and find ways to cope with our present, the place where social change and family history have brought us.

POSTSCRIPT

Are American Families in Decline?

Family living arrangements in the 1990s are diverse. Events and circumstances have left many people confused about the present and concerned about the future of families. Some of the questions raised by social commentators cause us to reflect on the meaning of the changes we observe in our own families. For example, do we as a society value families less today than in the past? As a result of putting individual concerns above family concerns, have we allowed family functions to be lost? Are families so diminished in power and authority that they serve solely as centers of affection and companionship and as places to rear children?

Popenoe believes that the answer to all of these questions is yes. He points to changes since 1960 that indicate family decline—retreat from marriage, fewer children born per family, more employed mothers, more divorced parents, greater numbers of single-parent families, and higher rates of cohabitation. Is it possible to successfully raise children in settings other than families? Can individuals get the affection and companionship usually provided in a family from other sources? Popenoe worries that in the future the answers to these two questions could also be yes.

Skolnick's view is that a majority of individuals continue to marry and have children. She claims that most changes in family life are a result of the changing social environment—recession, inflation, and the decline and relocation of industries. According to Skolnick, families do not have to resemble the traditional nuclear family for children to be well cared for.

Do Americans regularly talk about the problems of children but take few actions? Is it true that as a nation we invest less in our children than do other advanced nations? Can you think of programs in your own community that serve to improve the lives of children? Would it be productive to alter expectations to more accurately reflect the new realities of family life in the 1990s?

SUGGESTED READINGS

A. C. Acock & D. H. Demo, *Family Diversity and Well-Being* (Sage Publications, 1994).

D. Blankenhorn, *Fatherless America* (Basic Books, 1995).

D. Elkind, *Ties That Stress: The New Family Imbalance* (Harvard University Press, 1994).

L. B. Rubin, *Families on the Fault Line* (HarperCollins, 1994).

J. Stacey, *Brave New Families* (HarperCollins, 1991).

ISSUE 2

Is the Two-Parent Family Best?

YES: Barbara Dafoe Whitehead, from "Dan Quayle Was Right," *The Atlantic Monthly* (April 1993)

NO: June Stephenson, from *The Two-Parent Family Is Not the Best* (Diemer, Smith, 1991)

ISSUE SUMMARY

YES: Freelance writer Barbara Dafoe Whitehead reviews a wide range of literature and concludes that, in contemporary American culture, former vice president Dan Quayle was correct in advocating the two-parent family as best for children.

NO: Psychologist June Stephenson argues that the case for two parents being "the best" is grossly overstated. She concludes, based on her research, that a variety of family forms, including single-parent families, can produce children who are as well-adjusted as or better adjusted than those who are reared by two parents.

Why is the two-parent family considered best? Can we say that one family form is superior to all others, and if so, how do we define the superior family? For that matter, how do we consider all others? Are some politicians blinded by a nostalgic view of the American family?

This set of readings addresses one debate on family values that has continued for some time among politicians, theologians, scholars, and the general population. Americans seem preoccupied with the question of which family form is best and other related questions, for which there often is no one, uncomplicated answer.

As recently as the late 1950s and early 1960s, terms such as "atomistic family" and "nuclear family" were used to describe the state or form of the family that was purported to be dominant in the culture of the time. Television portrayals of the American family tended to depict families that were white, middle-class, and intact. Divorced, widowed, African American, Asian American, interracial, or single-parent families, for example, rarely received much, if any, positive attention. People knew what "real families" were supposed to be like, and television writers and producers reinforced those stereotypes. But those stereotypical formulas did not necessarily apply to reality: today, social scientists estimate that less than 15 percent of U.S. families fit the two-parent, two-child mold.

Family sociologist and historian Stephanie Coontz, in her book *The Way We Never Were: American Families and the Nostalgia Trap* (Basic Books, 1992), challenges many notions cited about what families were like in days gone by. For example, traditional families never asked for handouts, a man's home was his castle, and the television series *Leave It to Beaver* was a documentary on American family life. Coontz concludes that, on the contrary, throughout its history the United States has been home to many forms of families that have been part of the country's melting pot evolution. Coontz also maintains that today, in some retrospective analyses, we have a greater appreciation of this fact. The chapter titled "Toxic Parents, Supermoms, and Absent Fathers: Putting Parenting in Perspective" provides insight into the notion of "normal families" and "normal childhood" while looking at issues such as maternal employment, child-rearing practices, day care, latchkey children, divorce, single parenthood, and the myth of parental omnipotence.

Considerable debate continues to exist at the national, state, and local levels about what kind of family is best for the procreation and rearing of children. The debate occurs in the courtroom during custody hearings, from the pulpit during religious services, on the soapbox during elections, and even among families themselves as they come to grips with the ever-changing world. The selections that follow by Barbara Dafoe Whitehead and June Stephenson add fuel to the fires regarding what is the best parenting family form.

YES   Barbara Dafoe Whitehead

DAN QUAYLE WAS RIGHT

Divorce and out-of-wedlock childbirth are transforming the lives of American children. In the postwar generation more than 80 percent of children grew up in a family with two biological parents who were married to each other. By 1980 only 50 percent could expect to spend their entire childhood in an intact family. If current trends continue, less than half of all children born today will live continuously with their own mother and father throughout childhood. Most American children will spend several years in a single-mother family. Some will eventually live in stepparent families, but because stepfamilies are more likely to break up than intact (by which I mean two-biological-parent) families, an increasing number of children will experience family breakup two or even three times during childhood.

According to a growing body of social-scientific evidence, children in families disrupted by divorce and out-of-wedlock birth do worse than children in intact families on several measures of well-being. Children in single-parent families are six times as likely to be poor. They are also likely to stay poor longer. Twenty-two percent of children in one-parent families will experience poverty during childhood for seven years or more, as compared with only two percent of children in two-parent families. A 1988 survey by the National Center for Health Statistics found that children in single-parent families are two to three times as likely as children in two-parent families to have emotional and behavioral problems. They are also more likely to drop out of high school, to get pregnant as teenagers, to abuse drugs, and to be in trouble with the law. Compared with children in intact families, children from disrupted families are at a much higher risk for physical or sexual abuse.

Contrary to popular belief, many children do not "bounce back" after divorce or remarriage. Difficulties that are associated with family breakup often persist into adulthood. Children who grow up in single-parent or stepparent families are less successful as adults, particularly in the two domains of life —love and work—that are most essential to happiness. Needless to say, not all children experience such negative effects. However, research shows that many children from disrupted families have a harder time achieving intimacy in a relationship, forming a stable marriage, or even holding a steady job....

[I]t is... risky to ignore the issue of changing family structure. In recent years the problems associated with family disruption have grown. Overall child well-being has declined, despite a decrease in the number of children per family, an increase in the educational level of parents, and historically high levels of public spending. After dropping in the 1960s and 1970s, the proportion of children in poverty has increased dramatically, from 15 percent in 1970 to 20 percent in 1990, while the percentage of adult Americans in poverty has remained roughly constant. The teen suicide rate has more than tripled. Juvenile crime has increased and become more violent. School performance has continued to decline. There are no signs that these trends are about to reverse themselves.

If we fail to come to terms with the relationship between family structure and declining child well-being, then it will be increasingly difficult to improve children's life prospects, no matter how many new programs the federal government funds. Nor will we be able to make progress in bettering school performance or reducing crime or improving the quality of the nation's future work force—all domestic problems closely connected to family breakup. Worse, we may contribute to the problem by pursuing policies that actually increase family instability and breakup....

In the 1960s the rate of family disruption suddenly began to rise. After inching up over the course of a century, the divorce rate soared. Throughout the 1950s and early 1960s the divorce rate held steady at fewer than ten divorces a year per 1,000 married couples. Then, beginning in about 1965, the rate increased sharply, peaking at twenty-three divorces per 1,000 marriages by 1979. (In 1974 divorce passed death as the leading cause of family breakup.) The rate has leveled off at about twenty-one divorces per 1,000 marriages—the figure for 1991. The out-of-wedlock birth rate also jumped. It went from five percent in 1960 to 27 percent in 1990. In 1990 close to 57 percent of births among black mothers were nonmarital, and about 17 percent among white mothers. Altogether, about one out of every four women who had a child in 1990 was not married. With rates of divorce and nonmarital birth so high, family disruption is at its peak. Never before have so many children experienced family breakup caused by events other than death. Each year a million children go through divorce or separation and almost as many more are born out of wedlock.

Half of all marriages now end in divorce. Following divorce, many people enter new relationships. Some begin living together. Nearly half of all cohabiting couples have children in the household. Fifteen percent have new children together. Many cohabiting couples eventually get married. However, both cohabiting and remarried couples are more likely to break up than couples in first marriages. Even social scientists find it hard to keep pace with the complexity and velocity of such patterns. In the revised edition (1992) of his book *Marriage, Divorce, Remarriage*, the sociologist Andrew Cherlin ruefully comments: "If there were a truth-in-labeling law for books, the title of this edition should be something long and unwieldy like *Cohabitation, Marriage, Divorce, More Cohabitation, and Probably Remarriage*." ...

Given its dramatic impact on children's lives, one might reasonably expect that this historic level of family disruption would be viewed with alarm, even regarded as a national crisis. Yet this has not been the case. In recent years some people have argued that these trends pose a serious threat to children and to the nation as a whole, but they are dismissed as declinists, pessimists, or nostalgists, unwilling or unable to accept the new facts of life. The dominant view is that the changes in family structure are, on balance, positive.

A SHIFT IN
THE SOCIAL METRIC

There are several reasons why this is so, but the fundamental reason is that at some point in the 1970s Americans changed their minds about the meaning of these disruptive behaviors. What had once been regarded as hostile to children's best interests was now considered essential to adults' happiness. In the 1950s most Americans believed that parents should stay in an unhappy marriage for the sake of the children. The assumption was that a divorce would damage the children, and the prospect of such damage gave divorce its meaning. By the mid-1970s a majority of Americans rejected that view. Popular advice literature reflected the shift. A book on divorce published in the mid-1940s tersely asserted: "Children are entitled to the affection and *association* of two parents, not one." Thirty years later another popular divorce book proclaimed just the opposite: "A two-parent home is not the only emotional structure within which a child can be happy and healthy.... The parents who take care of themselves will be best able to take care of their children." At about the same time, the long-standing taboo against out-of-wedlock childbirth also collapsed. By the mid-1970s three fourths of Americans said that it was not morally wrong for a woman to have a child outside marriage.

Once the social metric shifts from child well-being to adult well-being, it is hard to see divorce and nonmarital birth in anything but a positive light. However distressing and difficult they may be, both of these behaviors can hold out the promise of greater adult choice, freedom, and happiness. For unhappy spouses, divorce offers a way to escape a troubled or even abusive relationship and make a fresh start. For single parents, remarriage is a second try at marital happiness as well as a chance for relief from the stress, loneliness, and economic hardship of raising a child alone. For some unmarried women, nonmarital birth is a way to beat the biological clock, avoid marrying the wrong man, and experience the pleasures of motherhood. Moreover, divorce and out-of-wedlock birth involve a measure of agency and choice; they are man- and woman-made events. To be sure, not everyone exercises choice in divorce or nonmarital birth. Men leave wives for younger women, teenage girls get pregnant accidentally—yet even these unhappy events reflect the expansion of the boundaries of freedom and choice.

This cultural shift helps explain what otherwise would be inexplicable: the failure to see the rise in family disruption as a severe and troubling national problem. It explains why there is virtually no widespread public sentiment for restigmatizing either of these classically disruptive behaviors and no sense—no public consensus—that they can or should be avoided in the future. On the contrary, the prevailing opinion is that we should accept the changes in family structure as inevitable and devise new forms of public and private support for single-parent families....

No one would claim that two-parent families are free from conflict, violence, or abuse. However, the attempt to discredit the two-parent family can be understood as part of what Daniel Patrick Moynihan has described as a larger effort to accommodate higher levels of social deviance. "The amount of deviant behavior in American society has increased beyond the levels the community can 'afford to recognize,'" Moynihan argues. One response has been to normalize what was once considered deviant behavior, such as out-of-wedlock birth. An accompanying response has been to detect deviance in what once stood as a social norm, such as the married-couple family. Together these responses reduce the acknowledged levels of deviance by eroding earlier distinctions between the normal and the deviant. . . .

[T]he popular portrait of family life does not simply reflect the views of a cultural elite, as some have argued. There is strong support at the grass roots for much of this view of family change. Survey after survey shows that Americans are less inclined than they were a generation ago to value sexual fidelity, lifelong marriage, and parenthood as worthwhile personal goals. Motherhood no longer defines adult womanhood, as everyone knows; equally important is the fact that fatherhood has declined as a norm for men. In 1976 less than half as many fathers as in 1957 said that providing for children was a life goal. The proportion of working men who found marriage and children burdensome and restrictive more than doubled in the same period. Fewer than half of all adult Americans today regard the idea of sacrifice for others as a positive moral virtue.

DINOSAURS DIVORCE

It is true that many adults benefit from divorce or remarriage. According to one study, nearly 80 percent of divorced women and 50 percent of divorced men say they are better off out of the marriage. Half of divorced adults in the same study report greater happiness. A competent self-help book called *Divorce and New Beginnings* notes the advantages of single parenthood: single parents can "develop their own interests, fulfill their own needs, choose their own friends and engage in social activities of their choice. Money, even if limited, can be spent as they see fit." Apparently, some women appreciate the opportunity to have children out of wedlock. "The real world, however, does not always allow women who are dedicated to their careers to devote the time and energy it takes to find—or be found by—the perfect husband and father wanna-be," one woman said in a letter to *The Washington Post*. . . .

[A] telling glimpse into the meaning of family disruption can be found in the growing children's literature on family dissolution. Take, for example, the popular children's book *Dinosaurs Divorce: A Guide for Changing Families* (1986), by Laurene Krasny Brown and Marc Brown. This is a picture book, written for very young children. The book begins with a short glossary of "divorce words" and encourages children to "see if you can find them" in the story. The words include "family counselor," "separation agreement," "alimony," and "child custody." The book is illustrated with cartoonish drawings of green dinosaur parents who fight, drink too much, and break up. One panel shows the father dinosaur, suitcase in hand, getting into a yellow car.

The dinosaur children are offered simple, straightforward advice on what to do about the divorce. *On custody decisions:* "When parents can't agree, lawyers and judges decide. Try to be honest if they ask you questions; it will help them make better decisions." *On selling the house:* "If you move, you may have to say good-bye to friends and familiar places. But soon your new home will feel like the place you really belong." *On the economic impact of divorce:* "Living with one parent almost always means there will be less money. Be prepared to give up some things." *On holidays:* "Divorce may mean twice as much celebrating at holiday times, but you may feel pulled apart." *On parents' new lovers:* "You may sometimes feel jealous and want your parent to yourself. Be polite to your parents' new friends, even if you don't like them at first." *On parents' remarriage:* "Not everyone loves his or her stepparents, but showing them respect is important."

These... books point to an uncomfortable and generally unacknowledged fact: what contributes to a parent's happiness may detract from a child's happiness. All too often the adult quest for freedom, independence, and choice in family relationships conflicts with a child's developmental needs for stability, constancy, harmony, and permanence in family life. In short, family disruption creates a deep division between parents' interests and the interests of children.

One of the worse consequences of these divided interests is a withdrawal of parental investment in children's well-being. As the Stanford economist Victor Fuchs has pointed out, the main source of social investment in children is private. The investment comes from the children's parents. But parents in disrupted families have less time, attention, and money to devote to their children. The single most important source of disinvestment has been the widespread withdrawal of financial support and involvement by fathers. Maternal investment, too, has declined, as women try to raise families on their own and work outside the home. Moreover, both mothers and fathers commonly respond to family breakup by investing more heavily in themselves and in their own personal and romantic lives.

Sometimes the tables are completely turned. Children are called upon to invest in the emotional well-being of their parents. Indeed, this seems to be the larger message of many of the children's books on divorce and remarriage. *Dinosaurs Divorce* asks children to be sympathetic, understanding, respectful, and polite to confused, unhappy parents. The sacrifice comes from the children: "Be prepared to give up some things." In the world of divorcing dinosaurs, the children rather than the grown-ups are the exemplars of patience, restraint, and good sense.

THREE SEVENTIES ASSUMPTIONS

As it first took shape in the 1970s, the optimistic view of family change rested on three bold new assumptions. At that time, because the emergence of the changes in family life was so recent, there was little hard evidence to confirm or dispute these assumptions. But this was an expansive moment in American life.

The first assumption was an economic one: that a woman could now afford to be a mother without also being a wife. There were ample grounds for believing this. Women's work-force participation had been gradually increasing in the postwar period, and by the beginning of the 1970s women were a strong presence in the workplace. What's more, even though there was still a substantial wage gap between men and women, women had made considerable progress in a relatively short time toward better-paying jobs and greater employment opportunities. More women than ever before could aspire to serious careers as business executives, doctors, lawyers, airline pilots, and politicians. This circumstance, combined with the increased availability of child care, meant that women could take on the responsibilities of a breadwinner, perhaps even a sole breadwinner. This was particularly true for middle-class women....

Feminists, who had long argued that the path to greater equality for women lay in the world of work outside the home, endorsed this assumption. In fact, for many, economic independence was a stepping-stone toward freedom from both men and marriage. As women began to earn their own money, they were less dependent on men or marriage, and marriage diminished in importance. In Gloria Steinem's memorable words, "A woman without a man is like a fish without a bicycle."...

The second assumption was that family disruption would not cause lasting harm to children and could actually enrich their lives. *Creative Divorce: A New Opportunity for Personal Growth*, a popular book of the seventies, spoke confidently to this point: "Children can survive any family crisis without permanent damage—and grow as human beings in the process...." Moreover, single-parent and stepparent families created a more extensive kinship network than the nuclear family. This network would envelop children in a web of warm and supportive relationships. "Belonging to a stepfamily means there are more people in your life," a children's book published in 1982 notes. "More sisters and brothers, including the step ones. More people you think of as grandparents and aunts and uncles. More cousins. More neighbors and friends.... Getting to know and like so many people (and having them like you) is one of the best parts of what being in a stepfamily... is all about."

The third assumption was that the new diversity in family structure would make America a better place. Just as the nation has been strengthened by the diversity of its ethnic and racial groups, so it would be strengthened by diverse family forms. The emergence of these brave new families was but the latest chapter in the saga of American pluralism.

Another version of the diversity argument stated that the real problem was not family disruption itself but the stigma still attached to these emergent family forms. This lingering stigma placed children at psychological risk, making them feel ashamed or different; as the ranks of single-parent and stepparent families grew, children would feel normal and good about themselves.

These assumptions continue to be appealing, because they accord with strongly held American beliefs in social progress. Americans see progress in the expansion of individual opportunities for choice, freedom, and self-expression. Moreover, Americans identify progress with growing tolerance of diversity. Over the past half century, the pollster Daniel Yankelovich writes, the United States has steadily grown more open-minded and accepting of groups that were previously perceived as alien, untrustworthy, or unsuitable for public leadership or social esteem. One such group is the burgeoning number of single-parent and stepparent families.

THE EDUCATION OF SARA McLANAHAN

In 1981 Sara McLanahan, now a sociologist at Princeton University's Woodrow Wilson School, read a three-part series by Ken Auletta in *The New Yorker.* Later published as a book titled *The Underclass,* the series presented a vivid portrait of the drug addicts, welfare mothers, and school dropouts who took part in an education-and-training program in New York City. Many were the children of single mothers, and it was Auletta's clear implication that single-mother families were contributing to the growth of an underclass. McLanahan was taken aback by this notion. "It struck me as strange that he would be viewing single mothers at that level of pathology." ...

One of the leading assumptions of the time was that single motherhood was economically viable. Even if single mothers did face economic trials, they wouldn't face them for long, it was argued, because they wouldn't remain single for long: single motherhood would be a brief phase of three to five years, followed by marriage. Single mothers would be economically resilient: if they experienced setbacks, they would recover quickly. It was also said that single mothers would be supported by informal networks of family, friends, neighbors, and other single mothers. As McLanahan shows in her study [on single motherhood, published in 1986], the evidence demolishes all these claims.

For the vast majority of single mothers, the economic spectrum turns out to be narrow, running between precarious and desperate. Half the single mothers in the United States live below the poverty line. (Currently, one out of ten married couples with children is poor.) Many others live on the edge of poverty. Even single mothers who are far from poor are likely to experience persistent economic insecurity. Divorce almost always brings a decline in the standard of living for the mother and children.

Moreover, the poverty experienced by single mothers is no more brief than it is mild. A significant number of all single mothers never marry or remarry. Those who do, do so only after spending roughly six years, on average, as single parents. For black mothers the duration is much longer. Only 33 percent of African-American mothers had remarried within ten years of separation. Consequently, single motherhood is hardly a fleeting event for the mother, and it is likely to occupy a third of the child's childhood. Even the notion that single mothers are knit together in economically supportive networks is not borne out by the evidence. On the contrary, single parenthood forces many women to be on the move, in search of cheaper housing and better jobs. This need-driven restless mobility makes it more difficult for them to sustain supportive ties to family and friends, let alone other single mothers....

McLanahan cites three reasons why single-mother families are so vulnerable economically. For one thing, their earnings are low. Second, unless the mothers are widowed, they don't receive public subsidies large enough to lift them out of poverty. And finally, they do not get much support from family members—especially the fathers of their children. In 1982 single white mothers received an average of $1,246 in alimony and child support, black mothers an average of $322. Such payments accounted for about 10 percent of the income of single white mothers and for about 3.5 percent of the income of single black mothers. These amounts were dramatically smaller than the income of the father in a two-parent family and also smaller than the income from a second earner in a two-parent family. Roughly 60 percent of single white mothers and 80 percent of single black mothers received no support at all.

Until the mid-1980s, when stricter standards were put in place, child-support awards were only about half to two-thirds what the current guidelines require. Accordingly, there is often a big difference in the living standards of divorced fathers and of divorced mothers with children. After divorce the average annual income of mothers and children is $13,500 for whites and $9,000 for nonwhites, as compared with $25,000 for white nonresident fathers and $13,600 for nonwhite nonresident fathers. Moreover, since child-support awards account for a smaller portion of the income of a high-earning father, the drop in living standards can be especially sharp for mothers who were married to upper-level managers and professionals.

Unwed mothers are unlikely to be awarded any support at all, partly because the paternity of their children may not have been established. According to one recent study, only 20 percent of unmarried mothers receive child support.

Even if single mothers escape poverty, economic uncertainty remains a condition of life. Divorce brings a reduction in income and standard of living for the vast majority of single mothers. One study, for example, found that income for mothers and children declines on average about 30 percent, while fathers experience a 10 to 15 percent increase in income in the year following a separation. Things get even more difficult when fathers fail to meet their child-support obligations. As a result, many divorced mothers experience a wearing uncertainty about the family budget: whether the check will come in or not; whether new sneakers can be bought this month or not; whether the electric bill will be paid on time or not. Uncertainty about money triggers other kinds of uncertainty. Mothers and children often have to move to cheaper housing after a divorce. One study shows that about 38 percent of divorced mothers and their children move during the first year after a divorce. Even several years later the rate of moves for single mothers is about a third higher than the rate for two-parent families. It is also common for a mother to change her job or increase her working hours or both following a divorce. Even the composition of the household is likely to change, with other adults, such as boyfriends or babysitters, moving in and out.

Sara McLanahan's investigation and others like it have helped to establish a broad consensus on the economic impact of family disruption on children. Most social scientists now agree that single motherhood is an important and growing cause of poverty, and that children suffer as a result. (They continue to argue, however, about the relationship between family structure and such economic factors as income inequality, the loss of jobs in the inner city, and the growth of low-wage jobs.) By the mid-1980s, however, it was clear that the problem of family disruption was not confined to the urban underclass, nor was its sole impact economic. Divorce and out-of-wedlock childbirth were affecting middle- and upper-class children, and these more privileged children were suffering negative consequences as well.

It appeared that the problems associated with family breakup were far deeper and far more widespread than anyone had previously imagined.

THE MISSING FATHER

Judith Wallerstein is one of the pioneers in research on the long-term psychological impact of family disruption on children. The California Children of Divorce Study, which she directs, remains the most enduring study of the long-term effects of divorce on children and their parents....

When, in 1971, Wallerstein and her colleagues set out to conduct clinical interviews with 131 children from the San Francisco area, they thought they were embarking on a short-term study. Most experts believed that divorce was like a bad cold. There was a phase of acute discomfort, and then a short recovery phase. According to the conventional wisdom, kids would be back on their feet in no time at all. Yet when Wallerstein met these children for a second interview more than a year later, she was amazed to discover that there had been no miraculous recovery. In fact, the children seemed to be doing worse.

The news that children did not "get over" divorce was not particularly welcome at the time. Wallerstein recalls, "We got angry letters from therapists, parents, and lawyers saying we were undoubtedly wrong. They said children are really much better off being released from an unhappy marriage. Divorce, they said, is a liberating experience." One of the main results of the California study was to overturn this optimistic view. In Wallerstein's cautionary words, "Divorce is deceptive. Legally it is a single event, but psychologically it is a chain—sometimes a never-ending chain—of events, relocations, and radically shifting relationships strung through time, a process that forever changes the lives of the people involved."

Five years after divorce more than a third of the children experienced moderate or severe depression. At ten years a significant number of the now young men and women appeared to be troubled, drifting, and underachieving. At fifteen years many of the thirtyish adults were struggling to establish strong love relationships of their own. In short, far from recovering from their parents' divorce, a significant percentage of these grownups were still suffering from its effects. In fact, according to Wallerstein, the long-term effects of divorce emerge at a time when young adults are trying to make their own decisions about love, marriage, and family. Not all children in the study suffered negative consequences. But Wallerstein's research presents a sobering picture of divorce. "The child of divorce faces many additional psychological burdens in addition to the normative tasks of growing up," she says.

Divorce not only makes it more difficult for young adults to establish new relationships. It also weakens the oldest primary relationship: that between parent and child. According to Wallerstein, "Parent-child relationships are permanently altered by divorce in ways that our society has not anticipated." Not only do children experience a loss of parental attention at the onset of divorce, but they soon find that at every stage of their development their parents are not available in the same way they once were. "In a reasonably happy intact family," Wallerstein observes, "the child gravitates first to one parent and then to the other, using skills and attributes from each in climbing the developmental ladder." In a divorced family, children find it "harder to find the needed parent at needed times." This may help explain why very young children suffer the most as the result of family disruption. Their opportunities to engage in this kind of ongoing process are the most truncated and compromised.

The father-child bond is severely, often irreparably, damaged in disrupted families. In a situation without historical precedent, an astonishing and disheartening number of American fathers are failing to provide financial support to their children. Often, more than the father's support check is missing. Increasingly, children are bereft of any contact with their fathers. According to the National Survey of Children, in disrupted families only one child in six, on average, saw his or her father as often as once a week in the past year. Close to half did not see their father at all in the past year. As time goes on, contact becomes even more infrequent. Ten years after a marriage breaks up, more than two thirds of children report not having seen their father for a year....

Even for fathers who maintain regular contact, the pattern of father-child relationships changes. The sociologists Andrew Cherlin and Frank Furstenberg, who have studied broken families, write that the fathers behave more like other relatives than like parents. Rather than helping with homework or carrying out a project with their children, nonresidential fathers are likely to take the kids shopping, to the movies, or out to dinner. Instead of providing steady advice and guidance, divorced fathers become "treat" dads.

Apparently—and paradoxically—it is the visiting relationship itself, rather than the frequency of visits, that is the real source of the problem. According to Wallerstein, the few children in the California study who reported visiting with their fathers once or twice a week over a ten-year period still felt rejected. The need to schedule a special time to be with the child, the repeated leave-takings, and the lack of connection to the child's regular, daily schedule leaves many fathers adrift, frustrated, and confused. Wallerstein calls the visiting father a parent without portfolio....

LONG-TERM EFFECTS

Since most children live with their mothers after divorce, one might expect that the mother-child bond would remain unaltered and might even be strengthened. Yet research shows that the mother-child bond is also weakened as the result of divorce. Only half of the children who were close to their mothers before a divorce remained equally close after the divorce. Boys, particularly, had difficulties with their mothers. Moreover, mother-child relationships deteriorated over time. Whereas teenagers in disrupted families were no more likely than teenagers in intact families to report poor relationships with their mothers, 30 percent of young adults from disrupted families have poor relationships with their mothers, as compared with 16 percent of young adults from intact families. Mother-daughter relationships often deteriorate as the daughter reaches young adulthood. The only group in society that derives any benefit from these weakened parent-child ties is the therapeutic community. Young adults from disrupted families are nearly twice as likely as those from intact families to receive psychological help.

... Obviously, not all children in two-parent families are free from emotional turmoil, but few are burdened with the troubles that accompany family breakup. Moreover, as the sociologist Amitai Etzioni explains in a new book, *The Spirit of Community*, two parents in an intact family make up what might be called a mutually supportive education coalition. When both parents are present, they can play different, even contradictory, roles. One parent may goad the child to achieve, while the other may encourage the child to take time out to daydream or toss a football around. One may emphasize taking intellectual risk, while the other may insist on following the teacher's guidelines. At the same time, the parents regularly exchange information about the child's school problems and achievements, and have a sense of the overall educational mission....

THE BAD NEWS ABOUT STEPPARENTS

Perhaps the most striking, and potentially disturbing, new research has to do with children in stepparent families. Until quite recently the optimistic assumption was that children saw their lives improve when they became part of a stepfamily. When Nicholas Zill and his colleagues began to study the effects of remarriage on children, their working hypothesis was that stepparent families would make up for the shortcomings of the single-parent family. Clearly, most children are better off economically when they are able to share in the income of two adults. When a second adult joins the household, there may be a reduction in the time and work pressures on the single parent.

The research overturns this optimistic assumption, however. In general the evidence suggests that remarriage neither reproduces nor restores the intact family structure, even when it brings more income and a second adult into the household. Quite the contrary. Indeed, children living with stepparents appear to be even more disadvantaged than children living in a stable single-parent family. Other difficulties seem to offset the advantages of extra income and an extra pair of hands. However much our modern sympathies reject the fairy-tale portrait of stepparents, the latest research confirms that the old stories are anthropologically quite accurate. Stepfamilies disrupt established loyalties, create new uncertainties, provoke deep anxieties, and sometimes threaten a child's physical safety as well as emotional security.

Parents and children have dramatically different interests in and expectations for a new marriage. For a single parent, remarriage brings new commitments, the hope of enduring love and happiness, and relief from stress and loneliness. For a child, the same event often provokes confused feelings of sadness, anger, and rejection. Nearly half the children in Wallerstein's study said they felt left out in their stepfamilies. The National Commission on Children, a bipartisan group headed by Senator John D. Rockefeller, of West Virginia, reported that children from stepfamilies were more likely to say they often felt lonely or blue than children from either single-parent or intact families. Children in stepfamilies were the most likely to report that they wanted more time with their mothers. When mothers remarry, daughters tend to have a harder time adjusting than sons. Evidently, boys often respond positively to a male presence in the household, while girls who have established close ties to their mother in a single-parent family often see the stepfather as a rival and an intruder. According to one study, boys in remarried families are less likely to drop out of school than boys in single-parent families, while the opposite is true for girls....

One of the most severe risks associated with stepparent-child ties is the risk of sexual abuse. As Judith Wallerstein explains, "The presence of a stepfather can raise the difficult issue of a thinner incest barrier." The incest taboo is strongly reinforced, Wallerstein says, by knowledge of paternity and by the experience of caring for a child since birth. A stepfather enters the family without either credential and plays a sexual role as the mother's husband. As a result, stepfathers can pose a sexual risk to the children, especially to daughters. According to a study by the Canadian researchers Martin Daly and Margo Wilson, preschool children in stepfamilies are forty times as likely as children in intact families to suffer physical or sexual abuse. (Most of the sexual abuse was committed by a third party, such as a neighbor, a stepfather's male friend, or another nonrelative.) Stepfathers discriminate in their abuse: they are far more likely to assault nonbiological children than their own natural children.

Sexual abuse represents the most extreme threat to children's well-being. Stepfamilies also seem less likely to make the kind of ordinary investments in the children that other families do. Although it is true that the stepfamily household has a higher income than the single-parent household, it does not follow that the additional income is reliably available to the children. To begin with, children's claim on stepparents' resources is shaky. Stepparents are not legally required to support stepchildren, so their financial support of these children is entirely voluntary. Moreover, since stepfamilies are far more likely to break up than intact families, particularly in the first five years, there is always the risk —far greater than the risk of unemployment in an intact family—that the second income will vanish with another divorce. The financial commitment to a child's education appears weaker in stepparent families, perhaps because the stepparent believes that the responsibility for educating the child rests with the biological parent....

DIMINISHING INVESTMENTS

There are several reasons for [stepparents'] diminished interest and investment [in their stepchildren]. In the law, as in the children's eyes, stepparents are shadowy figures. According to the legal scholar David Chambers, family law has pretty much ignored stepparents. Chambers writes, "In the substantial majority of states, stepparents, even when they live with a child, have no legal obligation to contribute to the child's support; nor does a stepparent's presence in the home alter the support obligations of a noncustodial parent. The stepparent also has ... no authority to approve emergency medical treatment or even to sign a permission slip...." When a marriage breaks up, the stepparent has no continuing obligation to provide for a stepchild, no matter how long or how much he or she has been contributing to the support of the child. In short, Chambers says, stepparent relationships are based wholly on consent, subject to the inclinations of the adult and the child. The only way a stepparent can acquire the legal status of a parent is through adoption. Some researchers also point to the cultural ambiguity of the stepparent's role as a source of diminished interest, while others insist that it is the absence of a blood tie that weakens the bond between stepparent and child....

In short, as Andrew Cherlin and Frank Furstenburg put it, "Through divorce and remarriage, individuals are related to more and more people, to each of whom they owe less and less." Moreover, as Nicholas Zill argues, weaker parent-child attachments leave many children more strongly exposed to influences outside the family, such as peers, boyfriends or girlfriends, and the media. Although these outside forces can sometimes be helpful, common sense and research opinion argue against putting too much faith in peer groups or the media as surrogates for Mom and Dad....

THE TWO-PARENT ADVANTAGE

All this evidence gives rise to an obvious conclusion: growing up in an intact two-parent family is an important source of advantage for American children. Though far from perfect as a social institution, the intact family offers children greater security and better outcomes than its fast-growing alternatives: single-parent and stepparent families. Not only does the intact family protect the child from poverty and economic insecurity; it also provides greater noneconomic investments of parental time, attention, and emotional support over the entire life course. This does not mean that all two-parent families are better for children than all single-parent families. But in the face of the evidence it becomes increas-

ingly difficult to sustain the proposition that all family structures produce equally good outcomes for children.

[T]he case against the two-parent family is remarkably weak. It is true that disaggregating data can make family structure less significant as a factor, just as disaggregating Hurricane Andrew into wind, rain, and tides can make it disappear as a meteorological phenomenon. Nonetheless, research opinion as well as common sense suggests that the effects of changes in family structure are great enough to cause concern. Nicholas Zill argues that many of the risk factors for children are doubled or more than doubled as the result of family disruption. "In epidemiological terms," he writes, "the doubling of a hazard is a substantial increase ... the increase in risk that dietary cholesterol poses for cardiovascular disease, for example, is far less than double, yet millions of American have altered their diets because of the perceived hazard."

The argument that family conflict, rather than the breakup of parents, is the cause of children's psychological distress is persuasive on its face. Children who grow up in high-conflict families, whether the families stay together or eventually split up, are undoubtedly at great psychological risk. And surely no one would dispute that there must be societal measures available, including divorce, to remove children from families where they are in danger. Yet only a minority of divorces grow out of pathological situations; much more common are divorces in families unscarred by physical assault. Moreover, an equally compelling hypothesis is that family breakup generates its own conflict. Certainly, many families exhibit more conflictual and even violent behavior as a consequence of divorce than they did before divorce.

Finally, it is important to note that clinical insights are different from sociological findings. Clinicians work with individual families, who cannot and should not be defined by statistical aggregates. Appropriate to a clinical approach, moreover, is a focus on the internal dynamics of family functioning and on the immense variability in human behavior. Nevertheless, there is enough empirical evidence to justify sociological statements about the causes of declining child well-being and to demonstrate that despite the plasticity of human response, there are some useful rules of thumb to guide our thinking about and policies affecting the family.

For example, Sara McLanahan says, three structural constants are commonly associated with intact families, even intact families who would not win any "Family of the Year" awards. The first is economic. In intact families, children share in the income of two adults. Indeed, as a number of analysts have pointed out, the two-parent family is becoming more rather than less necessary, because more and more families need two incomes to sustain a middle-class standard of living.

McLanahan believes that most intact families also provide a stable authority structure. Family breakup commonly upsets the established boundaries of authority in a family. Children are often required to make decisions or accept responsibilities once considered the province of parents. Moreover, children, even very young children, are often expected to behave like mature adults, so that the grown-ups in the family can be free to deal with the emotional fallout of the failed relationship. In some instances family disruption creates a complete vac-

uum in authority; everyone invents his or her own rules. With lines of authority disrupted or absent, children find it much more difficult to engage in the normal kinds of testing behavior, the trial and error, the failing and succeeding, that define the developmental pathway toward character and competence. McLanahan says, "Children need to be the ones to challenge the rules. The parents need to set the boundaries and let the kids push the boundaries. The children shouldn't have to walk the straight and narrow at all times."

Finally, McLanahan holds that children in intact families benefit from stability in what she neutrally terms "household personnel." Family disruption frequently brings new adults into the family, including stepparents, live-in boyfriends or girlfriends, and casual sexual partners. Like stepfathers, boyfriends can present a real threat to children's, particularly to daughters', security and well-being. But physical and sexual abuse represents only the most extreme such threat. Even the very best of boyfriends can disrupt and undermine a child's sense of peace and security. McLanahan says. "It's not as though you're going from an unhappy marriage to peacefulness. There can be a constant changing until the mother finds a suitable partner."

McLanahan's argument helps explain why children of widows tend to do better than children of divorced or unmarried mothers. Widows differ from other single mothers in all three respects. They are economically more secure, because they receive more public assistance through Survivors Insurance, and possibly private insurance or other kinds of support from family members. Thus widows are less likely to leave the neighborhood in search of a new or better job and a cheaper house or apartment. Moreover, the death of a father is not likely to disrupt the authority structure radically. When a father dies, he is no longer physically present, but his death does not dethrone him as an authority figure in the child's life. On the contrary, his authority may be magnified through death. The mother can draw on the powerful memory of the departed father as a way of intensifying her parental authority: "Your father would have wanted it this way." Finally, since widows tend to be older than divorced mothers, their love life may be less distracting.

Regarding the two-parent family, the sociologist David Popenoe, who has devoted much of his career to the study of families, both in the United States and in Scandinavia, makes this straightforward assertion:

Social science research is almost never conclusive. There are always methodological difficulties and stones left unturned. Yet in three decades of work as a social scientist, I know of few other bodies of data in which the weight of evidence is so decisively on one side of the issue: on the whole, for children, two-parent families are preferable to single-parent and stepfamilies.

NO

June Stephenson

THE TWO-PARENT FAMILY
IS NOT THE BEST

INTRODUCTION

This is ... about parenting and the human relationships involved in the process of raising children. It evaluates how well parents did in raising their children by what the children, now grown, say about their childhood. ...

The children ..., now grown to adulthood, speak out from four different family groups. These groups are composed of 368 women who were raised by single fathers, or by single mothers, or by both biological parents, or by a step parent. Their answers to a lengthy questionnaire asking a multitude of questions were compared from group to group. ...

This ... is about young girls, how they were raised and how they are now adults. The initial quest was to learn about girls raised by single fathers, but the study was then expanded for comparison purposes. ...

This study should dampen the assumption that the two biological parent family is the best for all children, because that did not prove to be true.

Among the other things that were learned were that single parent families have advantages over two-parent families, that girls growing up in single father homes have strong feminine characteristics, and girls growing up in single mother homes have strong masculine characteristics, and most girls growing up in step mother families are emotionally and physically abused. ...

Just "*to test the waters,*" I put an advertisement in the Berkeley, California weekly newspaper, *The Bay Area Guardian,* asking women who had been raised by fathers to volunteer for a research study. I was surprised to get several responses from women enthusiastic to participate. All of the women said they had never known anyone else raised by a single father and were eager to communicate. Encouraged, and now wanting to expand my initial curiosity into a reliable research study, I needed to find research participants from different geographical, economic, ethnic and educational backgrounds. I also needed to find women willing to participate who were not raised by their fathers so I would have one or more control groups for comparison. ...
To secure a more balanced sample, I then put advertisements in *Ms. Magazine,*

*Graduate Woman, 50 Plus, National En-
quirer, True Romance, Modern Romance,
Psychology Today, Mother Jones, Globe, The
Sun, and The Examiner, and True Story.*

The ads asked for volunteers in four
categories: women raised by fathers only,
women raised by mothers only, women
raised by both biological parents, and
women raised by one biological parent
and one step parent, where the biological
parent had died at about the time the
woman had been five years old. This
latter category was set up so that there
would not be respondents with two
sets of parents. The ads asked simply
for women to volunteer to answer a
questionnaire for a research project and
to indicate their category.

... [A]pproximately seventy percent of
all women who volunteered returned the
nine page questionnaire. There are over
120 questions.... Respondents were also
encouraged to write personal narratives
about their growing up. These are
heartfelt explorations which illuminated
the individual lives of women in all
groups.

... There are 119 respondents from the
"Single Fathers" group, 106 from the *"Single Mothers"* group, 92 from the *"Biological Parents"* group, and 51 from the *"Step
parents"* group, with a diversity of ethnic,
religious, educational, economic, and geographical backgrounds, ages 18–83....

In addition to the questionnaire which
we developed... we also used The
Gough Adjective Check List.... This is
a standardized test of 300 adjectives. The
respondent is asked to check which adjectives describe herself. We believe that
the use of this check list, in conjunction
with our own questionnaire, helps to validate our findings. When applicable, the
results of the questionnaire on certain
questions and the results of the Adjective

Check List are correlated. For instance,
one question on the questionnaire asks
if the respondent was permitted risks
which other girls were not permitted. The
results from this question were then compared with the results on the Adjective
Check List, specifically the Creative Personality Scale. Are girls who are permitted more risks more apt to develop creative personalities compared to girls who
are not permitted risks? The Adjective
Check List indicated that the answer to
that question was *"Yes."*

WHAT HAS BEEN LEARNED?

The results of this research represent
the group of women who responded
and the results *may* also represent most
women in this country in each particular
group. The results suggest a variety of
indications about women who have been
raised by both biological parents, or by
single fathers, or single mothers, or by
step parents. Five of the major indications
are these:

1. The Two-Parent Family
Is Not the Best

... This research indicated that, contrary
to a long-held belief, the two-parent family is not the best family for children.
Though a large percentage of this group
responded that their childhood had been
happy, followed closely by the two single
parent groups, and though, on the Adjective Check List, the biological parent
group had the highest percentage who
scored above 51% on a number of positive traits, there are indications from the
women's answers and written comments
on the Research Questionnaire that the
family situation with two parents, while
sometimes very good, was, also, just as
often, not good at all. This does not say

that the results concerning the biological parents group are wholly negative. But it does say that this group, which has always been thought to be the best family combination for raising children, appears to provide no clear advantage.

For example, only slightly over half of the women responded that their fathers were *"there for them"* when needed. Most have negative relationships with men. There is a higher percentage of women among *single* parent families who felt their families were *close knit* than did women in two-parent families. Where there were brothers in the family, fewer boys in this biological parents group shared in the household work than did brothers in the other three groups. This was also true of fathers sharing in household work. As a result, girls in the biological parents group did an unequal share of the housework. There was a general complaint among women in this group that their fathers spent much more time with their sons than with their daughters. Most wished their fathers had been at home more....

In a recent conference of the 4400 member National Council on Family Relations, Graham Spanier spoke of an assessment of various family structures. He referred specifically to a report which pulled together the results of more than 100 studies of different family situations and their effect on children. The report was written by David Demo of Virginia Polytechnic Institute and Alan Acock of Louisiana State University. What they found was that there was no definite evidence that the family structure *per se* was crucial to the children's psychological and social well-being. What was important was the quality of the *relationship* between parent and child and, if there were two parents,

the quality of the *relationship* between parents.

Negative impact on children's self-esteem was affected by parents not spending much time with their children and greatly affected by persistent family discord. Spanier also referred to a study by Paul Amato, University of Nebraska, who found that adults who had experienced their parents divorce or a parent's death when they were young were no different in self-esteem than those raised in a family that had not experienced such disruption.

This appears to be contrary to the results written in a book by Judith Wallerstein, *"Second Chances."* In her book, Wallerstein tracks 60 families who had experienced divorce and concludes that *"almost half the children entered adulthood as worried, underachieving, self-deprecating and sometimes angry young men and women."* Wallerstein's methodology is criticized by other researchers because she used no control group for comparison. It is possible she could have tracked 60 families which had remained intact and found the same results with the children. There is no definitive study on the long-term effects of divorce. Wallerstein's results are criticized by Mel Krantzler, author of *"Creative Divorce,"* who says *"Any book that gives the impression to people that divorce is such a traumatizing experience that kids are permanently damaged for the rest of their lives is destructive. A child can understand that life has adversities ... children can learn that they have the capacity to overcome a difficulty rather than wallow in it."*

A 1991 article in the journal, *Science,* reported that 18,700 families were studied over a period of years in England and in the United States. What was learned was that the children of divorced parents had behavioral problems long before the actual divorce. This, the article stated, should cause people to question the blame they put on divorce for the children's problems. If Wallerstein had studied the children in her research before their parents divorced, she may have found they had the same problems then as they had after the divorce.

Dr. Lindsay Chase-Lansdale, one of the study's psychologists at the University of Chicago, said the findings indicate, *"if a marriage is in trouble, there are effects on the children whether or not the parents divorce."* The co-author, Dr. Andrew Cherlin, a sociologist at Johns Hopkins University, added, *"More attention needs to be paid to the children when there is marital conflict. Conflict hurts children, regardless of whether it leads to divorce or not. If there is conflict, the children need to be sheltered from it, not caught in the middle between warring parents."* The conclusion is that more of the problems which children had could be attributed to marital discord than to divorce. The study indicated that staying together for the sake of the children can be harmful to the children if the marriage is filled with conflict and discord. Difficult as it is, divorce is often a relief for many children.

There are also indications that children growing up in two-parent families where the mother does not work outside the home may develop excessive dependency. Because there is no particular prestige for women who are full-time homemakers, they are apt to overinvest in their children and to slow down their children's personal growth by not permitting adventuresome activities....

This research, based on a comparison of four groups of women raised in four different kinds of family situations, is one in the over 100 already existing which says that whether a child has two biological parents or only one, or only one remaining step parent, or only one friend or grandmother or grandfather or whomever to raise her, she has a good chance of doing well if the personal relationships are wholesome, caring and supportive. The myth that the two biological parents group is the best for children leaves people who were raised differently feeling at times like outsiders. And it leaves people who divorce feeling guilty because they are led to believe that they are harming their children. That is not so, as long as the relationship between remaining parent and child is good.

Perpetuating the myth that the two-parent family is the best serves the *status quo*. It is politically and economically expedient to keep women in jobs which pay less than men, or to keep them in a position where they are in and out of the labor force depending on the needs to take care of their children which prevents them from building up job promotions, seniority or retirement benefits....

2. Single Father Daughters Develop Strong Feminine Traits

Though most women in single father families felt *older than their years* and most said they had *lost their childhood* because of their responsibilities as children, at least three-quarters had fathers who were *there for them* when they were needed. Also, more fathers were *helpful in their daughters' bereavement* when their mother died than were single mothers helpful when a child had lost a father. If there were brothers in the family, more were helpful with household chores than were brothers in the biological parents group.

As might be expected in single father families where most fathers worked all day, most girls were *on their own* much of the time. Also within this group there was the highest percentage of fathers who *permitted risks*. Yet a higher percentage of women who reported being *permitted risks* scored over the 60th percentile range on the Adjective Check List Creative Personality Scale than did women who were not permitted risks. . . .

The single father group is the group which grew up without mothers, yet apparently they feel comfortable in the role of mother, as most evaluated themselves as *very good* mothers. This group had the highest percentage who scored above 51% on the Nurturing Scale of the Adjective Check List which is described as *"To engage in behaviors that provide material or emotional benefits to others."* Having a single father and no mother did not diminish the women's *mothering* or nurturing skills.

Also, the single father group had the highest percentage of women who said that *"nurturing"* was the most important quality for mothering and for fathering. The women in this group had the highest percentage who said that a father can be a good substitute for a mother.

Also 71% said that *"nurturing"* was the most important quality for *fathering* compared with 57% who said the same thing in the biological parents group. Fifty-one percent (compared with 42% in the biological parents group) have positive relationships with men. Having been brought up almost exclusively by a man, more girls in this group are comfortable with men than are those brought up by a man and a woman. However, not as many in the single father group (56%) have positive relationships with women as do the women (72%) in the biological parents group. When asked if their childhood had been happy, 64% reported that they had had a happy childhood. . . .

Though most said they felt *different,* and most of these because they believe they had more masculine traits than others, which correlates with their high percentage on the upper ranges of the Adjective Check List Masculine Attributes Scale, they also had the highest percentage who scored 51%–100% on *Feminine* Attributes Scale. This group has the highest percentage which desires feminine characteristics of listening and caring in a mate. It would appear that the girl raised by her father has an excellent opportunity to develop an androgenous personality with both well developed masculine and feminine traits.

3. Single Mother Daughters Develop Strong Masculine Traits

In addition to financial security, what the women in the single mother families missed most in not having a father in the home was an appearance of being *"normal,"* or *"traditional."* Though three-quarters in the single father group said they had not known anyone else raised by a single *father,* and only one-quarter of the single mother group said they had not known anyone else raised by a single *mother,* that is, there are many more children who were raised and are now being raised by single mothers, it is the women in the single mother group who seemed to have suffered a stigma or a sense of shame for their family situation.

Most likely this feeling *different* or not *normal* was because when mothers, who traditionally earn less money than fathers, raise children by themselves, it causes financial hardship on children and they compare themselves with their peers, who not only have two parents, but also have more *things.* One of the prerequisites for being *"normal"* may mean being able to be equal.

In their earliest years, life was lonely for many of these girls. Only slightly over half of their mothers were *there for them* when needed, and only one-quarter were helpful to their daughters when the girl's father died or left because of divorce or desertion. Nevertheless, women in the single mother group have the highest percentage who felt they had a *close knit* family, and the highest percentage where, if there were brothers, the boys shared equally in the housework. Sharing housework can contribute to a feeling of working together, being a team, and being *close knit.*

The women in this group also had the highest percentage who were *the little mothers,* taking care of younger siblings when their mother worked. Sixty-four percent said they felt *older than their years* though a lesser percentage said they had *lost their childhood* than women in the single father families. This group had the highest percentage who were *on their own,* slightly higher than the women in the single father families, and over half were *permitted risks* which were not permitted to other girls.

The negative result of being on their own was that many of these girls felt lonely. Yet others *on their own* explored and developed their creativity which was a positive result of being permitted risks. Being on their own, as with women in the single father family, these women were free to make many of their own decisions. About two-thirds described their childhood as *happy.* . . .

Women in this group have the highest percentage who have negative relationships with men. When answering the question of how life would have been different if they had had a father, the highest percentage said they would have had financial security, and the next high-est percentage said they would have better relationships with men. This is the group which had the highest percentage of women who do not vote and who said they would not vote for any man. Their relationships with women are very good. . . .

When asked what qualities they desire in a mate, most desired androgenous qualities such as sense of humor, honesty, friendship, and companionship. They had the lowest percentage of women who desired stereotypical feminine qualities. As a comparison, 62% of the women in the single *father* group desired sterotypical feminine qualities of caring, listening, understanding, and only 20% of the women in the single *mother* group desired these qualities. . . .

In all likelihood, the father who finds himself or chooses to place himself in the position of raising children has either been conditioned to permit his feminine side and is a nurturing type man to begin with, or the act of raising children has brought out the nurturing side of his personality. . . .

Therefore women raised by nurturing single fathers not only have strong masculine traits but also strong feminine traits. But women raised by single *mothers* have more masculine traits than feminine traits. This is borne out by their perception of themselves in the Adjective Check List where a higher percentage scored in the upper percentile range in Masculine Attributes Scale (51%) than in the Feminine Attributes Scale (39%). The girl who grows up with a caring father in the home has the opposite sex on which to *"bounce off"* her adolescent sexual development. If it is a healthy father-daughter relationship he will assure her that she is doing all right in her role of growing up to be a woman. The girl in the single mother home does not have that opposite sex parent who will approve of her feminine side.

4. Single Parent Families Have Advantages

A father in the home gives the appearance of stability, even though he may be uncommunicative, often absent, or abusive. A mother in the home gives the appearance of wholesomeness, even though she may be alcoholic, demanding, or intrusive. Under the best circumstances, with a father who is present, communicative, supportive and caring, and a mother who is gentle, loving and understanding, and because she does not work outside her home has unlimited time for her children, and where there is enough financial security in the home, a child is blessed. And there are such families. But they are the exception rather than the rule. Actually a family with a father and a mother who does not work outside the home represents only 8% of the families today.

Tradition, which is important in the biological parents group, has been destroyed in the single parent group. When one parent dies or leaves, whatever habitual patterns of family life there were come to an end. For a long time, maybe even for years, there is a void. What to do at Christmas? Can the family take a vacation? As time goes on, the trauma of the shock subsides and new patterns evolve, usually without planning. One might say, *"new traditions"* replace the old.

People learn that they can survive what might have been seen as impossible to bear. Widows and divorcees find jobs to support their children and widowers pick up the threads of their lives and arrange for child care. The children go back to school after the funeral or after the shock of being deserted by one of their parents. Though they are hurting inside, they play on the swings and teeter-totters and force themselves to learn their multiplication tables. They realize earlier than other children that a lot of the work of keeping the household running rests on their shoulders. No doubt reluctantly and sadly at first they absorb the jobs of vacuuming rugs, getting dinner started, caring for younger children to keep them off the streets. But what they have learned in all of this is how to adapt, how to shed the old, and how to get on with the new.

These are hard lessons, and it is not recommended that children live through this kind of trauma in order to learn adaptation. But children who have survived hardship, and have had a supportive remaining parent, claim they are the stronger for it. Having to make a major life change in their future will probably not be devastating. Many in all groups, including the biological parents group, have said that the problems they have survived have made them stronger.

Girls who are brought up by single parents, whether mothers or fathers, develop strong, independent personalities, but society has a problem with strong, independent women. These women are apt to be assertive, to know that they can get along without men, that they can try new things, that they can test authority. Many have had tremendous responsibilities most of their lives and most are ready and eager to open new doors for themselves because, for them, tradition is not sacred.

As one woman in the single father group wrote, *"I feel that I have obtained a great benefit from my childhood. I think because I had to be responsible for taking care of myself and my sister, etc., that I got a 'jump' on maturity, in relation to others my age. This has meant that there are levels of growth which I feel I have access to, which a majority of people don't seem to have."* Other women in the single father group wrote, *"I believe that one good parent—mother or father—is better than one or two lousy ones. But I am well aware of the burdens of raising children alone. I would not choose to do it that way. It was not my father's choice either." "I think it would be an advantage to have both parents, only if they were happy together, or course." "I feel like being raised by my dad was beneficial. I saw a man's point of view clearer than many women ever see." ...*

[Another woman in the single father group wrote,] *"I feel that having been raised by my father was both an advantage and a disadvantage. Of course it would have been better to have had both a mother and father, loving and supportive of each other and their children. This is Utopia. I feel the perfect family does not exist, and am only now beginning to be mature enough to make the best of what we had. I think I have an inner strength many women never will have. Because of growing up with no female role model, I was forced to learn to rely on my own intuition and intelligence. This makes me no better or worse than other women. However it does make me inherently stronger." ...*

While the loss of a parent was not without trauma for the women in this study, for some there is compensation. For instance, for women in the single father family who never knew their mother, or women in any group who were badly treated by their mothers, it is said that in adulthood, in having and caring for their own children these women experience themselves as the *"mothered child"* which they never were. These women transfer to their children the love and understanding which they did not receive and in so doing restore their own lack of mothering to themselves.

There is also the advantage in single parent families that a girl does not have to compete with her mother for the affection of her father, or a boy does not have to compete with his father for the affection of his mother....

[One woman] who mentions both the advantages and disadvantages wrote, *"I don't feel as if I've missed very much. I have had a lot of wonderful experiences. Yet I do believe I missed a wonderful experience when I grew up without a mother. I grew up as a happy person, yet I do believe that on the sub-conscious level something was always missing."* In families where there are two parents, many children have been exposed to severe parental fighting from which children of single parents were spared, though many related to fighting before a divorce. One in the single father group wrote, *"I used to witness fights among my friends' parents and remember feeling lucky I didn't have to see my own parents fight."* ...

Most statistics on single families refer to single mothers. It is as if the single father family does not exist. Yet, even without statistics, there is an awareness that fathers raising their children by themselves is a growing phenomenon. Eventually the statistics may tell us about the level of education of a single father, his salary range and type of employment as the statistics now tell us about single mothers. For instance, in a study made by the National Association of Social Workers of single mothers in 12 states in 1987, 60% of the mothers said they believed their families were stronger than two-parent families; and 25% said they were just as strong.

Generally conceded to be the root of many social problems, the single parent family, which invariably means the single mother family, has been the scapegoat for many of this country's ills. It is usually the female who is either directly or indirectly blamed. The common erroneous complaint has been, "*If only women would stay home and take care of their kids there wouldn't be so many divorces, kids wouldn't be dropping out of school and getting into trouble. There would be better morals.*" As history has recorded, the virtue of a country rests on the virtue of its women. A woman raising children by herself, or even an employed mother in a two-parent family, is not held up as an ideal mother. . . .

5. Most Children With Step Mothers Are Emotionally and Otherwise Abused

While there were some disturbingly sad anecdotes from women in all groups in this research, the most consistently cruel came from the women who had grown up with a step mother. Not that all step mothers were cold and uncaring. There were several who were dearly loved by their step daughters. But these were rare. Not only did the step mothers cause grievous unhappiness for the girls in these families, but their own biological fathers, married to their step mothers, failed their daughters.

These girls had nowhere else to go. One of their parents had died so it wasn't as though there had been a divorce and then remarriages and a second set of parents. Sometimes relatives of the deceased parent attempted to help, but often the step parent prevented the girl from seeing these relatives. It is almost as though the step parent was more or less jealous of the ghost of their spouse's first spouse.

On every question, when comparing answers from women who had step mothers with those of women who were in the step parent group but had their own biological mother, there is almost a two to one difference in the degree of either helpfulness or loss. For instance, on the question, "*Do you feel because of your family situation that you lost your childhood?*" 30% of the women who had biological mothers in this group answered, "*Yes,*" compared with 58% of the women with step mothers. To the question, "*Was your childhood happy?*" 63% with biological mothers in this step parent group answered, "*Yes,*" compared with 37% of the women with step mothers.

To the question, "*Was your father there for you?*" 36% with step fathers answered, "*Yes,*" compared with . . . 32% with biological fathers in this group. "*Was your mother there for you?*" 32% of the women with step mothers answered, "*Yes,*" compared with 60% of the women with biological mothers in this step parent group. Biological fathers were not very helpful for their daughters when the mother had died. . . .

This group, as a whole, has the highest percentage (27%) of women who had been sexually abused. When the group is separated as to those with step mothers and those with step fathers, it is the group with step fathers that has the highest rate of sexual abuse. Thirty-eight percent of the women with step fathers had been sexually abused, mostly by their step fathers, though neighbors, step brothers, family friends, a janitor and a teacher contributed to this percentage. Sixteen percent of women with step mothers had been sexually abused; the abusers included brothers, step brothers, an uncle and a cousin.

This step parent group has the highest percentage of women who had fantasy mothers (56%) of those with step mothers, and the highest percentage of those with fantasy fathers (42%) of those with step fathers. Almost half of the women with step mothers did not get along with their step mothers at all. The group as a whole has the highest percentage who have *hostile* relationships with women, the highest which have *negative* relationships with women, the highest which have *difficult* relationships with women, and the highest percentage which have *hostile* relationships with men. Thirty-one percent of women in this group are overweight....

It is the step parent group that had the highest percentage scoring over the 50th percentile range on Autonomy on the Adjective Check List. Autonomy is described by the Scale as *"To act independently of others or of social values and expectations."* If one survives emotional hardship, one apparently develops a strong sense of independence. Though many were emotionally and some physically and sexually abused, most of the women in this group were capable of getting on with their lives. Being autonomous, they have achieved a separation from their earlier traumatizers. And as they have the highest percent which scored high in the personality trait, *"Change,"* on the Adjective Check List, described as *"seeks novelty of experience and avoids routine,"* most of the women in this group may very well keep life interesting for themselves and others....

IMPLICATIONS FOR THE FUTURE

Rewriting the Myth of the Two-Parent Family

Changing myths seems impossible, especially when there are advantages to some people to keep them. The myth that the two-parent family is the best is just that —a myth. Myths serve an important purpose and are the basis of religion and governments. But they are not based on fact. Our government is founded on the myth of equality. Actual equality does not exist but it is something to aspire to. The myth that the two-parent family is best for children served a purpose. It was something to aspire to and no doubt kept fathers in families who might otherwise have left their wives and children, at a time in history when women did not work and were therefore dependent on a man for subsistence.

Many happy two-parent families have existed throughout history, and many unhappy two-parent families have survived, locked in emotional misery because divorce was scandalous (a method for preserving the myth), because women could not earn a living, and because of the power of the myth. Unhappy people stayed in marriages *"for the sake of the children"*—a great burden to put on children —and themselves.

Because women in the biological parents group in this research had as much strife in their childhood as the women in other groups, it is time to rewrite the myth of the two-parent family being best for children.

Among much of what has been learned in this research is that maintaining the myth of the superiority of the two-parent family not only lends itself to deceit but it is also harmful to those *not* in a two-parent family. If a child is not in what is considered the *best* or the *normal* family arrangement, she/he feels *different* as most of the women in this research felt who were not in the biological parents group. Being in what is perceived as a second class situation can tarnish a child's self-esteem. Many women expressed a sense of shame which they felt in their childhood because of their single parentage.

While most of the women in this research who lived in single or step parent families overcame that sense of being outside the norm, it was something the children today should *not* have to overcome. There are and will be so many children growing up in single parent homes that their numbers should help relieve stress about not having both parents and should keep them from feeling so different. But more importantly, they should know that the two-parent family, which is held up to them as the ideal, in which they have no part, is, *as a category,* no better than *their* family category.

The increase in the number of single parent families and the lower financial ability of single parent families means that there will be more children living in poverty because most single parents are women. When the media refers to single parent families it is understood that the single parent is a woman. The growing number of single *father* families is practically ignored. It is known that single father families fare better economically than single mother families because men generally earn more money.

Now and in the future, conferences on family life must include some recognition that families *other* than two-parent families deserve respect, support, encouragement and praise for doing a difficult job. Single parents and children of single parents need to know that *any* family, *including single and step parent families,* which has financial security, good personal relationships, which cares about its children and promotes their healthy interests, is a good family for children.

POSTSCRIPT
Is the Two-Parent Family Best?

Stephenson's attack on the traditional two-parent family as being the best situation for nurturing young children may offend some, but it grants credibility to successful parents in nontraditional systems. Her research-based conclusions may not set well with those who tend to hold conservative, traditional beliefs. But her questioning of the stereotype provides a necessary parry to the foil presented by Whitehead's writings supporting the conservative "family values" position touted by many in the political and religious arenas.

Human services professionals, business and industry employers, government bureaucrats, educators, court workers, physicians, judges, and childcare providers deal frequently with the questions that are raised about parenting form and style in these two selections. Current discussions have yet to provide any easy answers about how to handle the many situations that arise.

The issue is not likely to go away. Perhaps by studying various family lifestyles and learning from the parenting styles that are used within them we can build a set of principles and practices that are in the best interests of the children. For example, in *Social Origins of Private Life: A History of American Families, 1600–1900*, Stephanie Coontz tells the story of a Native American in the sixteenth century whose parenting style was being criticized by a French missionary. The Jesuit missionary was trying to introduce "civilized family norms" to the New World native. The Naskapi Indian with whom the missionary was talking responded, "You French people love only your own children; but we love all the children of the tribe."

SUGGESTED READINGS

S. Coontz, *Social Origins of Private Life: A History of American Families, 1600–1900* (Verso, 1988).

S. Coontz, *The Way We Never Were: American Families and the Nostalgia Trap* (Basic Books, 1992).

J. Held and A. Shreve, *Remaking Motherhood: How Working Mothers Are Shaping Our Children's Future* (Viking Penguin, 1987).

R. Kagan, *Families in Perceptual Crisis* (W. W. Norton, 1989).

J. Wallerstein and S. Blakeless, *Second Chances: Women and Children a Decade After Divorce* (Ticknor & Fields, 1989).

ISSUE 3

Are Stepfamilies Inherently Problematic?

YES: David Popenoe, from "The Evolution of Marriage and the Problem of Stepfamilies: A Biosocial Perspective," in Alan Booth and Judy Dunn, eds., *Stepfamilies: Who Benefits? Who Does Not?* (Lawrence Erlbaum, 1994)

NO: Lawrence A. Kurdek, from "Remarriages and Stepfamilies Are Not Inherently Problematic," in Alan Booth and Judy Dunn, eds., *Stepfamilies: Who Benefits? Who Does Not?* (Lawrence Erlbaum, 1994)

ISSUE SUMMARY

YES: David Popenoe, dean of the College of Arts and Sciences at Rutgers University, argues that stepfamilies are biologically and culturally inferior to intact and single-parent families for raising children, and he recommends that every effort be made to halt their growth.

NO: Psychologist Lawrence A. Kurdek calls into question several of the major arguments advanced by Popenoe. Kurdek characterizes stepfamilies as a natural outgrowth of societal change and states that most stepparents and stepchildren are coping successfully.

After World War II the typical family pattern was for children to live to late adolescence with their married biological parents. Much has changed since then. According to projections from family demographers, no longer will even half of the children born since 1980 have that experience. Divorce and remarriage will likely be a major part of many children's lives.

Children in stepfamilies face a sequence of three major life events. First, the dissolution of their parents' marriage. Second, the establishment of a single-parent family. Finally, the reorganization of their lives into a stepfamily arrangement. Each of these stressful life circumstances requires major adjustments on the part of children and parents.

Some research indicates that children raised in stepfamilies are at higher risk of school failure, fragmented social relationships, and psychological problems than other children. Other studies conclude that living in a step-family is just one of the many factors that influence how children develop as they grow into adulthood, that only a minority of children have long-term problems. Lawrence Ganong and Marilyn Coleman, in their book *Remarried Family Relationships* (Sage Publications, 1994), argue that family scholars who talk excessively about risk factors and negative outcomes are assuming that stepfamilies are dysfunctional compared to first-married families. Such comparisons, which they label "deficit-comparison," are said to stigmatize stepfamilies and make it more difficult for them to gain useful knowledge, kin and community support, and needed improvements in government policies and programs.

Much of the recent literature on stepfamilies takes a problem-solving approach. For example, in an article in the *Journal of Divorce and Remarriage* (vol. 14, 1990, pp. 3–12), Emily Visher and John Visher describe six characteristics of successful stepfamilies:

1. Losses have been mourned.
2. Expectations are realistic.
3. Parents form a strong, unified bond.
4. Constructive new family traditions and rituals are established.
5. Satisfactory steprelationships are formed.
6. Separate households cooperate rather than compete.

The same journal contains a report of a survey in which 200 remarried couples were asked what advice they would give to other couples that were considering remarriage. They gave the following recommendations (ranked in order of importance): have open, honest communication; clarify expectations and reasons for remarriage; ensure compatibility of values and philosophies; be patient, supportive, and compromising with new family members; work hard; seek counseling, if needed; and learn from prior experiences.

Do overly negative images of stepparents and their children impinge on a stepfamily's ability to construct a successful new relationship? Do overly positive images fare any better? Each may prompt parents and children to miscalculate the tasks before them. Perhaps it would be more productive to ask, Can we identify parents and children who have benefited from remarriage? How have well-functioning stepfamilies gone about building successful relationships? Are there coping strategies and negotiation styles that seem to facilitate better parent-child relationships in stepfamilies? Can we identify policies and programs that are most helpful to stepfamilies? How do age of parents, age of children, gender, ethnicity, stage in the marital life cycle, and income affect stepfamily relationships? Do certain stepfamilies face a greater chance of family breakup?

As you read the two selections that follow, consider whether or not David Popenoe is correct in his belief that encouraging two-parent families to stay together would be better for children than providing support during the process of divorce and eventual remarriage. Or is Lawrence A. Kurdek's view that stepfamilies are coping well despite the social, economic, and cultural changes in American life since the 1950s more accurate?

YES

David Popenoe

THE EVOLUTION OF MARRIAGE AND THE PROBLEM OF STEPFAMILIES: A BIOSOCIAL PERSPECTIVE

One of the fastest growing family types in every advanced industrial nation has been the stepfamily....

Since 1960 ... the chances of spending part or all of one's childhood outside an intact family have grown dramatically. According to various estimates, the chances that a child born around 1980 will not be living at age 17 with both biological parents have increased to over 50% (Hernandez, 1993).... In 1960, an estimated 83% of all children are living with their two married, biological parents; by 1990, this figure was 58%.... More than 9 out of 10 stepchildren live with their biological mother and a stepfather....

THE PROBLEM OF STEPFAMILIES

Many, and perhaps most stepfamilies today lead contented home lives and produce happy and successful children. But a growing body of evidence suggests that the increase of stepfamilies has created serious problems for child welfare.... Contrary to the view of some social scientists in recent years, who believed that the effects of family fragmentation on children were both modest and ephemeral, there is now substantial evidence to indicate that the child outcomes of these alternative family forms are significantly inferior to those of families consisting of two biological parents. Compared to those in intact families, children in single-parent and stepfamilies are significantly more likely to have emotional and behavioral problems, to receive the professional help of psychologists, to have health problems, to perform poorly in school and drop out, and to leave home early. Moreover, some of these negative effects have been shown to persist into adult life.

Social scientists used to believe that, for positive child outcomes, stepfamilies were preferable to single-parent families. Today, we are not so sure. Stepfamilies typically have an economic advantage, but some recent studies indicate that the children of stepfamilies have as many behavioral and emotional problems as the children of single-parent families, and possibly more (e.g., Kiernan, 1992)....

Certain problems are more prevalent in stepfamilies than in other family forms. A common finding is that stepparents provide less warmth and communicate less well with their children than do biological parents (Thomson, McLenahan, & Curtin, 1992). A number of studies have found that a child is far more likely to be abused by a stepfather than by the biological father.... Compared to children in intact and single-parent households,... "stepchildren are not merely 'disadvantaged,' but imperiled" (Wilson & Daly, 1987, p. 230).

As in single-parent families, a major problem of the stepfamily phenomenon is the net loss of fathering in children's lives.... Many studies have shown that stepfathering acts to diminish contact between original fathers and their biological children (Furstenberg & Nord, 1985; Furstenberg, Nord, Peterson, & Zill, 1983; Mott, 1990; Seltzer & Bianchi, 1988). In their turn, stepfathers take a considerably less active role in parenting than do custodial biological fathers, according to many studies, and frequently become disengaged from their stepchildren following the establishment of a stepfamily....

Another problematic aspect of stepfamilies is their high breakup rate, higher than that of two-biological-parent families. According to the most recent census data, more than 62% of remarriages among women under age 40 will end in divorce, and the more that children are involved, the higher the redivorce rate.... By one estimate, about 15% of all children born in recent decades will go through at least two family disruptions before coming of age (Furstenberg, 1990).

In summary, according to the available evidence, stepfamilies tend to have less cohesive, more problematic, and more stressful family relationships than intact families, and probably also than single-parent families. Put more strongly by a recent article in *Psychology Today*, stepfamilies "are such a minefield of divided loyalties, emotional traps, and management conflicts that they are the most fragile form of family in America" ("Shuttle Diplomacy," 1993).

BIOSOCIAL BASES OF FAMILY LIFE

In order to better understand the special problems that stepfamilies pose, it is necessary to delve into the fundamental biosocial nature of human family life....

From the perspective of evolutionary biology, the organization of the human nuclear family is based on two inherited biological predispositions that confer reproductive success, one that operates between parent and child, and the other between parent and parent. The first is a predisposition to advance the interests of genetic relatives before those of unrelated individuals.... With respect to children, this means that men and women have likely evolved to invest more in children who are related to them than in those who are not....

The second biological predisposition is for males and females to have some emotional affinity for each other beyond the sexual act, and to establish pair bonds. We tend to fall in love with one person at a time. Although we think of love attachments as being highly social in character, they also have a strong biological component. There exists an "affective attachment" between men and women that causes us to be infatuated with each other, to feel a sense of well-being when we are together with a loved one, and to feel jealous when others attempt to intrude into our relationship. Around the world today, almost all adults pair-bond with someone of the opposite sex for at least a portion of their lives, and monogamous relationships are the rule....

One fundamental reason for family instability is that, at heart, human beings are probably more self-interested than truly altruistic, even toward our own relatives and intimates. We act, first and foremost, in the interest of self-survival. But another reason is that the male–female bond, especially when compared to the mother–infant bond, is notoriously fragile. Although marriage is universal, divorce has also been a central feature of human social life....

Possibly the most disintegrating force acting on the human pair bond is the male sexual drive.... Universally, men are the more sexually driven and promiscuous, while women are more relationship-oriented....

SEXUAL AND REPRODUCTIVE STRATEGIES

...Biologically, the primary reproductive function for males is to inseminate, and for females is to harbor the growing fetus.... Males, therefore, have more incentive to spread their numerous sperm more widely among many females, and females have a strong incentive to bind males to themselves for the long-term care of their more limited number of potential offspring.

The woman's best reproductive strategy is to ensure that she maximizes the survivability of the one baby she is able to produce every few years through gaining the provision and protection of the father.... The man's best strategy, however, may be twofold. He wants his baby to survive, yes, and for that reason he may provide help to his child's mother. But, at the same time, it is relatively costless to him... to inseminate other women, and thereby help to further insure that his genes are passed on....

Why aren't all men promiscuous cads? Because, in addition to the pull of the biological pair-bonding and parenting predispositions discussed previously, virtually all human societies have established strong cultural sanctions that seek to limit male promiscuity and protect the sanctity of the family....

If a man is to stay with one woman rather than pursue many different women, according to sociobiologists, the "paternal certainty" of his offspring is extremely important. An woman can be certain about her own offspring, but a man cannot be.... [A] male tends to invest in his mate's children only when his paternal confidence is high....

CULTURAL CONTEXTS

... During the most recent stages of the development of the human species, rapidly paced cultural evolution has overtaken slow-moving biological evolution as the main force of social change (Hallpike, 1986; Scott, 1989). One result if that family structures around the world today are widely variable, determined more by cultural differences than by biological predispositions....

Associated with the rise of horticultural and agrarian societies was fundamental shift in people's attitudes toward reproduction (Lancaster & Lancaster, 1987)....

[W]ith increased density of population and wealth, people came to perceive that resources were limited, that major differentials existed between who survived and who did not, and that survival was very much dependent on who controlled the most resources. It was no longer sufficient merely to rear as many offspring as possible and hope that they would survive to reproduce. Reproductive strategies became individually tailored to maximize the use and control of resources. It was necessary to try to guarantee children access to resources in the form of education or inheritance, for example, so that they would have an advantage over other parents' children.

Marriage and Divorce in Premodern Societies
The new perception of resource scarcity in complex societies generated a dramatic transformation in family life and kinship relations, including concern for the "legitimacy" of children, the rise of inheritance laws, and the careful control of female sexuality. The nuclear family gave way to the complex, extended family; the conjugal unit became imbedded in an elaborate kinship network. The father role of authority figure and head of household grew in importance, whereas the status of women deteriorated....

Through the institutionalization of cultural norms and sanctions, complex societies have become heavily devoted to socially controlling male and female sexual strategies. The most important social institution serving this purpose is marriage. Marriage can be defined simply as "a relationship within which a group socially approves and encourages sexual intercourse and the birth of children" (Frayser, 1985, p. 248).... Throughout most of recorded history, until recently, most marriages were arranged (although the principals typically had a say in the matter); they were less alliances of two individuals than of two kin networks, typically involving an exchange of money or goods.

Various theories have been put forth to explain the fundamental purposes of marriage. But certainly one purpose is, as noted previously, to hold men to the pair bond, thereby helping to ensure high quality offspring and, at the same time, helping to control the open conflict that would result if men were allowed unlimited ability to pursue the "cad" strategy with other men's wives....

Marriage and Divorce in Urban-Industrial Societies
... In urban-industrial societies, reproductive concerns about the quantity of children have largely given way to concerns about quality. Children in these societies require massive parental investments if they are to succeed, and child-rearing has become extraordinarily expensive in terms of time and money....

The modern nuclear family that accompanied the emergence of urban-industrialism and cultural modernity in the West was distinctly different from its preindustrial predecessor.... The new family form was emotionally intense, privatized, and child-oriented; in authority structure, it was relatively egalitarian; and it placed a high value on individualism in the sense of individual rights and autonomy....

The big winners from the emergence of the modern nuclear family... were... children. In preindustrial Europe, parental care of children does not seem to have been particularly prominent, and such practices as infanticide, wet nursing, child fosterage, and the widespread use of lower status surrogate caretakers were common (Draper &

Harpending, 1987).... Draper and Harpending (1987) suggested that one of the greatest achievements of the modern nuclear family was the return to the high-investment nurturing of children by their biological parents, the kind of parenting characteristic of our hunter-gatherer ancestors....

Family stability during this era, together with parental investments in children, may have been greater than at any other time in history. Cultural sanctions concerning marriage were powerfully enforce, and thanks to ever lowering death rates and low divorce rates, both parents were typically able to see their children through to adulthood. This remarkably high family stability helps to explain why the family situation in the United States today appears so troubled, particularly in the minds of the older generation.

RECENT FAMILY AND CULTURAL CHANGE IN AMERICA

In the past half century, the U.S. family has been on a social roller coaster. The ups and downs have been quite astonishing. Following World War II, the United States entered a two-decade period of extraordinary economic growth and material progress. Commonly referred to as simply "the 50s," it was the most sustained period of prosperity in U.S. history. Together with most other industrially developed societies of the world, this nation saw improvements in the levels of health, material consumption, and economic security that had scant historical precedent. For most Americans, the improvements included striking increases in longevity, buying power, personal net worth, and government-sponsored economic security.

The 1950s was also an era of remarkable familism and family togetherness, with the family as an institution undergoing unprecedented growth and stability within the middle and working classes. The marriage rate reached an all-time high, the birth rate returned to the high levels of earlier in the century, generating the baby boom, and the divorce rate leveled off. Home, motherhood, and child-centeredness reigned high in the lexicon of cultural values. A higher proportion of children were growing up in stable, two-parent families than ever before in U.S. history.

Beginning in the 1960s, however, a series of unanticipated social and cultural developments took place that shook the foundations of the modern nuclear family.... Men abandoned their families at an unprecedented rate, leaving behind broken homes and single-parent, female-headed households. Women relinquished their traditional mother/housewife roles in unexpectedly large numbers and entered the labor force. The percentage of births taking place outside of marriage skyrocketed. Highly permissive sexual behavior became acceptable....

Not only did the modern nuclear family become fragmented, but participation in family life went into a precipitous decline....

Underlying these family-related trends was an extraordinary shift in cultural values and self-definition.... Trust in, and a sense of obligation toward, the larger society and its institutions rapidly eroded; the traditional moral authority of social institutions such as schools, churches, and governments withered. What emerged, instead, was a new importance given by large segments of the population to the personal goal and even moral commandment of expressive individualism or "self-fulfillment" (Bellah, Madsen, Sullivan, Swidler, & Tipton, 1985)....

The institution of marriage was particularly hard hit....

The marriage rate has steadily declined over the past few decades, from 76.7 marriages per 1,000 unmarried women in 1970, to 54.2 in 1990. The divorce rate, although it has leveled off, remains at an historically high level. Marriage has become a voluntary relationship which individuals can make and break at will. As one indicator of this shift, the legal regulation of marriage and divorce has become increasingly lax. In summary, fewer people ever marry, those who marry do so at a later age, a smaller proportion of life is spent in wedlock, and marriages are of a shorter duration (Espanshade, 1985).

... One of the significant attitudinal changes of recent years is the rising acceptance of divorce, especially when children are involved....

The high voluntary dissolution of marriages might not be a serious problem if only adults were involved although, even then, it certainly generates considerable instability and anxiety. The problem is that young children, if they are to grow up successfully, still need strong attachments to parents. The evidence strongly suggests that parental bonds with children have suffered in recent years, and that the tremendous parenting advantages of the modern nuclear family are on the wane....

THE SOCIAL RESPONSE TO STEPFAMILIES

The decline of marriage and the increase of divorce are, of course, the major contributors to the recent growth of stepfamilies....

It is surely the case, especially in view of the diminutive of kinship and neighborhood groupings, that stepfamilies need our collective help and understanding more than ever. But we should not confuse short-run actions aimed at helping stepfamilies with long-run solutions. If the argument presented [here] is correct, and the family is fundamentally rooted in biology and at least partly activated by the "genetically selfish" activities of human beings, childrearing by nonrelatives is inherently problematic. It is not that unrelated individuals are unable to do the job of parenting, it is just that they are not as likely to do the job well. Stepfamily problems, in short, may be so intractable that the best strategy for dealing with them is to do everything possible to minimize their occurrence.

Unfortunately, many members of the therapeutic and helping professions, together with a large group of social science allies, now take the view that the trend toward stepfamilies cannot be reversed....

A close companion to this belief in stepfamily inevitability and optimum fit with a changing society is the view that we should now direct most of our attention toward understanding the familial processes of stepfamilies, and seek to develop social policies and interventions that will assist children's adjustment to them.... Once stepfamilies become more common and accepted, it is argued, and once our society comes to define the roles of stepparenthood more clearly, the problems of stepfamilies will diminish.

This may be a largely incorrect understanding of the situation. The reason why unrelated stepparents find their parenting roles more stressful and less satisfying than biological parents is probably due much less to social stigma and to the uncertainty of their obligations, as to the fact that they gain fewer intrinsic emotional rewards from carrying out those obligations....

If, as the findings of evolutionary biology strongly suggest, there is a biological basis to parenting, we must question the view, widespread in the social sciences, that parenthood is merely a social role anyone can play if only they learn the part....

The biosocial perspective presented in this essay leads to the conclusion that we as a society should be doing much more to halt the growth of stepfamilies. It is important to give great respect to those stepfamilies that are doing their job well, and to provide both assistance and compassion for those that are experiencing difficulties. But such efforts should not overshadow the paramount importance of public policies designed to promote and preserve two-biological-parent families, and of endeavors to reverse the cultural drift toward radical individualism and the decline of marriage.

REFERENCES

Bellah, R. N., Madsen, R., Sullivan, W. M., Swidler, A., & Tipton, S. M. (1985). *Habits of the heart: Individualism and commitment in american life.* Berkeley: University of California.

Daly, M., & Wilson, M. (1987). The Darwinian psychology of discriminative parental solicitude. *Nebraska Symposium on Motivation.*

Draper, P., & Harpending, H. (1987). Parent investment and the child's environment. In J. B. Lancaster, J. Altmann, A. S. Rossi, & L. R. Sherrod (Eds.), *Parenting across the life span: Biosocial*

dimensions (pp. 207–235). New York: Aldine De Gruyter.

Espenshade, T. J. (1985). The recent decline of american marriage. In K. Davis (Ed.), *Contemporary marriage* (pp. 53–90). New York: Russell Sage Foundation.

Frayser, S. (1985). *Varieties of sexual experience: An anthropological perspective on human sexuality,* New Haven, CT: HRAF Press.

Furstenberg, F. F., Jr. (1990). Divorce and the American family. *Annual Review of Sociology, 16,* 379–403.

Furstenberg, F. F., Jr., & Nord, C. W. (1985). Parenting apart: Patterns of childbearing after marital disruption. *Journal of Marriage and the Family, 47*(4), 893–905.

Furstenberg, F. F., Jr., Nord, C. W., Peterson, J. L., & Zill, N. (1983). The life course of children of divorce: Marital disruption and parental contact. *American Sociological Review, 48*(2), 656–658.

Hallpike, C. R. (1986). *The principles of social evolution.* Oxford: Clarendon.

Hernandez, D. J. (1993). *America's children.* New York: Russell Sage Foundation.

Kiernan, K. E. (1992). The impact of family disruption in childhood on transitions made in young adult life. *Population Studies, 46,* 213–234.

Lancaster, J. B., & Lancaster, C. S. (1987). The watershed: Change in parental-investment and family formation strategies in the course of human evolution. In J. B. Lancaster, J. Altmann, A. S. Rossi, & L. R. Sherrod (Eds.), *Parenting across the life span: Biosocial dimensions* (pp. 187–205). New York: Aldine de Gruyter.

Mott, F. L. (1990). When is father really gone? Paternal-child contact in father absent homes. *Demography, 27*(4), 499–517.

Scott, J. P. (1989). *The evolution of social systems.* New York: Gordon & Breach.

Seltzer, J. A., & Bianchi, S. M. (1988). Children's contact with absent parents. *Journal of Marriage and the Family, 50,* 663–677.

Shuttle diplomacy. (1993, July/August). *Psychology Today,* p. 15.

Thomson, E., McLanahan, S. S., & Curtin, R. B. (1992). Family structure, gender, and parental socialization. *Journal of Marriage and the Family, 54*(2), 368–378.

Wilson, M. I., & Daly, M. (1987). Risk of maltreatment of children living with stepparents. In R. J. Gelles & J. B. Lancaster (Eds.), *Child abuse and neglect: Biosocial dimensions* (pp. 215–232). New York: Aldine de Gruyter.

NO

Lawrence A. Kurdek

REMARRIAGES AND STEPFAMILIES ARE NOT INHERENTLY PROBLEMATIC

My strongest reactions to [professor of sociology David] Popenoe's chapter ["The Evolution of Marriage and the Problem of Stepfamilies: A Biosocial Perspective," in Alan Booth and Judy Dunn, eds., *Stepfamilies: Who Benefits? Who Does Not?*] were disappointment and irritation.... I had expected a critical review of the factors that determine both relationship commitment (e.g., Kurdek, 1993a) and relationship stability (e.g., Kurdek, 1993b) in remarriages involving children. No such review was presented.

Instead, Popenoe uses a biosocial perspective to make sweeping claims about the nature of family life that result in the conclusion that society should do more to halt the growth of stepfamilies....

CHILDREN OF STEPFAMILIES HAVE AS MANY BEHAVIORAL AND EMOTIONAL PROBLEMS AS THE CHILDREN OF SINGLE-PARENT FAMILIES, AND POSSIBLY MORE

My response to this claim has four parts: (a) comparisons between family structures should include mention of the size of any obtained differences between these family structures, (b) comparisons among divorce-related family structures need to take into account the number of parental divorces experienced, (c) the key family structure comparison involves stepfamilies and single divorced-parent families, and (d) comparisons involving stepfamilies need to consider the structural heterogeneity of stepfamilies. I expand on each of these parts.

In their influential meta-analysis of parental divorce and children's well-being, Amato and Keith (1991) presented information on the nature of differences between children in intact families and children in stepfamilies. True to the pattern Popenoe describes, relative to children in intact families, those in stepfamilies had more conduct problems, lower psychological adjustment, and lower self-esteem.... Although reliable, the differences between the two groups are fairly weak....

Based on evidence from the life events, attachment, and family process literatures, there is reason to expect that the children and adolescents most at risk for behavioral and emotional problems are not those in stepfamilies, but those who have experienced multiple parental divorces and, consequently, multiple parenting transitions. Although evidence on this point is limited, it is consistent.

Studies that have examined the effects of parenting transitions on child and adolescent outcomes have typically compared four groups. These are children living continuously with both biological parents, children who have experienced one parental divorce and live with a single mother, children who have experienced one parental divorce and have made the additional transition to living with a mother and stepfather, and children who have experienced more than one parental divorce. Because of their relatively small numbers, children living with single divorced fathers and children living in stepmother families are usually excluded (see Kurdek & Fine, 1993).

Across a range of outcome variables and sources of information, it is the multiple divorce group—not the stepfamily group—that differs most strongly and negatively from the two-parent group. In fact, few differences emerge between children living continuously with both biological parents and either children living with a singly divorced mother or children living in a stepfather family. These findings lead to the plausible conclusion that what negatively affects children's well-being is not so much the kind of family structure in which they happen to reside, but the history of the quality and consistency of the parenting they receive....

Despite the emphasis Popenoe places on family structure, he fails to recognize that stepfamilies themselves are quite structurally diverse. To his credit, he does note that stepfamilies may result from parental death, parental abandonment, or parental divorce. However, he does not mention that there may be important differences between stepfather families and stepmother families, or that the remarriage history of each spouse may affect the stability of the remarriage. Nor does he state that a joint consideration of the husbands' and wives' parent and custody status relevant to previous marriages leads to at least nine types of stepfamilies, and highlights the distinction between residential and nonresidential stepfamilies, or that a substantial number of children—as many as 300,000 children for women in second marriages alone —are born into stepfamilies (Wineberg, 1992). Given such diversity within stepfamily structures, the general and unqualified claim that stepfamilies are no better than single-parent families in unfounded.

STEPFAMILIES ARE MORE UNSTABLE THAN INTACT FAMILIES

Popenoe claims that one problematic aspect of stepfamilies is their high breakup rate. However, a close reading of the limited data on this topic reveals that the findings on this issue are actually inconsistent. Most of the evidence concerns the stability of second marriages. Some of these studies report no difference in the marital stability of second marriers with and without children. Others report slightly higher instability rates for second marriers with children compared to those without children. Still others report that for second-marriers, a slightly increased instability rate occurs only for dissolutions occurring within the first 5 years of remarriage and that the birth of children to a mother in a second marriage increases the stability of that remarriage (Wineberg, 1992).

In short, because stepfamilies are a diverse group, it is misleading to characterize their stability as if they represented a homogeneous group. The current evidence gives every reason to expect that stability rates of remarriages vary by divorce history and parent history of each spouse; length of remarriage; age, gender, and pattern of residence for stepchildren; and whether mutual children are born to spouses in the stepfamily.

A BIOSOCIAL PERSPECTIVE LEADS TO THE CONCLUSION THAT STEPFAMILIES ARE INTRACTABLY PROBLEMATIC

Popenoe claims that in order to understand the special problems posed by stepfamilies, one must consider the biosocial nature of human family life. Based on an evolutionary biology perspective, Popenoe states that the organization of the human nuclear family is based on two inherited biological predispositions that confer reproductive success. The first predisposition operates between parents and children and entails advancing the interests of genetic relatives over those of unrelated individuals. The second predisposition operates between parents and concerns affective attachments between males and females. These seem like reasonable propositions.

Popenoe further notes that family instability can be linked to the fact that human beings are more interested in themselves than in their own relatives, results from men being more sexually driven and promiscuous than women,

and that because human pair bonds are fragile, men and women follow different reproductive strategies: Men inseminate as many women as possible, whereas women withhold reproductive access until they can be certain that the male will commit his resources to his offspring.

I see two major problems with using these points to support the argument that childrearing by nonrelatives is inherently problematic. First, Popenoe ignores evidence that although the roles consistent with each gender's reproductive strategy do a reasonable job of accounting for differences between men and women in sexual attraction and mate selection, these same roles actually contribute to relationship problems and relationship instability. In what he termed the *fundamental paradox*, Ickes (1993) noted a tension between what genes predispose us to do in finding a mate and what current culture prescribes us to do in living happily with that mate. That is, although our evolutionary past may account for partner attraction, our cultural present accounts for how nonexploitative, equal partner relationships are established and maintained.

Second, Popenoe does not use the term *paternal investment* very clearly, but I assume he means that biological fathers in stable marriages are directly —and not just genetically—involved in childrearing. However, most of the normative descriptive data on this topic indicate that although fathers believe they should be directly involved in their children's lives, most are not (Thompson & Walker, 1989)....

Thus, the bystander role played by some stepfathers may be functionally similar to the indirect parenting role played by some biological fathers....

FAMILY LIFE IN THE 1950s WAS BETTER THAN CONTEMPORARY FAMILY LIFE

I agree with Popenoe that it is important to place family life within a larger socio-cultural context. Further, no one could disagree that divorce rates began to accelerate in the 1960s. However, I strongly disagree with Popenoe's claim that the 1950s were an era of remarkable familism and family togetherness. Certainly, marital stability rates were high at this time in history. Nonetheless, there is ample evidence that stable marriages are not necessarily happy or healthy marriages. In addition, prospective longitudinal studies that have assessed the same group of children when they lived with both parents as well as when they lived with a divorced single parent indicate that the relatively adverse functioning of children who have experienced parental divorce is predicted by conditions in the intact family that existed well before the divorce. . . .

What irritates me most about the claim of familism in the 1950s is that it seems to value marital stability for stability's sake. Home, motherhood, and children did rank high among U.S. cultural values, yet current data on middle-aged persons who were children during this era strongly suggest that what transpired in many of these families belied these values. That is, the culture of the family was at odds with the conduct of the family. How can Popenoe extol the somewhat superficial endorsement of familism during this era in light of evidence that many children in these highly stable families were exposed to an interconnecting web of family conflict, domestic violence, harsh and inconsistent discipline, alcoholism, and, in some instances, abuse and neglect?

Two biological parents were physically present in many of these families, but at what cost?

THE FAMILY IS BEING DEINSTITUTIONALIZED

Popenoe rightly notes that marriage as a social institution has evolved in form and function to adapt to new economic, social, cultural, and even phychological settings. But for some reason, Popenoe does not seem to think that the current nature of the institution of marriage reflects this continuous process of economic, social, cultural, and psychological change. One of the most peculiar aspects to Popenoe's chapter is that although he endorses a grand model of change (the biosocial, evolutionary perspective), he urges us as members of society to put an end to a family form that could be viewed as the result of the very economic, social, cultural, and psychological changes that preceded it.

... Like it or not, women are no longer economically dependent on their husbands. Like it or not, women no longer need to define themselves in terms of their social roles as wives and mothers. Like it or not, women benefit from participating in roles other than or in addition to that of mother. Like it or not, men and women are going to renege on vows of lifetime commitments to one person because life with that one person sometimes reaches intolerable limits that could not be foreseen at the time of marriage. Finally, like it or not, as a result of these economic, social, cultural, and psychological dimensions of contemporary life, many children will experience the stresses associated with parenting transitions.

REFERENCES

Amato, P. R., & Keith, B. (1991). Parental divorce and the well-being of children: A meta-analysis. *Psychological Bulletin, 110,* 26–46.

Ickes, W. (1993). Traditional gender roles: Do they make, and then break, our relationships? *Journal of Social Issues, 49,* 71–85.

Kurdek, L. A. (1993a). *Determinants of relationship commitment: evidence from gay, lesbian, dating heterosexual, and married heterosexual couples.* Manuscript submitted for publication.

Kurdek, L. A. (1993b). Predicting marital dissolution from demographic, individual-differences, interdependence, and spouse discrepancy variables: A 5-year prospective longitudinal study of newlywed couples. *Journal of Personality and Social Psychology, 64,* 221–242.

Kurdek, L. A., & Fine, M. A. (1993). The relation between family structure and young adolescents' appraisals of family climate and parenting behavior. *Journal of Family Issues, 14,* 279–290.

Thompson, L., & Walker, A. J. (1989). Women and men in marriage, work, and parenthood. *Journal of Marriage and the Family, 51,* 845–872.

Wineberg, H. (1992). Childbearing and dissolution of the second marriage. *Journal of Marriage and the Family, 54* 879–887.

POSTSCRIPT

Are Stepfamilies Inherently Problematic?

Remarriage may mean additional family income and an extra adult in the family, but it also results in numerous stressors that may put children at risk. Because the physical and emotional health of children is closely linked to successful parental functioning, how well parents manage life transitions like divorce and remarriage is of great significance.

If it is true that our genetic makeup as well as our cultural heritage leads us to designate "family" as a group of people with "blood" ties and assigns greater importance to the social, emotional, and material resources shared between people who demonstrate blood ties, then families of remarriage may have a double strike against them. Popenoe insists that biology and culture combine to determine parental behavior toward children. He believes that biological predispositions influence parents to make stronger commitments to their birth children and that cultural beliefs buttress those "natural" tendencies. Without evidence of blood ties, Popenoe professes, men are predisposed to be less involved and supportive of children. He reasons that programs and policies that reduce rates of divorce and remarriage would help children by securing the attention of two attached, caring parents.

In *Growing Up With a Single Parent* (Harvard University Press, 1994), Sara McLanahan and Gary Sandefur write that "stepfathers are less likely to be committed to the child's welfare than biological fathers, and they are less likely to serve as a check on mother's behavior." The authors assert that children often see the stepfather as a competitor for the mother's attention and love. McLanahan and Sandefur further state, "Children may reject their stepfathers because they resent having to share their mothers, or because they secretly hope their biological parents will get back together."

If, as Popenoe suggests, parents are biologically as well as culturally predisposed to be less supportive of stepchildren, and if, at the same time, stepchildren typically report having difficulty accepting stepparents as "real" parents with rightful roles and responsibilities as caregivers, are stepfamilies destined to be problematic, even to fail? Popenoe would say yes. He argues that there is sufficient reason to believe that children fare worse in stepfamilies. Given his presentation of the evidence, should society be doing more to ensure that two-parent families stay together and work out their problems?

On the other hand, if Kurdek is correct in his summary and evaluation of the research on stepfamilies, shouldn't society accept that divorce and remarriage are here to stay and begin to enact programs and policies that are more supportive of families of remarriage? If the traditional family of loving parents and cared-for children never really existed, as some believe, is it right to try to force families into cultural visions that do not match current societal expectations, values, and goals? Kurdek would say no. What do you say?

SUGGESTED READINGS

P. R. Amato, "Children's Adjustment to Divorce: Theories, Hypotheses, and Empirical Support," *Journal of Marriage and the Family*, 55 (1993): 23–38.

W. R. Beer, *American Stepfamilies* (Transaction, 1992).

A. Booth & J. N. Edwards, "Starting Over: Why Remarriages Are More Unstable," *Journal of Family Issues*, 13 (1992): 179–194.

A. J. Cherlin, *Marriage, Divorce, and Remarriage* (Harvard University Press, 1992).

A. J. Cherlin & F. F. Furstenberg, "Stepfamilies in the United States: A Reconsideration," *Annual Review of Sociology*, 20 (1994): 359–381.

R. M. Counts, "Second and Third Divorces: The Flood to Come," *Journal of Divorce and Remarriage*, 17 (1992): 193–200.

L. H. Ganong & M. Coleman, *Remarried Family Relationships* (Sage Publications, 1994).

S. McLanahan & G. Sandefur, *Growing Up With a Single Parent: What Hurts? What Helps?* (Harvard University Press, 1994).

P. L. Papernow, *Becoming a Stepfamily* (Jossey-Bass, 1993).

Internet: http://www.parentsplace.com/dialog/get/stepfamily.html

Internet: http://www.parentsplace.com/readroom/stepfamily/index.html

ISSUE 4

Should Gays and Lesbians Fight for the Right to Marry?

YES: Andrew Sullivan, from "Here Comes the Groom," *The New Republic* (August 28, 1989)

NO: Paula L. Ettelbrick, from "Since When Is Marriage a Path to Liberation?" *OUT/LOOK: National Lesbian and Gay Quarterly* (Fall 1989)

ISSUE SUMMARY

YES: Andrew Sullivan, former editor of *The New Republic*, proposes that allowing gay couples to marry would give them social and legal advantages that laws on "domestic partnerships" cannot provide.

NO: Gay rights activist Paula L. Ettelbrick argues that marriage would further constrain lesbians and gay men, making it easier for society to ignore evidence that there is a unique and distinctive gay identity and culture and to refuse to validate relationships that do not include marriage.

In his book *Gay and Lesbian Youth* (Hemisphere, 1990), Ritch C. Savin-Williams explains that there are two political perspectives on homosexuality. The first perspective advocates that gay men and lesbians are similar to everyone else. They only differ in whom they choose to love. He calls this a conservative position that promotes the benefits of accommodation. Promoters of this perspective believe that fitting in with society will lead to respectability and that gay people "will be normal, good citizens with civic responsibilities and appropriate behavior."

The second view, which Savin-Williams refers to as the gay radical perspective, promotes the belief that gay men and lesbians are "atypical." The reasons for this uniqueness may be either biological or cultural. Those who advocate biological origins want society to broaden its acceptance levels of what is biologically "normal" as well as its categorization of human traits as exclusively masculine or feminine. Those who believe in the cultural origins explanation hold out little hope that society will ever be very accepting of homosexuality. This group wants to end violence against gay men and lesbians and to have civil rights extended to them.

Marriage is one civil right that most people take for granted. The benefits of marriage include the right to file a joint income tax return, the right of a surviving spouse to inherit property, and the right of each spouse to share in health care insurance and pension benefits made available by many employers. In this way the law favors the marital union and helps foster and preserve the marital relationship.

In the eyes of the law, same-sex couples have none of these legal rights. Such couples are barred from forming a legal marital bond that would secure their relationship rights and publicly acknowledge their private commitments. It is true that a few states and cities prohibit discrimination based on marital status and recognize "domestic partnerships," which afford gay couples some of the rights enjoyed by married couples (such as inheritance rights and health insurance qualification), but such partnerships do not give gay and lesbian relationships the exact same rights as married couples. Is this an important difference? Should lesbian and gay couples have the right to marry just as heterosexual couples do? Should they want that right?

In the following selections, Andrew Sullivan argues in support of marriage between gay people because he feels that domestic partnership laws are inadequate and that such laws allow some heterosexual partners to escape the responsibilities and commitment implied by the marital contract. Marriage, Sullivan argues, is a much more secure and protective legal arrangement than is the domestic partnership. For lesbian and gay couples, marriage would symbolize a clear set of responsibilities and establish a more definite standard of partner commitment. This could lead to greater social approval because homosexuals would be viewed as being more family-oriented and less deviant.

Paula L. Ettelbrick strongly disagrees, asserting that marriage *would* provide greater social approval but at too great a cost. Liberation by means of marriage would render lesbians and gay men even more invisible to the larger community and undermine the movement to establish the existence of a separate gay and lesbian identity and culture, asserts Ettelbrick. Fervor for the notion that valid and committed relationships can exist in many forms other than in marriage would be diminished, if not lost. Justice, argues Ettelbrick, is much more important than rights. Justice means being accepted despite being different, while rights are legally dictated and morally dismissed. Ettelbrick claims that having the legal right to marry would mean that individuals in gay relationships would be expected to behave just like heterosexuals, amounting to the concession that heterosexual relationships represent the standard for what a good or successful relationship should be.

YES   Andrew Sullivan

HERE COMES THE GROOM

Last month in New York, a court ruled that a gay lover had the right to stay in his deceased partner's rent-control apartment because the lover qualified as a member of the deceased's family. The ruling deftly annoyed almost everybody. Conservatives saw judicial activism in favor of gay rent control: three reasons to be appalled. Chastened liberals (such as the *New York Times* editorial page), while endorsing the recognition of gay relationships, also worried about the abuse of already stretched entitlements that the ruling threatened. What neither side quite contemplated is that they both might be right, and that the way to tackle the issue of unconventional relationships in conventional society is to try something both more radical and more conservative than putting courts in the business of deciding what is and is not a family. That alternative is the legalization of civil gay marriage.

The New York rent-control case did not go anywhere near that far, which is the problem. The rent-control regulations merely stipulated that a "family" member had the right to remain in the apartment. The judge ruled that to all intents and purposes a gay lover is part of his lover's family, inasmuch as a "family" merely means an interwoven social life, emotional commitment, and some level of financial interdependence.

It's a principle now well established around the country. Several cities have "domestic partnership" laws, which allow relationships that do not fit into the category of heterosexual marriage to be registered with the city and qualify for benefits that up till now have been reserved for straight married couples. San Francisco, Berkeley, Madison, and Los Angeles all have legislation, as does the politically correct Washington, D.C., suburb, Takoma Park. In these cities, a variety of interpersonal arrangements qualify for health insurance, bereavement leave, insurance, annuity and pension rights, housing rights (such as rent-control apartments), adoption and inheritance rights. Eventually, according to gay lobby groups, the aim is to include federal income tax and veterans' benefits as well. A recent case even involved the right to use a family member's accumulated frequent-flier points. Gays are not the only beneficiaries; heterosexual "live-togethers" also qualify.

There's an argument, of course, that the current legal advantages extended to married people unfairly discriminate against people who've shaped their lives in less conventional arrangements. But it doesn't take a genius to see that enshrining in the law a vague principle like "domestic partnership" is an invitation to qualify at little personal cost for a vast array of entitlements otherwise kept crudely under control.

To be sure, potential DPs have to prove financial interdependence, shared living arrangements, and a commitment to mutual caring. But they don't need to have a sexual relationship or even closely mirror old-style marriage. In principle, an elderly woman and her live-in nurse could qualify. A couple of uneuphemistically confirmed bachelors could be DPs. So could two close college students, a pair of seminarians, or a couple of frat buddies. Left as it is, the concept of domestic partnership could open a Pandora's box of litigation and subjective judicial decision-making about who qualifies. You either are or are not married; it's not a complex question. Whether you are in a "domestic partnership" is not so clear.

More important, the concept of domestic partnership chips away at the prestige of traditional relationships and undermines the priority we give them. This priority is not necessarily a product of heterosexism. Consider heterosexual couples. Society has good reason to extend legal advantages to heterosexuals who choose the formal sanction of marriage over simply living together. They make a deeper commitment to one another and to society; in exchange, society extends certain benefits to them. Marriage provides an anchor, if an arbitrary and weak one, in the chaos of sex and relationships to which we are all prone. It provides a mechanism for emotional stability, economic security, and the healthy rearing of the next generation. We rig the law in its favor not because we disparage all forms of relationship other than the nuclear family, but because we recognize that not to promote marriage would be to ask too much of human virtue. In the context of the weakened family's effect upon the poor, it might also invite social disintegration. One of the worst products of the New Right's "family values" campaign is that its extremism and hatred of diversity has disguised this more measured and more convincing case for the importance of the marital bond.

The concept of domestic partnership ignores these concerns, indeed directly attacks them. This is a pity, since one of its most important objectives—providing some civil recognition for gay relationships—is a noble cause and one completely compatible with the defense of the family. But the way to go about it is not to undermine straight marriage; it is to legalize old-style marriage for gays.

* * *

The gay movement has ducked this issue primarily out of fear of division. Much of the gay leadership clings to notions of gay life as essentially outsider, antibourgeois, radical. Marriage, for them, is co-optation into straight society. For the Stonewall generation, it is hard to see how this vision of conflict will ever fundamentally change. But for many other gays—my guess, a majority—while they don't deny the importance of rebellion 20 years ago and are grateful for what was done, there's now the sense of a new opportunity. A need to rebel has quietly ceded to a desire to belong. To be gay and to be bourgeois no longer seems such an absurd proposition. Certainly since AIDS, to be gay and to be responsible has become a necessity.

Gay marriage squares several circles at the heart of the domestic partnership debate. Unlike domestic partnership, it allows for recognition of gay relationships, while casting no aspersions on traditional marriage. It merely asks that gays be allowed to join in. Unlike domestic partnership, it doesn't open up avenues for heterosexuals to get benefits without the responsibilities of marriage, or a nightmare of definitional litigation. And unlike domestic partnership, it harnesses to an already established social convention the yearnings for stability and acceptance among a fast-maturing gay community.

Gay marriage also places more responsibilities upon gays: it says for the first time that gay relationships are not better or worse than straight relationships, and that the same is expected of them. And it's clear and dignified. There's a legal benefit to a clear, common symbol of commitment. There's also a personal benefit. One of the ironies of domestic partnership is that it's not only more complicated than marriage, it's more demanding, requiring an elaborate statement of intent to qualify. It amounts to a substantial invasion of privacy. Why, after all, should gays be required to prove commitment before they get married in a way we would never dream of asking of straights?

Legalizing gay marriage would offer homosexuals the same deal society now offers heterosexuals: general social approval and specific legal advantages in exchange for a deeper and harder-to-extract-yourself-from commitment to another human being. Like straight marriage, it would foster social cohesion, emotional security, and economic prudence. Since there's no reason gays should not be allowed to adopt or be foster parents, it could also help nurture children. And its introduction would not be some sort of radical break with social custom. As it has become more acceptable for gay people to acknowledge their loves publicly, more and more have committed themselves to one another for life in full view of their families and their friends. A law institutionalizing gay marriage would merely reinforce a healthy social trend. It would also, in the wake of AIDS, qualify as a genuine public health measure. Those conservatives who deplore promiscuity among some homosexuals should be among the first to support it. Burke could have written a powerful case for it.

The argument that gay marriage would subtly undermine the unique legitimacy of straight marriage is based upon a fallacy. For heterosexuals, straight marriage would remain the most significant —and only legal—social bond. Gay marriage could only delegitimize straight marriage if it were a real alternative to it, and this is clearly not true. To put it bluntly, there's precious little evidence that straights could be persuaded by any law to have sex with—let alone marry— someone of their own sex. The only possible effect of this sort would be to persuade gay men and women who force themselves into heterosexual marriage (often at appalling cost to themselves and their families) to find a focus for their family instincts in a more personally positive environment. But this is clearly a plus, not a minus: gay marriage could both avoid a lot of tortured families and create the possibility for many happier ones. It is not, in short, a denial of family values. It's an extension of them.

Of course, some would claim that any legal recognition of homosexuality is a de facto attack upon heterosexuality. But even the most hardened conservatives recognize that gays are a permanent minority and aren't likely to go away. Since persecution is not an option in a civilized society, why not coax gays into traditional values rather than rail incoherently against them?

* * *

There's a less elaborate argument for gay marriage: it's good for gays. It provides role models for young gay people who, after the exhilaration of coming out, can easily lapse into short-term relationships and insecurity with no tangible goal in sight. My own guess is that most gays would embrace such a goal with as much (if not more) commitment as straights. Even in our society as it is, many lesbian relationships are virtual textbook cases of monogamous commitment. Legal gay marriage could also help bridge the gulf often found between gays and their parents. It could bring the essence of gay life—a gay couple—into the heart of the traditional straight family in a way the family can most understand and the gay offspring can most easily acknowledge. It could do as much to heal the gay-straight rift as any amount of gay rights legislation.

If these arguments sound socially conservative, that's no accident. It's one of the richest ironies of our society's blind spot toward gays that essentially conservative social goals should have the appearance of being so radical. But gay marriage is not a radical step. It avoids the mess of domestic partnership; it is humane; it is conservative in the best sense of the word. It's also practical. Given the fact that we already allow legal gay relationships, what possible social goal is advanced by framing the law to encourage those relationships to be unfaithful, undeveloped, and insecure?

NO
Paula L. Ettelbrick

SINCE WHEN IS MARRIAGE A
PATH TO LIBERATION?

"Marriage is a great institution... if you like living in institutions," according to a bit of T-shirt philosophy I saw recently. Certainly, marriage is an institution. It is one of the most venerable, impenetrable institutions in modern society. Marriage provides the ultimate form of acceptance for personal intimate relationships in our society, and gives those who marry an insider status of the most powerful kind.

Steeped in a patriarchal system that looks to ownership, property, and dominance of men over women as its basis, the institution of marriage long has been the focus of radical feminist revulsion. Marriage defines certain relationships as more valid than all others. Lesbian and gay relationships, being neither legally sanctioned or commingled by blood, are always at the bottom of the heap of social acceptance and importance.

Given the imprimatur of social and personal approval which marriage provides, it is not surprising that some lesbians and gay men among us would look to legal marriage for self-affirmation. After all, those who marry can be instantaneously transformed from "outsiders" to "insiders," and we have a desperate need to become insiders.

It could make us feel OK about ourselves, perhaps even relieve some of the internalized homophobia that we all know so well. Society will then celebrate the birth of our children and mourn the death of our spouses. It would be easier to get health insurance for our spouses, family memberships to the local museum, and a right to inherit our spouse's cherished collection of lesbian mystery novels even if she failed to draft a will. Never again would we have to go to a family reunion and debate about the correct term for introducing our lover/partner/significant other to Aunt Flora. Everything would be quite easy and very nice.

So why does this unlikely event so deeply disturb me? For two major reasons. First, marriage will not liberate us as lesbians and gay men. In fact, it will constrain us, make us more invisible, force our assimilation into the mainstream, and undermine the goals of gay liberation. Second, attaining the right to marry will not transform our society from one that makes narrow, but dramatic, distinctions between those who are married and those who are not married to one that respects and encourages choice of relationships and family diversity. Marriage runs contrary to two of the primary goals of the lesbian and gay movement: the affirmation of gay identity and culture; and the validation of many forms of relationships.

When analyzed from the standpoint of civil rights, certainly lesbians and gay men should have a right to marry. But obtaining a right does not always result in justice. White male firefighters in Birmingham, Alabama have been fighting for their "rights" to retain their jobs by overturning the city's affirmative action guidelines. If their "rights" prevail, the courts will have failed in rendering justice. The "right" fought for by the white male firefighters, as well as those who advocate strongly for the "rights" to legal marriage for gay people, will result, at best, in limited or narrowed "justice" for those closest to power at the expense of those who have been historically marginalized.

The fight for justice has as its goal the realignment of power imbalances among individuals and classes of people in society. A pure "rights" analysis often fails to incorporate a broader understanding of the underlying inequities that operate to deny justice to a fuller range of people and groups. In setting our priorities as a community, we just combine the concept of both rights and justice. At this point in time, making legal marriage for lesbian and gay couples a priority would set an agenda of gaining rights for a few, but would do nothing to correct the power imbalances between those who are married (whether gay or straight) and those who are not. Thus, justice would not be gained.

* * *

Justice for gay men and lesbians will be achieved only when we are accepted and supported in this society *despite* our differences from the dominant culture and the choices we make regarding our relationships. Being queer is more than setting up house, sleeping with a person of the same gender, and seeking state approval for doing so. It is an identity, a culture with many variations. It is a way of dealing with the world by diminishing the constraints of gender roles which have for so long kept women and gay people oppressed and invisible. Being queer means pushing the parameters of sex, sexuality, and family, and in the process transforming the very fabric of society. Gay liberation is inexorably linked to women's liberation. Each is essential to the other.

The moment we argue, as some among us insist on doing, that we should be treated as equals because we are really just like married couples and hold the same values to be true, we undermine the very purpose of our movement and begin the dangerous process of silencing our different voices. As a lesbian, I am fundamentally different from non-lesbian women. That's the point. Marriage, as it exists today, is antithetical to my liberation as a lesbian and as a woman because it mainstreams my life and voice. I do not want to be known as "Mrs. Attached-To-Somebody Else." Nor do I want to give the state the power to regulate my primary relationship.

Yet, the concept of equality in our legal system does not support differences, it only supports sameness. The very standard for equal protection is that people who are similarly situated must be treated equally. To make an argument for equal protection, we will be required to claim that gay and lesbian relationships are the same as straight relationships. To gain the right, we must compare ourselves to married couples. The law looks to the insiders as the norm, regardless of how flawed or unjust their institutions, and requires that those seeking the law's equal protection situate themselves in a similar posture to those who are already protected. In arguing for the right to legal marriage, lesbians and gay men would be forced to claim that we are just like heterosexual couples, have the same goals and purposes, and vow to structure our lives similarly. The law provides no room to argue that we are different, but are nonetheless entitled to equal protection.

The thought of emphasizing our sameness to married heterosexuals in order to obtain this "right" terrifies me. It rips away the very heart and soul of what I believe it is to be a lesbian in this world. It robs me of the opportunity to make a difference. We end up mimicking all that is bad about the institution of marriage in our effort to appear to be the same as straight couples.

By looking to our sameness and deemphasizing our differences, we don't even place ourselves in a position of power that would allow us to transform marriage from an institution that emphasizes property and state regulation of relationships to an institution which recognizes one of many types of valid and respected relationships. Until the constitution is interpreted to respect and encourage differences, pursuing the legalization of same-sex marriage would be leading our movement into a trap; we would be demanding access to the very institution which, in its current form, would undermine *our* movement to recognize many different kinds of relationships. We would be perpetuating the elevation of married relationships and of "couples" in general, and further eclipsing other relationships of choice.

Ironically, gay marriage, instead of liberating gay sex and sexuality, would further outlaw all gay and lesbian sex which is not performed in a marital context. Just as sexually active non-married women face stigma and double standards around sex and sexual activity, so too would non-married gay people. The only legitimate gay sex would be that which is cloaked in and regulated by marriage. Its legitimacy would stem not from an acceptance of gay sexuality, but because the Supreme Court and society in general fiercely protect the privacy of marital relationships. Lesbians and gay men who do not seek the state's stamp of approval would clearly face increased sexual oppression.

* * *

Undoubtedly, whether we admit it or not, we all need to be accepted by the broader society. That motivation fuels our work to eliminate discrimination in the workplace and elsewhere, fight for custody of our children, create our own families, and so on. The growing discussion about the right to marry may be explained in part by this need for acceptance. Those closer to the norm or to power in this country are more likely to see marriage as a principle of freedom and equality. Those who are more acceptable to the mainstream because of race, gender, and economic status are more likely to want the right to marry. It is the final acceptance, the ultimate affirmation of identity.

On the other hand, more marginal members of the lesbian and gay community (women, people of color, working class and poor) are less likely to see marriage as having relevance to our struggles for survival. After all, what good is the affirmation of our relationships (that is, marital relationships) if we are rejected as women, black, or working class?

The path to acceptance is much more complicated for many of us. For instance, if we choose legal marriage, we may enjoy the right to add our spouse to our health insurance policy at work, since most employment policies are defined by one's marital status, not family relationship. However, that choice assumes that we have a job *and* that our employer provides us with health benefits. For women, particularly women of color who tend to occupy the low-paying jobs that do not provide healthcare benefits at all, it will not matter one bit if they are able to marry their woman partners. The opportunity to marry will neither get them health benefits nor transform them from outsider to insider.

Of course, a white man who marries another white man who has a full-time job with benefits will certainly be able to share in those benefits and overcome the only obstacle left to full societal assimilation—the goal of many in his class. In other words, gay marriage will not topple the system that allows only the privileged few to obtain decent health care. Nor will it close the privilege gap between those who are married and those who are not.

Marriage creates a two-tier system that allows the state to regulate relationships. It has become a facile mechanism for employers to dole out benefits, for businesses to provide special deals and incentives, and for the law to make distinctions in distributing meager public funds. None of these entities bothers to consider the relationship among people; the love, respect, and need to protect that exists among all kinds of family members. Rather, a simple certificate of the state, regardless of whether the spouses love, respect, or even see each other on a regular basis, dominates and is supported. None of this dynamic will change if gay men and lesbians are given the option of marriage.

Gay marriage will not help us address the systemic abuses inherent in a society that does not provide decent health care to all of its citizens, a right that should not depend on whether the individual 1) has sufficient resources to afford health care or health insurance, 2) is working and receives health insurance as part of compensation, or 3) is married to a partner who is working and has health coverage which is extended to spouses. It will not address the underlying unfairness that allows businesses to provide discounted services or goods to families and couples—who are defined to include straight, married people and their children, but not domestic partners.

Nor will it address the pain and anguish of the unmarried lesbian who receives word of her partner's accident, rushes to the hospital and is prohibited from entering the intensive care unit or obtaining information about her condition solely because she is not a spouse or family member. Likewise, marriage will not help the gay victim of domestic violence who, because he chose not to marry, finds no protection under the law to keep his violent lover away.

* * *

If the laws change tomorrow and lesbians and gay men were allowed to marry, where would we find the incentive to continue the progressive movement we have started that is pushing for societal and legal recognition of all kinds of family relationships? To create other options and alternatives? To find a place in the law for the elderly couple who, for companionship and economic reasons, live together but do not marry? To recognize the right of a long-time, but unmarried, gay partner to stay in his rent-controlled apartment after the death of his lover, the only named tenant on the lease? To recognize the family relationship of the lesbian couple and the two gay men who are jointly sharing child-raising responsibilities? To get the law to acknowledge that we may have more than one relationship worthy of legal protection?

Marriage for lesbians and gay men still will not provide a real choice unless we continue the work our community has begun to spread the privilege around to other relationships. We must first break the tradition of piling benefits and privileges on to those who are married, while ignoring the real life needs of those who are not. Only when we de-institutionalize marriage and bridge the economic and privilege gap between the married and the unmarried will each of us have a true choice. Otherwise, our choice not to marry will continue to lack legal protection and societal respect.

The lesbian and gay community has laid the groundwork for revolutionizing society's views of family. The domestic partnership movement has been an important part of this progress insofar as it validates non-marital relationships. Because it is not limited to sexual or romantic relationships, domestic partnership provides an important opportunity for many who are not related by blood or marriage to claim certain minimal protections.

It is crucial, though, that we avoid the pitfall of framing the push for legal recognition of domestic partners (those who share a primary residence and financial responsibility for each other) as a stepping stone to marriage. We must keep our eyes on the goals of providing true alternatives to marriage and of radically reordering society's view of family.

The goals of lesbian and gay liberation must simply be broader than the right to marry. Gay and lesbian marriages may minimally transform the institution of marriage by diluting its traditional patriarchal dynamic, but they will not transform society. They will not demolish the two-tier system of the "haves" and the "have nots." We must not fool ourselves into believing that marriage will make it acceptable to be gay or lesbian. We will be liberated only when we are respected and accepted for our differences and the diversity we provide to this society. Marriage is not a path to that liberation.

POSTSCRIPT

Should Gays and Lesbians Fight for the Right to Marry?

In the first federal lawsuit of its kind, a surviving lesbian partner filed charges of discrimination against a large American corporation because it refused to pay her the benefits normally paid to marital partners after the death of a spouse. She claims that the relationship she had with her partner was as much a marriage as any heterosexual union.

Tamar Lewin describes this situation and its implications in an article in the *New York Times* (September 21, 1990). She explains that more and more companies are finding their policies coming under attack as increasing numbers of homosexual couples live more openly in long-term relationships. Within the next five years domestic partnership laws are expected to resolve some of the legal situations in which these couples find themselves. Currently, while marriage offers clearly defined expectations and responsibilities, domestic partnerships do not.

According to Sullivan, legalizing marriage between gay and lesbian couples would facilitate social approval of homosexual relationships, foster emotional security among lesbian and gay partners, and enable better economic well-being in such partnerships. Ettelbrick contends that extending the right to marry to lesbian and gay couples would grant them rights but would deny them social justice. What would society gain or lose from removing the legal barriers to gay and lesbian marriages? Would the definition of all marriages (heterosexual, homosexual, and interracial, for example) change if gay and lesbian marriages became legal?

SUGGESTED READINGS

R. M. Berger, "Men Together: Understanding the Gay Couple," *Journal of Homosexuality*, 19 (1990): 31–50.

J. Miranda and M. Stroms, "Psychological Adjustment of Lesbians and Gay Men," *Journal of Counseling and Development*, 68 (1989): 41–45.

J. Penelope, "The Lesbian Perspective," in J. Allen, ed., *Lesbian Philosophies and Cultures* (State University of New York Press, 1990).

L. A. Peplau and S. O. Cochran, "A Relationship Perspective on Homosexuality," in D. P. McWirther, S. A. Sanders, and J. M. Reinisch, eds., *Homosexuality/Heterosexuality* (Oxford University Press, 1990).

PART 2

Challenges to Successful Relationships

Couples continually strive to create and sustain satisfying and rewarding relationships. Partners talk of strengthening their commitment, working out problems, effecting positive change, communicating feelings, and renegotiating expectations. These are some of the current buzzwords of relational competence. The discussions in this section focus on some relational issues that often surface as challenges to successful relationship development. Gender is a prominent topic of debate when relationships are discussed, both in lay and in academic settings, and it is therefore examined closely in several of the debates.

- Is Intimate Attachment the Key to Successful Relationships?

- Do Men and Women Speak Different Languages?

- Are Women's Lives More Stressful Than Men's?

- Do Men Avoid Family Work?

ISSUE 5

Is Intimate Attachment the Key to Successful Relationships?

YES: Susan Johnson and Hara Estroff Marano, from "Love: The Immutable Longing for Contact," *Psychology Today* (March/April 1994)

NO: Geraldine K. Piorkowski, from "Back Off!" *Psychology Today* (January/February 1995)

ISSUE SUMMARY

YES: Susan Johnson, director of the Marital and Family Clinic at Ottawa Civic Hospital, and Hara Estroff Marano, editor of *Psychology Today*, argue that couples often break up because they fail to form an emotionally intimate and secure attachment to each other.

NO: Clinical psychologist Geraldine K. Piorkowski maintains that couples expect too much intimacy in their closest relationships. She claims that couples in satisfying relationships need to maintain some distance from each other.

Couples in intimate relationships help and protect each other, say they are devoted to each other, and feel distressed when separated. People who are emotionally attached speak of being committed to each other. They indicate surrendering control and dropping their defenses when with one another. Lovers typically display intimacy by gazing and smiling at each other, sitting close to one another, and touching each other softly.

Intimacy denotes emotional openness, honesty, caring, warmth, and attentiveness. Although intimacy has been described in various ways, most family scientists agree that for a relationship to develop intimately, both members of the couple must be willing to forge intimate connections through mutual self-disclosure. Goals, roles, expectations, rules, values, and beliefs must be communicated and responded to in kind. Only then, say experts on relationships, will a couple experience "real" intimacy.

All of this closeness can also have a dark side: disclosing personal thoughts and feelings opens the very real possibility of getting hurt. In a seminal article in 1984 entitled "The Dangers of Intimacy," educator and marital therapist Elaine Hatfield reported that people are often reluctant to become intimate with others because of various well-founded fears: fear of disclosing too much; fear of being abandoned after disclosing deeply personal information; fear of having private information shared with others outside the relationship;

fear of losing control—of being manipulated by the partner; and fear of losing individuality—of being engulfed by the partner. These fears, says Hatfield, are all legitimate. They exist because they do happen in close relationships.

How do most people overcome their reluctance to get very close? Family studies professionals point to trust as the answer. For example, being able to trust a partner not to use personal information to gain advantage or control in a relationship enhances feelings of closeness. And equally significant is being able to trust a partner to keep one's secrets. Relationships are most satisfying when they meet our needs; and needs are voiced most freely in relationships in which partners trust each other. Trust promotes self-disclosure and the development of intimacy. Trust also allows the acceptance of a partner's need to retreat without fear of reprisal.

In the following selections, Susan Johnson and Hara Estroff Marano contend that an individual's sense of trust emerges in infancy through attachment to his or her primary caregiver, usually the mother. In adulthood, as a result of this first trusting relationship, the individual remains strongly motivated to bond emotionally with another, usually a romantic partner. People seem to hunger for accessible and responsive partners with whom they can connect. Being able to forge a deep emotional attachment pays off in feelings of security. Johnson and Marano assert that because security is so critical to individual well-being, a partner who senses that a loved one is distancing from the relationship may feel rejected, become frightened and angry, and might try to aggressively reconnect.

Geraldine K. Piorkowski maintains that although some partners certainly thrive on intimate sharing of personal thoughts and feelings, most people overfocus on closeness in relationships. She believes that maintaining distance is healthy both for the person and for the relationship. It keeps people from becoming too dependent on one special person for meeting all their emotional needs.

Johnson and Marano write that there's nothing wrong with being dependent on someone we love; dependent feelings are natural in intimate relationships. Adults, like children, need attention and reassurance from their romantic partners. Most want to talk about their day, like to be touched and hugged on a regular basis, and want to be in close contact with their loved ones. Although Piorkowski acknowledges these tendencies, she points out that wanting too much closeness and attaching too much emotional weight to expectations for intimacy can destroy an otherwise "good enough" relationship.

As you read the following selections, you will find compelling evidence presented by each author. Which side seems more consistent with your own experiences in intimate relationships?

YES
Susan Johnson and
Hara Estroff Marano

LOVE: THE IMMUTABLE LONGING
FOR CONTACT

As a marital therapist, my job is to help people experience love, to move from distance and alienation to contact and caring. But in order to help distressed couples change, I realized early on that I needed a model of what a good relationship is. For too long, the choices have been confined to two. There is the psychodynamic, or psychoanalytic, view, which holds that adult relationships are more or less reflections of childhood relationships—replays of old conflicts. And there is the behaviorist view: Love is a rational exchange in which couples make deals based on their needs, and they succeed to the degree that they master the negotiation process. Love is then either a crazy compulsion or, after couples calm down, a kind of rational friendship where the partners make good deals.

* * *

... The truth is that these conventional descriptions do not adequately reflect the process of marital distress or the rekindling of love that I observe as a marital therapist.... Neither addresses the intense emotional responses that consume distressed couples. As I watch couples, I see that raw emotion, hurt, longing, and fear are the most powerful things in the room. Couples seem to have a desperate need to connect emotionally—and a desperate fear of connecting.

There are, of course, many elements to a relationship. It is true that echoes of the past are present in relationships, but this focus does not capture enough of what goes on and ignores the power of present interactions. Couples do also make bargains. But the essence of their connection is not a bargain. It is, rather, a bond.

The bond between two people hinges on two things—their accessibility and responsiveness to each other. The notion that the tie between two people is created through accessibility and responsiveness is an outgrowth of attachment theory. First put forth by the late British psychiatrist John Bowlby 30 years ago and later elaborated both by him and psychologist Mary Ainsworth in America, attachment theory is only now gathering significant momentum. It promises to be one of the most significant psychological ideas put forth in the 20th century....

VIEWING LOVE THROUGH A LENS

Over the past decade, a number of psychologists, including myself, have begun to see in attachment theory an understanding of adult relationships. In my experience attachment is the best lens for viewing adult love. When viewed through this lens, love relationships do not seem irrational at all; we do not have to pronounce them mysterious or outside our usual way of being. Nor do we have to shrink them to fit the laws of economic exchange. They make perfect—many would say intuitive—sense. And attachment theory goes a long way toward explaining what goes wrong in relationships and what to do about it.

John Bowlby observed that the need for physical closeness between a mother and child serves evolutionary goals; in a dangerous world, a responsive caregiver ensures survival of the infant. Attachment theory states that our primary motivation in life is to be connected with other people —because it is the only security we ever have. Maintaining closeness is a bona fide survival need.

Through the consistent and reliable responsiveness of a close adult, infants, particularly in the second six months of life, begin to trust that the world is a good place and come to believe they have some value in it. The deep sense of security that develops fosters in the infant enough confidence to begin exploring the surrounding world, making excursions into it, and developing relationships with others—though racing back to mom, being held by her, and perhaps even clinging to her whenever feeling threatened. In secure attachment lie the seeds for self-esteem, initiative, and eventual independence. We explore the world from a secure base.

Thanks to Mary Ainsworth, a large and growing body of research supports attachment theory.... Ainsworth found that whenever children feel threatened or can no longer easily reach their attachment figure, they engage in behavior designed to regain proximity—they call, they protest, they seek, they cry, they reach out. Closeness achieved, they do all they can to maintain it: They hug, they coo, they make eye contact, they cling— and, that all-time pleaser, they smile.

* * *

Ainsworth noticed that children differ in their attachment security and their patterns of behavior sort into three basic "attachment styles." Most children are securely attached: They show signs of distress when left with a stranger, seek their mother when she returns, hold her for a short time, then go back to exploring and playing. These infants develop attachment security because they have mothers who are sensitive and responsive to their signals.

On the other hand, she found, 40 percent of kids are insecurely attached. Some are anxious/ambivalent. They show lots of distress separating, and on reunion, they approach and reject their mother. Their mothers usually respond inconsistently to them, sometimes unavailable, other times affectionate. So preoccupied are these infants with their care-giver's availability that they never get to explore their world.

The third group of children have an avoidant attachment style. They do not seem distressed during separation, and they don't even acknowledge their mother during reunion. These infants keep their distress well-hidden; though they appear to dismiss relationships entirely, internally they are in a state of physiological arousal. These children are usually reared by caregivers who rebuff their attempts at close bodily contact....

Attachment bonds are particularly durable, and once an infant is attached, separation—or the threat of it—is extremely stressful and anxiety-producing. In the absence of attachment danger, children explore the world around them. But if the accessibility of a caregiver is questionable or threatened, the attachment behavior system shifts into high gear. Facing the loss or unreliability of an attachment figure, infants typically are thrust into panic and they mount an angry protest. Eventually, however, the protest dies down and they succumb to a despair that looks like classic depression.

The implications of attachment theory are extraordinary and extend to the deepest corners of our psyche. Attachment impacts the way we process information, how we see the world, and the nature of our social experience. Our attachment experience influences whether we see ourselves as lovable. Research now shows that we carry attachment styles with us into life, where they serve as predispositions to later behavior in love relationships.

* * *

We seek close physical proximity to a partner, and rely on their continuing affections and availability, because it is a survival need. What satisfies the need for attachment in adults is what satisfies the need in the young: Eye contact, touching, stroking, and holding a partner deliver the same security and comfort. When threatened, or fearful, or experiencing loss, we turn to our partner for psychological comfort. Or try to.

The core elements of love are the same for children and adults—the need to feel that somebody is emotionally there for you, that you can make contact with another person who will respond to you, particularly if you are in need. The essence of love is a partner responding to a need, not because it's a good deal—but even when it's not. That allows you to sense the world as home rather than as a dangerous place. In this sense, we never grow up.

It is growing clear that the dynamics of attachment are similar across the life span. Implicit in the anger of a couple who are fighting over everything is the protest of the child who is trying to restore the closeness and responsiveness of a parent. In the grief of adults who have lost a partner is the despair of a child who has lost a parent and experiences helplessness and withdrawal.

THE MUSICALITY OF EMOTION

Attachment theory makes sense of a matter that psychology has just begun to puzzle over—how we come to regulate our emotions. We regulate feelings, specifically negative ones—fear, sadness, anger—through the development of affectional bonds with others, and continuing contact with them. Through the lens of attachment we also come to understand that the expression of emotion is the primary communication system in relationships; it's how we adjust closeness and distance. Emotion is the music of the interpersonal dance. And when attachment is threatened—when we feel alienated from a partner or worry about our partner's availability—the music either gets turned way up, into the heavy metal of angry protest, or way down, shut off altogether.

The lens of attachment sharply illuminates the dangerous distortion personified in a popular icon of Western culture: the John Wayne image of the self-contained man, the man who is never dependent and never needs anyone else. Our need for attachment ensures that we become who we are as individuals because of our connection with other people. Our personality evolves in a context of contact with other people; it doesn't simply arise from within. Our attachment needs make dependence on another person an integral part of being human. Self-sufficiency is a lie.

A PLACE FOR VULNERABILITY

The most basic message of attachment theory is that to be valid adults, we do not need to deny that we are also always, until the end of our life, vulnerable children. A good intimate adult relationship is a safe place where two people can experience feelings of vulnerability —being scared, feeling overwhelmed by life, being unsure of who they are. It is the place where we can deal with those things, not deny them, control them, or regulate them, the old John Wayne way. Relatedness is a core aspect of our selves.

Yet Western psychology and psychiatry have often labeled feelings of dependency as pathologic and banished them to childhood. Our mistaken beliefs about dependency and self-sufficiency lead us to define strength as the ability to process inner experience and regulate our emotions all by ourselves. Attachment theory suggests that, not only is that not functional, it is impossible. We are social

beings not constituted for such physiological and emotional isolation. For those who attempt it, there are enormous costs. A great deal of literature in health and psychology shows that the cost of social isolation is physical and psychological breakdown. Under such conditions, we simply deteriorate.

* * *

There is nothing inherently demeaning or diminishing in allowing someone else to comfort you. We need other people to help us process our emotions and deal with the slings and arrows of being alive—especially the slings and arrows. In fact, the essence of making intimate contact is sharing hurts and vulnerability with someone else. You allow someone into a place where you are not defended. You put contact before self-protection. In marital distress the opposite happens, self-protection comes before contact. If you cannot share, then a part of your being is excluded from the relationship.

The couples I see have taught me that it is almost impossible to be accessible, responsive, emotionally engaged with someone if you are not able to experience and express your own vulnerabilities. If you cannot allow yourself to experience and show your vulnerability, you cannot tell others what you need and explicitly ask others to respond to you. But troubled couples naturally want to hide and protect their vulnerability, although that usually precludes any satisfying kind of emotional contact.

Like psychoanalytic theory, attachment theory sees early relationships as formative of personality and relationships later on. But unlike Freudian theory, it sees our view of ourselves and relationship styles as subject to revision as we integrate new experiences. This capacity makes growth possible. The past influences the present, but we are not condemned to repeat it....

A NEW WAY OF CONTACT

That may be what passionate love really is—we find someone who connects with us and alleviates our attachment fears, which opens up a whole new possibility of acceptance and responsiveness. Love is transforming—not just of the world but of the self. We find a whole new way of contacting another human being, and this emotional engagement opens up new possibilities of becoming ourselves. That is the intoxicating thing about the relationship. It modifies how people experience themselves and how they see other people....

So perhaps now the mystery of love is becoming clear. We fall in love when an attachment bond is formed. We stay in love by maintaining the bond. We use our repertoire of emotions to signal the need for comfort through contact, the need for a little distance. We help each other process our inner and outer worlds and experience each other's pain, fear, joy.

What, then, goes wrong in couples? As I see it, healthy, normal attachment needs go unmet and attachment fears begin to take over the relationship.

We know that distressed couples settle into rigid interaction patterns. Perhaps the most distressed pattern is that of the disappointed, angry, blaming wife demanding contact from a man who withdraws. Couples can stay stuck in this for years. We know from the research of John Gottman that this is a sure killer of marriages.

But it is only through the lens of attachment that we come to understand what makes such patterns of behavior

so devastating. The answer is, they block emotional engagement; they stand in the way of contact and exacerbate attachment fears. As partners hurl anger and contempt at each other or withdraw, emotional engagement becomes more and more difficult. Patterns of attack—defend or attack—withdraw are highly corrosive to a relationship because they preclude a safe way for a couple to emotionally engage each other and create a secure bond.

What couples are really fighting about is rarely the issue they seem to be fighting about—the chores, the kids. It is always about separateness and connectedness, safety and trust, the risk of letting someone in to see the exposed, vulnerable self.

Marital distress, then, is not a product of personality flaws. Nor is anger in relationships irrational. It is often a natural part of a protest that follows the loss of accessibility and responsiveness to a partner. It is an adaptive reaction —anger motivates people to overcome barriers to reunion. Self-defeating as it may be, anger is an attempt to discourage a partner from further distancing.

A COMPELLING EMOTION

But fear is the most compelling emotion in a distressed relationship. Hostility in a partner is usually a sign that the fear level has gone way up—the partner feels threatened. Attachment fears—of being unlovable, abandoned, rejected—are so tied to survival that they elicit strong fight or flee responses. In protecting ourselves, we often undermine ourselves as a secure base for our partner, who becomes alarmed. Our partner then confirms our fears and becomes the enemy, the betrayer.

Such fear sets off an alarm system. It heightens both the anger of those experiencing anxiety in attachment and the dismissal of emotional needs by those given to avoidance.

A NEW FRAME FOR BEHAVIOR

The lens of attachment puts a whole new frame on our behavior in relationships. The angry, blaming wife who continues to pursue with blame, even though she understands this behavior may drive her husband away, is not acting irrationally. Nor do her actions necessarily reflect a lack of communication skill. She is engaged in a desperate intensification of attachment behaviors—hers is an entreaty for contact. She perceives her husband as inaccessible and emotionally unresponsive: a threat that engages the attachment behavioral system. Of course, the defensiveness and conflict make safe contact increasingly less likely, and the cycle of distress escalates. It keeps going because the person never gets the contact and the reassurance that will bring closure and allow the attachment fears to be dealt with.

In working with couples, my colleague Les Greenberg and I have elaborated a therapy, "Emotionally Focused Couples Therapy," that views marital distress in terms of attachment insecurities. It recognizes that relationship problems are created by how individuals react to, cope with, and disown their own attachment needs and those of their spouse. A major goal of therapy is owning and validating needs for contact and security, helping people to expand their emotional range, rather than shut their feelings down or constantly control them. It is not about ventilating feelings, but about allowing people to immerse themselves more deeply in their experience and process elements of it they usually protect against —the desperation and loneliness behind anger, the fear and helplessness behind silent withdrawal.

The most powerful change agent in a distressed relationship seems to be the expression of the tender, more disarming emotions, such as longing, fear, and sadness. It is the most powerful tool to evoke contact and responsiveness from a significant other. If I help couples create contact, couples can then solve their own problems.

Most couples begin by declaring how incredibly angry they are. They have good reason to be angry. As they come to feel more of their anger, not justify or contain it, they usually begin to explore and experience more of what it is about. The experience starts to include elements they don't usually focus on, which they may even [see] as inappropriate. In fact one reason for feeling so angry is that they feel totally helpless and unlovable, which scares them.

Soon one partner begins talking to the other about what happened one second before lashing out—an incredible sense of helplessness, a voice that comes into the head and said, "I'm not going to feel this way. I refuse to feel so helpless and needy. This is unacceptable." And now the experience has been expanded beyond anger and partners start to contact hidden parts of themselves—in the presence of the other.

This is a new and compelling experience for them that enables one partner to turn to the spouse and confide, "Somehow, some part of me has given up the hope of ever feeling cherished, and instead I've become enraged because I am so sure that you could never really hold me and love me." This kind of dialogue redefines the relationship as one where a person can be vulnerable and confide what is most terrifying about him or herself or the world. And the partner, with the therapist's help, is there both for comfort and as a validating mirror of those experiences of the self.

BUILDING A SECURE BASE

The relationship is then starting to be a secure base where people can be vulnerable, bring out the neediness or other elements of themselves that frighten them, and ask for their attachment needs to be met. In this safe context, the husband or wife doesn't see the partner as weak but as available—not dangerous. I may hear one say: "That's the part I fell in love with?" In a sense, the language of love is the language of vulnerability. While Western psychology focuses on the value of self-sufficiency, in our personal lives we struggle to integrate our needs for contact and care into our adult experience.

Attachment theory is an idea whose time has finally come because it allows us to be whole people. It views behavior gone awry as a well-meaning adaptation to past or present experience. And it views the desire for contact as healthy. Secure attachments promote emotional health and buffer us against life's many stresses. Love then becomes the most powerful arena for healing and for growth, and from this secure base, both men and women can go out and explore, even create, the world.

NO

Geraldine K. Piorkowski

BACK OFF!

We are overfocused on intimate relationships, and I question whether our current preoccupation with intimacy isn't unnatural, not entirely in keeping with the essential physical and psychological nature of people. The evidence suggests that there is a limit to the amount of closeness people can tolerate and that we need time alone for productivity and creativity. Time alone is necessary to replenish psychological resources and to solidify the boundaries of the self.

All our cultural focus on relationships ultimately has, I believe, a negative impact on us. It causes us to look upon intimate relationships as a solution to all our ills. And that only sets us up for disappointment, contributing to the remarkable 50 percent divorce rate.

Our overfocus on relationships leads us to demand too much of intimacy. We put all our emotional eggs in the one basket of intimate romantic relationships. A romantic partner must be all things to us—lover, friend, companion, playmate, and parent.

We approach intimate relationships with the expectation that this new love will make up for past let-downs in life and love. The expectation that this time around will be better is bound to disappoint, because present-day lovers feel burdened by demands with roots in old relationships.

We expect unconditional love, unfailing nurturance, and protection. There is also the expectation that the new partner will make up for the characteristics we lack in our own personality—for example, that he or she will be an outgoing soul to compensate for our shyness or a goal-oriented person to provide direction in our messy life.

If the personal ads were rewritten to emphasize the emotional expectations we bring to intimacy, they would sound like this. "WANTED: Lively humorous man who could bring joy to my gloomy days and save me from a lifetime of depression." Or, "WANTED: Woman with self-esteem lower than mine. With her, I could feel superior and gain temporary boosts of self-confidence from the comparison."

From my many years as a clinical psychologist, I have come to recognize that intimacy is not an unmitigated good. It is not only difficult to achieve, it is treacherous in some fundamental ways. And it can actually harm people.

From Geraldine K. Piorkowski, "Back Off!" *Psychology Today* (January/February 1995). Copyright © 1995 by Sussex Publishers, Inc. Reprinted by permission.

The potential for emotional pain and upset is so great in intimate relationships because we are not cloaked in the protective garb of maturity. We are unprotected, exposed, vulnerable to hurt; our defenses are down. We are wide open to pain.

Intuitively recognizing the dangers involved, people normally erect elaborate barriers to shield themselves from closeness. We may act superior, comical, mysterious, or super independent because we fear that intimacy will bring criticism, humiliation, or betrayal—whatever an earlier relationship sensitized us to. We develop expectations based on what has happened in our lives with parents, with friends, with a first love. And we often act in anticipation of these expectations, bringing about the result we most want to avoid.

The closer we get to another person, the greater the risks of intimacy. It's not just that we are more vulnerable and defenseless. We are also more emotionally unstable, childish, and less intelligent than in any other situation. You may be able to run a large company with skill and judgment, but be immature, ultra-sensitive, and needy at home. Civilized rules of conduct often get suspended. Intimacy is both unnerving and baffling.

HEALTHY RETREATS

Once our fears are aroused in the context of intimacy, we tend to go about calming them in unproductive ways. We make excessive demands of our partner, for affection, for unconditional regard. The trouble is, when people feel demands are being made of them, they tend to retreat and hide in ways that hurt their partner. They certainly do not listen.

Fears of intimacy typically limit our vulnerability by calling defensive strategies into play. Without a doubt, the defense of choice against the dangers of intimacy is withdrawal. Partners tune out. One may retreat into work. One walks out of the house, slamming the door. Another doesn't call for days. Whatever the way, we spend a great deal of time avoiding intimacy.

When one partner unilaterally backs off, it tends to be done in a hurtful manner. The other partner feels rejected, uncared about, and unloved. Typically, absolutely nothing gets worked out.

However, avoidance is not necessarily unhealthy. Partners can pursue a time out, where one or both work through their conflict in a solitary way that is ultimately renewing. What usually happens, however, is that when partners avoid each other, they are avoiding open warfare but doing nothing to resolve the underlying conflicts.

Fears of intimacy can actually be pretty healthy, when they're realistic and protective of the self. And they appear even in good relationships. Take the fears of commitment that are apt to surface in couples just before the wedding. If they can get together and talk through their fears, then they will not scare one another or themselves into backing off permanently.

After many years of working with all kinds of couples, I have come to believe that human nature dictates that intimate relationships have to be cyclical. There are limitations to intimacy and I think it is wise to respect the dangers. Periods of closeness have to be balanced with periods of distance. For every two steps forward, we often need to take one step back.

An occasional retreat from intimacy gives individuals time to recharge. It offers time to strengthen your sense of who you are. Think of it as constructive avoidance. We need to take some emphasis off what partners can do for us and put it on what we can do for ourselves and what we can do with other relationships. Developing and strengthening same-sex friendships, even opposite-sex friendships, has its own rewards and aids the couple by reducing the demands and emotional expectations we place on partners.

In our culture, our obsession with romantic love relationships has led us to confuse all emotional bonds with sexual bonds, just as we confuse infatuation with emotional intimacy. As a result, we seem to avoid strong but deeply rewarding emotional attachments with others of our own sex. But having recently lost a dear friend of several decades, I am personally sensitive to the need for emotionally deep, same-sex relationships. They can be shared as a way of strengthening gender identity and enjoying rewarding companionship. We need to put more energy into nonromantic relationships as well as other activities.

One of the best ways of recharging oneself is to take pleasure in learning and spiritual development. And there's a great deal to be said for spending time solving political, educational, or social ills of the world.

Distance and closeness boundaries need to be calibrated and constantly readjusted in every intimate relationship. Such boundaries not only vary with each couple, they change as the relationship progresses. One couple may maintain their emotional connection by spending one evening together a week, while another couple needs daily coming together of some sort. Problems arise in relationships when partners cannot agree on the boundaries. These boundaries must be jointly negotiated or the ongoing conflict will rob the relationship of its vitality.

S.O.S. SIGNALS

When you're feeling agitated or upset that your partner is not spending enough time with you, consider it a signal to step back and sort out internally what is going on. Whether you feel anxiety or anger, the emotional arousal should serve as a cue to back off and think through where the upset is coming from, and to consider whether it is realistic.

That requires at least a modest retreat from a partner. It could be a half hour, or two hours. Or two days—whenever internal clarity comes. In the grip of emotion, it is often difficult to discriminate exactly which emotion it is and what its source is. "What is it I am concerned about? Is this fear realistic considering Patrick's behavior in the present? He's never done this to me before, and he's been demonstrating his trustworthiness all over the place, so what am I afraid of? Is it coming from my early years of neglect with two distant parents who never had time for me? Or from my experiences with Steve, who dumped me two years ago?"

Introspective and self-aware people already spend their time thinking about how they work, their motives, what their feelings mean. Impulsive people will have a harder time with the sorting-out process. The best way to sort things out is to pay attention to the nature of the upset. Exactly what you are upset about suggests what your unmet need is, whether it's for love, understanding, nurturance, protection, or special status. And once you identify the need, you can figure out its antecedents.

The kinds of things we get upset about in intimacy tend to follow certain themes. Basically, we become hurt or resentful because we're getting "too much" or "too little" of something. Too many demands, too much criticism, too much domination. Or the converse, too little affectional, conversational, or sexual attention (which translates into "you don't feel I'm important" or "you don't love me"). Insufficient empathy is usually voiced as "you don't understand me," and too little responsibility translates into failure to take on one's share of household and/or financial tasks. All these complaints require some attention, action, or retreat.

SHIFTING GEARS

It's not enough to identify the source of personal concern. You have to present your concerns in a way your partner can hear. If I say directly to my partner, "I'm afraid you're going to leave me," he has the opportunity to respond, "Darling, that's not true. What gave you that idea?" I get the reassurance I need. But if I toss it out in an argument, in the form of "you don't care about me," then my partner's emotional arousal keeps him from hearing me. And he is likely to back away—just when I need reassurance most.

If people were aware that intimate relationships are by nature characterized by ambivalence, they would understand the need to negotiate occasional retreats. They wouldn't feel so threatened by the times when one partner says, "I have to be by myself because I need to think about my life and where I'm going."

Or "I need to be with my friends and spend time playing." If people did more backing off into constructive activities, including time to meditate or to play, intimate relationships would be in much better shape today.

If couples could be direct about what they need, then the need for retreat would not be subject to the misrepresentation that now is rampant. The trouble is, we don't talk to each other that openly and honestly. What happens is, one partner backs off and doesn't call and the partner left behind doesn't know what the withdrawal means. But he or she draws on a personal history that provides room for all sorts of negative interpretations, the most common being "he doesn't care about me."

No matter how hard a partner tries to be all things to us, gratifying all of another's needs is a herculean task—beyond the human calling. Criticism, disappointment, and momentary rejection are intrinsic parts of intimate life; developing a thicker skin can be healthy. And maintaining a life apart from the relationship is necessary. Energy invested in other people and activities provides a welcome balance.

GOOD-ENOUGH INTIMACY

Since our intimate partner will never be perfect, what is reasonable to expect? The late British psychiatrist D.W. Winnicott put forth the idea of "good-enough mothering." He was convinced that mothering could never be perfect because of the mother's own emotional needs. "Good-enough mothering" refers to imperfect, though adequate provision of emotional care that is not damaging to the children.

In a similar vein, I believe there is a level of imperfect intimacy that is good enough to live and grow on. In good-enough intimacy, painful encounters occasionally occur, but they are balanced by the strength and pleasures of the relationship. There are enough positives to balance the negatives. People who do very well in intimate relationships don't have a perfect relationship, but it is good enough.

The standard of good-enough intimacy is essentially subjective, but there are some objective criteria. A relationship must have enough companionship, affection, autonomy, connectedness, and separateness, along with some activities that partners engage in together and that they both enjoy. The relationship meets the needs of both partners reasonably well enough, both feel reasonably good about the relationship. If one person is unhappy in the relationship, then by definition it is not good enough for them.

People looking for good-enough intimacy are bound to be happier than those seeking perfect intimacy. Their expectations are lower and more realistic. Time and time again, those who examine the intricacies of happiness have found the same thing—realistic expectations are among the prime contributors to happiness.

POSTSCRIPT

Is Intimate Attachment the Key to Successful Relationships?

For the past 20 years intimacy has been considered the ultimate goal of couples in loving relationships. In his book *Triangle of Love* (Basic Books, 1988), Robert J. Sternberg describes love as having three components: intimacy, passion, and commitment. He defines intimacy as feelings of closeness and connectedness, of being bonded to the other person. In an article in *Family Relations* (1993), Barry Moss and Andrew Schwebel write that skill in achieving intimacy enables individuals to develop closer friendships and attain greater marital happiness. They further proclaim that an individual who fails to make an intimate connection with a romantic partner runs a greater risk of developing mental and physical health problems.

One of the biggest issues that people in romantic relationships confront is the constant struggle to find a comfortable balance between the need to establish emotional closeness and the desire to create some distance from their partners. People seem to have contradictory impulses between being open and sharing confidences and being closed and protective of the self. Both Johnson/Marano and Piorkowski offer explanations for people's anxiety about intimacy. Each describes the process by which individuals come together to share love and develop intimacy and then inevitably want to withdraw to protect their sense of privacy and independence. Nevertheless, the authors disagree about what withdrawal signals to the partner and how couples should handle distancing behaviors. Which theory seems most reasonable to you?

The following questions may help you to explore your thoughts and feelings about intimacy in close relationships: What types of behaviors would you consider a betrayal of trust on the part of an intimate partner? Once trust is breached, do you think it can ever be regained? How might a person go about convincing a loved one of his or her trustworthiness, despite a serious transgression? What factors do you think would influence a person to self-disclose in a romantic relationship? What past experiences might cause a partner to be fearful of intimacy? Should a person sometimes hold back certain thoughts and feelings for the good of her or his partner or for the good of the relationship? Are there types of information that should never be disclosed to a romantic partner? Do you think that attachment patterns set in infancy are fixed for life? Do adults have the same needs for emotional support and security as do children? Who besides parents and spouses serve as primary attachment figures in one's life? Are some attachment figures more important to one's well-being than others? Do you believe that there is such a thing as "good enough" intimacy? Do you think that couples can place too much emphasis on sharing their thoughts and feelings with each other?

SUGGESTED READINGS

S. S. Brehm, *Intimate Relationships* (Random House, 1992).

V. J. Derlega, S. Metts, S. Petronis, and S. T. Margullis, *Self-Disclosure* (Sage Publications, 1993).

S. W. Duck, ed., *Understanding Relationship Processes, vol. 2: Learning About Relationships* (Sage Publications, 1993).

J. Pearson, *Lasting Love: What Keeps Couples Together* (William C. Brown, 1992).

L. M. Register and T. B. Henley, "The Phenomenology of Intimacy," *Journal of Social and Personal Relationships*, 9 (1992): 467–481.

A. L. Weber and J. H. Harvey, *Perspectives on Close Relationships* (Allyn & Bacon, 1994).

J. T. Wood and C. C. Inman, "In a Different Mode: Masculine Styles of Communicating Closeness," *Journal of Applied Communication Research*, 21 (1993): 279–295.

Internet: http://www.scri.fsu.edu/~sollohub/wwme/wwme.html

ISSUE 6

Do Men and Women Speak Different Languages?

YES: Robert Bly and Deborah Tannen, from "Where Are Women and Men Today?" *New Age Journal* (January/February 1992)

NO: Mary Crawford, from *Talking Difference: On Gender and Language* (Sage Publications, 1995)

ISSUE SUMMARY

YES: Robert Bly, a leader of workshops on men's issues, and professor of sociolinguistics Deborah Tannen team up for a dialogue in which they propose that conversational differences exist between men and women.

NO: Professor of psychology Mary Crawford argues that gendered talking styles are media hype, the result of flawed scholarship and popular opinion. She fears that publicity will heighten the stereotype that women's talk is ineffective.

Currently, there is a debate over whether or not women and men have different talking styles. Some claim that men are driven by a need for hierarchy in their social relationships. During conversations men plot to capture the floor, state their issues with forthright clarity, and make decisions with impunity. They loath being interrupted and revel in giving information and advice.

By contrast, the argument goes, women are culturally predisposed to be inclusive and nurturing in their conversational style. They approach problems indirectly, wait their turn for the floor, and make cooperative decisions after hearing from all sides. Women like to keep the conversation flowing, interrupt each other, fill silences, and ask questions. Expressing sympathy and sharing similar experiences and feelings is a regular part of women's conversations. The result of women's more inclusive style is strengthened feelings of emotional closeness. According to some researchers, the overarching goal of women's talk is to create intimacy rather than to engage in competition. Disagreement is often taken personally—signs of a less caring attitude and a lack of concern for the conversational partner.

Those who believe that these gendered patterns of communication exist say that the contrasting styles may lead to misunderstandings between men and women in close relationships. To improve relational quality and partner satisfaction, some argue, it is necessary to develop an understanding and sympathy for differences in how women and men talk and to make sincere efforts to listen and appreciate the other's ways of speaking.

Opponents of this view say that one must dig deeper than obvious sex differences to understand people's communication patterns. Ways of speaking may depend more on the social status and power of the speaker and less on gender. Patterns of talk, say opponents, probably evolve from the unequal resources of relational partners. The person with more power—greater income, education, job status—most likely uses it to gain a better position. The more powerful person in a relationship, usually the male partner, seems to consider it "only natural" that he controls what the couple talks about, when they talk about it, and who does most of the talking on important matters.

As you read the following two selections, ask yourself, Do girls and boys learn different rules of social behavior that result in gendered scripts and that continue to guide their personal communication even into adulthood? Do men and women have unique styles of talking that culminate in hurt feelings, misinterpretations of motives, disagreements, and confused problem solving among marital partners, friends, and colleagues?

Consider whether or not this proposed conversational dichotomy is simply a case of slim research findings being misinterpreted by the mass media. Does believing that one's gender determines how one talks mean that conversational difficulties are a personal problem rather than a societal concern? If a problem is labeled personal, is it then up to the individual to find a solution? For example, is it a woman's own fault if she gets pushed aside, hushed up, and blamed for miscommunications at home and at work? And if we accept the notion that conversation is a gendered activity, are we buying into existing stereotypes and myths about men and women in general?

YES   Robert Bly and Deborah Tannen

WHERE ARE WOMEN AND MEN TODAY?

ROBERT BLY: The first time I came in contact with your book, my wife and I were having dinner up in northern Minnesota and someone started to read out of it. We both fell off our chairs laughing, because it illuminated every mistake we had made, including every misunderstanding. I remember the first example that was read: On their way home, a woman asks a man if he'd like to stop for a drink. My wife has made remarks like that to me many times, and I always thought she was asking for information. I'd check my body. My body would say, "No, I don't want a drink." And so I'd report it and say, "No thanks." And that was it. I had always thought I was doing what was asked of me. But it turns out she was imagining maybe a little conversation before the day ends. . . .

Another thing that I thought was wonderful in the book was this: At home the woman says to the man, "Why don't you ever talk to me?" Then they go to a party and a half-hour later he's giving this long lecture on the Galapagos tortoises to thirty people. And she says, "How come you talk to them, but you don't talk to me?"

TANNEN: Or in your case it might be, "You talk to a thousand people, but you don't talk to me."

BLY: Right. And these are hard questions, but you give a wonderful answer. Women engage in rapport talk—using conversation to gain rapport—to increase the unity between two people, whereas men's conversation is a report —a report of all the fantastic things that have happened in the universe. So, for a man, when you're sitting home there's nothing to report about, but when you get with three or four other people your adrenaline rises and you realize that you can talk about how much you love the world, which includes the Galapagos tortoises. I think a lot of forgiveness comes from simply naming these differences, and it doesn't mean that either one is wrong.

TANNEN: But it also doesn't mean that it's not frustrating. So we have to talk about what we can do from there. Maybe you can tell us how you and your wife have worked it out now.

BLY: *Hmmm.* Have you got an hour or two? (*Laughter.*)

... I think that women and men have a very different definition of what the comfort of home is. He's been using language all day in the struggle to make sure he gets the respect that he deserves, to make sure that people don't push him around in his job, to establish his position in the group. And that's very tiring and wearing. So at the end of the day he feels, "Now I'm home with somebody whom I trust. I have nothing to prove, so I'm free to not talk." And so the demand to talk in that situation is experienced as an unfair one.

And, of course, she feels, quite rightly, that she's had to be careful how she's used language all day. If she talks too much people will call her aggressive, pushy, and all the other words that we have for women who talk too much. Or she might spark a conflict, hurt somebody's feelings. She's been monitoring what she says all day long, so when she gets home she feels, "Now I'm home with somebody I feel close to, so I'm free to talk."

BLY: I just want to emphasize how much shame the man takes in during the day when he's having these conversations at business. This business of checking to see who's on top in the conversation means that the ones down below are receiving shame all day. And when you go home, you say to yourself, "Thank God, now I'm not going to get shamed." And then what does your wife say? "Would you talk to me?"

And you say, "Oh God, now she's going to be better at it than me, and I'm going to be a fool again. I can't do it. Isn't there a *New York Times* somewhere that I can read?"

TANNEN: I think this is particularly hurtful for women, because coming home and telling everything that's hap-pened is a ritual that they've engaged in from the time they were very little. And in order to feel that life is going on as it should, we want to play out these rituals. But because this is not a ritual that men understand—it's not one that they've done—the man will look for the literal reason for the talk. And he can't find one. And it's very frustrating to do something when you don't understand the reason for it.

This applies to the desire of women to talk about their problems without having the man jump in with a solution. I've had people say, "Well, just say to him, 'I don't want you to tell me what to do, just listen to me.'" And though that makes perfect sense on the surface, it will drive the man crazy to sit and listen to something when he doesn't understand why he's listening and what the conversation is getting at. And so here's another compromise I learned. One time I was talking with my husband, and he said, "Well, I know you just want to talk about this and you don't want me to give you the solution, but it's too frustrating for me to sit here and listen when I know the solution. (*Laughter.*) So let me tell you the solution, and then you can keep talking about it if you want to keep talking about it." And that's worked fine....

BLY: You've said that one thing women learn is how to listen well. And when they begin to say something, they really want you to listen and not to fix it. They want you to hear what's being said, because women feel unseen and unheard.

Now, you can train a man to listen. That's not too difficult. But the problem is that in some way that's not part of the male mode of feeling. I can't explain it exactly, but men don't want women to listen well. When a man is talking and the woman is listening and saying things like "I hear that" or "that's interesting," he says, "Listen, I'm going nuts here. This whole thing is running out of me." The man wants the woman to say something like "that's not true in the South" or "that's only true of a Republican." I mean, he wants to *hear* something. When you're looking at it as a man, you're looking at the content. So to talk well with a man, you've got to object. You've got to say, "I don't think so. Let me tell you what Heraclitus said." And immediately the man goes, "Wow, she knows something about Heraclitus." It's very strange.

TANNEN: Yes. I think women often feel that what they can give the other person in conversation is agreement and matching. In my book I give the example of a couple who had been married for a long, long time—maybe thirty years. One morning he said, "I didn't sleep well last night." And she said, "Yeah, I didn't sleep well, either. I never do." And he said, "Why are you belittling me?" She was very hurt, and said, "But I'm not, I'm just trying to show you that I understand." And it amazed me that I got perhaps half a dozen letters from men saying to me, She really *was* belittling him in that conversation. She's putting him down because he said he didn't sleep well last night, and she's saying "I *never* do." So, my situation is worse than yours. It's bigger. I'm more. . . .

You think you're giving the person what he wants, and he acts as if you hit him in the face. . . .

I think this misunderstanding comes from a difference in focus. We all need to feel involved with other people, to know that we're not alone, but we also all need to feel independent and unique. Women seem to focus more on that need for involvement, which is what she was doing by saying, "I'm going through the same thing. I feel the same way." And he was focusing on the need for independence. And so he saw her attempt to say "we're the same" as an offense to his uniqueness.

BLY: Another way to look at that is to say that it was a little bit too much comforting for him. Here's what I mean. A few years ago, I was teaching small groups in Boulder, and a woman would come every time with a certain man. She was a very feisty woman who had been very badly abused in childhood. I liked her. She caused a lot of trouble.

One year when I came back, she wasn't there. And when I asked the man what happened, he said: "About three months ago we were skiing down the mountain and her ski broke. The edge of it went into her jugular vein and she died right there." And so I said, "What happened?" And he said, "Well, a lot of people in Boulder knew about it. And the women would come up to me and be very comforting. And they would say things like 'How do you feel?' and so on and so on." And, he said, "Eventually, I was getting too much comfort. I couldn't do it anymore. It was wrong to get that amount of sympathy." But, he said, "I found that when I talked to men, they would hear me, and then they might say something like, 'Well, what are you going to do about it? Are you gonna tell this story the rest of your life?' That was more help to me than the comfort the women gave me." So I think there's something about the male mode of feeling in which we don't comfort quite as much. There's a limited amount of comforting that feels right to a man.

TANNEN: Comfort can somehow be belittling. Maybe there was that, too. I make that point in my book.

BLY: Well, one of the things you can say is that if someone comforts you a lot, it turns you into a boy.

TANNEN: Yes, a parent comforts a child. A mother comforts a child.

BLY: That's right. So he began to feel like he was a boy when he told this story to the women in Boulder, but when the men heard it, it was like two adults talking with each other.

TANNEN: I think women experience the matching of feeling as putting us on an equal footing, but I can see how you could perceive comfort as putting you in a one-down position.

BLY: Indeed.

TANNEN: There's a conversation in my book that illustrates this. It's from a tape recording of two tenth-grade boys talking to each other. And it's the kind of conversation that I think most women cringe at, because each one belittles the other's problem. The boys are talking about very significant feelings—one of them is talking about a problem he has with drinking, and the other is saying that he's been feeling alienated and left out and doesn't feel that he belongs anywhere. In response, they just dismiss each other's problems....

A woman told me that when her boyfriend reacts to her talking about problems in that way she feels put down, dismissed. And I told her that I think he was trying to dismiss the problem to make her feel better, because if he said, "Oh yeah, that's a terrible problem," in a way he'd be saying, "You're really a problem-ridden, unfortunate person." And that can be experienced as a put-down. So, in a sense, dismissing the problem and making little of it can be like building a person back up rather than rubbing his nose in it.

BLY: Yes, and once again, I'd like to emphasize how easy it is for the two genders to shame each other. In 1985 or so they found that the corpus callosum —the bridge that binds the two sides of the brain—is thicker in the female song sparrow than in the male song sparrow. And about two years ago, after further investigation, they found that even in the fetus of the human female, the corpus callosum is thicker.

Words are in one lobe of the brain and feelings in the other. So that means that women have an ability to mingle those much quicker than men can. Women have a superhighway going on there! And, as Michael Meade remarked, men have this little crookedy country road, and you're lucky if a word gets over. So the woman, with the larger corpus callosum, can shame the man without intending to at all, simply by talking to him the swift way. But I think it's significant for this reason: Let's say a woman wakes up at eight o'clock one morning, and when she takes the garbage out, she kicks the garbage can. So what does she do? She goes back in the house, calls up one of her girlfriends, and says, "You know, something weird happened. I just kicked the garbage can. I think I must be angry." So they talk about it and within forty-five minutes she's figured out why she's angry.

Now, I want to tell you that some men do not know they're angry until four in the afternoon when they've done something like hit their son. That's the first indication they have. If they did kick a garbage can, they didn't call up a friend and say, "Listen, Jack, I just kicked the garbage can." This is definitely a flaw in the male mode of feeling. But the reason is that the corpus callosum is thinner and not much goes across. Sometimes the man doesn't know he's angry until his fist goes out, and then he feels terribly ashamed. He feels stunned by what's happened. And what's he going to do? Defend his action? Try to find a reason *why* he hit his son?

To me, one of the purposes of art and poetry is to thicken the corpus callosum. My corpus callosum is much thicker than when I was twenty. Women's are still wider than mine, but at least I've got two lanes now. And I think one of the jobs of older men is to try to help the corpus callosum of the younger men get thicker. TANNEN: But I also want to add something, because I don't want to leave us with the idea that women talk more freely and more easily than men in *all* situations. While there are some situations where women talk and perhaps shame men for not talking, there are other situations where the reverse happens—women are shamed for not talking. Here's an example: I was talking to a group in a living room, and one particular couple sitting on the couch was noticeable because the woman didn't say anything the entire evening, while the man was the biggest talker in the group. Toward the end of the evening, when I mentioned that many women complain that the men they live with don't tell them anything, this man said, "That's absolutely right." And pointing to the woman sitting silently beside him, he said, "She's the talker in our family." Everybody laughed because she hadn't said anything. And he said, "But it's true. At the end of the day, I come home and have nothing to say, and she talks all evening."

I think we have to remember that, in public, many men talk more easily. The road is blocked in the public situation for many women. And this is particularly destructive for women in a society like ours. In business, in school—in so many situations where our careers and our futures are at stake, a woman is frequently seen as less competent and intelligent than she is because her words don't flow as freely as they do in private. It's very typical for women to talk much less than men at meetings.

BLY: Yes. A woman once said to me, "You know what a man is? Someone who takes up more space on the plane than is given to him." Anyway, as you said in your book, when women are in a public situation and the men are interrupting each other all the time, the women tend to get angry and say the men are trying to prevent them from speaking. But that isn't right. The men are just going through their contest thing, and they're enjoying it. Who can interrupt whom the most? The excitement of that raises the adrenaline level, and they actually *do* say more intelligent things. Meanwhile, the woman waits for a pause. Well, *there ain't gonna be no pause*. The pause is no fun. So the woman waits all afternoon, and then says these people are anti-female. It isn't so.

TANNEN: ... Both women and men accuse each other of interrupting, but typically, when the man accuses the woman of interrupting, it's because "you're finishing my sentences for me." When women accuse men of interrupting, it's taking the floor, changing the subject.

BLY: So it seems that women have to learn the public way of speaking just as the men have to go home and learn the private way of speaking—women have to learn to interrupt as men do, not waiting for a pause, just jumping in. It doesn't do any good if only the men learn a new way of speaking, because the woman will then feel down when she's in a business situation.

TANNEN: But I think we have to keep in mind that women don't always have the same options that men have. If she fights for the floor in the same way—if she talks as long, if she interrupts—then she'll be seen as aggressive and all those other words.... And that threat is always lurking there, hovering over women, making them quite cautious about talking in the same way as men....

Most women will avoid confrontation at all cost. It's very common for women to have experiences on the job where they feel that people have behaved inappropriately with them and they don't say anything about it. By the way, I don't think that's so different from men, either. I mean, if someone is your boss and your job is dependent upon him and you feel that this is the best job for your career—men put up with all kinds of junk on the job because they feel that they need the job, and ...

BLY: Men are *always* playing golf with people they can't stand—and don't even mention it....

TANNEN: I think that the impulse to be nice to people, to be good, to not make trouble, is something that is fundamental to most women....

BLY: So the willingness to cause trouble is a part of the male mode of feeling that the women might study.

[At this point Tannen and Bly invite questions from the audience.]

QUESTIONER: I'm always fascinated by the fact that in a group setting or a business meeting, women are not only reticent to speak up, but they often begin by asking for permission, whereas men will just simply state their minds. Can you comment on that?

TANNEN: I think that's because so many of women's rituals are based on the idea of not imposing on other people. Beginning by asking permission is a way of not imposing on others. I think it's crucial to see, though, that although this kind of indirect communication doesn't serve women well when they're communicating in a public situation with men, there's nothing inherently bad about doing it that way.... What's unfortunate about the difference between men's and women's rituals in our country is that they often put women at a disadvantage in interactions with men.

BLY: I'd like to follow that with a remark on the difference between consensus and hierarchy. It seems that men tend to be more comfortable with hierarchy and women with consensus—checking everything out. Men love hierarchy, and one of the reasons is that for 200,000 years we were hunters. And when you're hunting, one man has to make the decision as to where you're going to go and meet the animal. In the '60s there was a lot of shaming of men by women for being hierarchical, because consensus seemed to work well. But lately I've been realizing that that kind of shaming is not proper—both of these things are terrific. Hierarchy is very beautiful. Men love hierarchy, long for hierarchy, feel good in hierarchy. Women love consensus, feel good in consensus, honor consensus.

But I think the love of consensus can sometimes damage women's opportunities. Here's an example: A few years ago at a conference with men and women, we separated the men and the women for most of a day. Before going off, the women and the men agreed to each prepare a gift to present to the others when we returned at five o'clock. The women went off to their place, and Michael

Meade and I went off with the men in a bunch of canoes. And as soon as we got to the new place, we started to rave and carry on and tell stories, and we had a great time. At about a quarter to five or so we said, "We'd better get the gift ready." So Michael Meade suggested that we all sing an old Irish grieving song. It was a good idea, and all the men started to sing it. In ten minutes, they'd done the whole thing. Not a single argument.

So we went back, and when the women got there, we stood up in front and sang our song for them. And then there was this terrible pause. And, it turned out the women had spent three hours trying to prepare a gift for the men. They'd gotten the thing going. Everyone had learned her part, and ten minutes before the end one woman said, "I don't like it." And they were so devoted to consensus that they dropped the idea. But then they felt very bad at not having any gift at all to give the men.

TANNEN: There's another danger with consensus. If you have two people trying to make a decision, and one person feels that it's OK if we don't agree, he or she can say, "Well, you want this, and I want that, and I'm going to do that," and the other one feels they *have* to agree. You can see that the person who is seeking agreement will very often not get his or her way. Because they can't get the other person to say, "I agree." I think women in particular often give up what they want because they can't get the other person to agree, whereas it would actually be pretty fine with the other person if she said, "OK, you don't like it. I'm going to do it anyway." ...

An audience member then voices an objection that the speakers are making too many generalizations about women and men.

TANNEN: I would agree that there is something inherently dangerous about grouping people together—about saying "women," "men," or any other group. One of the worst things that people do is to lump other people into groups, label them, and then heap scorn on them. That's the opening for all kinds of evil things that people do to each other. I'm aware of that danger. But I believe that if there are patterns, the danger of *not* identifying them is greater than the danger *of* identifying them. And it's women in particular who suffer if we don't describe the differences, because we have one standard in this country—and that standard is based on men's way.

... I think it's crucial that we describe the differences between women and men so that we can begin to respect our own mode of communication. When I wrote my book, I was always very cautious to say "many," or "most" and to never say "all." Of course, when they write it up in the media, they take all the qualifiers out and make it sound absolute. But I've been astounded by the mail I've gotten. It's all positive. People say that what I describe is true of them and they've been blaming themselves or blaming their partner or their partner has been blaming them. They say it is such a relief to have the burden of pathology lifted off. So that has given me the courage to go out and actually talk about these differences, despite my very real awareness of the danger of generalizing. And I think it's important to realize that this is a description of one culture in one time. It's not the way it has to be....

Understanding the dynamics of what makes conversation work the way it does, understanding how one person's strategy affects the other person in interaction, gives us the tools, the flexibility, to begin making the changes we want to make. So describing the status quo doesn't mean that we want the status quo to go on forever. It gives us a way to begin to make the changes that we want to make.

And, finally, I'd like to say that the saddest part about making any statements about women and men is the possibility that people will hear just the word itself as an accusation....

[I]f we want to open the dialogue, we have to be open to listening to each other and not have our backs go up at anything any person of the other group says about us or about themselves. We need to begin to understand both our differences and our similarities and use that as a starting point for making the changes that we want to make.

NO   Mary Crawford

TWO SEXES, TWO CULTURES

CROSS-CULTURAL TALK

Consider the difficulties of talk between, say, a person of Italian background and one from Japan. Even if the two share a common language, they may have trouble communicating because they are likely to have different ways of expressing politeness, conversational involvement, and so forth. The 'two-cultures' approach proposes that talk between women and men is fraught with potential misunderstanding for much the same reasons that communication across ethnic groups is.

... Talk shows and best-sellers proclaim the frustrations of cross-sex talk (*You just don't Understand*) and describe a gender gap so great that the two sexes might as well be from different planets (*Men are from Mars, Women are from Venus*)....

Talking Across the Gender Divide

... When we think of distinct female and male subcultures we tend to think of societies in which women and men spend virtually their entire lives spatially and interactionally segregated.... In Western societies, however, girls and boys are brought up together. They share the use of common space in their homes; eat, work, and play with their siblings of both sexes; generally attend coeducational schools in which they are aggregated in many classes and activities; and usually participate in religious meetings and activities together. Both sexes are supervised, cared for, and taught largely by women in infancy and early childhood, with male teachers and other authority figures becoming more visible as children grow older. Moreover, they see these social patterns mirrored and even exaggerated in the mass media. How can the talk of Western women and men be seen as talk across cultures?

The two-cultures model was first applied to the speech of North American women and men by Daniel Maltz and Ruth Borker, who proposed that

From Mary Crawford, *Talking Difference: On Gender and Language* (Sage Publications, 1995), pp. 86–94, 97, 101–108. Copyright © 1995 by Sage Publications Ltd. Reprinted by permission. Some references omitted.

difficulties in cross-sex and cross-ethnic communication are 'two examples of the same larger phenomenon: cultural difference and miscommunication' (1982: 196). Maltz and Borker acknowledge the argument that American women and men interact with each other far too much to be characterized as living in different subcultures. However, they maintain that the social rules for friendly conversation are learned between the ages of approximately 5 and 15, precisely the time when children's play groups are maximally segregated by sex. Not only do children voluntarily choose to play in same-sex groups, they consciously exaggerate differences as they differentiate themselves from the other sex. Because of the very different social contexts in which they learn the meanings and goals of conversational interaction, boys and girls learn to use language in different ways.

Citing research on children's play, Maltz and Borker (1982) argue that girls learn to do three things with words:

1. to create and maintain relationships of closeness and equality;
2. to criticize others in acceptable (indirect) ways;
3. to interpret accurately and sensitively the speech of other girls.

In contrast, boys learn to do three very different things with words:

1. to assert one's position of dominance;
2. to attract and maintain an audience;
3. to assert oneself when another person has the floor.

The Two-Cultures Approach as Bandwagon

... The new twist in the two-cultures model of communication is to conceive relationship difficulties not as women's deficiencies but as an inevitable result of deeply ingrained male–female differences. The self-help books that encode a two-cultures model make the paradoxical claim that difference between the sexes is deeply socialized and/or fundamental to masculine and feminine natures, and at the same time subject to change and manipulation if the reader only follows prescribed ways of talking....

A best-selling exemplar of the genre is *Men are from Mars, Women are from Venus* (Gray, 1992). As its title proclaims, this book dichotomizes and stereotypes women and men to extremes....

Every aspect of personality, motivation, and language is polarized. Women's speech is indirect, men's is direct. Women respond to stress by becoming overwhelmed and emotionally involved, men by becoming focused and withdrawn. Women and men even lunch in restaurants for different reasons: for men, it is an efficient way to approach the task of eating; for women, it is an opportunity to build a relationship.

Women and men are so irredeemably and fundamentally different that they need translators to help them communicate.... They also need rules and routines to bridge the gender gap. (Oddly, some of these rules and routines are opposite to those endorsed in assertiveness training books. Instead of 'I would like you to take out the trash,' a wife is exhorted to ask, 'Would you take out the trash?' Like assertiveness prescriptions, however, they are promulgated with detailed specificity and total conviction. If she unthinkingly asks '*Could* you take out the trash?' the wife has doomed her relationship to a period of resistance and resentment.)...

Although the book makes prescriptions for both sexes, it leaves little doubt about its intended readership: women in middle-class heterosexual marriages. In this book, Martians come home after a long day at the office to waiting Venusians. Martians are obsessed with paid work and money, Venusians with home and feelings. Venusians seem to do almost all the domestic work, from taking children to the dentist to cooking, cleaning, and calling elderly relatives. Martians may be asked to help, but only if Venusians use carefully circumscribed request forms and recognize that Martians have every right to refuse. Helpful tips are provided for 'Programming a Man to Say Yes' and 'The Art of Empowering a Man.' If all else fails, one can read the section on 'How to Give up Trying to Change a Man.'

... Despite the endless lists of how to change each other, the ultimate promise is that women can earn love through acceptance of the status quo. Individual change is not really necessary, much less the restructuring of masculinity and femininity. 'Through understanding the hidden differences of the opposite [sic] sex we can... give and receive... love. Love is magical, and it can last, if we remember our differences' (Gray, 1992: 14).

Academic psychologists and linguists have tended to ignore self-help materials. The path along the journey to enlightenment and communication heaven in these books is not likely to be cluttered with any actual references to research....

The situation would be different if a prominent and well-respected academic were to claim expertise in male–female communication and write about it for the general public. And that is just what has happened with Deborah Tannen's *You just don't Understand: Women and Men in Conversation* (1990).... *You just don't*

Understand has been on the *New York Times* bestseller list for over three years and claims over one million copies in print.... It seems that the state of gender relations among the middle-class book-buying public demanded an explanation of communication difficulties and frustrations, an explanation that books like *Men are from Mars, Women are from Venus* and *You just don't Understand* promised to provide.

Although Tannen is a much-published and respected linguist, this particular work has been quite controversial among her peers. Scholarly review and commentary have been mixed....

Tannen claims that childhood play has shaped world views so that, when adult women and men are in relationships 'women speak and hear a language of connection and intimacy, while men speak and hear a language of status and independence' (1990: 42). The contrasting conversational goals of intimacy and independence lead to contrasting conversational styles. Women tell each other of their troubles, freely ask for information and help, and show appreciation of others' helping efforts. Men prefer to solve problems rather than talk about them, are reluctant to ask for help or advice, and are more comfortable in the roles of expert, lecturer, and teacher than learner or listener. Men are more talkative in public, women in private. These different styles are labelled 'report talk' (men's) and 'rapport talk' (women's).

Given the stylistic dichotomy between the sexes, miscommunication is almost inevitable; however, no one is to blame. Rather, another banner proclaims, 'The Key is Understanding:' 'Although each style is valid on its own terms, misunderstandings arise because the styles are different. Taking a cross-cultural approach to male–female conversations makes it possible to explain why dissatisfactions are justified without accusing anyone of being wrong or crazy' (1990: 47).

You just don't Understand makes its case for the two-cultures model skillfully and well using techniques that have become standard in popular writing about behavior: characterizations of 'most' women and men, entertaining anecdotes, and the presentation of research findings as fact. However, it is better written than most....

THE TWO-CULTURES APPROACH: AN EVALUATION

Beyond Deficiencies and Blame
Proponents of the two-cultures model maintain that it is an advance over approaches that blame particular groups for miscommunication....

Unlike earlier approaches, the two-cultures model does not characterize women's talk as deficient in comparison to a male norm.... To John Gray, neither Mars nor Venus is a superior home. To Deborah Tannen, 'report talk,' and 'rapport talk' are equally limiting for their users in cross-sex communication. The speech style attributed to men is no longer 'standard' speech or 'the language,' but merely one way of negotiating the social landscape.

... Although *Men are from Mars, Women are from Venus* prescribes rigid rules for talk, the much more sophisticated *You just don't Understand* presents a view of language that stresses its flexibility....

Doing Gender, Doing Power
The two-cultures approach fails to theorize how power relations at the structural level are recreated and maintained at the interactional level....

This failure to recognize structural power and connect it with interactional power has provoked the strongest criticisms of the two-cultures approach. In a review of *You just don't Understand*, Senta Troemel-Ploetz (1991) pointed out that if the majority of relationships between women and men in our society were not fundamentally asymmetrical to the advantage of men,

> we would not need a women's liberation movement, women's commissions, houses for battered women, legislation for equal opportunity, antidiscrimination laws, family therapy, couple therapy, divorce.... If you leave out power, you do not understand any talk, be it the discussion after your speech, the conversation at your own dinner-table, in a doctor's office, in the back yards of West Philadelphia, in an Italian village, on a street in Turkey, in a court room or in a day-care center, in a women's group or at a UN conference....

No one involved in debating the two-cultures approach denies that men have more social and political power than women. Maltz and Borker (1982: 199) acknowledge that power differentials 'may make some contribution' to communication patterns. However, they do not theorize the workings of power in interaction or advocate structural changes to reduce inequity.

THE BANDWAGON REVISITED
... Deborah Tannen's critics have charged that, despite the absence of overt woman-blaming and the positive evaluation of 'feminine' modes of talk, the interpretations she offers often disguise or gloss over inequity, and privilege men's interpretations. They have accused her of being an apologist for men, excusing their

insensitivity, rudeness, and dominance as mere stylistic quirks, and encouraging women to make the adjustments when needs conflict....

Differences and Dichotomies

In both *You just don't Understand* and *Men are from Mars, Women are from Venus*, women and men are presented as having non-overlapping and inherently conflictual conversational goals and styles....

Both books position cross-sex communication as fundamental. They do not set out to deal with communication across other categories that separate people: class, 'race,' ethnicity, age, sexual orientation, and so on.... With their erasure, the complexities of social position and situation are backgrounded; women become a global category and sex can take center stage....

When sex is the only conceptual category, differences attributable to situations and power relationships are made invisible....

The language of both books further constructs gender as difference. Gray repeatedly characterizes men and women as 'opposite sexes,' describes gender-differentiated behavior as 'instinctive,' and indulges in classic gender polarities: Martians are hard, Venusians soft; Martians are angular, Venusians round; Martians are cool, Venusians warm. 'In a magical and perfect way their differences seemed to complement each other' (1992: 44). Tannen's much more responsible and scholarly work is guilty of none of these excesses; it constructs gender as difference more subtly. The overlap between women and men is obscured by chapter titles ('Different Words, Different Worlds') and banner headings ('Male–Female Conversation is Cross-Cultural Communication') that suggest categorically different speech styles. The demands of mass-market writing preclude the use of numbers, tables, statistical analyses, graphs of distributions of results, or discussions of how persons and situations interact. Without these aids to conceptualizing *degrees* of differences and fluctuation, difference cannot readily be described except in terms of most/many women/men. This contributes to the fundamental attribution error. Instead of a flexible, situation-specific behavior, speech style becomes a static personality trait.

... Although Tannen notes that some women fear *with justification* that 'different' will be heard in reference to an implicit male norm, and that the conceptual step between 'different' and 'worse' is a short and perhaps inevitable one (1990: 14–15), she never develops these insights. Like the acknowledgment of status and power disparities, acknowledgement that difference may be read as women's deficiency appears, then disappears, without becoming a vehicle for further analysis.

... Tannen defends her choice not to write about dominance, control, and the politics of gender:

Asymmetries of Power

... In a chapter titled 'Damned if You Do,' Tannen reviews some of the research showing that the same behavior may be interpreted differently depending on whether it is done by a woman or a man, and that such interpretation is usually to women's disadvantage. The styles more typical of men, she acknowledges, are taken as the norm. Moreover, when women and men interact in mixed-sex groups, men's norms prevail. Women adjust to them, and it is this that gives the *appearance* of male dominance.

Women who attempt to emulate the male norms may be disliked and disparaged as unfeminine and aggressive. Although Tannen makes the poignant observation that 'The road to authority is tough for women, and once they get there it's a bed of thorns,' this observation *ends* her chapter on the double bind rather than providing a starting point for further analysis.

> These are important areas of research, and many books have been written about them; they are not new, and they are not the field in which I work. I wrote a book about the role of what I call 'conversational style' in everyday conversation, especially in the context of close relationships, because that has been the subject of my research throughout my academic career. (Tannen, 1992: 249)

... Thirty years of social science research has shown that men have more power in heterosexual marriage and dating relationships due to their ability to access external resources and their higher social status generally.... Though Tannen briefly and belatedly... acknowledges research showing that earning more money is probably the greatest source of marital power, she does not appear to recognize that the actual result of this phenomenon, which she presents as a gender-neutral fact, is greater *male* power....

A Rhetoric of Reassurance
The rhetoric of difference makes everyone—and no one—responsible for interpersonal problems. Men are not to blame for communication difficulties; neither is a social system in which gender governs access to resources. Instead, difference is reified: 'The culprit, then is not an individual man or even men's styles alone,

but the difference between women and men's styles' (Tannen, 1990: 95).

One of the most striking effects achieved in these books is to reassure women that their lot in heterosexual relationships is normal. Again and again, it is stressed that no one is to blame, that miscommunication is inevitable, that unsatisfactory results may stem from the best of intentions....

Tannen explains that when men do most of the talking in a group, it is not because they intend to prevent women from speaking or believe that women have nothing important to say. Rather, they see the women as *equals*, and expect them to compete in the same style they themselves use. Thus, an inequity that feminists have conceptualized in terms of power differentials is acknowledged, but explained as an accidental imbalance created by style and having little to do with a gendered social order.

... In the separate worlds of 'report talk' and 'rapport talk', the goal may be sex-specific but the desire is the same: to be understood and responded to in kind. In *You just don't Understand*, each anecdote is followed by an analysis of the intentions of *both* speakers, a practice that Tannen (1992) feels reflects her fairness to both sexes. But this symmetry is false, because the one kind of intention that is never imputed to any speaker is the intent to dominate. Yet people are aware of such intentions in their talk, and, when asked, can readily describe the verbal tactics they use to 'get their own way' in heterosexual interactions....

Many of the most compelling anecdotes describe situations in which a woman is hurt, frustrated or angered by a man's apparently selfish or dominating behavior, only to find that her feelings were unwarranted because the man's intentions were good. This is psychologically naive. There is no reason to believe that *post hoc* stated intentions are a complete and sufficient description of conversational motives. Accounts of one's intentions are a socially constructed product in which face-saving and self-justification surely play a part. And even if intentions are innocent, language is a form of social action. Speech acts do things, and these things cannot be undone by declaring good intentions.

The emphasis on interpreting a partner's intentions is problematic in other ways as well. As Nancy Henley and Cheris Kramarae (1991: 42) point out, '[F]emales are required to develop special sensitivity to interpret males' silence, lack of emotional expressiveness, or brutality, and to help men express themselves, while men often seem to be trained deliberately to misinterpret much of women's meaning.' Young girls are told that hitting, teasing, and insults are to be read as signs of boys' 'liking.' Adolescent girls are taught to take responsibility for boys' inexpressiveness by drawing them out in conversation, steering talk to topics that will make them feel comfortable, and being a good listener. Girls and women learn from the discourse of popular fiction to reinterpret men's verbal and physical abuse. Indeed, a central theme in the romance novel is that cold, insensitive and rejecting behavior by men is to be read as evidence of their love (Unger and Crawford, 1992). Interpreting their partners' behavior in these ways may func-

tion to keep women in unrewarding relationships by making them more bearable.

Analyzing conversation in terms of intentions has a very important implication: it deflects attention from *effects*, including the ways that everyday action and talk serve to recreate and maintain current gender arrangements. Instead, readers are left to analyze what goes on in people's heads—what they say they intend to accomplish, not what they do accomplish, when they are engaged in 'doing gender.' Entering a larger discourse in which women are blamed for the consequences of societal sexism and for their own powerlessness, popularizations of the two-cultures model may be used to deflect responsibility from men.

REFERENCES

Gray, J. (1992) *Men are from Mars, women are from Venus.* New York: Harper Collins.

Henley, N. M. and Kramarae, C. (1991) Gender, power, and miscommunication. In N. Coupland, H. Giles, and J. M. Wiemann (eds), '*Miscommunication and problematic talk* (pp. 18–43). Newbury Park, CA: Sage.

Maltz, D. N. and Borker, R. A. (1982) A cultural approach to male–female miscommunication. In J. Gumperz (ed.), *Language and social identity.* Cambridge: Cambridge University Press.

Tannen, D. (1990) *You just don't understand: women and men in conversation.* New York: Ballantine.

Tannen, D. (1992) Response to Senta Troemel-Ploetz's 'Selling the apolitical' (1991). *Discourse and Society, 3,* 249–254.

Troemel-Ploetz, S. (1991) Review essay: selling the apolitical. *Discourse and Society, 2,* 489–502.

Unger, R. and Crawford, M. (1992) *Women and gender: a feminist psychology.* New York and Philadelphia: McGraw-Hill and Temple University Press. [2nd edn in press]

POSTSCRIPT

Do Men and Women Speak Different Languages?

Couples continue to seek ways to improve communication in their relationships. Young adults often blame communication difficulties for their failed romances. When married couples seek professional counseling, they often point to a lack of communication as the foremost source of their unhappiness. Divorced spouses commonly blame faulty communication for their separation.

This may explain why two of the best-selling books in the past decade are Tannen's *You Just Don't Understand: Women and Men in Conversation* (William Morrow, 1990) and John Gray's *Men Are from Mars, Women Are from Venus* (HarperCollins, 1992). Many readers of these books have trooped to lectures and workshops and tried various strategies and techniques "guaranteed" to bridge the communication gap between themselves and their intimate partners.

Bly and Tannen maintain that there are conversational style differences between women and men. They recommend that partners attempt to recognize and appreciate each other's styles instead of blaming each other for relationship impasses. They claim that there is no one right way to listen, discuss, or talk to a loved one; the styles of men and women are equally valid.

Although Crawford admits that women and men may, at times, use different conversational styles, she asserts that these differences depend more on social status, role, and power disparities than on gender. According to Crawford, society may shape how we relate to our partners, but it is unlikely that childhood socialization has much to do with it. Differences between women and men may have more to do with daily, ongoing conversations in which women typically have less power to be heard.

SUGGESTED READINGS

S. Bem, *Lenses of Gender* (Yale University Press, 1993).

A. Eagly, "On Comparing Women and Men," *Feminism and Psychology*, 4 (1994): 513–522.

M. A. Fitzpatrick and A. L. Vangelisti, eds., *Explaining Family Interactions* (Sage Publications, 1995).

D. Tannen, *Talking from Nine to Five* (William Morrow, 1994).

J. T. Wood, *Gendered Lives: Communication, Gender, and Culture* (Wadsworth, 1994).

ISSUE 7

Are Women's Lives More Stressful Than Men's?

YES: Jeff Grabmeier, from "The Burden Women Bear: Why They Suffer More Distress Than Men," *USA Today Magazine* (July 1995)

NO: Warren Farrell, from *The Myth of Male Power: Why Men Are the Disposable Sex* (Simon & Schuster, 1993)

ISSUE SUMMARY

YES: Jeff Grabmeier, managing editor of research news at Ohio State University, makes the case that in comparison to men, women experience more distress, less happiness, and, as a result, a poorer quality of life.

NO: Warren Farrell, a leader of workshops on men's issues, argues that men suffer greater life stress and, as a consequence, have a significantly shorter life expectancy than women.

The 1980s and 1990s have been called the "age of stress." During this time stress was discovered by the general public and became a greatly discussed and researched topic. Currently, businesses organize stress management workshops for employees, school administrators arrange stress seminars for teachers, and people read about managing stress in their favorite magazines. Stress has become a large part of daily life: Stress terminology pops up in daily conversations, personal accounts of its results are reported in the local newspaper, and people deal with it on live television. National conferences, university courses, and weekend seminars target specific populations to teach people how to successfully cope with the outcomes of particular stressful situations—divorce, unemployment, death of a family member, alcoholism of a friend, loss of a close relationship, and so forth. Stressors can be categorized as unexpected crises, normal life events, or chronic daily concerns that trigger within us various unpleasant physical and emotional responses—sweaty palms, nervous stomach, aching neck, sadness, frustration, anger, depression, or feelings of being overwhelmed.

The general public is well educated about what causes feelings of being stressed out. It is also known that prolonged, unabated stress can lead to health complications such as heart disease, hypertension, and a depressed immune system. However, many believe that people can learn to successfully cope with most types of stress.

Stress researchers continue to focus on identifying the causes of chronic stress-related diseases. They hope to find a key to better health and longer life. Researchers searching for answers have increasingly targeted gender as a vital link. The impact of stress on health has been shown to differ for women and men.

In the following selections, Jeff Grabmeier maintains that women suffer a greater stress burden than men. The reasons for this include biological, psychological, and social factors, particularly the changing roles of women and men and how cultural traditions that favor men are being preserved despite altered family and work circumstances that are especially burdensome to women. He also argues that women do not cope as well as men. Women, Grabmeier states, get angry and depressed, blame themselves, and consequently fail to find solutions to their problems. He makes various suggestions for improving women's quality of life and health.

Warren Farrell strongly disagrees with the position that women are more stressed than men. Using health statistics from various sources, Farrell presents historical evidence to show that the changing nature of family and work roles have, over time, eroded men's health much more than women's. He asserts that men, in their efforts to protect women, have made themselves more vulnerable to stress-related health problems. As a consequence, men are susceptible to more chronic diseases and greater psychological distress and have a shorter life expectancy than women. Farrell discusses what he views as gendered myths that have kept men from receiving the health care they need. He concludes with a discussion of solutions to men's health problems.

As you read, identify the primary goal or purpose of each selection. Do the authors define *stress* in the same way? Note any flaws you detect in either author's logic and reasoning. Has each been fair and unbiased in his presentation of statistics and research findings?

YES

Jeff Grabmeier

THE BURDEN WOMEN BEAR: WHY THEY SUFFER MORE DISTRESS THAN MEN

Who suffers more in life, men or women? This was a great issue to bring up around the office coffee machine or at cocktail parties because it not only made for lively conversation, it also was one of those questions that couldn't be settled simply by calling the reference desk at the local library.

Recently, though, evidence is growing that women, in fact, do suffer more than men. Blame it on biology, the stress of combining parenthood and career, living in a male-centered society, or all of the above. A study at Ohio State University by sociologists John Mirowsky and Catherine Ross shows that females experience symptoms of psychological distress—including sadness, anger, anxiety, malaise, and physical aches and pains—about 30% more often than males. Their work complements earlier research that found women about twice as likely as men to experience major clinical depression.

"Women genuinely suffered more distress than men by all the measures in our study," Mirowsky indicates. He and Ross interviewed 1,282 women and 749 men aged 18 to 90 and asked them on how many of the last seven days they had experienced various emotions. In each case, women reported more days with symptoms of distress than men. Don't assume women feel more of everything than men, however. The female participants experienced happiness 3.3% less often than the males.

In the past, assertions about women's surplus of suffering have been dismissed because they were thought to be more emotional than men. In other words, females simply complained more than males, who hid their pain behind a stoic facade. Mirowsky and Ross examined that possibility and found that women did indeed express their emotions more than men. About 68% of the males in the study agreed or strongly agreed that they kept their emotions to themselves, compared to 50% of the females who responded similarly. Even after the researchers took these differences into account, women still showed more signs of distress than men. "Women do express their emotions more, but that doesn't mean they aren't truly more depressed," Mirowsky maintains.

There is no simple explanation for why women suffer more distress than men. Most experts believe a combination of factors, including biological differences, puts females at greater risk for some psychological troubles. Scientists have discovered that imbalances of certain neurotransmitters in the brain—particularly norepinepherine and serotonin—are related to depression. Low levels of serotonin may lead to depression, anxiety, anger, eating disorders, and impulsive behavior, points out Henry Nasrallah, chairperson of psychiatry. "We don't know why, but women may have less stable brain systems for regulating these neurotransmitters. Female hormones are believed to play a role in the regulation of neurotransmitters that affect mood and that may explain why females are more likely to experience clinical depression. Fluctuations in hormone levels, for example, have been associated with the well-known premenstrual syndrome, which afflicts some women."

Just how much of a role biology plays in women's distress remains unclear. "There is usually an interplay between biological, psychological, and social factors," says Nasrallah. "Clearly there are biological factors that contribute a great deal to behavior and mood in men and women."

Blaming biology for distress can be a two-edged sword. It can help to mobilize medical resources and make physicians take such problems seriously, but also may take the focus off social factors that contribute to the situation.

This two-edged sword is painfully apparent for those with a uniquely female form of distress—postpartum depression. Women suffering from this syndrome have formed national interest groups seeking, in part, to get more medical attention for their problems, notes Verta Taylor, a professor of sociology who has studied their cause. However, these women walk a fine line between looking for medical solutions and pushing for their partners to provide more help in caring for children.

For a book she is writing, Taylor interviewed more than 100 women who said they suffered emotional problems —ranging from "baby blues" to clinical depression—after the birth or adoption of a baby. This illness, which afflicts more than three-quarters of new mothers, may last weeks or, as one woman told Taylor, it "didn't end until [my son] left home for college."

Taylor indicates that the question of whether postpartum depression has biological roots is a hotly debated topic. She found that women physicians who suffered from it were more likely than male doctors to believe that the disorder is the result of a deficiency in the hormone progesterone. Accordingly, women physicians were more likely to advocate progesterone therapy to treat the biochemical basis of the illness.

Nasrallah says most medical professionals believe that postpartum depression is an illness with biochemical causes that must be treated with antidepressants. However, the less serious postpartum blues usually can be treated with rest, family support, and reassurance.

Even women who believe their postpartum depression has a biochemical aspect don't blame their condition simply on hormonal imbalances, Taylor points out. They echo the grievances of many working mothers—with and without postpartum depression—who complain of not getting enough support from husbands and partners. "A majority of the women I interviewed saw their excessive worry and irritability as the inevitable result of trying to combine and balance the demands of a 'second shift' of child care, housework, and a marriage with a paid job. Well over half the women expressed anger, hostility, and resentment toward their husbands or partners for failing to share child care and household responsibilities."

The problem, according to history professor Susan Hartmann, is that women now have more opportunities outside the home, but still do most of the household chores. "The old norms haven't changed that much. Women are still expected to take care of the home and children. But a majority of women also have taken on the responsibility of work. They've added new roles and responsibilities without significant changes in their old ones."

Although men sometimes may help out, there usually isn't a true sharing of household and child care responsibilities in American society. When men care for their children, for instance, it often is seen as "babysitting." When women do it, that simply is part of being a mother.

There is ample evidence that women still shoulder most of the responsibility of caring for kids, housework, and day-to-day chores. Margaret Mietus Sanik, an associate professor of family resource management, conducts studies of time use in families. She has found that, in couples with a new child, mothers spend about 4.6 hours per day in infant care, compared to about 1.3 for fathers. New mothers also lose more of their leisure time—about 3.8 hours a day—than their husbands, who give up approximately one hour. The result is that women often feel overworked and underappreciated.

A recent U.S. government survey of 250,000 working women found that stress was the most mentioned problem by respondents. The number-one issue females would like to talk about with Pres. Clinton is their inability to balance work and family, the survey found.

With the often overwhelming demands of juggling a career and family, it is no wonder that employed women suffer more depression than men. That doesn't mean that full-time homemakers have it better; in fact, research suggests they actually have higher levels of psychological distress than employed women. While working women can derive satisfaction from multiple roles at home and in the workplace, stay-at-home moms have only their homemaker role, Mirowsky indicates. They may feel isolated and out of step with the rest of society because parenting apparently is not highly valued in American culture.

Moreover, whether they want to work or not, housewives are economically dependent on their husbands, which is a powerful cause of distress. "In our culture, economic independence gives you status in the eyes of the community and a sense of security and self-worth," Mirowsky explains. "Housewives don't have that economic security. What we have found is that women are psychologically better off if they are employed."

In her studies of postpartum depression, Taylor has found that society's expectations of mothers also can put a suffocating burden on women. It is expected that a new mother will be happy, overjoyed even, and more than willing to put her baby's needs above her own. "But motherhood is often difficult, and women can find that their feelings are out of sync with societal expectations. They may feel as though their negative feelings are proof that they're not being a good mother, which compounds their feelings of distress, depression, anger, anxiety, and guilt."

If the stress of work and caring for children contributes to women's higher levels of distress, what about single, childless females? According to Mirowsky, they show less evidence of distress than other women, but more than men. That is because females face more than just role overload, she maintains. Women in the U.S. are paid about 75% of what men receive, are more likely to live in poverty, face a greater threat of physical and sexual abuse, and live in a culture that often promotes near-unattainable ideals for physical perfection. "Women just face a lot of problems and obstacles that men don't have to deal with. I'm surprised women don't feel more distress."

PSYCHOLOGICAL STRATEGIES

Adding to the situation is the fact that women tend to use psychological strategies that amplify and prolong their distress. Psychologists have found that, when females are faced with problems, they are more likely than males to think continually about troubling issues. They also are more apt to blame themselves. The result is that women can be caught in a cycle of worry and depression instead of working to find a way out. Men, on the other hand, tend to take action in dealing with problems. They are more likely to place the blame elsewhere and find activities such as sports or hobbies to distract them.

All of this ruminating about their troubles leads women to more than just depression. One of the key findings about women's distress is the amount of anger they feel, Mirowsky and Ross discovered. The stereotype has been that women get depressed and men get angry, but their study revealed that the female subjects actually experienced anger about 29% more often than the males. "Anger is depression's companion —not its substitute," Mirowsky notes.

The anger gap actually was larger than the difference in depression. The researchers found that women were more angry and anxious than men who were equally depressed. Females in the study also were more likely to express their anger through yelling at others. "We thought this was particularly interesting because yelling is crossing the line between an emotion and an action," Mirowsky says. "Our interpretation is that women are yelling at their children more often than their husbands do."

While women are at home getting angry and depressed, maybe men are handling their distress another way—by drinking alcohol and taking drugs. Research has shown that males are more likely than females to abuse alcohol and drugs, but Mirowsky doesn't think that explains the distress gap. "In one sense, if alcohol and drugs really did help eliminate distress, then our findings would make sense—it would explain why men feel less distressed than women. In actuality, there's no evidence that alcohol or drugs help people, or men in particular, feel better." One study, for instance, found that alcoholism and drug abuse increase the odds of a major depressive episode more than fourfold. "Alcohol and drug use probably produces more distress than it prevents," Mirowsky claims.

No matter how you look at the evidence, he suggests, it seems clear that women really do suffer more psychological distress. Is there anything that can be done about it? There is not much females can change concerning their biology, although serious depression often can be treated with anti-depressant drugs. Many of the problems require fundamental changes in how government, business, and society treat women. Taylor says they want their concerns taken seriously. Because females traditionally have been seen as emotional, their problems haven't been given much weight. "Whatever causes higher rates of distress in women, it's not treated. If women feel it and suffer from it, then it should be seen as real."

One thing they are doing is organizing to make their voices heard. Some groups, such as the National Organization for Women, are well-known for their efforts to improve the lot of females. Taylor notes that women with postpartum depression have organized two national groups to present their issues to the public and the medical community. Their efforts, while specifically for the benefit of those with postpartum depression, really involve issues of concern to many females, she states. "The leaders of these groups argue all the time in their speeches that we need men to get more involved in parenting. Women are under this tremendous strain because they are almost solely responsible for parenting. Men have to assume a larger role, and that's a societal problem that requires changing how we structure gender roles."

Working women face special problems that need to be addressed by business and government, experts say. A recent survey by the U.S. government of 250,000 working women has put the spotlight on some of the issues women face, such as lack of adequate child care and unequal pay with men. "I think that more and more businesses are trying to recognize the needs of women in the workforce, yet the progress has been slow," Hartmann points out. "The situation for working women may get incrementally better, but I don't see any major improvements soon."

Social change is always slow and uneven, Mirowsky feels, but it is necessary if the distress gap is to be eased. "People may debate whether there's a difference in the quality of life for men and women in the United States. The evidence, however, suggests the quality of life is poorer for many women, and it's something that needs to be addressed."

NO

Warren Farrell

WHY DO WOMEN LIVE LONGER?

IS IT BIOLOGY?

ITEM. In Bangladesh today, *men* live *longer* than women. In Harlem today, women live longer than men. Correction. In Harlem, women live *much* longer than men. If biology is the only variable, why these differences?

WHAT OUR LIFE SPAN TELLS US ABOUT WHO HAS THE POWER

When we learn that nonwhites have about 80 percent of the chance of whites to reach 85, we know that it is because of the relative powerlessness of nonwhites. But . . .

ITEM. A boy infant is only half as likely as a girl infant to live to age 85.

ITEM. When a man is about 25, his anxiety about "making it" is at its height. . . . [T]he odds of a person living out that year [are shown in Figure 1].

ITEM. Blacks die earlier than whites from *twelve* of the fifteen leading causes of death. Men die earlier than women from all *fifteen* of the leading causes of death.

THE INDUSTRIALIZATION FACTOR

ITEM. The more industrialized a society becomes, the more both sexes' life expectancies increase. But industrialization increases women's life expectancy roughly twice as much as men's.

In preindustrialized societies (e.g., Italy and Ireland in the nineteenth century), a gap of only one to two years between the life spans of women and men was common. . . . Women who lived in the countryside died more than men from tuberculosis, diphtheria, pneumonia, measles, heart disease, burns, and scalds. When women moved to the cities, as they did in England in the early 1800s, their death rate declined by more than a third. What happened?

When women and men have approximately equal life expectancies, it seems to be because women die not only in childbirth (fewer than thought) but about equally from contagious, parasitic diseases; poor sanitation and water; inadequate health care; and diseases of malnutrition. In industrialized societies, early deaths are caused more by diseases triggered by stress, which breaks down the immune system. *It is since stress has become the key factor that men have died so much sooner than women.*

Industrialization's Double Standard

Industrialization pulled men away from the farm and family and into the factory, alienating millions of men from their source of love. Industrialization allowed women to be connected with the family and, as we discussed above, increasingly surrounded with fewer children and more conveniences to handle those children, more control over whether or not to have children, less likelihood of dying in childbirth, and less likelihood of dying from almost all diseases. It was this combination that led to women living almost 50 percent longer in 1990 than in 1920. *What we have come to call male power, then, actually produced female power.* It literally gave women life....

Industrialization made performing away from home the male role. The fact that members of both sexes who performed away from home were vulnerable gives us a clue as to the impact of role over biology.

Don't women today perform away from home? Yes, but when the first child comes, *two thirds* of working women do not return to the workforce for at least a year. Husbands suddenly support three people rather than one. Overall, women are forty-three times more likely than men to leave the workforce for six months or longer for family reasons. *It is the options that allow a woman to tailor her role to her personality,* whereas the male mandate —to work full time—does not allow him flexibility to suit his personality. If he expects to provide well, he expects to wear a suit, not to wear what suits him.

Why has the gap between women's and men's life span been *reduced* slightly (from eight to seven years) between 1975 and 1990? In part because men's health habits are becoming more constructive, women's more destructive. Thus women are dying more from what the Chinese call "the disease of affluence"—breast cancer. But women are also working more away from home and suffering the stress-related diseases that go with the territory.

On the other hand, why has the gap not decreased even more? Because the husband of even the *full-time* working woman still works nine hours more per week *outside* the home and commutes yet another two hours more per week. Her equal work burden still provides more balance between work and home. If her husband is reasonably successful, she can tailor this balance not only to her personality but also to her stage in life. Her greater options, greater balance, and greater connection to the family still keep her alive seven years longer.

Industrialization, then, has broadened women's options and deepened men's mold. Her juggling act allows her connection to everything; his intensifying act creates disconnection from love. Both are better off than they were, but her connection creates life, his disconnection creates death....

THE GENETIC FACTOR

If men had genetically superior immune systems, this would be our rationale for paying more attention to female health: "women are fragile; women need protection." However, women's double-X chromosomes give them a kind of genetic backup system. That is, if a

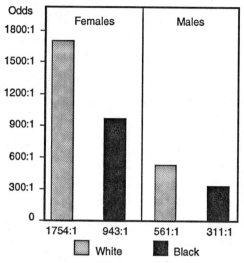

Figure 1
**Odds of Living Out This Year
(25-Year-Olds)**

hormones." For examples, testosterone is generated, but testosterone weakens his immune system; adrenaline (or epinephrine) is generated, but adrenaline also causes his blood to be more likely to clot, making him more vulnerable to heart failure....

WHY THE MALE ROLE IS SO LIFE DEPLETING

When boys and girls are young (1 to 4), boys die only slightly more frequently than girls. Once adult sex roles are experienced—between ages 15 and 24—men die at a rate more than three times that of women. The male role, then, might be thought of as being about three times as life depleting for men as is the female role for women.... [T]he need of boys to perform, pay, and pursue to be equal to girls' love [leads] boys to anxiety that sometimes resulted in suicide. It also leads to a series of coping mechanisms that prepare boys to die more quietly even as they are succeeding more overtly. Two examples:

woman has a defective gene along one thread of her X chromosome, the odds are very high that the matching gene on the other X will be perfect. Men don't have that backup system.

So while women have that initial advantage, it is not an all-encompassing advantage. In birds, butterflies, and moths, it is the males who have this genetic backup system and the males still die sooner. And in humans, almost all premature deaths after the first year are related to stress-induced diseases and pressures related to men's role—from suicides to heart attacks, from cancer to murder.

More powerfully, the vulnerability of men because of their social role cannot be separated from their vulnerability because of their biology. For example, when men reflexively rescue women, they are not only more likely to get physically stabbed, shot, or punched but these rescuing behaviors generate "emergency

Male Pattern Flaw Finding
If you've ever had an adolescent son (or been one), you know a boy's "best friend" is the one with whom he trades "wit-covered put-downs." Why is "the put-down trade" the commerce of male adolescence? And why is this "male pattern flaw finding" so damaging?

The put-down trade is our adolescent son's rehearsal for taking criticism as an adult. Taking criticism is a prerequisite to success. The upside is that it prepares men to handle criticism at work and in their personal relationships without taking it personally. The downside is the "hidden tax."

Table 1

Male–Female Ratio of Age-Adjusted Death Rates for the 15 Leading Causes of Death

Rank*	Cause	Male to Female
1.	Heart disease	1.9 to 1
2.	Cancerous cysts	1.5 to 1
3.	Cerebrovascular diseases	1.2 to 1
4.	Accidents and adverse effects	2.7 to 1
5.	Obstructive lung disease	2.0 to 1
6.	Pneumonia and influenza	1.8 to 1
7.	Diabetes mellitus	1.1 to 1
8.	Suicide	3.9 to 1
9.	Chronic liver disease and cirrhosis	2.3 to 1
10.	Hardening of the arteries	1.3 to 1
11.	Inflammation of the kidneys	1.5 to 1
12.	Homicide	2.0 to 1
13.	Blood infections	1.4 to 1
14.	Deaths around the time of birth**	1.3 to 1
15.	AIDS	9.1 to 1

*Rank based on number of deaths.
**Inasmuch as deaths from this cause occur among infants, ratios are based on infant mortality rates rather than on age-adjusted death rates.

The hidden tax? The *New England Journal of Medicine* has recently reported that speaking about one's faults creates abnormalities in the pulsations of our heart. Tiny abnormalities? No. Abnormalities as great as those produced by riding a stationary bicycle to the point of either exhaustion or chest pain. Perhaps the criticism, then, contributes to men being four times more likely than women to suffer heart disease before age fifty. In essence, our sons might be practicing heart-disease training.

While men are bonding by giving each other criticism, women are bonding by giving each other support. The price men pay is the feeling of isolation and loneliness. Only now we are discovering that *loneliness is a strong predictor of heart disease.* Heart disease, then, is the hidden tax of the put-down trade. Male pattern flaw finding becomes male pattern heart attacks.

Male Nurturance

In almost every men's group I have formed, men discuss problems they face at work—especially feelings of being unappreciated or criticized by bosses and colleagues. If we ask a man whether he has discussed this with his wife or womanfriend, he usually says he has, but only superficially. Why? He says he doesn't want to worry her.

Not worrying his wife about work fears is one of many male forms of nurturance —protecting the woman he loves from insecurity. So he puts on a facade of security that prevents him from asking for help through his deepest insecurities.

It is this male dilemma that creates the stress that silently damages men's immune systems. He might seek temporary satisfaction from a "substitute wife" (a second woman, second job, second drink, or second needle)... which is one reason he is three times more likely than a woman to have a drinking problem. If he doesn't turn to an escape, an escape turns to him: cancer, a heart attack....

Killing Him Softly

These coping mechanisms—or defense mechanisms—kill men a lot more softly than in the past. Fewer men die in coal mines, more die inside when a lifetime of doing everything he could to support a family leads to his income becoming an incentive for his wife to leave him....

When the demands to perform outpace the resources to perform, men become the disposable sex....

No group of men is more a victim of the demands to perform without the resources to perform than the black boy and his dad.

THE BLACK MALE: NOT-SO-BENIGN NEGLECT

The only group that can expect to live shorter lives in 1990 than in 1980 is black men. Why? For starters, it is black men who experience the greatest gap between the Stage I expectation to survive by being a physical slave and the Stage II need to be a master of technology. Thus the black male now lives nine years fewer than the black female. Nevertheless, we hear more about the double jeopardy of racism and sexism encountered by the black female.

More black males are in the prison system than are in the college system. That is, an incredible one out of four black males is either in jail, prison, on probation, or on parole. That's almost

50 percent greater than the number in college. This does not even come close to being true of black women. If it were, imagine the number of job training, education, and rehabilitation programs we'd be sponsoring for black women. The black male does not face double jeopardy, he faces quadruple jeopardy: racism, sexism, antagonism, and neglect....

DOESN'T MEDICAL RESEARCH NEGLECT WOMEN?

The belief that sexism has led to a focus on men's health at the expense of women's has led both the federal government and private industry to focus on women's health at the expense of men's. Thus the government has recently established an Office of Research on Women's Health but no Office of Research on Men's Health. It has also established an Office of Minority Health that defines women as a minority, but no Office of Minority Health that defines men as a minority (due to only men dying at a younger age from all fifteen of the major causes of death). The belief in women's neglect has led private hospitals and health-care companies to start women's health-care centers but almost no men's health-care centers. So let's look at the myths versus the realities.

Overall Myth. *Less money and attention are given to female health than male health.*

Supporting Myth #1. "Less than 20 percent of the research budget of the National Institutes of Health [NIH] is spent on women's health."

Fact. *No governmental agency focusing on health spends as much on men's health as on women's health.* The reason less than 20 percent of the research budget of the NIH is spent on women's health is because 85 percent of the research budget is spent on *non*gender-specific health issues (or basic science); 10 percent is spent on women's health; 5 percent is spent on men's health. (This is the analysis of the NIH's Office of Research on *Women's* Health.)

Supporting Myth #2. Sexism is the reason that more studies have been done on men in almost all areas of medical research.

Fact. In a search of more than three thousand medical journals listed in *Index Medicus, twenty-three* articles were written on women's health for each *one* written on men's.

Fact/Perspective. With that larger picture in mind, it is true new products and potentially dangerous drugs were often tested on prisoners. But this is because we care less about prisoners; and they were often tried on men because we care less about men. Similarly, sulfa drugs, LSD, and other experimental research was often conducted by making guinea pigs of military men. Did the men in the military get anything in return? Yes. Time off from time which only men were required to serve. In brief, *we do more research on men in prison, men in the military, and men in general than we do on women for the same reason we do more research on rats than we do on humans.*

Supporting Myth #3. If diseases were killing men as fast as breast cancer is killing women, men would get the funding to solve the problem.

Fact. A woman is 14 percent more likely to die from breast cancer than a man is from prostate cancer, yet funding for breast cancer research is 660 percent greater than funding for prostate cancer research. The death-to-funding ratio is 47 to 1 in women's favor.

Fact. The death rate for prostate cancer has grown at almost *twice the rate* of breast cancer in the last five years.

Fact. Black men in the United States have the highest incidence in the *world* of cancer of the prostate.

Supporting Myth #4. Virtually all of women's health has been neglected —from ovarian cancer to menopause. The neglect comes in both research and treatment.

Fact. There is a neglect in research for women's health such as ovarian cancer and menopause that is now being remedied by the new Office of Research on Women's Health of the NIH; there is *also* a neglect in research in the following seventeen areas of men's health that is *not* being adequately remedied by anyone:

- A men's birth control pill
- Suicide
- Posttraumatic stress syndrome
- Circumcision as a possible trauma-producing experience
- The male midlife crisis
- Dyslexia
- The causes of male violence
- Criminal recidivism
- Homelessness
- Steroid abuse
- Color blindness
- Testicular cancer
- Prostate cancer
- Hearing loss over age 30
- Sexual impotence
- Nonspecific urethritis

- Epididymitis (a disease of the tubes that transmit sperm)
- Klinefelter's disease, ALD, and other male-only inherited diseases

Fact. Men are more likely to suffer from mental illness; women are almost twice as likely to be treated for mental illness.

Yes, there is a need for more research on women's health—as there is a need for more basic research and more research on men's health. Yet all of these needs for specific research must not be dictated so much by gender politics that the basic research (DNA, cellular, transplant, etc.) gets neglected—research which can help both sexes live longer. . . .

Supporting Myth #5. Woman are now as vulnerable as men to death from heart attacks, but sexism is why only men have been studied.

First, the vulnerability to death from heart attacks. . . .

Fact. Compared to other diseases, heart attacks have now become the number one killer of women. But men are still far more vulnerable to death from heart attacks than women: before the age of 65, men still die from heart attacks at a ratio of almost 3 to 1 vis-à-vis women. Even after the age of 85, men's death rate is still slightly higher.

Put another way, *almost three quarters of women who die of heart attacks are 75 or older. By this time, the average man has been dead for three years.*

Second, concerning the cause célèbre of medical sexism—that only men had been studied related to the effects of aspirin on heart attacks. . . .

Fact. Yes, there was a study on only male physicians on the effects of aspirin

on heart attacks. *And* there was a simultaneous study conducted only on female nurses (also on the effects of aspirin on heart attacks). The press touted only the male study as sexism. Yet the women's study was longer in duration and there were four women studied for each man. . . .

Supporting Myth #6. Sexism is the reason men with heart attack symptoms are more likely to receive the most advanced tests and most effective operations: coronary bypass and angioplasty.

Fact. Coronary bypass operations are more than twice as likely to lead to death for women than for men. Why? In part, because women as a group have smaller coronary arteries which are more likely to close after the operation. And in part because almost three quarters of women who have heart disease are over 75 and are also much more likely to have cancer of the breast or other complications that make the demands of surgery far more likely to lead to death. As a result, a woman is more likely than a 60-year-old man to refuse a coronary bypass or angioplasty operation. Which is why she is also less likely to ask for a costly and somewhat demanding diagnostic test. . . .

Fact. When age and other complicating factors (e.g., diabetes, hypertension, obesity) are controlled for, there is no difference between the treatment of men versus women with heart attacks.

In brief, medical research has been perhaps the single biggest contributor to women's life span increasing almost 50 percent since 1920. Medical research was responsible for a female pill (but no male pill), fewer female deaths in childbirth, and research on the diseases women once died of in equal numbers to men (TB, diphtheria, polio). It is ironic that feminists are calling it sexism against women when it is women's lives that have gone from one year longer than men's to seven years longer than men's. What would feminists be calling the medical community if men lived longer? Or if women died at a younger age of every one of the fifteen major causes of death?...

TOWARD SOLUTIONS

Although a government study found that men's health was much worse than women's health or the health of any minority group, headlines around the country read: "Minorities Face Large Health Care Gap." They did *not* say: "*Men* Face Large Health Care Gap." Why? Because we associate the sacrifice of men's lives with the saving of the rest of us, and this association leads us to carry in our unconscious an incentive not to care about men living longer....

If we care enough to start an Office of Men's Health, will it really make any difference? Yes. An Office of Men's Health can introduce us to men's problems we haven't even heard of....

A good education program could keep more men from dying of prostate cancer each year than were killed each year in the Vietnam War. And good research can help us know to what degree the vasectomies that are linked to prostate cancer in mice are also linked to prostate cancer in men....

An Office of Men's Health can pioneer suicide crisis hotlines nationwide, create support networks for elderly men who are 1,350 percent more likely to commit suicide than women their age, and education programs for high school guidance counselors on the connections between adolescent male stress and adolescent male suicide.

An Office of Men's Health could educate men about why men are seven times more likely than women to be arrested for drunk driving while only three times more likely than women to be hospitalized for alcoholism.

We often interpret women's increased drinking and smoking as reflections of women's increased stress level (which if often is) but rarely interpret the facts that men are three times more likely to be alcoholics and more likely to die of lung cancer as reflections of men's continuing higher stress level. In brief, we keep ourselves open to new ways of understanding (and helping) women, which is wonderful, but fail to use the same mind-set to better understand (and help) men.

POSTSCRIPT

Are Women's Lives More Stressful Than Men's?

A number of studies have found that men and women are confronted with life problems that are unique to their gender. Studies also show that women typically react more emotionally to stressors and generally choose coping strategies that are different from men's. Some social analysts speculate that these gender differences explain why women live longer than men but are more susceptible to depression and other psychological disorders. In one study by Catherine Ross and Chloe Bird published in *Journal of Health and Social Behavior* (June 1994), men were found to have more stress-protecting resources than women—better jobs and higher incomes, for example. Furthermore, men reported finding their work more rewarding, indicated having significantly lower emotional distress levels, and demonstrated better physical health than women. Men also did less household work and engaged in strenuous exercise more often than women. But, compared to women, men smoked more and were more likely to be overweight.

Ross and Bird concluded that over a lifetime women typically are in worse health than men, despite statistics showing that they live longer. Women, they found, have more chronic health problems, such as thyroid conditions, migraines, and arthritis—diseases that are long-lasting but nonfatal. Men, on the other hand, suffer more from life-threatening chronic diseases that take decades to develop but ultimately kill, such as heart disease, cancer, and emphysema.

SUGGESTED READINGS

V. L. Banyard and S. A. Graham-Bermann, "Can Women Cope? A Gender Analysis of Theories of Coping With Stress," *Psychology of Women Quarterly*, 17 (1993): 303–318.

D. Erickson, "Work and Health: Are Women and Men That Different?" *Harvard Business Review* (September–October 1995): 12–15.

L. Goldberger and S. A. Breznitz, *Handbook of Stress* (Free Press, 1993).

L. S. Porter and A. A. Stone, "Are There Really Gender Differences in Coping? A Reconsideration of Previous Data and Results from a Daily Study," *Journal of Social and Clinical Psychology*, 14 (1995): 184–202.

J. T. Ptacek, R. E. Smith, and J. Zanas, "Gender, Appraisal, and Coping: A Longitudinal Analysis," *Journal of Personality*, 60 (1992): 747–770.

R. W. Simon, "Gender, Multiple Roles, Role Meaning, and Mental Health," *Journal of Health and Social Behavior*, 36 (1995): 182–194.

ISSUE 8

Do Men Avoid Family Work?

YES: Bickley Townsend and Kathleen O'Neil, from "American Women Get Mad," *American Demographics* (August 1990)

NO: Joseph H. Pleck, from "Are 'Family-Supportive' Employer Policies Relevant to Men?" in Jane C. Hood, ed., *Men, Work, and Family* (Sage Publications, 1993)

ISSUE SUMMARY

YES: Bickley Townsend and Kathleen O'Neil, both with the Roper Organization, argue that the division of family work is inequitable and that women are becoming increasingly vocal about the need for change.

NO: Joseph H. Pleck, the Luce Professor of Families, Change, and Society at Wheaton College in Norton, Massachusetts, states that significant numbers of men have substantially increased their involvement in family roles but are given neither credit nor respect for their efforts.

Many executives in top positions continue to expect male employees to put in long days and leave family concerns to their wives. When women are hired, supervisors often assume that they will behave according to the male career model and give work priority over other life roles. Most management publications portray the corporate world as a domain governed by men in traditional families. For example, a manager at Corning Inc. is quoted in the June 28, 1993, edition of *Business Week* as saying, "Ninety percent of our senior managers are males who have spouses at home taking care of the kids. But 75 percent of the staff are in dual-career households." To many executives, taking time off from work or reducing hours for family reasons remains a sign of low job commitment and lack of achievement motivation.

A poll conducted by Robert Half International found that nearly 8 out of 10 men would choose to advance in their careers at a slower pace if they could work more flexible hours and spend more time with their families. Although many men report yearning for family time, they rarely go against cultural norms and cut back on work time to accommodate family roles. Fear persists that men who take company offers of flexible scheduling or family leave will be labeled as insufficiently committed to their work. Most family leave programs and support systems are geared toward working women. Many women are reluctant to use leave, but they do so more often than men.

A Conference Board survey released in June 1995 showed that fewer than 15 percent of employees use flexible scheduling options such as job-sharing, part-time employment, or telecommuting, even when available and promoted by companies. When the consulting firm Kwasha Lipton surveyed managers from 116 companies, they found that 37 percent consider work-family benefits "fluff." Another 34 percent thought such programs were inequitably distributed among employees (see the *Washington Post*, July 17, 1995). In *The Overworked American: The Unexpected Decline of Leisure* (Basic Books, 1993), Juliet B. Schor claims that employees today work more hours than they did 25 years ago, putting in about one extra month per year.

When both spouses are employed it is often the woman who performs most of the household work. Work-Family Directions surveyed 10,000 managers and other employees at major corporations and found that "working mothers averaged 44 hours a week on the job and 31 on family responsibilities; fathers put in three more hours at the office but logged just half as much time as their wives on child care and household chores" (see *Fortune*, March 21, 1994).

In the following selections, Bickley Townsend and Kathleen O'Neil argue that men's roles in the family have not changed despite women's expanded commitment to the workforce and that women are angry about men's limited contribution. Townsend and O'Neil state that women are feeling stressed by the lopsided nature of the traditional family arrangement, blame men for the situation, and are beginning to ask for change.

Joseph H. Pleck argues that men's contributions to household work and child care are greater than conventionally believed and that they tend to be overlooked and misrepresented. According to Pleck, men have increased their family involvement in defiance of a society that devalues and minimizes their efforts to be more caring husbands and fathers.

As you read these two selections, think about the family lives of the dual-employed couples you know. Can you think of examples that fit Townsend and O'Neil's descriptions of family work? Do you know men who have increased their share of the family work?

YES

Bickley Townsend and
Kathleen O'Neil

AMERICAN WOMEN GET MAD

Over the past two decades, the lives of American women have undergone unparalleled change. The Virginia Slims Opinion Poll has chronicled that change in national surveys conducted six times since 1970. Together, these surveys provide a comprehensive picture of women's changing status, and of their views of the future.

One of the most striking findings of the 1990 Virginia Slims Opinion Poll is the degree of consensus—rather than conflict—in women's and men's attitudes about the changing roles of women. In many respects, the two sexes agree. Men express strong and consistent support for women's improved status in society. They, like women, believe that sex discrimination remains an important problem in the workplace. And they agree that the most tangible way in which they could help women balance jobs and family is to take on more household work.

But men are also a major cause of resentment and stress for American women. In 1970, most women were concerned about getting men to share household chores. Now, a generation of sweeping change later, women's expectations have outpaced the change in men's behavior. Token help with the dishes or the children no longer inspires women's gratitude; instead, as women contribute more to the family income, they expect in return a more equal division of the household responsibilities.

Increasingly, the kitchen table has become the bargaining table. There is evidence in the poll that waiting for men to live up to the ideal of equal responsibility is a major irritant for most women today. Next to money, "how much my mate helps around the house" is the single biggest cause of resentment among women who are married or living as if married, with 52 percent citing this as a problem. Improvement in this area is one of the top things women cite when they consider what would make their lives better....

WORKER, MOTHER, WIFE

Most women in the course of their lives wear three hats—worker, mother, wife. With more women working today than ever before, many women are wearing three hats at once, and the triple role of worker, mother, wife has become as familiar as that of worker, father, husband.

Since the mid-1970s, a majority of women have said that a lifestyle combining marriage, career, and children is the ideal. The 1990 poll finds that 57 percent of women prefer this option, while 27 percent would rather marry and have children but no career. For 53 percent of women, the ideal kind of marriage is one of shared responsibility, in which both partners work and share housekeeping responsibilities. Thirty-eight percent would prefer a traditional marriage in which the husband is the sole breadwinner and the wife cares for the home and children.

A large majority of women get satisfaction from their jobs. More working women today than in 1985 think of their work as a career, not "just a job." In fact, for the first time, a majority of full-time working women consider their work as a career.

The primary reasons women work are the same as men's. Fifty-five percent work because they need the money to support themselves and their families, up from 46 percent ten years ago. Another 32 percent say they work to bring in extra money.

However, though most working women with children say that, all in all, they do a good job of balancing their job and family, this balancing act comes at a price. Six in ten mothers working full-time feel the demands of family and job put them under a lot of stress. Most feel guilty that they don't spend more time with their families, and most say they feel badly about leaving their kids in the morning when they go to work.

Women face tensions and difficulties in attempting to balance work and family. More women now than in 1985 feel that something gets slighted when women work—and they think children suffer the most. The conventional six-week maternity leave is considered ideal by only 1 woman in 20. The greatest number of women (and men) say that the ideal would be for a woman to stay at home until her children go to school. Yet few women believe that, as a practical reality, they could do this.

What could change to help women balance their triple role of worker, mother, wife? Far and away the answer, cited by seven in ten women, is more help from men with household and child-care responsibilities. And almost as many men as women—64 percent—agree that by doing more at home, men could help women balance work and family.

Resentment toward men is also evident in the fact that women today think less of men than they did in the 1970 Virginia Slims Opinion Poll. By significantly higher margins today, women agree that most men are selfish (42 percent of women agree), too absorbed in their outside lives to pay attention to things going on at home (53 percent), interested mainly in their own sexual satisfaction (50 percent), and driven by their egos to "keep women down" (55 percent). And while two-thirds of women in 1970 believed that men are basically kind, gentle and thoughtful, barely half (51 percent) now agree.

WHAT'S NEXT

As women struggle and negotiate for change, and as society responds to women's needs, new initiatives are likely

Figure 1
Percent of Women Agreeing With These Statements, 1970 and 1990

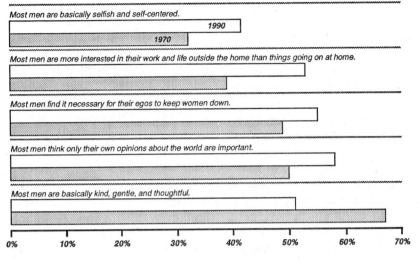

Most men are basically selfish and self-centered.

1990
1970

Most men are more interested in their work and life outside the home than things going on at home.

Most men find it necessary for their egos to keep women down.

Most men think only their own opinions about the world are important.

Most men are basically kind, gentle, and thoughtful.

0%   10%   20%   30%   40%   50%   60%   70%

Many women don't think very highly of men. These feelings are growing stronger.

Source: The 1990 Virginia Slims Opinion Poll, the Roper Organization

Most Satisfying Lifestyle for Women, in Percent, 1974–1990

Shared*

Traditional**

60%
50%
40%
30%
0%

1975   1980   1985   1990

*Marriage where both husband and wife work and share housekeeping and child-care responsibilities
**Marriage with husband providing for family and wife running house and caring for children

Though the proportion of women who favor a marriage of shared responsibilities has fallen by 4 percentage points since 1985, most women still say it is the most satisfying lifestyle.

Source: The 1990 Virginia Slims Opinion Poll, the Roper Organization

Figure 2

Reasons Employed Women Work, in Percent, 1980 and 1990

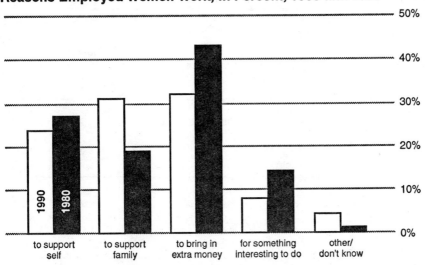

A growing proportion of women work to support their families.

Source: The 1990 Virginia Slims Opinion Poll, the Roper Organization

---

Among Women Who Think Things Could Change to Help Them Better Balance Work, Marriage, and Children, Percent Citing Factors That Would Help Most, 1990

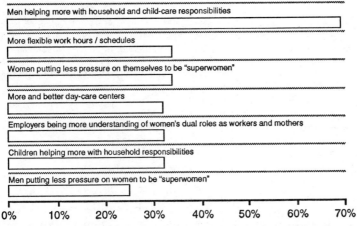

More help from their husbands is the single biggest factor that would help women balance work and family responsibilties.

Source: The 1990 Virginia Slims Opinion Poll, the Roper Organization

Table 1

Career Women

	think of work as a career	think of work as "just a job"
All Employed Women	45%	53%
All Employed Men	57%	40%

What Women Say About Their Work

	"it's a career"	"it's just a job"		"it's a career"	"it's just a job"
Age			**Household Income**		
18 to 29	37%	61%	Under $15,000	26%	72%
30 to 39	52	46	$15,000 to $25,000	37	61
40 to 49	48	51	$25,000 to $35,000	48	51
50 and older	43	54	$35,000 and over,	59	40
Education			**Employment Status**		
Less than high school	19%	78%	Employed full-time	51%	47%
High school graduate	34	65	Employed part-time	29	69
At least some college	59	39			
Race			**Occupation**		
White	46%	52%	Executive/professional	81%	18%
Black	40	57	White collar	37	61
			Blue collar	24	74

A growing proportion of women regard their work as a career rather than "just a job." Today, 45 percent of women think of their work as a career, up from 41 percent in 1985. Most working women aged 30 to 39 think of their work as a career, as do most with at least some college experience, most with household incomes of $35,000 or more, and most employed full-time. Fully 81 percent of women executives and professionals are on the career track. Today, women are almost as career oriented as men: 57 percent of men regard their work as a career, no signficant shift from 1985.

Note: Rows do not total to 100 percent because of "don't know" responses.

Source: The 1990 Virginia Slims Opinion Poll, the Roper Organization

both in the home and the workplace. Look for these changes in the 1990s.

- *The "old-boy network" will go co-ed.* Growing confidence in women's abilities as workers and leaders suggests that women will become increasingly prominent in government and business. Look for more women to break through the "glass ceiling" to positions of top leadership.

- *Family issues will be the focus in the workplace.* From flexible work schedules to parental leave, employment policies once targeted at working mothers will be redirected toward working *parents.* Look for growing pressure on American businesses to incorporate family policies as standard personnel practices.

- *Money will matter... even more.* Despite the unprecedented economic expansion the U.S. has enjoyed for most of the 1980s, financial concerns are at the top of American women's agenda. Look for financial issues—pay equity above all—to dominate women's demands for change.

- *Women's home life will become easier.* Men's performance at home has failed to measure up to women's expectations. But the outlook is positive, because men know they need to become more involved in household responsibilities. Look for beliefs to be transformed into behavior.

NO

Joseph H. Pleck

ARE "FAMILY-SUPPORTIVE" EMPLOYER POLICIES RELEVANT TO MEN?

As the rate of labor force participation among married women with children steadily increased in the last two decades in the United States, policy analysts argued that U.S. workplaces should change their policies to make it easier for employed mothers to combine their work and family roles. Rather quickly, however, the language used to describe what had originally been labeled "working mothers'" issues became gender neutral. By the late 1980s, "work and family" had clearly become the dominant term for these concerns. ...

However, at conferences and workshops, I have observed negative responses to the inclusion of men that the "work and family" language implies. Many react to the term cynically or view it as a wistful fantasy. One leading policy analyst told me, for example, "Of course, no one seriously thinks these issues impact on fathers the way they do on mothers." Some women have told me they feel affronted by "work and family" and other gender-neutral terms that make women invisible. "They're not work and family issues, they are *working mothers'* issues!" ...

To view family-supportive policies as relevant to men, one must believe that a significant proportion of men has a substantial level of family responsibility. Recent publications arguing that men accept little family responsibility and are not doing more in the family than they used to (Hochschild, 1989; LaRossa, 1988) have reinforced doubts that men will use family-supportive policies to any significant degree.

In addition, data on men's use of parental leave ("paternity leave") often trigger a variety of strong positive and negative responses. To some, the availability of paternity leave is central to future change in gender roles. To others, data on paternity leave show how truly uninterested most fathers are in greater paternal responsibility. Depending on underlying assumptions one makes about the structural constraints faced by men and what kinds of behaviors represent real accommodations, these data indicate that men are making accommodations in their work life to meet their family needs either a lot or hardly at all. ...

THE CONTEXT: LEVELS AND TRENDS IN MEN'S FAMILY PARTICIPATION

In earlier publications (Pleck, 1985, 1987), I reported that U.S. men's average level of housework and child care combined was about 1.85 hours per day in 1975. I also recounted research findings showing that men's time in these activities increased between the mid-1960s and the early 1980s, with men's share of the total performed by both sexes rising from 20% in 1965 to 30% in 1981. In some studies the increase is evident among males or husbands overall, whereas in others it is evident only among those with young children. Later investigations, employing time use data collected through 1986, have provided further documentation that time spent in family roles has continued to increase among men as a whole, as well as among married and unmarried men, and among fathers and nonfathers. Women's average time in family roles has correspondingly decreased, both among women as a whole, and among married, single, employed, nonemployed, mother and nonmother subgroups. In the most recent available national data, married men do 34% of the housework performed by couples (Robinson, 1988). Although married men's 34% share of housework in 1985 is still far from the 50% that would denote equality, the increase from men's 20% share of housework and child care in 1965 is substantial.

Two other recent and widely cited analyses have offered different conclusions about men's levels of housework and child care, and trends in these levels. First, Hochschild (1989, p. 4) stated that in U.S. national data in 1965, husbands' average time in housework averaged 17 minutes

per day and child care 12 minutes. These figures are the only quantitative estimates for men's average time in family roles provided in Hochschild's book, and they have been widely repeated in the media. Hochschild also asserted that husbands' time in housework and child care did not increase between 1965 and 1975.

However, the two figures Hochschild cites are actually the time spent by employed fathers only on *workdays*, when both employed men and women spend less time in family roles.... When nonworkdays are factored in, and time spent in all housework and child care is included, these 1965 data show that employed fathers actually spent an average of 91 minutes per day in housework and child care combined. This figure is close to other published calculations based on these data, for example, Juster's (1985) estimate of 1.6 hours per day for men as a whole. It is also noteworthy that although more current data were easily available, the data Hochschild selected to report were over two decades old.[1]

Hochschild's (1989) further assertion that "between 1965 and 1975... men weren't doing more housework" (p. 272) is incorrect. This study she cites on this point (Robinson, 1977), which used a narrower definition of family tasks that most other studies, actually reported that men's time in housework and child care rose from 9.0 to 9.7 hours per week between 1965 and 1975.[2] In this respect as well as by highlighting the 17- and 12-minute figures as summary estimates of men's housework and child care, Hochschild does not accurately convey what time use research has found about men's family involvement.

In a critical overview of men's family role performance focusing on fatherhood, LaRossa (1988) asserts that since the turn of the century "fatherhood has not changed (at least significantly), if one looks at the conduct of fatherhood —how fathers behave vis-a-vis their children" (p. 451). However, the two specific sources of data LaRossa discusses to support this point contradict this conclusion....

Other data since 1981 further corroborate that father's average level of child care involvement is rising. Robinson et al. (1988) provides the most recent data on men's time in child care that makes a comparison to earlier decades....

Another more recent indicator of levels and trends in men's child care responsibility derives from large-scale surveys of child care arrangements in families with employed mothers. According to the fall 1987 Current Population Survey (U.S. Bureau of the Census, 1990), in two-earner families with a child under 5 years, 18% of mothers reported that the father was the primary child care arrangement during the mother's working hours. Fathers are the primary care arrangement almost as often as are family day care homes (22%), and far more often than group care centers (14% or grandparents (9%). Presser (1989) also reports evidence that father care for children during mothers' working hours increased between 1965 and 1985.

Father care is so frequent not because many fathers are unemployed, but because mothers and fathers often have nonoverlapping work schedules. Such "two-shift" families sometimes select these schedules as a conscious strategy to reduce child care costs, although they also occur involuntarily. The fact that fathers are the primary arrangement during mothers' work hours in almost one our of five dual-earner families with preschool children suggests that a much higher proportion of fathers have significant child care responsibility than is usually thought.

No one questions that men perform less housework and child care than women, and that the rate of change in males' share of these family responsibilities has been relatively slow. However, the level and rate of increase in men's family involvement are greater than Hochschild and LaRossa suggest. Recent evidence that husbands on average perform one third of the housework and one of five fathers with an employed wife is the primary child care arrangement for his preschool child suggests that family-supportive policies may be more relevant to men than is generally realized.

THE EVIDENCE

If men are spending more time in family roles, is there corresponding evidence that men experience conflict between their work and family responsibilities? If they do, what do we know about the extent to which men make use of the three most important family-supportive workplace policies: child care supports, flexible schedules, and parental leave? And what do we know about the impact of these policies on men's family behavior?

Levels and Consequences of Work-Family Stress
Many surveys of workers have documented that substantial proportions of working fathers report stress in combining work and family roles, or say they are interested in suing specific policies to reduce this stress. In some surveys, men's stress levels or desire to use policies equals or exceeds women's....

Other studies find that fathers report lower rates of work-family problems. Nonetheless, the proportion of fathers reporting difficulties in these studies is substantial, for example, 23% in a 1987 survey of employees in Portland, Oregon (Regional Research Institute for Human Services, 1987). Some research also finds that although fathers report work-family problems less frequently than mothers, when stress occurs it has more negative consequences for men than for women (Bolger, DeLongis, Kessler, & Wethington, 1989). Another study found that although men were less likely to miss work when child care arrangements broke down, missing work for this reason is more strongly associated with stress, poor health, and diminished well-being among men than among women (Shinn, Ortiz-Torres, Morris, & Simko, 1987). It has also been documented that fathers miss work and are late for work more frequently than nonfathers.

Men's interest in using specific policies to reduce work-family stress is also increasing.... The percentage expressing personal interest in leave to care for newborn children increased from 15% in 1986 to 35% in 1991; the proportion interested in leave to care for sick children rose from 40% to 64% in the same period ("Labor Letter," 1991).

Child Care Supports

Affordable, high-quality child care is perhaps working parents' greatest need. It is becoming widely recognized that employers can help workers meet their needs for child care. Companies can do this not only or primarily by providing on-site centers, but by purchasing slots or otherwise subsidizing local child care centers, fostering family day care networks, providing information and referral services, and by making it possible for workers to pay for child care with pretax income (dependent care reimbursement programs).

No systematic data concerning the availability or utilization of these child care policies by men are available.... The reports and the findings noted earlier that fathers miss and are late for work more often than nonfathers and that child care problems have a negative effect on fathers' health suggest that fathers will use employer-provided child care supports when present.

Flextime and Other Alternative Work Schedules

The second main workplace policy supporting families is flexible work schedules. A particularly important example is "flextime," in which workers have some latitude to set their starting and ending times, but continue to work a full day....

In my experience when fathers use flextime and other alternative work schedules to increase their time with their children, it is generally not recognized as such. This use of flextime as a male work-family "accommodation" strategy tends to be invisible because of gender role stereotypes. If a father with flextime changes his schedule, it may simply not occur to co-workers and supervisors that a child care need or a desire to spend more time with his child is the reason for the change. Many fathers may likewise find it simplest to let others thank that something else motivated their change in schedule. The resulting invisibility of flextime as a male work-family accommodation then further reinforces the stereotype that fathers do not adjust or limit their work role to meet family obligations.

Formal Paternity Leave

... When employers began to provide child care supports and flexible work schedules over the last two decades, many probably assumed that all or most users would be women. Even so, companies adopting these policies routinely made them available to both sexes.... Men who take parental leave invariably generate considerable interest. Unlike child care supports and flexible schedules, employers offering, and fathers using, parental leave requires a fundamental shift in how employers view men....

Only two U.S. studies have collected systematic data on fathers' utilization of parental leave. Of the 119 companies offering unpaid leave to fathers in a 1984 investigation, only 9 reported that a father had taken leave under this policy, and in most of these, only 1 father had done so (Catalyst, 1986). A survey conducted by a national recruiting firm in 1990 concluded that slightly more than 1% of eligible fathers use leave (Vrazo, 1990). Recent reports about specific companies indicate that the number of fathers taking leave is zero or extremely low in many companies.

However, these recent accounts also suggest that in some other large firms, fathers' use of parental leave is becoming more common. At Commonwealth Edison (Chicago), 25 fathers applied for child care leave between 1985 and 1988 (Trost, 1988). The number of fathers taking leave is increasing at Aetna, Eastman Kodak, American Telephone and Telegraph (AT&T), 3M, and Lotus Development (Hammonds, 1991). For example, 23 fathers took leaves at Lotus in 1990, compared with 29 in the previous 2 years combined. At Eastman Kodak, 61 men took paternity leave in the last 3 years. At AT&T, men account for 1 of every 50 employees taking family leave, compared to 1 in 400 a decade ago; 85% do so for 3 months or longer, a higher rate than for women. About 10% of the employees taking family leave at IBM are men (Vrazo, 1990)....

"Informal" Paternity Leave

The data considered so far concern the extent to which fathers take parental leave made available through formal policies. Almost all the U.S. data derive from surveys of companies, in which personnel offices report how many fathers have used these policies. Because I was concerned that such information might not fully reflect what fathers actually do, I collected relevant data directly from fathers themselves. In surveys conducted in 1988, 1990, and 1991, I interviewed 142 fathers with preschool children to find out whether and how much time they took off from work when their child was born. These fathers came from a college-sponsored nursery school, the hometown networks of college students, and the birth records of a working-class town.

Of the sample of 142 fathers, 124 (87%) reported they had taken at least some days off work. The average number of days taken was 5.3. On the average, about half this time consisted of vacation and sick days, but the other half appeared to be discretionary days off. That is, following a birth, supervisors and co-workers appeared to allow a father to take a few extra days off without loss of pay as long as he does not abuse this flexibility. It is also noteworthy that fathers generally did not label this time as "paternity leave"; 82% of the fathers who took days off work in my 1988 survey reported that they did *not* think of their days off in this way.

Two studies conducted since I first collected these data confirm fathers' high rates of leave taking when it is assessed by measures asking whether fathers take time off from work rather than whether they used a formal leave policy. The Four State Parental Leave Study found that 75% of a sample of 1,395 fathers of newborns in Minnesota, Oregon, Rhode Island, and Wisconsin took at least some leave from work (Bond, Galinsky, Lord, Staines, & Brown, 1991). Essex and Klein (1991) also found that 75% of a sample of 55 Wisconsin fathers took some leave.

Some may question the meaningfulness of taking vacation and sick days off after a birth and be skeptical of the value of leaves averaging 5 to 6 days. Use of vacation and sick days may seem trivial, until one realizes that many workers' vacations are scheduled by the employer, not the worker, and that many employers require medical certification, often from a company doctor, to take paid sick days. Another indicator that use of vacation or sick days for parental leave is not to be taken for granted is that several company surveys show that substantial proportions of employers have explicit policies either permitting or prohibiting such use.

Although longer leaves would no doubt have greater value, one should not minimize the benefits to mother and family of even these few days. Perhaps those who think 5 workdays off makes no difference should ask the new mother whose husband took *no* days off. In addition, I analyzed the relationship between the amount of time fathers took off and their later involvement in child care. In two of the three samples (1988 and 1991), the more days the father took off from work, the higher his reported current involvement in child care, even after controlling for the child's age and sex, mother's employment status, and father's work hours....

Thus, although few fathers use formal parental leave policies, the large majority *do* take informal parental leave by arranging to take a small number of days off work, without loss of pay, in other ways. What makes this possible is that informal paternity leave involves no loss of pay, and usually no formal application procedure. By contrast, taking a formal parental leave almost always leads to loss of pay (a particularly important factor if the mother is also taking unpaid job leave or leaving her job), besides requiring formal application and approval.

What Influences Whether Fathers Take Paternity Leave?

The way the question is often put is "Why do so few fathers take paternity leave?" The data presented above, however, suggest that the question should really be why so few fathers take formal, long-term, unpaid leaves. The most important reason is that the majority of fathers simply do not feel a desire to take this kind of leave. For most men, taking such a leave is not part of their conception of their role as father. Unlike mothers, fathers have not grown up believing there is a special bond between themselves and their child that requires their being home full-time during the first months of their child's life.

Several other factors reinforce fathers' low motivation to take formal long-term leaves. These additional influences also act as disincentives to formal leave taking among the minority of fathers who *do* want to take such leaves. Formal paternity leave for men is almost always unpaid. Even among fathers motivated to take time off, most will be reluctant to lose pay, especially at a time when the birth of a child has increased the family's economic responsibilities. In addition, fathers' choice about leave occurs in the context of the choices mothers make. Because most employed new mothers either take leave (usually unpaid) or stop working, most couples will perceive the father taking an unpaid leave at this time to be a luxury they cannot afford. There is also a disincentive for the alternative option of the father, but not mother taking leave, in that fathers usually earn more than mothers, and paternity leave thus "costs" more....

A second general disincentive to paternity leave is that employers and co-workers have negative attitudes about it.... A human resource manager observed that "There's something in the corporate culture that says to men, 'Don't do it' " (Lawson, 1991, p. C1). As one father described it, "There was nothing in the policy that said that men could not take the leave, but there was an unwritten rule that men do not do it" (Lawson, 1991, p. C8). Another observer who interviewed fathers in a variety of businesses reported, "At a number of companies, there's a joke—'Sure, we have parental leave, and the first guy who uses it will have an arrow in this back' " (Levin, quoted in Vrazo, 1990, p. 17). In addition to being viewed as uncommitted to the job, men who take leaves are perceived as unmasculine. One researcher noted, "We haven't escaped the notion that house-husbands are, to a certain degree, wimpier than persons who are not" (Alexander, 1990, p. B1). The relatively high numbers of fathers noted earlier to take leave in a few companies indirectly corroborates the role of corporate cultures: Certain firms seem to have climates in which a father taking a formal paternity leave is more acceptable....

Finally, an additional reason that most U.S. fathers do not take long-term formal leave may be that it is relatively easy to take short-term informal leave. That is, most fathers have available an alternative that meets, at least to a limited degree, their need to be at home. Although this alternative is limited, it has the advantage that it does not lead to loss of pay or to being labeled as uncommitted to their jobs, odd, or unmasculine.

CONCLUSIONS

Men use flextime to about the same degree as women, and with the same consequences for their family participation, although these effects tend to be less visible. Most men do take time off from work when children are born. However, they typically do so on an informal, short-term basis in contrast to women's taking long-term, formal leave. There is also evidence that men experience work-family stress, and that this stress has negative consequences for them—in several studies actually greater than for women. Thus, to a far greater extent than is usually realized, men *do* engage in work-family accommodations or adaptations, that is, they negotiate the demands of their jobs to meet family needs. In spite of the assumption that only women accommodate their jobs to their family, many men do so as well.

Men's work-family accommodations tend to be less visible than women's. Some male adaptations, such as use of flextime, are usually perceived as motivated by other purposes. Other accommodations, such as informal paternity leave, are often not noticed at all, and when they are noticed, their significance is minimized or interpreted in other ways. On several occasions when managers have told me they have never seen any father take paternity leave, I have asked them to describe what happened the last time a male in their immediate work group had a child. Invariably managers describe a pattern of the man using vacation days, sick days, compensatory time off, and other informal time off totaling a week or more. When I respond that in some ways this sounds like paternity leave, they become extremely uncomfortable. To others, the data on informal paternity leave just show that men don't want to take *real* parental leave. In effect, many observers do not acknowledge men's parental leave patterns because they are comparing men's behavior to a standard derived from women, and because men do not fit this standard, conclude that men are not taking parental leave. This judgment parallels the way women's employment behavior has traditionally been discounted because it departs from the male model (e.g., women are not really attached to the labor force if they work part-time or interrupt employment for early child rearing).

... Workplace culture can create expectations for male performance that exceed "official" demands of the job. In some companies, if a father leaves work at 5:00 or 5:30, male co-workers will joke, "Are you working part time now?" (Levine, 1991, p. 3). Workplace norms also define some informal work-family accommodations, as in informal paternity leave, as well as stimulate the development of others. As illustrations of the latter, Levine (1991) identifies a number of strategies fathers use to leave work on time without appearing uncommitted: the "avoid the supervisor ploy" (not leaving until just after the supervisor leaves or parking in the back lot to avoid being seen leaving by others) and the "another meeting ploy" (saying you have to break away from work for a "meeting").

To reduce employed fathers' work-family conflicts and to promote greater family involvement, further attention to how men actually use formal family-supportive policies as well as the adaptations men develop informally are needed.

NOTES

1. Hochschild (1989, p. 279, note 2) cites Szalai (1972, p. 668) as the source for the 17- and 12-minute estimates, but these numbers are actually taken from p. 642 and concern the subgroup of men who are employed and have children. My calculation is based on data reported on pp. 642, 644, and 646 for employed married men with children. Also, although Hochschild (pp. 3, 271–273) does discuss data from other and more recent studies concerning men's *total* time spent in work and family roles compared to women's (the "leisure gap"), she does not report their estimates of men's time in family roles by themselves, all of which are dramatically higher than the 17- and 12-minute figures she highlights.

2. Some other analyses of changes in men's family time comparing these two surveys find a decrease. Pleck (1985, pp. 143–146) discusses the inconsistencies among these analyses.

REFERENCES

Alexander, S (1990, August 24). Fears for careers curb paternity leaves. *Wall Street Journal*, pp. B1, B4.

Bolger, N., DeLongis, A., Kessler, R. C., & Wethington, E. (1989). The contagion of stress across multiple roles. *Journal of Marriage and Family, 51,* 175–183.

Bond, J. T., Galinsky, E., Lord, M., Staines, G. L., & Brown, K. R. (1991). *Beyond the parental leave debate: The impact of laws in four states.* New York: Families and Work Institute.

Catalyst. (1986). *Report on a national study of parental leaves.* New York: Author.

Essex, M. J., & Klein, M. H. (1991). The Wisconsin parental leave study: The roles of fathers. In J. S. Hyde & M. J. Essex (Eds.) *Parental leave and child care: Setting a research and policy agenda* (pp. 280–293). Philadelphia: Temple University Press.

Hammonds, K. (1991), April 15). Taking steps toward a daddy track *Business Week,* pp. 90–92.

Hochschild, A. (1989) *The second shift: Working parents and the revolution at home.* New York: Viking.

Juster, F. T. (1985). A note on recent changes in time use. In F. T. Juster & F. Stafford, (Eds.), *Time, goods, and well-being* (pp. 313–332). Ann Arbor: University of Michigan, Institute for Social Research.

Labor letter (1991, April 30). *Wall Street Journal,* p. 1.

LaRossa, R. (1988). Fatherhood and social change. *Family Relations, 37,* 451–457.

Lawson, C. (1991, May 26). Baby beckons: Why is daddy at work? *New York Times,* pp. C1, C8.

Levine, J. A. (1991, June 11). *The invisible dilemma: Working fathers in corporate America* (Testimony at the hearing "Babies and briefcases. Creating a family-friendly workplace for fathers"). Washington, DC: U.S. House of Representatives, Select Committee on Children. Youth, and Families.

Pleck, J. H. (1985). *Working wives, working husbands.* Newbury Park, CA: Sage.

Pleck, J. H. (1987). The contemporary man. In M. Scher, G. Eichenfield, M. Stevens, & G. Good (Eds.) *Handbook on counseling and psychotherapy with men* (pp. 16–27. Beverly Hills, CA: Sage.

Presser, H. B. (1989). Can we make time for children? The economy, work schedules, and child care. *Demography, 26,* 523–543.

Regional Research Institute for Human Services (1987). *Employee Profiles: 1987 Dependent Care Survey.* Unpublished report, Portland State University.

Robinson, J. P. (1977). *Changes in Americans' use of time, 1965–75: A progress report.* Cleveland, OH: Cleveland State University, Communications Research Center.

Robinson, J. P. (1988). Who's doing the housework. *American Demographics, 10* (12), 24ff.

Shinn, M. Ortiz-Torres, B., Morris, A., & Simko, P. (1987, August). *Child care patterns, stress, and job behaviors among working parents.* Paper presented to the American Psychological Association, New York.

Trost, C. (1988, November 1). Men too, wrestle with career-family stress. *Wall Street Journal.* p. 33.

U.S. Bureau of the Census. (1990). *Who's minding the kids? Child care arrangements: Winter 1987–7* (Current Population Reports, Series, P-70, No. 20). Washington, DC: U.S. Government Printing Office.

Vrazo, D. (1990, October 15). Paternity leaves offered more often. *Providence Journal,* p. 17

POSTSCRIPT

Do Men Avoid Family Work?

One of the most consistent research findings is that employed women who exhibit fewer symptoms of stress say that the key to their well-being is having a supportive husband. A husband's ways of providing support are described as listening, offering advice, and providing comfort when their wives are under stress. Although these emotionally supportive gestures are valued, various investigations indicate that women's overload and stress are best eased by husbands who become more involved in family roles—taking on more responsibility for household chores and child care. Researchers point out that men who share more of the family work actually benefit by experiencing higher self-esteem and greater well-being.

If sharing responsibilities in marital relationships is beneficial to both women and men, why aren't more husbands energetically engaged in family roles? And why aren't more wives pointing out the unhealthy consequences of a lopsided family workload? Townsend and O'Neil say that women are increasingly aware of and resentful over chore-sharing arrangements, which they view as inequitable and threatening to their well-being. Pleck asserts that there is growing interest among men in improving their status as good husbands and fathers.

There are signs that the situation is changing. Several national conferences on men in families have been held in major cities across the United States, including one recent gathering on fatherhood featuring Vice President Al Gore, the Reverend Jesse Jackson, and country singer Garth Brooks. In her book *No Man's Land: Men's Changing Commitments to Family and Work* (Basic Books, 1993), Kathleen Gerson states that growing numbers of men are facing down reluctant employers to become more involved in family life.

SUGGESTED READINGS

N. R. Ahlander and K. S. Bahr, "Beyond Drudgery, Power, and Equity: Toward an Expanded Discourse on the Moral Dimensions of Housework in Families," *Journal of Marriage and the Family*, 57 (1995): 54–68.

A. Bayfield, "Juggling Jobs and Kids: The Impact of Employment Schedules on Fathers' Caring for Children" *Journal of Marriage and the Family*, 57 (1995): 321–332.

D. Blankenhorn, *Fatherless America* (Basic Books, 1995).

P. Schwartz, *Peer Marriage: How Love Between Equals Really Works* (Free Press, 1994).

PART 3

Parenthood

Changing attitudes about childbearing and childrearing have expanded the pool of personal choices potential parents may make. This has led to new questions about how children should be brought into the world. For instance, if a couple finds that they cannot produce children together, should that couple be offered the alternative of surrogate mothering? Another example is the teenager who finds herself pregnant: Should she marry the father of the baby? What roles does the father play in childrearing and in the family in general? Does the dramatic increase of mothers in the workplace mean that corporations must establish new policies to allow women to balance career and family? This section examines some of the choices that men and women must make about bearing and raising children.

- Have Men Lost Their Sense of Fatherhood?
- Are Mothers the Main Barrier to Fathers' Involvement in Childrearing?
- Would a "Mommy Track" Benefit Employed Women?
- Should Surrogate Parenting Be Permitted?
- Should Pregnant Teens Marry the Fathers of Their Babies?

ISSUE 9

Have Men Lost Their Sense of Fatherhood?

YES: David Blankenhorn, from *Fatherless America: Why Men Are Increasingly Viewed as Superfluous to Family Life* (Basic Books, 1995)

NO: Haya Stier and Marta Tienda, from "Are Men Marginal to the Family? Insights from Chicago's Inner City," in Jane C. Hood, ed., *Men, Work, and Family* (Sage Publications, 1993)

ISSUE SUMMARY

YES: David Blankenhorn, chair of the National Fatherhood Initiative, argues that America is becoming a fatherless society because increasing numbers of men are refusing to face the responsibility of caring for their own children.

NO: Sociologists Haya Stier and Marta Tienda maintain that fathers are not irresponsible scoundrels who have retreated from their family ties.

In his book *Man Enough: Fathers, Sons, and the Search for Masculinity* (Berkley, 1993), Frank Pittman writes that most men today suffer from "father hunger" —longing for a father to love, value, advise, protect, and teach them. Have fathers become too busy earning a living to spend time with their children? Has there been a mass defection of fathers from families—an unwillingness among men to face the responsibility of caring for their own children?

Organizations like the Promise Keepers and the National Institute for Responsible Fatherhood and Family Revitalization base their growing membership on people's conviction that America has become a fatherless nation. These and similar organizations continue to fill conference rooms with men eager to regain their status as husbands and fathers. The 1995 Million Man March on Washington, D.C., captured the attention of the general public as black men gathered to reaffirm their commitment to families and communities. Responsible fathering is now a grassroots initiative in many major American cities.

David Blankenhorn declares that society no longer appreciates, respects, or teaches men to be good fathers. Social analysts link rising rates of juvenile crime, teenage pregnancy, and poverty to fatherlessness. As some view it, rising rates of divorce, wife battering, child abuse, increasing imprisonment of young adult males, and women raising their children alone are among the consequences of a mass defection of men from fatherhood. Blankenhorn reasons that fatherhood has come to be defined by providing rather than by nurturing. The provider father is increasingly identified as being out of the family circle as job demands claim his heart and time and as men become content with being "good enough" fathers.

Yet even as the new men's movements flourish and public concerns about families are hammered into purposeful programs, some argue that these represent bandwagon politics built on false assumptions and misleading information. For example, in 1993 a publication by the Population Reference Bureau titled *Where's Papa: Father's Role in Child Care* reported that more fathers were involved in child care than at any time in the previous 10 years. In a survey by Theodore Cohen reported in Jane C. Hood, ed., *Men, Work, and Family* (Sage Publications, 1993), fathers corroborated those findings. Fathers in Cohen's study indicated that having children made a dramatic impact on their lives. Fatherhood led to changes in what the men thought and worried about. It changed the way the men viewed themselves, their relationships with wives and kin, even the kinds of activities in which they engaged. Cohen found that fathers, regardless of class and ethnicity, ranked wage earning as secondary to parenting responsibilities, which included being a role model, a teacher and socializer, a nurturer, a companion, and a playmate to their children. A primary goal voiced by the fathers surveyed was to be a better, more involved parent than their own fathers. Cohen also found that, despite the greater involvement of these men in the lives of their children and their determination to be better parents, work schedules and job demands were the strongest influence on how much time they could devote to fathering activities.

Haya Stier and Marta Tienda argue that fathers who cannot provide financial and emotional support to their children often have compelling grounds for what is commonly labeled irresponsible behavior. They propose broadening the examination of causes of so-called fatherlessness to include social explanations, such as limited access to jobs, restrictive visitation rules after separation or divorce, and strained finances from supporting additional children from second families. It is not accurate, say Stier and Tienda, to portray fathers as irresponsible parents who always shirk their parental duties. Minority men, in particular, have been hurt by such public derision.

As you read the following selections, consider whether or not there is evidence to justify the contention that fathers are abdicating their parental responsibilities by personal choice. Have we become a fatherless society?

YES

David Blankenhorn

THE DIMINISHMENT OF AMERICAN FATHERHOOD

A growing number of American children have no relationship with their fathers. Court and school officials report that many children do not even know what to put in the "Father's Name" blank on printed forms. An even larger proportion of children have only the slightest acquaintance with their fathers. In its 1991 survey of children in the United States, the National Commission on Children described the spreading phenomenon of father-child relationships that "are frequently tenuous and all too often nonexistent."

Fathers are vanishing legally as well as physically. About one-third of all childbirths in the nation now occur outside of marriage. In most of these cases, the place for the father's name on the birth certificate is simply left blank. In at least two of every three cases of unwed parenthood, the father is never legally identified. Not surprisingly, paternity suits are on the rise.

... "There are different kinds of daddies," one book for preschoolers states, and "sometimes a Daddy goes away like yours did. He may not see his children at all."[1] Another children's book is equally candid: "Some kids know both their mom and dad, and some kids don't." One child in this book says: "I never met my dad, but I know that he lives in a big city." Another says: "I'll bet my dad is really big and strong."[2]

... It is the story of an increasingly fatherless society. The moral of this new narrative is that fathers, at bottom, are unnecessary. The action of the story centers on what can be best understood as the fragmentation of fatherhood.

Imagine something big, made out of glass, called fatherhood. First imagine it slowly shrinking. Then imagine it suddenly shattering into pieces. Now look around. Try to identify the shards. Over here is marriage. Over there is procreation. Over here, manhood. Over there, parenthood. Here, rights. There, responsibilities. In this direction, what's best for me. In that direction, what's best for my child.

Off to one side, looking nervous, is an emaciated fellow we must now call a biological father, filling out forms and agreeing to mail in child-support payments. Off to the other side is some guy the experts now call a social father, wondering what to do next and whether he wants to do it. In the

From David Blankenhorn, *Fatherless America: Why Men Are Increasingly Viewed as Superfluous to Family Life* (Basic Books, 1995). Copyright © 1995 by The Institute for American Values. Reprinted by permission of Basic Books, a division of HarperCollins Publishers, Inc. Some notes omitted.

middle, poking through the rubble and deciding when to leave, are mothers and children. There is much anger and much talk of "rights." People are phoning their lawyers. People are making excuses. People are exclaiming at how complicated things have become.

Indeed, as fatherhood fragments, things do become complicated. Culturally, the story of fatherhood becomes harder to figure out. For, as we witness the collapse of fatherhood as a social role for men, we become confused and divided about the very nature and meaning of fatherhood.

Parenting experts question whether there is anything truly gendered about fatherhood. Scholars win research grants to investigate whether father absence harms children. Social workers debate whether it helps children, especially poor children, to press for fathers' names on birth certificates. Judges try to sort out tangled custody conflicts, often pitting unmarried biological fathers against "father figures" such as the mother's boyfriend or even former boyfriend. Journalists write stories alternately condemning "deadbeat dads" and sympathizing with the plight of teenage fathers.

... What does it mean to be a father in the United States today? What does our society require of fathers? Are some fathers excused from these requirements? For example, are unemployed men excused? What about minority males from disadvantaged backgrounds? What about prominent elected officials who are candid about their personal lives?

Do we stigmatize unwed fatherhood or do we not? Do we jail deadbeat dads or enroll them in jobs programs? How long is a father financially responsible for his child? As long as a child needs his help? Until court-ordered child support expires? Until the child holds a press conference?

Our society is deeply ambivalent and divided about each of these questions. For as fatherhood disintegrates around us, we grow more confused about just what fatherhood is....

THE SHRINKING AMERICAN FATHER

Prior to fragmenting—breaking into pieces, like Humpty Dumpty—fatherhood in our society spent a long time shrinking. Historically, the contraction of fatherhood both preceded and precipitated its disintegration. In this sense, today's fragmentation of fatherhood represents the end point a long historical process: the steady diminishment of fatherhood as a social role for men.

Over the past two hundred years, fathers have gradually moved from the center to the periphery of family life. As the social role for fathers has diminished, so our cultural story of fatherhood has by now almost completely ceased to portray fathers as essential guarantors of child and societal well-being. Not to be overly gloomy, but in some respects it has been all downhill for fathers since the Industrial Revolution.

In colonial America, fathers were seen as primary and irreplaceable caregivers. According to both law and custom, fathers bore the ultimate responsibility for the care and well-being of their children, especially older children. Throughout the eighteenth century, for example, child-rearing manuals were generally addressed to fathers, not mothers. Until the early nineteenth century, in almost all cases of divorce, it was established practice to award the custody of children to fathers. Throughout this period, fathers, not mothers, were the chief correspondents with children who lived away from home.

More centrally, fathers largely guided the marital choices of their children and directly supervised the entry of children, especially sons, into the world outside the home. Most important, fathers assumed primary responsibility for what was seen as the most essential parental task: the religious and moral education of the young. As a result, societal praise or blame for a child's outcome was customarily bestowed not (as it is today) on the mother but on the father.[3]

Of course, all of this eventually changed: not marginally, but fundamentally. First, industrialization and the modern economy led to the physical separation of home and work. No longer could fathers be in both places at once. No longer, according to Alexander Mitscherlich, could children typically acquire skills "by watching one's father, working with him, seeing the way he handled things, observing the degree of knowledge and skill he had attained as well as his limitations." The nineteenth century's "progressive fragmentation of labor, combined with mass production and complicated administration, the separation of home from the place of work, [and] the transition from independent producer to paid employee who uses consumer goods" led to "a progressive loss of substance of the father's authority and a diminution of his power in the family and over the family.[4]

The major change in family life in the nineteenth century was the steady feminization of the domestic sphere. Accompanying this radical change were a host of new ideas about gender identity and family life—some focusing on childhood as a special and separate "tender years" stage of life, others on what were believed to be the special capacities of women to care for children and to create, in contrast to the outside world dominated by men, a secure moral ethos for family life.

One important consequence of these new ideas was the relative decline of patriarchy and the shift toward more companionate models of marriage and parenthood. The historian Carl Degler, describing the increasingly "attenuated character" of nineteenth-century patriarchy, concludes that "the companionate marriage placed limits on the power of the husband" and led to the "relatively democratic role of the father in the nineteenth-century family."[5] As early as the 1830s, Alexis de Tocqueville could praise the "influence of democracy" on fatherhood in America, even as it led to the fact that "paternal authority, if not destroyed, is at least impaired."[6]

From a modern perspective, this philosophical shift, this emerging ethos of the companionate family, is praiseworthy. Certainly our society could not, and does not wish to, recreate for our time the model of the agrarian patriarchal father. Regarding the cultural meaning of paternity, however, the historical evidence is clear: Both the new economy and the new philosophy of the nineteenth century contributed to the sharp contraction of fatherhood as a social role....

Increasingly, men looked outside the home for the meaning of their maleness. Masculinity became less domesticated, defined less by effective paternity and more by individual ambition and achievement. Fatherhood became a thinner social role. Paternal authority declined as the fatherhood script came to be anchored in, and restricted to, two paternal tasks: head of the family and bread-winner....

In sum, over the past two hundred years, fatherhood has lost, in full or in part, each of its four traditional roles: irreplaceable caregiver, moral educator, head of family, and family breadwinner. As the historian Peter N. Stearns put it: "An eighteenth-century father would not recognize the distance contemporary men face between work and home... or the parental leadership granted to mothers or indeed the number of bad fathers."[7]

The result is that fatherhood as a social role has been radically diminished in three ways. First, it has become, in the most literal sense, smaller: There are simply fewer things that remain socially defined as a father's distinctive work. The script has been shortened to only a few pages.

Second, fatherhood has been devalued. Within the home, fathers have been losing authority; within the wider society, fatherhood has been losing esteem. Many influential people in today's public debate argue that, when all is said and done, fathers are simply not very important.

Third, and most important, fatherhood has been diminished as paternity has become *decultured*—denuded of any authoritative social content or definition. A decultured paternity is a minimalist paternity. It is biology without society. As an extreme example, consider the phenomenon of the sperm bank: fatherhood as anonymous insemination. No definition of fatherhood could be tinier.

A decultured paternity necessarily fractures any coherent social understanding of fatherhood. As fewer children live with their biological fathers, and more live with or near stepfathers, mothers'

boyfriends, or other male "role models," biological fatherhood is being separated from social fatherhood. In turn, social fatherhood, once detached from any one man, becomes more diffuse as an idea and elastic as a role—less a person than a style of relating to children.

... To use a military metaphor, our cultural story no longer conscripts men into a uniform fatherhood service. Instead, fathers increasingly comprise an all-volunteer force, small and flexible. No longer unambiguously responsible for a fixed number of mandatory tasks, today's decultured fathers must largely select for themselves, from a complex menu of lifestyle options, the meaning of their paternity. Ultimately, a decultured paternity is incompatible with fatherhood as a defined role for men.

Finally, a decultured paternity signals the growing detachment of fatherhood from wider norms of masculinity. Consider several aspects of this phenomenon. In our elite discourse, masculinity is widely viewed as a problem to be overcome, frequently by insisting upon "new" fathers willing to disavow any inherited understandings of masculinity. In popular culture, the traditional male fantasy of sex without responsibility—the anti-father world view of the adolescent male, as emblematized in the philosophy of *Playboy* magazine, James Bond movies, and Travis McGee novels—is an increasingly accepted cultural model in our society, less an accusation than an assumption about male behavior. In addition, in what the sociologist Elijah Anderson calls the "street culture" of our inner cities, men's glorification of casual and even predatory sex, completely divorced from responsible fatherhood, now constitutes the core of what Anderson calls the "sex code" of young minority males.[8]

All three of these otherwise distinct trends are linked by an underlying idea: the disintegrating connection between masculinity and responsible paternity. Being male is one thing. Being a good father is another. The latter is no longer the pathway to proving the former. "Man" and "father" become separate and even dissimilar cultural categories.

Consequently, as paternity is decultured, the larger meaning of masculinity in our society becomes unclear and divisive. A decultured fatherhood thus produces a doubtful manhood. For without norms of effective paternity to anchor masculinity, the male project itself is increasingly called into question and even disrepute. . . .

THE COLLAPSING BASES OF GOOD-ENOUGH FATHERHOOD

Structurally, the preconditions for effective fatherhood are twofold: coresidency with children and a parental alliance with the mother. These two foundations do not guarantee effective fatherhood, but they do sustain the possibility of good-enough fatherhood. Conversely, when one or both of these enabling conditions are absent, good-enough fatherhood is not possible for most men.

. . . With each passing year, fewer and fewer men are living with their children. Fewer and fewer fathers are willing or able to sustain cooperative partnerships with the mothers of their children.

. . . Scholars estimate that, before they reach age eighteen, more than half of all children in the nation will live apart from their fathers for at least a significant portion of their childhoods.

For most of these children, the possibility of being fathered has largely evaporated. When a man does not live with his children and does not get along with the mother of his children, his fatherhood becomes essentially untenable, regardless of how he feels, how hard he tries, or whether he is a good guy. Almost by definition, he has become de-fathered.

Yet these two father-disabling phenomena have become the distinguishing traits of the fatherhood trend of our time. In historical terms, the spread of these new conditions of paternity marks the essential difference between a fatherhood that is shrinking and a fatherhood that is fragmenting.

When fatherhood is *shrinking*, a father is doing less, and perhaps doing it less well, but he is still a father. His role may be diminishing, but it is still coherent. He is still on the premises. His children see him every day. He is still a husband and a partner to their mother. He is responsible for protecting and nurturing his children. He may not win any Father's Day prizes —he may not be a very good father at all —but he is still recognizably a father.

But when fatherhood is *fragmenting*, the identity and social definition of the father change not in degree but in kind. The new conditions, driven by divorce and out-of-wedlock childbearing, split the nucleus of the nuclear family. Now the father is physically absent. When he comes "home," his children are not there. He is not a husband. Because the parental alliance has either ended or never begun, the mother has little reason or opportunity to defend or even care about his fatherhood. In the most important areas, he is not responsible for his children.

. . . His paternity has become disabled, cut off from its essential supports. In sociological terms, his fatherhood has become deinstitutionalized, or detached from socially cognizable expectations and goals. Consequently, the very meaning of his fatherhood becomes fractured and disorganized. To his children and to the larger society, he becomes largely unrecognizable as a father....

Moreover, as fatherhood fragments, so do other institutions that depend on fatherhood. Marriage is an obvious example....

What results is men who impregnate women, and who at times assert paternal rights, but who find themselves hopelessly tangled up by a rather basic question: Who is this child's rightful father? ...

In sum, a new fatherhood has emerged in our society. But what is new is not the hands-on, nurturing "new" fatherhood so widely proclaimed and urged in the media and by parenting experts. Instead, measured according to demographic reach and social impact, what is truly new in our generation is a fatherhood that is increasingly estranged from mothers and removed from where children live. Unlike previous fatherhood shifts in our nation's history, these newly dominating conditions of paternity do not simply change or even shrink fatherhood. They end it.

THE RISE OF VOLITIONAL FATHERLESSNESS

Historically, the principal cause of fatherlessness was paternal death. By the time they turned fifteen, about 15 percent of all American children born in 1870 had experienced the death of their fathers....

Today, the principal cause of fatherlessness is paternal choice. Over the course of this century, the declining rate of paternal death has been matched, and rapidly surpassed, by the rising rate of paternal abandonment....

Though paternal death and paternal abandonment are frequently treated as sociological equivalents, these two phenomena could hardly be more different in their impact upon children and upon the larger society. To put it simply, death puts an end to fathers. Abandonment puts an end to fatherhood....

When a father dies, a child grieves. (I have lost someone I love.) When a father leaves, a child feels anxiety and self-blame. (What did I do wrong? Why doesn't my father love me?) Death is final. (He won't come back.) Abandonment is indeterminate. (What would make him come back?)

When a father dies, his fatherhood lives on, inside the head and heart of his child. In this sense, the child is still fathered. When a father leaves, his fatherhood leaves with him to wither away. The child is unfathered. When a father dies, the mother typically sustains his fatherhood by keeping his memory alive. When a father leaves, the mother typically diminishes his fatherhood by either forgetting him or keeping her resentments alive.

... The fact that paternal death caused such pain and social concern, while paternal departure is now accepted with relative equanimity, tells us with great precision what is truly new about contemporary fatherhood.

NOTES

1. Jeanne Warner Lindsay, *Do I Have a Daddy? A Story About a Single-Parent Child* (Buena Park, Calif: Morning Glory Press, 1991).

2. Michele Lash, Sally Ives Loughridge, and David Fassler, *My Kind of Family: A Book for Kids in Single-Parent Homes* (Burlington, Vt.: Waterfront Books, 1990), 20–21, 93.

3. See John Demos, *Past, Present, and Personal: The Family and the Life Course in American History* (Oxford, U.K.: Oxford University Press, 1986), 44–46; Carl N. Degler, *At Odds: Women and the Family in America from the Revolution to the Present* (Oxford, U.K.: Oxford University Press, 1981), 73; E. Anthony Rotundo, "American Fatherhood: A Historical Perspective," *American Behavioral Scientist* 29, no. 1 (September/October 1985): 7–25; and Stephen M. Frank, " 'Their Own Proper Task': The Construction of Meanings for Fatherhood in Nineteenth-Century America," paper presented at the conference "The History of Marriage and the Family in Western Society" (Ottawa: Carleton University, April 1992).

4. Alexander Mitscherlich, *Society Without the Father: A Contribution to Social Psychology* (New York: Harper Collins, 1993), 147. The effects of industrialization on family life, and especially on the father's role, are widely acknowledged by historians. Allan Carlson, for example, describes "the great divorce of labor from the home" as "one of the defining features of American domestic life since the 1840s." See Allan Carlson, *From Cottage to Work Station: The Family's Search for Social Harmony in the Industrial Age* (San Francisco: Ignatius Press, 1993), 4.

5. Degler, *At Odds*, 74, 77. Similarly, to the historian and literary scholar Ann Douglas, "it seems indisputable that paternal authority was a waning force in the middle-class American family" in the nineteenth century. For example, Douglas finds that during this period "mothers increasingly took over the formerly paternal task of conducting family prayers." See Ann Douglas, *The Feminization of American Culture* (New York: Anchor Press, 1988), 74–75.

For a description of the spread of the ideal of the "companionate family" in the 1920s and 1930s, accompanied in part by the further "diminution of fatherhood," see Ralph LaRossa et al., "The Fluctuating Image of the 20th-Century Father," *Journal of Marriage and the Family* 53, no. 4 (November 1991): 988, 996; and Steven Mintz and Susan Kellogg, *Domestic Revolutions: A Social History of American Family Life* (New York: Free Press, 1988), 107–31.

6. Alexis de Tocqueville, *Democracy in America*, vol. 2 (New York: Schocken, 1961), 229.

7. Peter N. Stearns, "Fatherhood in Historical Perspective: The Role of Social Change," in Frederick W. Bozett and Shirley M. H. Hanson, eds., *Fatherhood and Families in Cultural Context* (New York: Springer, 1991), 50.

8. Elijah Anderson, *Streetwise: Race, Class, and Change in an Urban Community* (Chicago: University of Chicago Press, 1990,) 112–37. See also Anderson, "The Code of the Streets," *Atlantic Monthly* (May 1994): 81–94. In many respects, Anderson's work is a successor to Elliot Liebow's classic anthropological study, *Tally's Corner* (Boston: Little, Brown, 1967).

NO

Haya Stier and Marta Tienda

ARE MEN MARGINAL TO THE FAMILY? INSIGHTS FROM CHICAGO'S INNER CITY

INTRODUCTION

Both the rise in the number of children living in poverty and the deteriorating economic status of households headed by women have been attributed to the absence of a male provider in the household (Eggebeen & Lichter, 1991). Child poverty rates have been aggravated by the minimal child support provided by noncustodial fathers (Garfinkel & McLanahan, 1986; Weitzman, 1985). According to Garfinkel and McLanahan (1986), about 60% of absent white fathers and 80% of blacks pay no child support (p. 24). Moreover, child support payments are generally low and usually comprise a tiny share of household income (10% for whites and 3.5% for blacks). But father absence is more than an economic problem. Because fathers are key agents of socialization, their presence is critical for healthy child development (Garfinkel & McLanahan, 1986; Hetherington, Camara, & Featherman, 1983).

Academic and policy discussion about the linkages between family structure and poverty have generated a picture of poor, unmarried minority women abandoned by irresponsible men who shirk their parental responsibilities (e.g., Murray, 1984). In fact, many noncustodial parents either never married or never lived with their children (Furstenberg, 1991; Hannerz, 1969; Sullivan, 1989). Whereas some men actually deny their fatherhood, others who acknowledge paternity renege on obligations to provide support, despite their best intentions. A third group of noncustodial fathers marry the mother of their children, but like many men who marry before children come, lose contact with the children after subsequent separation. Thus, because of rising divorce rates and high rates of nonmarital fertility, growing numbers of children receive inadequate emotional and financial support from their biological fathers.

Do declining levels of support from noncustodial fathers mean that men, especially minority men, are becoming marginal to the family? This provocative thesis is implicit in many recent accounts about the growth of an urban underclass, but it has not been explicitly posed. We explore this thesis by

From Haya Stier and Marta Tienda, "Are Men Marginal to the Family? Insights from Chicago's Inner City," in Jane C. Hood, ed., *Men, Work, and Family*, pp. 23–28, 36–41, 43–44 (Sage Publications, 1993). Copyright © 1993 by Sage Publications, Inc. Reprinted by permission. Notes and some references omitted examining the circumstances underlying father absence for a sample of parents residing in Chicago's inner city....

THEORETICAL CONSIDERATIONS

Men's familial roles have undergone substantial changes since preindustrial times. Although all family members contributed to subsistence activities during preindustrial times, men were the dominant source of authority *within* the household. As family heads, men were considered to be primary providers because they were credited with their wives' and children's work. With the relocation of economic activity outside the household that accompanied modernization, men's family roles acquired an almost exclusive concern with economic support functions (Damos, 1986). Although fathers continued involvement with their children, particularly at an emotional level, mothers became the principals in socialization except in unusual circumstances. For example, Furstenberg (1988) noted that until the middle of the 19th century, fathers usually assumed custody over the children in case of a marital disruption. When rates of female labor force activity were low, this arrangement protected children's economic well-being. The belief that children are better off with their mother, especially during their early years of life, gradually led to changes in this practice so that by the end of the 19th century, mothers usually became custodial parents in the event of marital disruption.

The "good provider" role of fathers dominated family ideology until the 1960s, when according to Ehrenreich (1985) and others, men began to retreat from their instrumental familial roles (Bernard, 1981; Furstenberg, 1988; Ro-

tundo, 1985). This retreat manifested itself in two ways: Men either *increased* their familial responsibilities by taking more active roles in child rearing and household duties, or greatly diminished their involvement in domestic and parenting roles. Thus, changes in the division of labor within families resulted in two extreme styles of modern parenthood. Whereas some fathers have become heavily involved in child rearing and have extended their familial roles beyond that of breadwinners (Marsiglio, 1991; Pleck, 1987), other fathers deny responsibility for their children, refusing to support them altogether (Furstenberg, 1988).

Many researchers have argued that men in general and minority men in particular are retreating from the family. The primary evidence for this claim derives from levels of financial and emotional support provided by noncustodial fathers. Alternative interpretations build on differences in the form and content of child support provided by men of varying economic means and ethnic group membership. These two views of child support patterns undergird our analysis of whether or not men are becoming marginal to the family.

The growing number of fathers who fail to provide child support for noncustodial children and who have minimal contact with them is socially problematic because it results in both economic and emotional deprivation (Furstenberg, Nord, Peterson, & Zill, 1983; Garfinkel & McLanahan, 1986; Weitzman, 1985). But it is unclear whether noncustodial fathers' failure to provide child support reflects their irresponsibility in dealing with familial obligations, denial of access to their children, or economic constraints. To be sure, men who lack steady incomes find it difficult to provide regular support to their noncustodial children (Furstenberg, 1991; Furstenberg et al., 1983). Before judging men's disregard of child support as evidence of their marginality to the family, it is essential to establish why they fail to provide child support. For example, learning that lack of access to jobs is the reason for neglect shifts the locus of policy debate from concerns about how to force "the scoundrels" to pay their due to concerns about the circumstances underlying their precarious labor market position (Wilson, 1987; Wilson & Neckerman, 1986). Such considerations are particularly germane to the recent debates about the growth of an urban underclass.

There is compelling evidence that some men refuse to support children even when they have resources do so. For example, economic explanations for limited child support stress the low potential benefits noncustodial fathers receive from nonresident children with whom they have limited contact. Presumably, restricted access to children reduces incentives for working fathers to invest in their children. Further, when noncustodial fathers establish new families, they usually give primary attention to their co-resident (often adopted) offspring. This circumstance further decreases incentives to provide child support to nonresident children, reinforcing Weitzman's (1985) contention that able fathers provide inadequate support even when they are financially capable.

Aggregate statistics reveal inadequate levels of financial support by noncustodial fathers, but qualitative studies that disclose more subtle forms of child support tell another story (Furstenberg, 1991; Stack, 1974). For example, both Furstenberg (1991) and Stack (1974) found that many fathers provide in-kind support to their children and to the mothers of their children, albeit on an irregular basis. Furstenberg makes a distinction between "daddies" and "fathers" as indicating those who "do" and "don't do" for their children. Doing for one's child includes support ranging from regular financial contributions to purchasing an occasional box of diapers or looking after the child on occasion. Stack showed that when fathers were unable to provide in-kind support themselves, they engaged the services of their close female kin to take an active role in caring for their children. Stack's thick description portrays men as bridges in a broad kin network that functions as a normative extended family. Thus, although the fathers themselves may play a minor role in their children's lives, they often perform a crucial, but indirect support function by ensuring the replacement of functions they are unable to perform.

In sum, with the increasing rates of out-of-wedlock childbirth and divorce, absent fathers are becoming numerous. These men are most likely to lose interest in their nonresident children because many have limited contacts with them and do not provide adequate support. In our judgment these men are marginal to the family because they have lost their traditional roles as providers and are not involved emotionally with the rearing of their children. One consequence of this behavior is a growing number of children, but especially minority children, being reared in poverty (Eggebeen & Lichter, 1991). To date, most empirical work on living arrangements and support patterns of noncustodial fathers has been restricted to blacks or comparisons between blacks and whites. As a result, ethnic differences in parenting styles, living arrangements, and support activities are neither well documented nor understood. In particular, relatively little is known about Hispanic men's roles as fathers and providers.

... Our analyses... compare black, white, Mexican, and Puerto Rican fathers residing in inner-city neighborhoods where father absence is pervasive. In addition to documenting the living arrangements of inner-city fathers and their children, we examine the circumstances that undergird their support patterns.

DATA AND METHODS

Our analyses are based on the Urban Poverty and Family Life Survey of Chicago (UPFLS) conducted by National Opinion Research Center.... The UPFLS is based on a multistage, stratified probability sample of parents aged 18–44 who resided in census tracts representing diverse socioeconomic environments.

... This sampling strategy deliberately overrepresented poor neighborhoods because it was the most cost-efficient way to study social behavior in deprived neighborhoods, but it is important to distinguish between sampling poor places and poor people. Although poor people have a greater probability of selection in areas with the highest poverty rates, respondents were randomly selected within tracts, hence there is appreciable socioeconomic variability among respondents.... Completed interviews were obtained from 2,490 respondents, which include 1,186 blacks, 368 whites, 484 Mexicans, and 453 Puerto Ricans. The current study is based on 811 men, all of whom were fathers at the time of the survey.

...Determining whether or not men are deliberately abdicating their family responsibilities requires evidence that decisions to avoid child support are personal *choices* and not merely reflections of material circumstances. In particular, given similar resources, are minority men less likely to provide child support to noncustodial children? ...

FATHERHOOD, MARRIAGE, AND PARENTAL OBLIGATIONS

... On balance, our results support Wilson's (1987; Wilson & Neckerman, 1986) premises about the enabling role of economic position—education or work—in raising the propensity of inner-city men to marry. That the act of fathering a child itself propels men into marriage indicates that they are inclined to accept their parental obligations when they have the means to support their children. These results also corroborate with Stack's (1974) finding that couples often do not formalize their marriage until the advent of a birth. Finally, our results show that there exist alternative pathways into adult roles in the inner city. In other words, marriage often follows rather than precedes parenting in impoverished environments. The sequencing of these two life course events differs markedly by race and Hispanic origins.

Yet, marriage is not a sufficient condition to ensure the economic well-being of children. Divorce can reverse this status, and marriage per se does not guarantee that fathers will be stably employed. Further, the advent of a marriage following a birth does not necessarily result in legitimation of the child in question. In fact, the living arrangements of men in our sample reveal that many fathers live apart from their own children. These children experience the highest risk of poverty and long-term problems with intellectual and social development (Garfinkel & McLanahan, 1986). Therefore it is important to examine directly whether and how noncustodial fathers support their children.

Absent fathers may take an active role in their child's upbringing by showing involvement in either the economic or the emotional needs of the child. As Stack (1974) argued, participation in child support can be done either in person or through female kin. Of course, some absent fathers chose to ignore their children altogether, thus playing only a marginal role in the children's lives. Other fathers face logistical difficulties in providing support. For example, over 80% of Mexican fathers in our sample are foreign born, and if their children reside in Mexico, frequent visits and regular in-kind support are impractical.

... Of the population of fathers who reported having nonresident children, most reported providing economic support to their offspring. There is limited ethnic variation in the practice of providing financial support, except that Mexican men, who were less likely to have nonresident children to begin with, were somewhat more likely to provide financial support—probably because they often live far away from their offspring. Puerto Ricans were the least likely to support their children financially. Although there may be limited ethnic variation in the tendency of noncustodial fathers to support their children, the nature and level of support may vary greatly both in its regularity and the amounts provided.

Most fathers also report providing in-kind support (e.g., toys, clothes) to the children. That noncustodial Mexican fathers report a lower incidence of in-kind support reflects practical difficulties: For those who left dependent children in Mexico, monetary transfers are more practical than in-kind support, which often involves services and miscellaneous goods. This interpretation is consistent with other ethnic differences in child support (e.g., the actual contact with the children discussed below).

Not only do noncustodial fathers provide economic contributions to their children, but so do their relatives. This practice is especially evident among black fathers: Nearly one in four report that their noncustodial children receive financial support from other relatives, and over half reported that other relatives provide some in-kind support. Kin-based financial support to children is less common among whites, Mexicans, and Puerto Ricans, but the frequency of in-kind support from other white and Puerto Rican relatives is comparable to that of blacks.

Economic support of any kind is more frequent than direct interaction with children. However, tabulations on visitation behavior reveal that black fathers visit their children more than any other category of men. One third of black fathers reported daily contact with the nonresident children, whereas one third see the child only once or twice a month, and the remainder have no contact at all. This pattern is consistent with Stack's (1974) account of father-child interaction in a poor black community. In comparison, only 18% of the whites, 15% of the Puerto Ricans, and 9% of Mexicans reported daily visits with the children. Half of all Puerto Ricans, three fourths of Mexicans, and nearly half of the whites say they never see their children. On balance, and with the exception of blacks, noncustodial fathers have very limited if any contact with their children.

As a path to separation of fathers from their children, divorce often involves mobility of one parent, thus inhibiting frequent and regular contact with children left behind. For blacks, whose children are conceived out of wedlock at higher rates than the other groups, marriage and co-residence seem to play less decisive roles in shaping child-parent interaction. According to Stack (1974), Sullivan (1989), and Hannerz (1969), men (or their close relatives) are expected to take care of the children, regardless of the living arrangements or the marital relationships to the mother....

Fathers who are currently employed are almost three times more likely to support their nonresident children compared to fathers who are not working. Also, high school graduates are 20% more likely to support their children compared to dropouts. That the ethnic differences are not statistically significant conveys an important message about the cultural underpinnings of distinct forms of support for noncustodial children. Stated differently, *ethnicity and race appear to be proxies for economic rather than family marginality.* This is not to dismiss the role of culture in shaping patterns of co-residence and the differential involvement of kin in providing for noncustodial children, but rather to stress that ethnic differences give way to indicators of fathers' economic status as determinants of material support to noncustodial children.

SUMMARY AND DISCUSSION

Are inner-city fathers marginal to their families? Our analyses documented the support roles of noncustodial inner-city fathers. That these men have diverse lifestyles is evident in their marital behavior and fulfillment of child responsibilities. This diversity, which corresponds to race and ethnic group divisions, results from cultural and normative differences in the way groups define familial responsibility and behavior. On the one hand, Mexican and white fathers represent the traditional mainstream view of men's familial behavior: Most of them are married and they fulfill their roles as providers within their economic means and within normative family settings. Blacks, and to a lesser extent, Puerto Ricans, are considerably less likely to adopt the "normative" path to family and parenthood. Many more bear children out of wedlock, and of these, relatively few live with their own children.

Earnings prospects... and labor market status appear to be the key determinants of child support activity for all fathers, regardless of ethnicity. Although black fathers are more likely than white or Hispanic men to be noncustodial parents, they compensate for this loss of family responsibility through frequent contact with their offspring and by invoking the financial contributions of their kin. Similar practices, although less prevalent, are reported by white, Mexican, and Puerto Rican fathers. Thus, it appears that through their economic, but especially their social relationships with other relatives, unmarried inner-city fathers provide an alternative family context for their noncustodial children.

Our analyses of inner-city fathers' child support patterns refute the idea that these men are becoming marginal to the family. Despite the severe financial constraints faced by minority men residing in Chicago's inner city, we were most struck by the relatively high proportions of men who reported providing financial and in-kind support to their noncustodial children. Unfortunately, we were unable to assess the regularity of the support provided or to consider whether it covered a reasonable share of their children's living expenses. Given the high rates of joblessness in the inner city (Tienda & Stier, 1991), it is unlikely that child support provided by inner-city fathers was adequate to cover all costs of child rearing. However, it is inappropriate to conclude that these men have retreated from the family, or that they are "irresponsible scoundrels" who neglect their children. Our results show that noncustodial fathers make great efforts to maintain ties with their children. That black fathers report the highest levels of contact with their noncustodial children corroborates Stack's (1974) interpretation about men's interactions with kin. When they lack financial resources, they contribute their own time and solicit support from other kin. We cannot determine whether or not visits compensate for income contributions, but visitation is certainly important for emotional development.

More generally, our study raises questions about the origins of men's marginality in the inner city. There is widespread agreement that minority men, particularly those residing in declining inner cities, have been marginalized from the labor market (Wilson, 1987). Despite their precarious economic position, it is remarkable that inner-city fathers manage to maintain ties with their noncustodial children. However, men's economic marginality, which is clearly reflected in declining rates of labor force participation and higher rates of unemployment, does reverberate in their family roles. Poor labor market standing influences the likelihood of marrying and fathering children, and the sequencing of these major life course events (Testa et al., 1989; Wilson & Neckerman, 1986). The provider roles assumed by inner-city men may not conform to the norms of middle-class whites, but this difference

should not be translated as "flight from the family."

REFERENCES

Bernard J. (1981). The good provider role: Its rise and fall. *American Psychologist, 36*(1), 1–12.

Damos, J. (1986). *Past, present, and personal: The family and life course in American history.* New York: Oxford University Press.

Eggebeen, D., & Lichter, D. T. (1991). Race, family structure, and changing poverty among American children. *American Sociological Review, 56*(6), 801–817.

Ehrenreich, B. (1985). *The hearts of men: American dreams and the flight from family commitment.* New York: Anchor.

Furstenberg, F. F. (1988). Good dads—bad dads: Two faces of fatherhood. In A. J. Cherlin (Ed.), *The changing American family and public policy* (pp. 193–218). Washington, DC: Urban Institute.

Furstenberg, F. F. (1991). *Daddies and fathers: Men who do for their children and men who don't.* Unpublished manuscript, University of Pennsylvania.

Furstenberg, F. F., Nord, C. W., Peterson, J. L., & Zill, N. (1983). The life course of children of divorce: Marital disruption and parental contact. *American Sociological Review, 48*, 656–668.

Garfinkel, I., & McLanahan, S. S. (1986). *Single mothers and their children: A new American dilemma.* Washington, DC: Urban Institute.

Hannerz, U. (1969). *Soulside: Inquiring into ghetto culture and community.* New York: Columbia University Press.

Hetherington, M. E., Camara, K. A., & Featherman, D. L. (1983). Achievement and intellectual functioning of children in one-parent households. In J. Spence (Ed.), *Achievement and achievement motives* (pp. 205–285). San Francisco: W. H. Freeman.

Marsiglio, W. (1991). Parental engagement activities with minor children. *Journal of Marriage and the Family, 53*, 973–986.

Murray, C. (1984). *Losing ground: American social policy, 1950–1980.* New York: Basic Books.

Pleck, J. H. (1987). American fathering in historical perspective. In M. S. Kimmel (ed.), *Changing men: New directions in research on men and masculinity* (pp. 83–97). Newbury Park, CA: Sage.

Rotundo, E. A. (1985). American fathering in historical perspective. *American Behavioral Scientist, 29*(1), 7–25.

Stack, C. B. (1974). *All our kin: Strategies for survival in the black community.* New York: Harper & Row.

Sullivan, M. L. (1989, January). Absent fathers in the inner city. *Annals of the American Academy of Political and Social Sciences, 501*, 48–58.

Testa, M., Astone, N. M., Krogh, M., & Neckerman, K. M. (1989, January). Employment and marriage among inner city fathers. *Annals of the American Academy of Political and Social Sciences, 501*, 79–91.

Tienda, M., & Stier, H. (1991). Joblessness and shiftlessness: Labor force activity in Chicago's inner city. In C. Jencks & P. Peterson (Eds.), *The urban underclass* (pp. 135–154). Washington, DC: Brookings Institution.

Weitzman, L. J. (1985). *The divorce revolution: The unexpected social and economic consequences for women and children in America.* New York: Free Press.

Wilson, W. J. (1987). *The truly disadvantaged: The inner city, the underclass, and public policy.* Chicago: University of Chicago Press.

Wilson, W. J., & Neckerman, K. M. (1986). Poverty and family structure: The widening gap between evidence and public issues. In S. H. Danziger & D. H. Weinberg (Eds.), *Fighting poverty: What works and what doesn't* (pp. 232–259). Cambridge, MA: Harvard University Press.

POSTSCRIPT

Have Men Lost Their Sense of Fatherhood?

From their research, Stier and Tienda conclude that fathers who could not find family-sustaining jobs or who lost such jobs had difficulty forming economically secure families. Despite discovering that jobs and family life were restricted by their economic circumstances, the fathers surveyed continued to provide whatever support they could. Some noncustodial fathers made it their mission to persuade other relatives to extend the family circle and give care and support to their children.

Blankenhorn worries that fathers' role in the family has shrunk dramatically over the past several generations. He fears that the very idea of fatherhood is being lost, or fragmented. He speculates that society no longer seems to have a basic set of core expectations or goals for fathers. He concludes that Americans are no longer sure of what being a good father means. Today, men strive to be merely "good enough" fathers.

Social critics have been quick to point out that, given the economic and social times we live in, it would be advantageous to find ways of fostering intimacy, caring, responsibility, and interdependence that extend beyond ourselves and our immediate families. In her book *It Takes a Village* (Scholastic, 1996), Hillary Clinton suggests broadening our definition of nurturing and obligation to encompass more than the nuclear family unit. Her message seems to be that families need stronger connections to the larger social world and that communities, work environments, and government need to be more supportive of children and families.

SUGGESTED READINGS

H. B. Biller, *Fathers and Families* (Auburn House, 1993).

M. H. Bornstein, ed., *Handbook of Parenting, vol. 4: Applied and Practical Parenting* (Lawrence Erlbaum, 1995).

S. Coltrane and K. Allan, "New Fathers and Old Stereotypes: Representations of Masculinity in 1980s Television Advertising," *Masculinities*, 2 (1994): 1–25.

N. A. Crowell and E. M. Leeper, *America's Fathers and Public Policy* (National Academy Press, 1994).

W. Marsiglio, ed., *Fatherhood: Contemporary Theory, Research, and Social Policy* (Sage Publications, 1995).

Internet: gopher://gopher-cec.mes.umn.edu:1300/11/FatherNet

ISSUE 10

Are Mothers the Main Barrier to Fathers' Involvement in Childrearing?

YES: Denise Schipani, from "The Mothering Double Standard," *Child* (September 1991)

NO: Brent A. McBride, from "The Effects of a Parent Education/Play Group Program on Father Involvement in Child Rearing," *Family Relations* (July 1990)

ISSUE SUMMARY

YES: Denise Schipani, a writer who publishes frequently on women's and family issues, portrays mothers as the primary roadblock to fathers' active participation in childrearing.

NO: Brent A. McBride, a professor of human development and family studies, argues that fathers' limited parental involvement is strongly linked to their own lack of knowledge and experience.

Mothers have traditionally been more involved than fathers in the daily lives of their children. Several attempts have been made to explain this lopsided arrangement, including the much-debated notion, briefly popular in the 1980s, that women have an instinctive drive to mother, termed by one writer as "mother hunger." Regardless of which theory enjoys public attention, most people are now convinced that fathers need to be more involved with their children.

In the 1990s a concerted effort has been made to convince fathers that they make unique and important contributions to their children's development; that fathers really do matter as parents. One only has to look at the cover of *Vanity Fair* with actor Jack Nicholson surrounded by babies, watch movies such as *Three Men and a Baby, Undercover Blues,* or *Sleepless in Seattle,* or read interviews in which celebrity fathers Eddie Murphy and Tom Cruise talk about the joys of fatherhood to understand that being a father—as far as the media is concerned—is in. A favorite pose of print advertisers, enamored of the images of fathers and children, is of a half-naked father cuddling a bare-bottomed infant. Lead articles in news and women's magazines herald the emergence of the new father as an aware, concerned, and involved parent.

According to a recent Gallup poll, American mothers who are tired of having an overload of responsibilities at home and in the workplace are asking where this new father can be found. Men, feeling the rising pressure to take on a larger share of parenting responsibilities, respond that they would like to help out or even share equally child-care responsibilities—but many seem at a loss on how to proceed. There appears to be a problem with moving from attitude adjustment to actual behavior.

Barriers line the passage from the old fatherhood to the new fatherhood. Men claim that employers, families, friends, and colleagues act as gatekeepers to parenthood—offering little in the way of support but much in the way of criticism for behavior construed as "slacking off" from the male breadwinner role. Fathers get the message that fathering is okay but that work must always come first. They also complain of having to struggle for any quality time alone with their children.

Is fathers' lower parental involvement part of a much broader social and cultural problem, as Brent A. McBride proposes? Or is men's neglect of their parenting responsibilities simply a result of women not wanting to give up control of the family domain, as Denise Schipani suggests? According to Schipani, mothers give verbal support to greater father involvement, saying they need and want husbands to be more active parents. But, she argues, mothers do not truly trust fathers' parenting skills and so they keep fathers at arm's length from many meaningful parent-child interactions. Mothers, men complain, want perfection. They have unbending standards on how a child is to be fed, bathed, dressed, soothed, and put to bed. There seems to be no room for fathers to develop their own parenting skills. Schipani advocates a five-step plan for making room for daddy.

McBride, in contrast, views fathers' parental reluctance as the result of a lack of a preparation for fatherhood and a dearth of social and institutional support for the fathering role. He advocates father support groups where men can meet and discuss parental concerns, offer advice to each other, and learn child-rearing skills.

YES

Denise Schipani

THE MOTHERING DOUBLE STANDARD

The tension in the car was almost palpable. JoAnn Myers [these people's names have been changed at their request], a college professor in Iowa City, Iowa, sat in the backseat with her 8-week-old daughter Kaylin, while her husband Ted, an advertising executive, concentrated grimly on the road. They had spent the day at Ted's parents' house, and that afternoon Kaylin started fussing. "I think she's tired," Ted had offered. "I'll put her down on her quilt on the floor; she'll fall asleep there."

"No, you're wrong," JoAnn announced. "She's hungry. I'll nurse her and then she'll fall asleep in the car." JoAnn briskly took her daughter from Ted's arms. Soon, a familiar argument ensued. Ted accused JoAnn of ignoring—even ridiculing—his attempts to help care for Kaylin; JoAnn insisted she simply knew better.

"I told Ted, 'If I came to your office and started suggesting ideas for ads, you'd probably tell me how to do it.' Well, motherhood is *my* job. *I* read the parenting books. *I'm* with her all day. I feel like I'm the expert," JoAnn says.

But Ted saw things differently. "JoAnn would say she needed help—but when I offered to take Kaylin, she handed me the baby and then stood over me. It was like she didn't trust me," he says.

For many parents like the Myerses, a double standard appears to be in operation. Today's mothers are determined to tackle everything from career concerns to cleaning bathrooms to bringing up kids. Their big complaint: a lack of help—primarily from dad. In a 1990 Roper Organization poll, 70 percent of working mothers reported that if men simply increased their participation at home, the strain of doing it all would be eased.

Not only is it in mom's best interest to let her husband into the parenting circle, it's also good for the child. "In the past, the mark of a good father was his ability to act as a 'babysitter,' to pinch-hit for his wife," says Martin Greenberg, M.D., a San Diego psychiatrist and author of *The Birth of a Father.* "But good fathering goes beyond merely lending a hand. Kids actually need a father's parenting contributions."

Barriers keeping dads off the primary-care track range from professional pressure to cultural ideals about men. But a major reason may be mom: Why do moms crave control, and how can they give some of it up—for everyone's good?

THE PSYCHOLOGY OF TERRITORIALITY

The evidence is overwhelming: Kids need their dads, dads want to be with their kids, and moms need a break. Yet the sneaky secret remains that women are territorial when it comes to child-rearing. Part of the reason stems from basic psychology. "Mothers, who learn from an early age that caretaking is their domain, are reassured by sticking to their own routine," notes Karen Shanor, Ph.D., a clinical psychologist in private practice in Washington, D.C. "In order to let her husband take over some child-rearing tasks, a woman may feel she has to 'train' him in the 'right' way to do it—that is, *her* way." Thus, as much as a woman protests that she wants her husband to lend a hand, she may ultimately decide that it's not worth the trouble to teach him how.

Territorial feelings are not limited to stay-at-home moms, although they may be more pronounced for them. "Because the stay-at-home mother has given up her employment to be her child's primary caregiver, she begins to see the home as her domain," says Dr. Shanor. "It's her instinct to protect her 'turf,' her 'identity.'"

Mattie Gershenfeld, Ph.D., a psychologist and president of the Couples Learning Center near Philadelphia, agrees: "Mothers who are with their kids during the day often complain that their husbands are the 'stars' in the family—when daddy comes home, the kids flock to him. On an unconscious level, she may be jealous of her husband's 'star status.'" If dad then feeds the kids dinner or plays with them, he rises in their estimation of him—while mom may end up feeling somewhat displaced.

A working mother may experience another pitfall of the double standard: guilt. "She gets home and is faced with an evening of childcare chores," says Dr. Gershenfeld. "She may see evening hours as a way to make up for the caretaking time she's missed all day, or worry that accepting her husband's help is a tacit admission of her failure to handle her dual role as dedicated mom and career person."

Of course, all the blame for the parenting double standard should not fall on mothers; fathers play a part, too. "Men receive cultural messages from the time they are little boys," asserts Dr. Gershenfeld. "They are told they must be in control of any situation. And most men are taught very little about babies. Handling a tiny, helpless infant can be very daunting—and he may not admit he needs direction."

THE DISCONTENTED DAD

What happens to dads who try to do the right thing, but are eclipsed by their wives' super-efficient mothering skills? "A father doesn't like being 'watched' as he takes care of his child. He gets the message that his wife places little confidence in his abilities," says Dr. Shanor.

Eventually, "he falls out of the loop," adds Dr. Gershenfeld. "He gets the idea that there is a coalition between his wife and child—to which he can't contribute."

Feeling left out can have lasting effects on his desire to parent. One outcome: "The father may no longer view childcare as a normal or enjoyable responsibility. He'll only pitch in grudgingly when his wife insists, to keep her from being angry with him," says Dr. Gershenfeld. He may even stop offering assistance altogether —something no mother would like to see happen.

The "distant dad" problem is most obvious during infancy. Many fathers, uncomfortable with their real or perceived ineptness at the care and handling of a baby, may unconsciously opt out until a later date—say, when the kid's old enough to throw a baseball—and the mystery of infancy is long past. But that's a mistake. "The relationship between father and child is constantly revitalized —it's not something you can pick up somewhere along the line," says Dr. Greenberg. Starting the father-child relationship early on is easier and more satisfying than trying to establish connection with a child at a later date.

MAKING ROOM FOR DADDY

Mothers who want—and deserve—more help with kids and home are justified. But experts all agree that resolving this issue is a challenge both partners must face —as individuals, and then together. The most important step for a mother may be discovering how her own emotions affect the double standard. "Realize that you may have mixed feelings on the subject," says Dr. Shanor. "What you may ideally want—that your husband be the perfect co-parent—may not really be what you're asking for with your actions and your attitude. Most mothers have quite a lot invested in being their children's primary caregivers—it's a point of pride." The

THE 5-STEP PLAN FOR LETTING GO

These steps can help too-possessive moms let go of the idea that they have to do it all—and build the foundation for a better father-child relationship.

1. GIVE HIM A CHANCE. Allow your spouse time alone with the baby on a regular basis so he can start to form a one-on-one relationship with his child.

2. ACKNOWLEDGE DIFFERENCES. Praise his parenting efforts—even when he does things in a way you ordinarily might not. His way isn't necessarily *wrong*.

3. BE FAIR. Provide him with a range of parenting experiences—from diaper duty to bathing—so he's sharing the chores as well as the fun stuff.

4. GRANT HIM CONFIDENCE. Fight the impulse to call home every time you leave him alone in the house with the baby for a few hours.

5. STEP ASIDE. If you still feel the urge to hover over your spouse or correct his parenting behavior, leave the house—he'll manage.

father faces the task of breaking into the close mother-child relationship. The good news, notes Dr. Shanor: There's plenty of baby for everyone.

"One thing a mother should *not* do is try to 'train' her husband to father— either physically or emotionally," advises Dr. Greenberg. "She doesn't want a substitute mom; she wants an involved dad. She has to allow him *room*, the space to learn to do it himself his own way." In some cases, she may need to step completely out of the picture to keep from hovering. "Try to trust that, even though he doesn't parent just like you, however he does it is okay in its own way," says Dr. Gershenfeld.

Dad, too, may be at fault if he gives in too easily, Dr. Gershenfeld says. He may gamely agree to do bedtime duty, but then, frustrated that he can't find the pajamas with the feet or the favorite storybook, call for his wife to rescue him. If that is the case, she should simply tell him what he needs to know, and then leave the room.

Interestingly, note experts, the *child* has a hand in perpetuating the problem. A toddler who catches on to his father's discomfort may ask for his mother to feed him or put him to bed instead, But eventually kids whose fathers persist in caring for them come around. "Soon enough, even a very young child will realize that 'bedtime with Mommy' is one thing, and 'bedtime with Daddy' is another, but that both are fine," says Dr. Shanor. An older child will usually help her father. "If he's getting her dressed, she might say, 'No, Dad, I always wear sneakers to daycare.' This *should* happen; fathers and children need to learn routines together," says Dr. Shanor.

As tough as it may be for parents to shatter the double standard, the benefits of doing so outweigh the difficulties. Four months after that strained car ride home, for example, the Myerses are back on track. "It became obvious that if I continued to correct Ted, I would risk alienating him," says JoAnn. "Once we aired our feelings, we could work them out. Now, I leave him alone with Kaylin and enjoy my freedom. That's best for all of us."

That new attitude has had a marked effect on family dynamics. "It's wonderful to witness Ted's relationship with Kaylin," says JoAnn. "There are certain songs he sings to her, for example, that she loves. Also, he has a special way of calming her. It's great; if what I try doesn't work, he tries his way. Instead of fighting, we're enjoying her, each in our own way."

NO

Brent A. McBride

THE EFFECTS OF A PARENT EDUCATION/PLAY GROUP PROGRAM ON FATHER INVOLVEMENT IN CHILD REARING

Contrary to popular belief, increased levels of father involvement may not always have positive outcomes. Lamb, Pleck, and Levine (1985) have suggested that for paternal involvement to have positive consequences, it must be the result of the desires of both parents. Instead of insisting that increased levels of paternal involvement are universally desirable, Lamb and his colleagues have suggested that more attempts need to be made to increase the options available to fathers so that those who wish can become more involved in raising their children. There are different ways in which fathers can become involved in child rearing; some forms of involvement may suit some fathers better than others. The interesting question then becomes how parental options might be expanded or what factors constrain or limit these options.

At the present time there are limited options available to men for involvement in raising their children. Two factors may contribute to these limited options. The first is a lack of preparation for fatherhood. For a variety of reasons, many men feel unprepared to assume an active parental role and as a result, are reluctant to become deeply involved in the raising of their children. This lack of preparation can be seen in such areas as knowledge of normal child development (Klinman & Vukelich, 1985; Smith & Smith, 1981; Tomlinson, 1987), developmentally appropriate parenting skills (Palkovitz, 1984), and sensitivity to their children's needs (Easterbrooks & Goldberg, 1984; Russell, 1982a; Sagi, 1982). Palkovitz (1984) has suggested several reasons why fathers might be unprepared for an active parental role. Fathers often have little exposure to paternal role models, few social opportunities to prepare for fatherhood, limited institutional supports for the parental role, and a lack of father-child interactions that are obligatory.

A second constraining factor may be the lack of social and institutional support for the paternal role. In our society boys are not given opportunities

From Brent A. McBride, "The Effects of a Parent Education/Play Group Program on Father Involvement in Child Rearing," *Family Relations*, vol. 39, no. 3 (July 1990), pp. 250–256. Copyright © 1990 by The National Council on Family Relations, 3989 Central Avenue NE, Suite 550, Minneapolis, MN 55421. Reprinted by permission.

to develop skills needed to become a nurturing parent (Berman & Pedersen, 1987; Klinman, 1986). Further, when these boys reach adulthood and are ready to start families of their own, the social support and educational systems available to help mothers develop parenting skills are not available to them as fathers (Bolton, 1986; DeFrain, 1977; Levant & Doyle, 1983; Smith & Smith, 1981). This lack of preparation and parenting support limits the options open to fathers as they determine the amount and type of involvement they will have with their children. The purpose of this study is to examine whether a parent education program geared specifically for fathers would increase the type or amount of involvement men have with their young children, thereby overcoming the constraints limiting the parenting options available to them.

LITERATURE REVIEW

Researchers have recently looked more closely at the roles of fathers in child rearing. Early studies of paternal involvement tended to focus on outcomes such as the cognitive and sex-role development of the child rather than father involvement itself (Lamb, 1986). However, little empirical work has been done examining the various factors associated with paternal involvement, or how parent education and support programs designed specifically for fathers may influence this involvement (Dembo, Sweitzer, & Lawritzen, 1985; Lamb, 1986)....

The lack of a clear and consistent definition of father involvement has been a major obstacle to research and to the design and evaluation of parent programs for fathers (Baruch & Barnett, 1986a). Lamb and his colleagues (Lamb, Pleck, Charnov, & Levine, 1987) have recently proposed a three-part taxonomy (I. Interaction; II. Accessibility; III. Responsibility) that may help to overcome this limitation. Category I of the Lamb taxonomy (Interaction) involves the father interacting one-on-one with his children in activities such as playing with them or reading to them. In category II (Accessibility) the father may or may not be directly engaged in interaction, but is still available to his child. In category III (Responsibility) the father assumes responsibility for the welfare and care of his child. This involvement includes such tasks as making child care and baby-sitting arrangements or knowing when the child needs to go to the pediatrician. Lamb suggests that being responsible doesn't necessarily involve direct interaction with the child; the anxiety, worry, and contingency planning that comprise paternal responsibility often occurs when the father is doing something else.

The effects of father participation in a parent education/play group program on each of these types of involvement was investigated in the present study. Thus, one goal of the study was to assess a program designed to increase the parenting options of fathers who wish to become more involved with their children....

METHOD

Subjects

Participants were 30 fathers (15 treatment, 15 control) and their preschool-aged children. All subjects were volunteers identified through flyers placed in various preschools in the communities surrounding the university where the study took place....

Mean age for the fathers in the study was 34.97 years (range, 26 to 43 years). Mean age for the children was 34.8 months (range, 25 to 44 months). There were 17 (57%) boys and 13 (43%) girls participating in the study. Fourteen (47%) of the participating fathers had only one child, 13 (43%) had two, and 3 (10%) had three children. The majority of the fathers (70%) signed up to participate with their firstborn child. The ethnic make-up of the subjects included 80% white, 7% black, 7% Arabic, 3% Hispanic, and 3% Asian....

Treatment

Treatment group father-child pairs participated in a parent education/play group program that met for 2 hours on 10 consecutive Saturday mornings. This 10-week program had two major components; group discussion and father-child play time. Because many men lack a general knowledge of normal child development and parenting skills (Klinman & Vukelich, 1985; Palkovitz, 1984; Smith & Smith, 1981; Tomlinson, 1987) along with the motivational desire or societal options which would encourage them to actively participate in the ways described by Lamb (1986), one hour of each weekly treatment session was spent in group discussions focusing on these various issues....

During the second hour of the program fathers and their children participated in structured and nonstructured preschool-type group activities.... This portion of the program allowed the fathers to explore and discover different ways of interacting with their children and to develop sensitivity to the needs of their children....

As predicted..., the parent education/play group program is successful in increasing fathers' sense of competence in parenting skills....

This effect coincides with the nature of the discussion group portion of the treatment program. The main goal of this part of the program was to encourage the men to share their feelings and desires about involvement in child rearing. The fathers actively participated in discussions on topics such as discipline, education, sibling rivalry, ages and stages of development, and in the process, contributed their own personal feelings and experiences as parents. Taking these discussions into account, along with the support provided by the peer group and indirectly by the sponsoring institution, it is not surprising to find... significant increases in fathers' sense of competence....

IMPLICATIONS FOR PROGRAM DEVELOPMENT

Implications for future program development can be drawn from this study. The creation of parent education/play group programs such as the one assessed in this study may be one means by which family life and parent educators can help fathers become more comfortable with their paternal role and better prepare them to meet the demands of new role expectations. The results of this study have shown this program to be effective in helping fathers become more comfortable with their paternal role (a component of parental competence) and in increasing the amount of responsibility they assume in child rearing. Lamb (1986) suggests that "responsibility" is the most important type of involvement (when viewed in the context of equal opportunity for mothers and fathers), yet research indicates that fathers typically assume little or no responsibility. Research also indicates there is a strong relationship between parental competence and paternal involvement....

The present program and evaluation should be viewed as a "first step" in developing support programs for fathers of preschool-aged children. It is through these efforts that researchers and practitioners alike will develop a better understanding of the modifiability of father involvement. This improved understanding may lead to the development and implementation of parent education and support programs which can effectively increase fathers' parenting options.

REFERENCES

Berman, P. W., & Pedersen, F. A. (1987). Research on men's transitions to parenthood: An integrative discussion. In P. W. Berman & F. A. Pedersen (Eds.), *Men's transitions to parenthood: Longitudinal studies of early family experience* (pp. 217–242). Hillsdale, NJ: Lawrence Erlbaum.

Bolton, F. G. (1986). Today's father and the social services delivery system: A false promise. In M. E. Lamb (Ed.), *The father's role: Applied perspectives* (pp. 429–441). New York: Wiley.

DeFrain, J. D. (1977). Sexism in parenting manuals. *Family Coordinator, 26,* 245–251.

Dembo, M. H., Sweitzer, M., & Lawritzen, P. (1985). An evaluation of group parent education: Behavioral, P.E.T., and Adlerian programs. *Review of Educational Research, 55,* 155–200.

Easterbrooks, M. A., & Goldberg, W. A. (1984). Toddler development in the family: Impact of father involvement and parenting characteristics. *Child Development, 55,* 740–752.

Klinman, D. G. (1986). Fathers and the educational system. In M. E. Lamb (Ed.), *The father's role: Applied perspectives* (pp. 413–428). New York: Wiley.

Klinman, D. G., & Vukelich, C. (1985). Mothers and fathers: Expectations for infants. *Family Relations, 34,* 305–313.

Lamb, M. E. (1986). The changing roles of fathers. In M. E. Lamb (Ed.), *The father's role: Applied perspectives* (pp. 3–27). New York: Wiley.

Lamb, M. E., Pleck, J. H., & Levine, J. A. (1985). The role of the father in child development: The effects of increased paternal involvement. In B. B. Lahey & A. E. Kazdin (Eds.), *Advances in clinical child psychology* (Vol. 8, pp. 229–266). New York: Plenum.

Lamb, M. E., Pleck, J. H., Charnov, E. L., & Levine, J. A. (1987). A biosocial perspective on paternal behavior and involvement. In J. B. Lancaster, J. Altman, A. Rossi, & L. Sherrod (Eds.), *Parenting across the lifespan: Biosocial perspectives* (pp. 111–142). Chicago: Aldine.

Levant, R. F., & Doyle, G. F. (1983). An evaluation of a parent education program for fathers of school-aged children. *Family Relations, 32,* 29–37.

Palkovitz, R. (1984). Parental attitudes and fathers' interactions with their 5-month-old infants. *Developmental Psychology, 20,* 1054–1060.

Russell, G. (1982a). Highly participant Australian fathers: Some preliminary findings. *Merrill-Palmer Quarterly, 28,* 137–156.

Sagi, A. (1982). Antecedents and consequences of various degrees of paternal involvement in child rearing: The Israeli Project. In M. E. Lamb (Ed.), *Nontraditional families: Parenting and child development* (pp. 205–232). Hillsdale, NJ: Lawrence Erlbaum.

Smith, R. M., & Smith C. W. (1981). Childrearing and single parent fathers. *Family Relations, 30,* 411–417.

Tomlinson, P. S. (1987). Father involvement with first-born infants: Interpersonal and situational factors. *Pediatric Nursing, 13,* 101–105.

POSTSCRIPT

Are Mothers the Main Barrier to Fathers' Involvement in Childrearing?

Two different rationales are used to explain fathers' neglect of child-rearing responsibilities. One rationale rests on the belief that the lack of a father's participation in parenting is really the mother's problem: mothers have a vested interest in keeping fathers isolated from meaningful parenting activities because mothers supposedly gain power and a sense of control from being the most significant parent. The second rationale relies on the conviction that a father's participation in parenting is essentially a societal issue, reflecting cultural assumptions about masculinity and male roles.

The selections by Schipani and McBride touch on each of these rationales. Which perspective do you find most plausible? Are fathers on the verge of significantly increasing the nurturing and caregiving time they spend with their children? Are mothers threatened by fathers' new interest in parenting, causing them to put obstacles in the path of improved father-child relations? Do mothers portray the body of knowledge and skills necessary for good parenting as vast and overwhelming, and do fathers face an educational void concerning parenting skills and patterns of child development? Or are mothers, grateful for fathers' active involvement with children, acting as support systems for fathers as they grapple with new parenting roles?

SUGGESTED READINGS

P. W. Berman and F. A. Pedersen, eds., *Men's Transitions to Parenthood: Longitudinal Studies of Early Family Experience* (Lawrence Erlbaum, 1987).

H. B. Biller, *Fathers and Families: Paternal Factors in Child Development* (Auburn House, 1993).

M. E. Lamb, *The Father's Role: Cross-Cultural Perspectives* (Lawrence Erlbaum, 1987).

K. D. Pruett, *The Nurturing Father* (Warner, 1987).

J. Snarey, *How Fathers Care for the Next Generation* (Harvard University Press, 1993).

B. C. Volling and J. Belsky, "Multiple Determinants of Fathering During Early Infancy in Dual-Earner and Single-Earner Families," *Journal of Marriage and the Family*, 53 (1991): 461–474.

L. Yablonsky, *Fathers and Sons* (Gardner, 1990).

Internet: http://ericps.ed.uiuc.edu/nccic/nccichome.html

ISSUE 11

Would a "Mommy Track" Benefit Employed Women?

YES: Felice N. Schwartz, from "Management Women and the New Facts of Life," *Harvard Business Review* (January/February 1989)

NO: Barbara Ehrenreich and Deirdre English, from "Blowing the Whistle on the 'Mommy Track,'" *Ms.* (July/August 1989)

ISSUE SUMMARY

YES: Felice N. Schwartz, president and founder of Catalyst, an organization that consults with corporations on the career and leadership development of women, argues that it is in the best interests of corporations to retain valued managerial women by creating two career paths within the organization, one for "career-primary" women and the other for "career-and-family" women.

NO: Journalists Barbara Ehrenreich and Deirdre English maintain that the "mommy track" notion is based on stereotypical assumptions about women and that it ignores the real issue of why corporations continue to promote work policies that are incompatible with family life.

The composition of the workforce is changing; women are comprising an increasing percentage of new workplace entrants. Many of these women have college degrees and seek management positions. As they advance in rank and status, the majority of managerial women marry, and most continue to work after having children, taking only a limited amount of time off for maternity leave. Upon returning to work after leave, women are usually expected to retain primary responsibility for taking care of the family and, at the same time, pursue active careers.

Such expectations create problems for women with children because traditional work schedules require excessive work hours. The workday generally begins very early or ends very late or both, which prevents employed women from spending time with their families. In addition, work scheduling typically does not mesh well with child-care arrangements. Finding reliable child care is among the most problematic and worrisome concerns for parents. Providing care for children when they are too ill to go to day care is particularly difficult. The result is that career mothers with small children often feel overloaded, anxious, and guilty.

Corporations typically respond to women's concerns by initiating seminars on stress management and advising women to focus on finding new ways to balance career goals and parenthood. Such programs are inexpensive to initiate and maintain and spare organizations the financial costs of instituting other, more comprehensive but more costly programs. These stopgap measures, currently used by many organizations, are not very beneficial for either women or corporations, and they have not been proven effective in reducing the absenteeism, tardiness, and employee turnover associated with child-care issues.

Another reason why corporations seem hesitant to implement policies that are friendlier to family concerns is that many supervisors in the managerial hierarchy made their career advances during a time when women were primarily homemakers and family caregivers. The career paths of these supervisors are characterized by the primacy of career goals over family roles. When new work patterns are proposed to ease the burden of work responsibilities on family life, supervisors often view them as alien to what seems appropriate and normative from their own personal perspectives and experiences.

Despite these barriers, some employers—aware of the changing demographics of the workforce, worried about losing productive female employees, and conscious of the need to attract talented women for future positions —have begun to listen more intently to women's concerns and to develop and implement policies that are targeted to family needs, such as maternity leave, flexible work hours, and part-time employment. Women are increasingly voicing unhappiness about being in positions where job expectations are incompatible with family life. Men with young children are also becoming more aware of work and family issues. Since women today are likely to be employed, their husbands are under greater pressure than in the past to assume more of the child-rearing responsibilities and household tasks. Men and women alike are becoming more vocal in supporting corporate policies that help combine work and family roles.

The authors of the following selections believe that corporations must adjust work policies to attract and keep talented women. Felice N. Schwartz believes that corporations should develop two career paths for women. One path would be for those who intend to pursue careers as their primary life goal, and the other path would be for women who want to combine career and family roles by temporarily working part-time after having children. Barbara Ehrenreich and Deirdre English maintain that Schwartz's "mommy track" would perpetuate gender role stereotypes. They also claim that the "mommy track" would be difficult to administer fairly and would continue to promote work policies that are incompatible with contemporary family life.

YES

Felice N. Schwartz

MANAGEMENT WOMEN AND
THE NEW FACTS OF LIFE

A new study by one multinational corporation shows that the rate of turnover in management positions is $2^1/_2$ times higher among top-performing women than it is among men. A large producer of consumer goods reports that one half of the women who take maternity leave return to their jobs late or not at all. And we know that women also have a greater tendency to plateau or to interrupt their careers in ways that limit their growth and development....

Career interruptions, plateauing, and turnover are expensive. The money corporations invest in recruitment, training, and development is less likely to produce top executives among women than among men, and the invaluable company experience that developing executives acquire at every level as they move up through management ranks is more often lost....

It is terribly important that employers draw the right conclusions from the studies now being done. The studies will be useless—or worse, harmful—if all they teach us is that women are expensive to employ. What we need to learn is how to reduce that expense, how to stop throwing away the investments we make in talented women, how to become more responsive to the needs of the women that corporations *must* employ if they are to have the best and the brightest of all those now entering the work force....

*　*　*

The one immutable, enduring difference between men and women is maternity. Maternity is not simply childbirth but a continuum that begins with an awareness of the ticking of the biological clock, proceeds to the anticipation of motherhood, includes pregnancy, childbirth, physical recuperation, psychological adjustment, and continues on to nursing, bonding, and child rearing. Not all women choose to become mothers, of course, and among those who do, the process varies from case to case depending on the health of the mother and baby, the values of the parents, and the availability, cost, and quality of child care.

In past centuries, the biological fact of maternity shaped the traditional roles of the sexes. Women performed the home-centered functions that related to the bearing and nurturing of children. Men did the work that required great physical strength. Over time, however, family size contracted, the community assumed greater responsibility for the care and education of children, packaged foods and household technology reduced the work load in the home, and technology eliminated much of the need for muscle power at the workplace. Today, in the developed world, the only role still uniquely gender related is childbearing. Yet men and women are still socialized to perform their traditional roles....

In the decades ahead, as the socialization of boys and girls and the experience and expectations of young men and women grow steadily more androgynous, the differences in workplace behavior will continue to fade. At the moment, however, we are still plagued by disparities in perception and behavior that make the integration of men and women in the workplace unnecessarily difficult and expensive.

Let me illustrate with a few broadbrush generalizations. Of course, these are only stereotypes, but I think they help to exemplify the kinds of preconceptions that can muddy the corporate waters.

Men continue to perceive women as the rearers of their children, so they find it understandable, indeed appropriate, that women should renounce their careers to raise families. Edmund Pratt, CEO of Pfizer, once asked me in all sincerity, "Why would any woman choose to be a chief financial officer rather than a full-time mother?" By condoning and taking pleasure in women's traditional behavior, men reinforce it. Not only do they see parenting as fundamentally female, they see a career as fundamentally male—either an unbroken series of promotions and advancements toward CEOdom or

stagnation and disappointment. This attitude serves to legitimize a woman's choice to extend maternity leave and even, for those who can afford it, to leave employment altogether for several years. By the same token, men who might want to take a leave after the birth of a child know that management will see such behavior as a lack of career commitment, even when company policy permits parental leave for men.

Women also bring counterproductive expectations and perceptions to the workplace. Ironically, although the feminist movement was an expression of women's quest for freedom from their homebased lives, most women were remarkably free already. They had many responsibilities, but they were autonomous and could be entrepreneurial in how and when they carried them out. And once their children grew up and left home, they were essentially free to do what they wanted with their lives. Women's traditional role also included freedom from responsibility for the financial support of their families. Many of us were socialized from girlhood to expect our husbands to take care of us, while our brothers were socialized from an equally early age to complete their educations, pursue careers, climb the ladder of success, and provide dependable financial support for their families. To the extent that this tradition of freedom lingers subliminally, women tend to bring to their employment a sense that they can choose to change jobs or careers at will, take time off, or reduce their hours.

Finally, women's traditional role encouraged particular attention to the quality and substance of what they did, specifically to the physical, psychological, and intellectual development of their children. This traditional focus may explain women's continuing tendency to search for more than monetary reward—intrinsic significance, social importance, meaning—in what they do. This too makes them more likely than men to leave the corporation in search of other values.

The misleading metaphor of the glass ceiling suggests an invisible barrier constructed by corporate leaders to impede the upward mobility of women beyond the middle levels. A more appropriate metaphor, I believe, is the kind of cross-sectional diagram used in geology. The barriers to women's leadership occur when potentially counterproductive layers of influence on women—maternity, tradition, socialization—meet management strata pervaded by the largely unconscious preconceptions, stereotypes, and expectations of men. Such interfaces do not exist for men and tend to be impermeable for women.

One result of these gender differences has been to convince some executives that women are simply not suited to top management. Other executives feel helpless. If they see even a few of their valued female employees fail to return to work from maternity leave on schedule or see one of their most promising women plateau in her career after the birth of a child, they begin to fear there is nothing they can do to infuse women with new energy and enthusiasm and persuade them to stay. At the same time, they know there is nothing they can do to stem the tide of women into management ranks.

Another result is to place every working woman on a continuum that runs from total dedication to career at one end to a balance between career and family at the other. What women discover is that the male corporate culture sees both extremes as unacceptable. Women who want the flexibility to balance their families and their careers are not adequately committed to the organization. Women who perform as aggressively and competitively as men are abrasive and unfeminine. But the fact is, business needs all the talented women it can get. Moreover, as I will explain, the women I call career-primary and those I call career-and-family each have particular value to the corporation.

* * *

Women in the corporation are about to move from a buyer's to a seller's market. The sudden, startling recognition that 80% of new entrants in the work force over the next decade will be women, minorities, and immigrants has stimulated a mushrooming incentive to "value diversity."

Women are no longer simply an enticing pool of occasional creative talent, a thorn in the side of the EEO officer, or a source of frustration to corporate leaders truly puzzled by the slowness of their upward trickle into executive positions. A real demographic change is taking place. The era of sudden population growth of the 1950s and 1960s is over. The birth rate has dropped about 40%, from a high of 25.3 live births per 1,000 population in 1957, at the peak of the baby boom, to a stable low of a little more than 15 per 1,000 over the last 16 years, and there is no indication of a return to a higher rate. The tidal wave of baby boomers that swelled the recruitment pool to overflowing seems to have been a one-time phenomenon. For 20 years, employers had the pick of a very large crop and were able to choose males almost exclusively for the executive track. But if future population remains fairly stable while the economy continues to expand, and if the new information society simultaneously creates a greater need for creative, educated managers, then the gap between supply and demand will grow dramatically and, with it, the competition for managerial talent.

The decrease in numbers has even greater implications if we look at the traditional source of corporate recruitment for leadership positions—white males from the top 10% of the country's best universities. Over the past decade, the increase in the number of women graduating from leading universities has been much greater than the increase in the total number of graduates, and these women are well represented in the top 10% of their classes.

The trend extends into business and professional programs as well. In the old days, virtually all MBAs were male. I remember addressing a meeting at the Harvard Business School as recently as the mid-1970s and looking out at a sea of exclusively male faces. Today, about 25% of that audience would be women. The pool of male MBAs from which corporations have traditionally drawn their leaders has shrunk significantly....

* * *

Under these circumstances, there is no question that the management ranks of business will include increasing numbers of women. There remains, however, the question of how these women will succeed—how long they will stay, how high they will climb, how completely they will fulfill their promise and potential, and what kind of return the corporation will realize on its investment in their training and development.

There is ample business reason for finding ways to make sure that as many of these women as possible will succeed. The first step in this process is to recognize that women are not all alike. Like men, they are individuals with differing talents, priorities, and motivations. For the sake of simplicity, let me focus on the two women I referred to earlier, on what I call the career-primary woman and the career-family woman.

Like many men, some women put their careers first. They are ready to make the same trade-offs traditionally made by the men who seek leadership positions. They make a career decision to put in extra hours, to make sacrifices in their personal lives, to make the most of every opportunity for professional development....

The secret to dealing with such women is to recognize them early, accept them, and clear artificial barriers from their path to the top. After all, the best of these women are among the best managerial talent you will ever see. And career-primary women have another important value to the company that men and other women lack. They can act as role models and mentors to younger women who put their careers first. Since upwardly mobile career-primary women still have few role models to motivate and inspire them, a company with women in its top echelon has a significant advantage in the competition for executive talent....

Clearing a path to the top for career-primary women has four requirements:

1. Identify them early.

2. Give them the same opportunity you give to talented men to grow and develop and contribute to company profitability. Give them client and customer responsibility. Expect them to travel and relocate, to make the same commitment to the company as men aspiring to leadership positions.

3. Accept them as valued members of your management team. Include them in every kind of communication. Listen to them.
4. Recognize that the business environment is more difficult and stressful for them than for their male peers. They are always a minority, often the only woman. The male perception of talented, ambitious women is at best ambivalent, a mixture of admiration, resentment, confusion, competitiveness, attraction, skepticism, anxiety, pride, and animosity....

Stereotypical language and sexist day-to-day behavior do take their toll on women's career development.... With notable exceptions, men are still generally more comfortable with other men, and as a result women miss many of the career and business opportunities that arise over lunch, on the golf course, or in the locker room.

* * *

The majority of women, however, are what I call career-and-family women, women who want to pursue serious careers while participating actively in the rearing of children. These women are a precious resource that has yet to be mined. Many of them are talented and creative. Most of them are willing to trade some career growth and compensation for freedom from the constant pressure to work long hours and weekends.

Most companies today are ambivalent at best about the career-and-family women in their management ranks. They would prefer that all employees were willing to give their all to the company. They believe it is in their best interests for all managers to compete for the top positions so the company will have the largest possible pool from which to draw its leaders....

These companies lose on two counts. First, they fail to amortize the investment they made in the early training and experience of management women who find themselves committed to family as well as to career. Second, they fail to recognize what these women could do for their middle management.

The ranks of middle managers are filled with people on their way up and people who have stalled. Many of them have simply reached their limits, achieved career growth commensurate with or exceeding their capabilities, and they cause problems because their performance is mediocre but they still want to move ahead. The career-and-family woman is willing to trade off the pressures and demands that go with promotion for the freedom to spend more time with her children. She's very smart, she's talented, she's committed to her career, and she's satisfied to stay at the middle level, at least during the early child-rearing years....

Consider a typical example, a woman who decides in college on a business career and enters management at age 22. For nine years, the company invests in her career as she gains experience and skills and steadily improves her performance. But at 31, just as the investment begins to pay off in earnest, she decides to have a baby. Can the company afford to let her go home, take another job, or go into business for herself? The common perception now is yes, the corporation can afford to lose her unless, after six or eight weeks or even three months of disability and maternity leave, she returns to work on a full-time schedule with the same vigor, commitment, and ambition that she showed before.

But what if she doesn't? What if she wants or needs to go on leave for six months or a year or, heaven forbid, five years? In this worst-case scenario, she works full-time from age 22 to 31 and from 36 to 65—a total of 38 years as opposed to the typical male's 43 years. That's not a huge difference. Moreover, my typical example is willing to work part-time while her children are young, if only her employer will give her the opportunity. There are two rewards for companies responsive to this need: higher retention of their best people and greatly improved performance and satisfaction in their middle management.

The high-performing career-and-family woman can be a major player in your company. She can give you a significant business advantage as the competition for able people escalates. Sometimes, too, if you can hold on to her, she will switch gears in mid-life and re-enter the competition for the top. The price you must pay to retain these women is threefold: you must plan for and manage maternity, you must provide the flexibility that will allow them to be maximally productive, and you must take an active role in helping to make family supports and high-quality, affordable child care available to all women....

* * *

Time spent in the office increases productivity if it is time well spent, but the fact that most women continue to take the primary responsibility for child care is a cause of distraction, diversion, anxiety, and absenteeism—to say nothing of the persistent guilt experienced by all working mothers. A great many women, per-haps most of all women who have always performed at the highest levels, are also frustrated by a sense that while their children are babies they cannot function at their best either at home or at work.

In its simplest form, flexibility is the freedom to take time off—a couple of hours, a day, a week—or to do some work at home and some at the office, an arrangement that communication technology makes increasingly feasible. At the complex end of the spectrum are alternative work schedules that permit the woman to work less than full-time and her employer to reap the benefits of her experience and, with careful planning, the top level of her abilities.

Part-time employment is the single greatest inducement to getting women back on the job expeditiously and the provision women themselves most desire. A part-time return to work enables them to maintain responsibility for critical aspects of their jobs, keeps them in touch with the changes constantly occurring at the workplace and in the job itself, reduces stress and fatigue, often eliminates the need for paid maternity leave by permitting a return to the office as soon as disability leave is over, and, not least, can greatly enhance company loyalty. The part-time solution works particularly well when a work load can be reduced for one individual in a department or when a full-time job can be broken down by skill levels and apportioned to two individuals at different levels of skill and pay.

I believe, however, that shared employment is the most promising and will be the most widespread form of flexible scheduling in the future. It is feasible at every level of the corporation except at the pinnacle, for both the short and the long term. It involves two people taking responsibility for one job....

Flexibility is costly in numerous ways. It requires more supervisory time to coordinate and manage, more office space, and somewhat greater benefits costs (though these can be contained with flexible benefits plans, prorated benefits, and, in two-paycheck families, elimination of duplicate benefits). But the advantages of reduced turnover and the greater productivity that results from higher energy levels and greater focus can outweigh the costs.

A few hints:

- Provide flexibility selectively. I'm not suggesting private arrangements subject to the suspicion of favoritism but rather a policy that makes flexible work schedules available only to high performers.
- Make it clear that in most instances (but not all) the rates of advancement and pay will be appropriately lower for those who take time off or who work part-time than for those who work full-time. Most career-and-family women are entirely willing to make that trade-off.
- Discuss costs as well as benefits. Be willing to risk accusations of bias. Insist, for example, that half time is half of whatever time it takes to do the job, not merely half of 35 or 40 hours....

* * *

Family supports—in addition to maternity leave and flexibility—include the provision of parental leave for men, support for two-career and single-parent families during relocation, and flexible benefits. But the primary ingredient is child care. The capacity of working mothers to function effectively and without interruption depends on the availability of good, affordable child care. Now that women make up almost half the work force and the growing percentage of managers, the decision to become involved in the personal lives of employees is no longer a philosophical question but a practical one. To make matters worse, the quality of child care has almost no relation to technology, inventiveness, or profitability but is more or less a pure function of the quality of child care personnel and the ratio of adults to children. These costs are irreducible. Only by joining hands with government and the public sector can corporations hope to create the vast quantity and variety of child care that their employees need.

Until quite recently, the response of corporations to women has been largely symbolic and cosmetic, motivated in large part by the will to avoid litigation and legal penalties. In some cases, companies were also moved by a genuine sense of fairness and a vague discomfort and frustration at the absence of women above the middle of the corporate pyramid. The actions they took were mostly quick, easy, and highly visible— child care information services, a three-month parental leave available to men as well as women, a woman appointed to the board of directors....

Now that interest is replacing indifference, there are four steps every company can take to examine its own experience with women:

1. Gather quantitative data on the company's experience with management-level women regarding turnover rates, occurrence of and return from maternity leave, and organizational level attained in relation to tenure and performance.

2. Correlate this data with factors such as age, marital status, and presence and age of children, and attempt to identify and analyze why women respond the way they do.

3. Gather qualitative data on the experience of women in your company and on how women are perceived by both sexes.

4. Conduct a cost-benefit analysis of the return on your investment in high-performing women. Factor in the cost to the company of women's negative reactions to negative experience, as well as the probable cost of corrective measures and policies. If women's value to your company is greater than the cost to recruit, train, and develop them—and of course I believe it will be—then you will want to do everything you can to retain them.

* * *

We have come a tremendous distance since the days when the prevailing male wisdom saw women as lacking the kind of intelligence that would allow them to succeed in business. For decades, even women themselves have harbored an unspoken belief that they couldn't make it because they couldn't be just like men, and nothing else would do. But now that women have shown themselves the equal of men in every area of organizational activity, now that they have demonstrated they can be stars in every field of endeavor, now we can all venture to examine the fact that women and men are different.

NO

Barbara Ehrenreich and
Deirdre English

BLOWING THE WHISTLE ON THE "MOMMY TRACK"

When a feminist has something bad to say about women, the media listen. Three years ago it was Sylvia Hewlett, announcing in her book *A Lesser Life* that feminism had sold women out by neglecting to win child-care and maternity leaves. This year it's Felice Schwartz, the New York–based consultant who argues that women—or at least the mothers among us—have become a corporate liability. They cost too much to employ, she argues, and the solution is to put them on a special lower-paid, low-pressure career track—the now-notorious "mommy track."

The "mommy track" story rated prominent coverage in the New York *Times* and *USA Today*, a cover story in *Business Week*, and airtime on dozens of talk shows. Schwartz, after all, seemed perfectly legitimate. She is the president of Catalyst, an organization that has been advising corporations on women's careers since 1962. She had published her controversial claims in no less a spot than the *Harvard Business Review* ("Management Women and the New Facts of Life," January-February 1989). And her intentions, as she put it in a later op-ed piece, seemed thoroughly benign: "to urge employers to create policies that help mothers balance career and family responsibilities."

Moreover, Schwartz's argument seemed to confirm what everybody already knew. Women haven't been climbing up the corporate ladder as fast as might once have been expected, and women with children are still, on average, groping around the bottom rungs. Only about 40 percent of top female executives have children, compared to 95 percent of their male peers. There have been dozens of articles about female dropouts: women who slink off the fast track, at age 30-something, to bear a strategically timed baby or two. In fact, the "mommy track"—meaning a lower-pressure, flexible, or part-time approach to work—was neither a term Schwartz used nor her invention. It was already, in an anecdotal sort of way, a well-worn issue.

Most of the controversy focused on Schwartz's wildly anachronistic "solution." Corporate employers, she advised, should distinguish between two categories of women: "career-primary" women, who won't interrupt their careers for children and hence belong on the fast track with the men, and "career-and-family" women, who should be shunted directly to the mommy track. Schwartz had no answers for the obvious questions: how is the employer supposed to sort the potential "breeders" from the strivers? Would such distinction even be legal? What about *fathers*? But in a sense, the damage had already been done. A respected feminist, writing in a respected journal, had made a case that most women can't pull their weight in the corporate world, and should be paid accordingly.

Few people, though, actually read Schwartz's article. The first surprise is that it contains *no* evidence to support her principal claim, that "the cost of employing women in management is greater than the cost of employing men." Schwartz offers no data, no documentation at all—except for two unpublished studies by two *anonymous* corporations. Do these studies really support her claim? Were they methodologically sound? Do they even exist? There is no way to know.

Few media reports of the "mommy track" article bothered to mention the peculiar nature of Schwartz's "evidence." We, however, were moved to call the *Harvard Business Review* and inquire whether the article was representative of its normal editorial standard. Timothy Blodgett, the executive editor, defended the article as "an expression of opinion and judgment." When we suggested that such potentially damaging "opinions" might need a bit of bolstering, he responded by defending Schwartz: "She speaks with a tone of authority. That comes through."

(The conversation went downhill from there, with Blodgett stating sarcastically, "I'm sure your article in *Ms.* will be

very objective." Couldn't fall much lower than the *Harvard Business Review*, we assured him.)

Are managerial women more costly to employ than men? As far as we could determine—with the help of the Business and Professional Women's Foundation and Women's Equity Action League— there is no *published* data on this point. A 1987 government study did show female managerial employees spending less time with each employer than males (5 years compared to 6.8 years), but there is no way of knowing what causes this turnover or what costs it incurs. And despite pregnancy, and despite women's generally greater responsibility for child-raising, they use up on the average only 5.1 sick days per year, compared to 4.9 for men.

The second surprise, given Schwartz's feminist credentials, is that the article is riddled with ancient sexist assumptions —for example, about the possibility of a more androgynous approach to child-raising *and* work. She starts with the unobjectionable statement that "maternity is biological rather than cultural." The same thing, after all, could be said of paternity. But a moment later, we find her defining maternity as "... a continuum that begins with an awareness of the ticking of the biological clock, proceeds to the anticipation of motherhood, includes pregnancy, childbirth, physical recuperation, psychological adjustment, and continues on to nursing, bonding, and child-rearing."

Now, pregnancy, childbirth, and nursing do qualify as biological processes. But slipping child-rearing into the list, as if changing diapers and picking up socks were hormonally programmed activities, is an old masculinist trick. Child-raising is a *social* undertaking, which may involve nannies, aunts, grandparents, day-care workers, or, of course, *fathers.*

Equally strange for a "feminist" article is Schwartz's implicit assumption that employment, in the case of married women, is strictly optional, or at least that *mothers* don't need to be top-flight earners. The "career-and-family woman," she tells us, is "willing" and "satisfied" to forgo promotions and "stay at the middle level." What about the single mother, or the wife of a low-paid male? But Schwartz's out-of-date—and class-bound—assumption that every woman is supported by a male breadwinner fits in with her apparent nostalgia for the era of the feminine mystique. "Ironically," she writes, "although the feminist movement was an expression of women's quest for freedom from their home-based lives, *most women were remarkably free already* [emphasis added]."

But perhaps the oddest thing about the "mommy track" article—even as an "expression of opinion and judgment"—is that it is full of what we might charitably call ambivalence or, more bluntly, self-contradictions. Take the matter of the "glass ceiling," which symbolized all the barriers, both subtle and overt, that corporate women keep banging their heads against. At the outset, Schwartz dismisses the glass ceiling as a "misleading metaphor." Sexism, in short, is not the problem.

Nevertheless, within a few pages, she is describing the glass ceiling (not by that phrase, of course) like a veteran. "Male corporate culture," she tells us, sees both the career-primary and the career-and-family woman as "unacceptable." The woman with family responsibilities is likely to be seen as lacking commitment to the organization, while the woman who *is* fully committed to the organization is likely to be seen as "abrasive and unfeminine." She goes on to cite the corporate male's "confusion, competitiveness," and his "stereotypical language and sexist... behavior," concluding that "with notable exceptions, men are still more comfortable with other men."

And we're supposed to blame *women* for their lack of progress in the corporate world?

Even on her premier point, that women are more costly to employ, Schwartz loops around and rebuts herself. Near the end of her article, she urges corporations to conduct their own studies of the costs of employing women—the two anonymous studies were apparently not definitive after all—and asserts confidently ("of course I believe") that the benefits will end up outweighing the costs. In a more recent New York *Times* article, she puts it even more baldly: "The costs of employing women pale beside the payoffs."

Could it be that Felice Schwartz and the editors of the *Harvard Business Review* are ignorant of that most basic financial management concept, the cost-benefit analysis? If the "payoffs" outweigh the costs of employing women—runny noses and maternity leaves included—then the net cost may indeed be *lower* than the cost of employing men.

In sum, the notorious "mommy track" article is a tortured muddle of feminist perceptions and sexist assumptions, good intentions and dangerous suggestions—unsupported by any acceptable evidence at all. It should never have been taken seriously, not by the media and not by the nation's most prestigious academic business publication. The fact that it was suggests that something serious *is* afoot: a backlash against America's high-status, better paid women, and potentially against all women workers.

We should have seen it coming. For the past 15 years upwardly mobile, managerial women have done everything possible to fit into an often hostile corporate world. They dressed up as nonthreatening corporate clones. They put in 70-hour workweeks; and of course, they postponed childbearing. Thanks in part to their commitment to the work world, the birthrate dropped by 16 percent since 1970. But now many of these women are ready to start families. This should hardly be surprising; after all, 90 percent of American women do become mothers.

But while corporate women were busily making adjustments and concessions, the larger corporate world was not. The "fast track," with its macho camaraderie and toxic work load, remains the only track to success. As a result, success is indeed usually incompatible with motherhood—as well as with any engaged and active form of fatherhood. The corporate culture strongly discourages *men* from taking parental leave even if offered. And how many families can afford to have both earners on the mommy track?

Today there's an additional factor on the scene—the corporate women who *have* made it. Many of them are reliable advocates for the supports that working parents need. But you don't have to hang out with the skirted-suit crowd for long to discover that others of them are impatient with, and sometimes even actively resentful of, younger women who are trying to combine career and family. Recall that 60 percent of top female executives are themselves childless. Others are of the "if I did it, so can you" school of thought. Felice Schwartz may herself belong in this unsisterly category. In a telling anecdote in her original article, she describes her own problems with an executive employee seeking maternity leave, and the "somewhat awkward conversations" that ensued.

* * *

Sooner or later, corporations will have to yield to the pressure for paid parental leave, flextime, and child care, if only because they've become dependent on female talent. The danger is that employers—no doubt quoting Felice Schwartz for legitimization—will insist that the price for such options be reduced pay and withheld promotions, i.e., consignment to the mommy track. Such a policy would place a penalty on parenthood, and the ultimate victims—especially if the policy trickles down to the already low-paid female majority—will of course be children.

Bumping women—or just fertile women, or married women, or whomever—off the fast track may sound smart to cost-conscious CEOs, but eventually it is the corporate culture itself that needs to slow down to a human pace. No one, male or female, works at peak productivity for 70 hours a week, year after year, without sabbaticals or leaves. Think of it this way. If the price of success were exposure to a toxic chemical, would we argue that only women should be protected? Work loads that are incompatible with family life are themselves a kind of toxin—to men as well as women, and ultimately to businesses as well as families.

POSTSCRIPT

Would a "Mommy Track" Benefit Employed Women?

There is little question that corporations need to address the unique problems that employed mothers face in the workplace. Some women eagerly resume their career activities at the end of their maternity leaves; others feel less committed but must continue to work because of family financial responsibilities. Still other career women with children opt to take additional time off and then work part-time for some months or years before returning to full-time employment.

Given that women do not always share the same needs, expectations, and motivations, what kinds of corporate policies should be implemented to help them successfully balance career and family roles? Schwartz believes that identifying "career-primary" women early in their careers and investing more heavily in their training as compared to "career-and-family" women is the best corporate response to this problem. Ehrenreich and English reply that policies that support stereotypical images and roles for women and relegate them to less powerful positions with lower pay and fewer company benefits early in their careers would not result in recruiting and retaining the most talented and productive women. They argue that corporations should acknowledge women's and men's changing roles in both family and work situations, and they challenge organizations to provide flexible options that better reflect the diversity of today's families.

In "A Mother's Dilemma," *Ms.* (July–August 1989), Kim Triedman discusses the middle-class mother who wants both a career and children. She describes the struggle of balancing these needs without much support from anyone. From her own experiences she writes, "Our fathers and mothers (who underwrote our higher education) remind us that 'our careers won't wait forever' and we 'didn't go to college for nothing.' Our employers give us explicit policy on maternity leave—and subtler shows of our bosses' displeasure. Our husbands let us know that the mortgage is due and our bank balances are dropping. And sadly, some of our career-oriented, childless female friends see us as total and unredeemable idiots."

Is a "mommy track" the answer? In what other ways might parents, friends, and employers be more supportive of career mothers? Some social commentators have suggested that corporations should also implement a "daddy track." Having both a "mommy track" and a "daddy track" would make balancing financial responsibilities and childrearing a *parental* concern rather than solely a *woman's* concern. Are fathers at least partially responsible for the evolution of the "mommy track" idea? That is, if fathers were more involved parents, would there be less need for a "mommy track"? Would this issue be less controversial if more women were corporate heads? What workplace policies might alleviate the need for a "mommy track"? Does corporate America have any obligation to be more supportive of parents in the workplace? Will businesses that continue to ignore or postpone support for parents suffer?

SUGGESTED READINGS

E. Ehrlich, "The Mommy Track: Juggling Kids and Careers In Corporate America Takes a Controversial Turn," *Business Week* (March 20, 1989): 126–134.

J. Fierman, "Why Women Still Don't Hit the Top," *Fortune,* 122 (1990): 40–58.

E. Hopkins, "Who Is Felice Schwartz and Why Is She Saying Those Terrible Things About Us?" *Working Woman* (October 1990): 116–120, 148.

G. W. Loveman, "The Case of the Part-Time Partner," *Harvard Business Review,* 68 (1990): 12–29.

K. O'Neill and A. Tocco, "Are Child Care Assistance Programs a Crucial Investment?" *Financial Executive,* 6 (1990): 19–23.

C. R. Stoner and R. I. Hartman, "Family Responsibilities and Career Progress: The Good, the Bad, and the Ugly," *Business Horizons,* 33 (1990): 7–14.

Internet: `gopher://gopher-cyfernet.mes.umn.edu:4242/11/ChildCare/EmployerOptions`

ISSUE 12

Should Surrogate Parenting Be Permitted?

YES: Monica B. Morris, from "Reproductive Technology and Restraints," *Society* (March/April 1988)

NO: Richard John Neuhaus, from "Renting Women, Buying Babies and Class Struggles," *Society* (March/April 1988)

ISSUE SUMMARY

YES: Sociology professor Monica B. Morris maintains that surrogate mothering represents a positive advance in reproductive technology and that carefully regulating its use will protect women from being exploited.

NO: Richard John Neuhaus, director of the Rockford Institute Center on Religion and Society, denounces surrogate mothering as "a new form of trade in human beings" and argues that the practice leads to increased division and hostility between the upper and lower classes.

Approximately 10 to 15 percent of married couples in the United States who want to have children find they are not able to bear children due to infertility problems attributable to one or both couple members. These problems can be the result of any of a number of conditions, such as a low sperm count, irreparably damaged fallopian tubes, or developmental anomalies. When infertility is discovered, there are options to be explored, choices to be made, and questions to be contemplated: Is marriage only for having children? What role would children play in our lives as married people? How important is it to us as individuals, as a couple, as members of extended families, and as members of a larger community to be parents? Can we adopt? Are infants available who are somewhat like us? Is artificial insemination a legitimate moral or religious option? Who would act as donor? How vital is it to carry on the family name? Should we consider adopting a "hard to place" or "unwanted" child? Can we afford the expenses? How will the extra efforts put into becoming parents affect our marriage?

Depending on the circumstances, surrogate mothering, in which a couple pays a woman to become pregnant with the husband's baby and then to give the baby to the couple once it is born, is one option for couples facing infertility. But it does pose dilemmas that are not easily resolved for the couple, the potential surrogate, and the larger social order.

Collaborative reproduction may have positive outcomes for the concerned couple: parenting needs may be met, sex-linked illnesses that could be passed on to the couple's children can be avoided, and marital needs based on the expectation to bear and raise children may be satisfied, all of which could contribute to a better marriage. However, the decision to take this route could spark moral or ethical dilemmas for the individuals involved, their extended families, and the larger community.

The debate presented here raises concerns about the possibility of exploitation by couples seeking surrogate contracts. One side objects to surrogate mothering as a form of human trafficking and argues that a couple who utilizes a surrogate to bear their child is essentially renting that woman. Also, because she is being paid to carry the child to term, the surrogate can be held to whatever stipulations the paying couple wishes to put in the contract, no matter how strict they may seem. The opposing side argues that any possible misuse or abuse of surrogate motherhood can be controlled through legal regulation. Furthermore, it is vital that the practice not be repressed because it is an important breakthrough in biotechnology that, properly utilized, can bring greater happiness to all involved.

In the following selections, Monica B. Morris argues that surrogate mothering is "miraculous" and that regulation will indeed prevent it from being misused. On the opposing side, Richard John Neuhaus argues that surrogate mothering should be outlawed, partly because it exploits the lower class.

YES
Monica B. Morris

REPRODUCTIVE TECHNOLOGY
AND RESTRAINTS

We are on the edge of a biotechnical revolution as profound in its implications as was the Industrial Revolution—and we are as unprepared for this one as we were for that. To believe we can outlaw surrogate parenting is to believe with the Luddites that the Industrial Revolution could be stopped by wrecking the machinery that made it possible.

Many thinkers, including Richard John Neuhaus, are adamant that surrogate motherhood should be outlawed. The reasons they give are many and, for the most part, sensible and humane. For Neuhaus, the main objection to surrogate motherhood is that it is a form of trade in which those with money exploit poor, or poorer, women and that, in the United States, in deciding matters like the Baby M case, money speaks louder than morality, ethics, or compassion.

As we spill gallons of ink on paper in discussion of social class and exploitation in the Baby M case, technological advances continue and the topic widens and deepens to include a dozen more issues, so that the "problem" becomes not one but many, so densely interwoven that solutions become ever more elusive. The speed of new discoveries and of refinements to existing technology becomes apparent when the kind of arrangement between Mary Beth Whitehead and the Sterns is referred to in a recent edition of the television program, "Nova," as "traditional surrogacy." This "traditional" surrogacy has been going on for over a decade. . . .

[Today's] biotechnical achievements are miraculous, offering hope to couples who long to have children but who, until now, have not been successful. Estimates of infertility vary between one in seven and one in five couples, and one must feel compassion for those who want children and cannot have them. Those so placed talk of their suffering, their pain, their "obsession," with having a baby. Women give up jobs, careers, to devote all their time to fertility treatments. There has even been a play on the subject, David Rudkin's bitter *Ashes*, that depicts one infertile couple's obsessive and, ultimately, fruitless efforts to procreate.

Human-made miracles appear to offend some who believe that only God can work miracles. Yet, since its beginning, technology has attempted to

From Monica B. Morris, "Reproductive Technology and Restraints," *Society*, vol. 25, no. 3 (March/April 1988). Copyright © 1988 by Transaction Publishers. Reprinted by permission.

conquer nature and make it work for us rather than against us. Scientific discoveries, from the time of Copernicus on, have been strongly resisted as against the will of God or as sacrilegious. According to the scriptures, women are to bring forth offspring in "sorrow"; science has eased our sorrow, and it has reduced the dangers that came "naturally" before we understood enough to wash our hands before plunging them into the bodies of women delivering babies.

Science, as has been repeatedly, and often passionately, argued, cannot determine morality. Given the large numbers of couples in despair over their infertility, the deep pool of poor women who might be recruited as surrogate mothers or as egg donors, and the skill of entrepreneurs in generating "needs" as yet unrealized, the potential for misuse of the reproductive technology, and for the abuse and exploitation of all parties, is vast. It raises disturbing questions about how we are to manage our technological marvels. How can we assure they are used for good? What, indeed, is "good," and for whom is it good?

BEST INTERESTS OF THE CHILD

The United States is not the only country grappling with these problems. A widely reported surrogacy case was ruled upon in Great Britain at about the same time as the Baby M case was going through the New Jersey Courts. On March 12, 1987, a surrogate mother was granted custody of six-month-old twins, a boy and a girl, conceived by artificial insemination. Like Mary Beth Whitehead, after the birth the surrogate refused to hand the babies over to the father and his wife. The judge, Sir John Arnold, said he had heard nothing that "might be

taken to outweigh the advantages to these children of preserving the link to the mother to whom they are bonded and who has exercised a satisfactory degree of maternal care." Sir John saw nothing shameful in the arrangements between the parties but that "ultimately, the welfare of the children is the first and paramount consideration which the court must, by statute, take into account and that is what I do." Unlike Judge Sorkow, in deciding the best interest of the child, Sir John did not weigh the wealth of the father as important. The birth mother was unmarried and on social security; one reason she offered herself as a surrogate mother was to raise money to bring up her seven-year-old son. At last report, the mother was seeking child support for the twins from their father who, under present legislation may have to pay maintenance costs until the twins are sixteen years old, even though he has no parental rights. Appeals by the father may set precedents in this hitherto uncharted area.

Although both Judge Arnold and Judge Sorkow stated their concerns with the children in these custody cases and what would be best for them, each ruled differently. For Judge Arnold, the best interest of a child lies in preserving the link to its mother. For Judge Sorkow, the close bonding of Mary Beth Whitehead to her child was dismissed as irrelevant. Under the terms of the contract, she should not have allowed herself to become emotionally involved. Yet, in discussing custody of children in adoption cases, when birth mothers change their minds and want to keep their babies, adoption and child-development experts, as well as judges, have seen some risk of long-term emotional disturbance to a child who is taken from the care of one woman and given into the care of another at between six months and two-and-a-half years of age. The adult most suited to making a child feel wanted is the one with whom the child has already had, and continues to have, an affectionate bond. This would seem to apply to Baby M, whose mother nursed her from birth and who was with her for most of the first several months of her life.

Given the Baby M case and, perhaps, similar cases to follow, how can we determine the best interest of the child. In the United States, will the Ph.D. always win out over the high-school dropout? One problem is that we do not yet have children of these arrangements who are old enough to be studied. The best we can do is consider "scholarly" opinions as well as extrapolate from what we know about children who have grown up in other unusual or nontraditional circumstances; these might include adopted children, children of gay parents, and children born to mothers, including unmarried mothers, who chose artificial insemination by a donor.

Looking again at Great Britain, the British Medical Association (BMA) has flipped, then flopped, then flipped again on surrogate motherhood, most recently considering the practice not in the best interests of the children. In February, 1984, the association recommended that doctors not become involved in any "rent-a-womb" surrogacy scheme, whether the surrogate is paid or not and regardless of whether the baby was conceived by artificial insemination or in vitro and is genetically the couple's child. It seemed not to object to the use of in vitro fertilization to allow another woman to donate an egg for a couple with an infertile wife.

In December, 1985, the British Medical Association voted to support surrogate motherhood under "careful controls," but the May 7, 1987, report by the association's Board of Science and Education states that the baby born to a surrogate mother is "doomed to second best from the start by being deliberately deprived of one of its natural parents," and that the practice should not be supported. The report concluded that the interests of such children cannot be guaranteed and their welfare is more important than the wishes of infertile couples. This may not be the last word on surrogacy from the BMA, and its vacillation is not surprising given how little is known about surrogacy's effects on its products.

Information is sparse, too, on children resulting from artificial insemination by a donor. Researchers have found it difficult to follow the progress of such children largely because the legal parents have resisted study. As with traditional adoption, secrecy has generally been the rule. Some children of these arrangements, discovering their unorthodox origins— and estimates indicate about half of such children are later told or find out—have been vocal in expressing their anger. One, Suzanne Rubin, has been particularly visible on television talk shows and in magazine articles. She, like others in her situation, is dismayed at the lack of information available to her about her father's genetic background. She expresses horror that men like her father are able to sell their sperm without any responsibility for the lives they will help create. Discovering their origins in adolescence or in adulthood has the effect of destroying all their past lives as unreal, as fictional. These days, single women choosing artificial insemination by a donor are more likely to speak out about their decision and, presumably, will tell their offspring as much as they know about the donor. Openness is now thought to be desirable in attuning the children to their condition and in helping them accept it with minimum trauma.

Adoption agencies, too, have been recommending more openness between birth mothers and adopting couples than once was the rule. Agency research indicates that many adopted children have suffered substantial emotional anguish at their inability to trace their biological mothers, an anguish that has discolored their lives. One of my students, J, a married man with several children of his own, told me of his desperation to find his "real" mother and father, despite the great love and appreciation he felt for his adoptive parents. Records had been sealed, but after years of effort and with much ingenuity and some guile, J did trace his mother, long-married and with other children, to a city on the other side of the country. His father, also married and with grown children, was also tracked down. The father, angry at first, refused to see J. Successful in business and fearful of schemes that might deprive his legitimate children of their inheritance, he resisted. J, risking arrest, pushed his way into his father's office and confronted him. In time, J's wife and children were accepted by the families of both his biological parents. "I can't tell you what it meant," he said, "to look into my mother's face and see my little daughter's face there! And to find all those brothers and sisters I never knew I had!" Biological ties can be important, it seems, and while William Stern's "compelling need" appears to have been in continuing his family "blood line," neither the feelings of Mary Beth Whitehead's older children at losing their sister, nor the existence of Baby M's older siblings and the meaning of their loss to her life have been considered of significance in the Baby M case. Baby M also has a "blood line," independent of her father's....

My own explorations into what it feels like to be the child of older parents, prompted by the current trend toward deferred parenting, also indicates the difficulties children face when they are different in any way from most of their peers. Having one's parents mistaken for one's grandparents, or realizing that Dad is not able to play catch with the lads like the other guys' dads may not seem terrible hardships, but to the children involved they can cause embarrassment and sadness. The fear of losing parents while one is still a child is real. The now-adult subjects offered suggestions about how today's older parents might ease the problems for their children. These included being open with children about such worrying matters as the possibility of early responsibility for ailing, elderly parents, and about the likelihood of being left without parents, especially without fathers, sooner than most of their peers. The need for openness is emphasized in all kinds of nontraditional or less-than-usual family patterns. Children of older parents also emphasized their need for their parents' time. Those whose parents had been generous in discussion and in time and attention were far less likely to be troubled in any way by their parents' ages than those whose parents were less open and less available. That older parents are more likely to be financially comfortable than younger ones was noted by several subjects as an advantage, but one that is outweighed by many other factors....

The requirement for subjects in my research was that their mothers were at least thirty-six-years-old when the subjects were born; the fathers' ages ranged from thirty-five to over fifty. Although little has been said about the matter, it cannot be overlooked that the Sterns are older parents, each forty or forty-one when Baby M was born, making her an ideal candidate for my research later on—were she not weighted down with a passel of problems unrelated to her parents' age.

Parents' age is seen as important in, for instance, the choice of adoptive parents for infants. Adoption counselors in three different agencies have told me, unofficially—officially they do not discriminate on the basis of age—that, given a choice of adoptive parents for an infant, they would probably not give the child to a couple aged forty or over. One reason among several is that while the couple might be energetic in their forties, by the time the baby was a teenager, they would be in their mid-fifties or older and perhaps less able to cope with stresses and strains of adolescence than would younger parents.

REPRODUCTIVE TECHNOLOGY TODAY AND TOMORROW

In the matter of Baby M, all the participants have been hurt, and they may never be entirely free of pain. We cannot assess how Baby M's life will be colored or, rather, discolored by her origins and by the publicity arising from the case for her custody. In light of the repugnance generated by talk of rented wombs and the commercialization of birth, of baby-selling, of children as commodities to be contracted for, and the outrage felt by many that an infant can be wrested from its birth mother against her will because of a bill of sale,

it is not unreasonable for Neuhaus and others to call for an end to surrogate mothering. But, even were it possible to stop surrogacy completely, it would be a mistake. It is possible and, given the doubts about the future well-being of the offspring, of vital importance that it be very tightly controlled and used only in special circumstances which should be clearly specified.

Why should we not outlaw surrogacy? The technology involved is a vital step toward solving other problems. Surrogate mothering, artificial insemination by a donor, in vitro fertilization, embryo suctioning and transplanting, embryo freezing, have been developed by researchers as part of the quest not only to help infertile couples but also to diminish life-long suffering of children with serious genetic conditions. For some time, we have been able to perform certain surgical procedures on fetuses in utero; now, an embryo suctioned after a few days of gestation can be examined for genetic flaws before replanting in its mother's uterus. These techniques, while still experimental, may become routine. Instead of waiting until the second trimester of pregnancy for amniocentesis, a pregnant woman may know within days of conception if the embryo will develop normally. The choice to abort is rarely easy; it is particularly difficult at sixteen or eighteen weeks of gestation....

Why must we regulate surrogacy and other procedures? Regulation is needed, not only to control exploitation of poor women but also to avoid the widespread misuse of these technologies. Neuhaus is right to deplore using one class of women for the benefit of those of another social class. This exploitation will know no bounds if allowed free rein. The ability to transplant a couple's own embryo into the uterus of a third party means that the third party need not be of the same race or ethnicity as the embryo. A black woman could bear a white child who has no genetic relationship to its "incubator." Gena Corea, author of *The Mother Machine*, raises the possibility that women in the Third World could be induced to provide baby-bearing services for far less money than American women, making the procedure attractive to couples who could not otherwise afford it. Rather than expressing horror at this idea, the studio audience of the Donahue show on which Corea appeared on August 7, 1987, as well as the rest of the panel, dismissed her as radical and shrill. Women in the audience, and those who called in, were attracted to the idea of surrogate mothering. One caller wanted to know how she could become a surrogate. A member of the audience suggested that a computerized list of would-be surrogates be made nationally available for couples to choose from. Another regarded surrogacy as "a wonderful option" for people who marry late and want children. This latter statement drew hearty applause from an audience that could gain little understanding of the implications of what they applauded from the superficial handling of the topic on a television talk show. These kinds of entertainments stir up enthusiasm and create markets. Manufacturers have not been slow to turn to workers in the Third World to keep labor costs down; entrepreneurs in the baby business will seize the same opportunities if they are cost-effective—and if they are allowed to do so.

LACK OF REGULATION

Unlike those of several other countries, the United States government has been slow to fund—and hence to regulate—research in reproductive technologies. It has been slow, too, to regulate the "private" areas of family and procreation, leaving both research and surrogacy wide open for commercial exploitation. Without regulations, lawyers and businessmen have been able to raise capital—even to sell public stock—to operate sperm banks, reproduction and fertility clinics, surrogacy agencies, and to promote the idea of "franchises" that will use patented techniques. This means that royalties would be paid to the patent holders every time a particular tool—a specialized catheter, for instance—were used. A company spokesman for Fertility and Genetic Research, Incorporated, in a sales pitch to stockbrokers, spoke of plans to tap the affluent market for egg donation. Market researchers, hired to survey the availability of women willing to serve as regular donors for $250 a procedure, discovered that "Donor women exist in cost-effective abundance." Another entrepreneur, lawyer Noel P. Keane, whose infertility center made the match between Mary Beth Whitehead and the Sterns, has a thriving business finding surrogates. His fee is about $10,000 for each match; this is apart from the fee paid to the surrogate and the cost of prenatal care and delivery, all of which is paid by the negotiating couple. It is reported that Keane is now expanding his services to include a pool of egg donors as well as surrogate mothers. The donors are available, as is a ready market of affluent couples willing to do almost anything to have children. Why not put the two together and make everybody, especially the money men, happy? It is the American way.

Indeed, Americans have not shown any great dismay or disgust with the profiting from these arrangements. Seventy-five percent of those polled by the Roper organization felt Judge Sorkow's ruling to give Baby M to the Sterns was right. "After all," people responded, "A contract is a contract." Business, in fact, is business. Only 20 percent of the personal sympathy of those polled lay with Mary Beth Whitehead. The contract for a woman to bear a child to give to another couple was viewed as no different from any other exchange of services for money.

A small part of this reasoning may be due to some, not all, feminists' insistence that women are to be treated under the law exactly as men are treated, that women should have control over their own bodies, including the right to use them to make money, and that to suggest that women's biological makeup might affect their emotions is to be sexist and paternalistic. Since the Baby M case, feminist thinking has converged and several prominent feminists, including Gloria Steinem, Betty Friedan, Phyllis Chesler, and Marilyn French, have joined with other groups to file an amicus curiae brief arguing that the commercialization of surrogate parenthood violates the Constitution and the dignity of women.

In making this distinction between surrogacy and commercial surrogacy, the feminists are following the guidelines of already established regulations in some other countries. As one example, under the Surrogacy Arrangements Act of 1985, Great Britain outlaws surrogacy agencies. It outlaws third-party intervention of any kind between a couple and the woman who is to bear a baby for them. Advertising for surrogacy arrangements is a criminal offense by the publisher or the distributor. Commercial surrogacy, then, is against the law, and although it is legal for a woman to be paid for bearing a child for someone else, contracts between the parties are not legally enforceable.

It is fascinating to watch how those profiting from surrogacy have attempted to subvert, or find loopholes, in the British law. The London *Sunday Times* reports that British women are being sought by one Washington-based agency to travel to the United States to serve as surrogate mothers for British couples, also being recruited, who are prepared to pay as much as £20,000 (approximately $32,000) for a child, thus removing the entire transaction from the United Kingdom. It may well be, as Patrick Steptoe, the pioneer in in vitro fertilization, has said, that we need international, rather than local, legislation.

REGULATING REPRODUCTIVE TECHNOLOGY

Guidelines on regulating surrogate mothering and all the other techniques are urgently needed. The lag between our technology and our social policy grows wider by the moment. At the very least, prospective parents should meet the criteria for eligibility to adopt a child under the current laws. Couples should not be able to arrange for a child, as they might arrange for an entertainment center or a BMW, simply because they want one and can afford it. Certainly, the doctrine of informed consent should prevail. That is, all parties should recognize and accept the risks and benefits involved and enter voluntarily, free of any kind of coercion. The psychological as well as the physical risks of childbearing must be understood by all and it should also be acknowledged that the emotional involvement in carrying a fetus to term and delivering it is of a different order from that involved in milking sperm into a jar. Informed consent is no simple matter; people do not always know in advance of an event how they will feel about it when it occurs.

We do not have to start with a blank sheet. We can look to countries more advanced than ours for guidelines to legislation. Britain, as already mentioned, has outlawed commercial surrogacy; the Australian state of Victoria, in The Infertility (Medical Procedures) Act of 1984 has also set firm limits, both on who is eligible for the procedures and on just how far the scientists may go. Control is firmly in government hands. Among other criteria, patients must have been under treatment for infertility for at least twelve months to assure they are seeking a "last resort" and that there is no other possibility of a pregnancy, or that the woman seeking treatment could pass on a hereditary disorder. The law prohibits any kind of payment for sperm, eggs, or embryos, other than travel or medical expenses incurred by the donor. It sets strict rules on the use by scientists of embryos in experiments, and makes it an offense, punishable by up to two years in prison, to give or receive payment for acting as a surrogate mother. Like the British law, it forbids advertising for surrogates or for offering to act as one and it declares void all contracts between the parties....

The Luddites' fear of the machine was well founded. Industrialization eventually raised the standard of living for millions, providing them with shoes and dishes and clothing and other goods of a quality once reserved for the rich; but at the beginning the factory system and the shift from rural to urban areas brought untold misery. Men, women, and children were hideously exploited, separated from their roots, forced to work long hours for little pay in filthy, backbreaking, and dangerous conditions. In many parts of the world, where they remain unregulated, working conditions and pay are still appalling. Regulation of surrogacy does not necessarily "make a public statement that it is all right." Good laws and regulations protect those who are least able to protect themselves or who are unaware of the implications of their actions. They also serve to protect a society from its own folly.

NO

Richard John Neuhaus

RENTING WOMEN, BUYING BABIES AND CLASS STRUGGLES

Quite suddenly, it seems, we have a new form of trade in human beings. It is called surrogate motherhood, and several states have already declared it legitimate by establishing regulations for the trade. Voices have been raised to oppose the baby traders before their business becomes a fait accompli. It may already be too late for that. The *New York Times* has editorially pronounced that regulation is the only way to go since, after all, "the business is probably here to stay." Numerous objections of a moral, legal, and commonsensical nature have been raised to surrogate motherhood. One aspect that has not been sufficiently explored is the way in which the baby trade so rudely rips the veil off class divisions and hostilities in American life.

SURROGATING TODAY AND YESTERDAY

The most celebrated, or notorious, case of surrogate motherhood is the one that has swirled around "Baby M" in a New Jersey courtroom. Some of the details are by now well known. Mr. William Stern, a biochemist married to Dr. Elizabeth Stern, a pediatrician who thought pregnancy might be bad for her health, contracted with Mrs. Mary Beth Whitehead to have his baby in return for $10,000 plus an equal amount in expenses. Mrs. Whitehead and her husband Richard, a sanitation worker, agreed. The surrogate contract is not uninteresting, including as it does provisions for amniocentesis and obligatory abortion if Mr. Stern did not like the results of the test. Also, Mrs. Whitehead would not receive the $10,000 but only a small payment for her troubles "in the event the child is miscarried, dies, or is stillborn." The Sterns were taking no chances. But they could not prevent Mary Beth Whitehead from changing her mind. "It's such a miracle to see a child born," she said. "The feeling is overwhelming. All the pain and suffering you've gone through is all gone." Within five minutes she is breastfeeding the baby, the bonding is effected, she runs away to avoid having to turn the baby over to the Sterns, the Sterns hire detectives to snatch the baby, and it all ends up in a court trying to decide who gets to keep the baby.

The liberal Catholic journal, *Common-weal*, observes: "Surrogate motherhood is a simple idea. It has become a critical issue today not because of the breakthrough in technology but because of a breakdown in moral understanding—namely, the understanding that human reproduction should be firmly placed in the matrix of personal sexuality, marital love, and family bonds." The point is an important one. Also in religious circles today, there is much prattle about changing moral rules because of technological advances and new discoveries about sexuality. It is highly doubtful that we know anything very significant about sexuality that, say, Saint Augustine did not know. As to surrogate motherhood, long before the dawn of modern science human males had mastered the technique of impregnating women other than their wives. Genesis 16 tells how Sarah and Abraham chose Hagar to be the surrogate mother of Ishmael. That too turned out badly, although Hagar did get to keep the child. Hagar, of course, was a slave.

Today it is at least gauche to speak of buying or renting women. The Sterns got over that awkwardness by hiring a Manhattan clinical psychologist who testified, "In both structural and functional terms, Mr. and Mrs. Stern's role as parents to Baby M was achieved by a surrogate uterus and not a surrogate mother." The contract did not call for Mrs. Whitehead to get involved. In fact *she* was supposed to stay out of this deal altogether. Mary Beth's problem, it would seem, is that she was not able to disaggregate herself from her uterus. She did not understand that she could rent out her uterus just as the Manhattan doctor could rent out his certified expertise. The capable lawyers hired by the Sterns had made it all very clear, and for a while she thought she under-

stood, but then somehow the whole thing began to seem surreal. (Not being an educated person, she did not say it seemed surreal. She said it just seemed wrong.)

TAKING ADVANTAGE

True, there are those who argue that there is nothing new in the rich renting of the nonrich, whether in whole or in part. A servant or employee, they say, is in effect a rented person. It is hard to argue with people who say such things. More often than not, they are the kind of people who also say that property is theft and tolerance is oppression. One can point out that the employee is free to quit, that a person's work "belongs" to him even if he is paid to do it, that the worker may find fulfillment in the work, and so forth. But such wrongheaded people do have one undeniable point: with respect to the negotiation of worldly affairs, rich people do generally have the advantage of nonrich people. That said, one can only hope it will be acknowledged that there is something singular about the connections between a woman, her sexuality, and her procreative capacity. It is not the kind of acknowledgment people can be argued into, and those to whom it must be explained probably cannot understand. Proabortion proponents of a woman's "reproductive rights" regularly appeal to the uniquely intimate relationship between a woman and her body. Strangely enough, many of them also approve surrogate motherhood as a further step in rationalizing sexual relationships and liberating society from the oppression of traditional mores. The recently discovered constitutional doctrine of "privacy," it would seem, is absolute—unless you have accepted money to have it violated. The inviolably intimate sphere of sexuality is one thing, but a deal is a deal.

As with abortion, there is another party involved. As is not the case with abortion, everyone here recognizes the other party involved. Baby M, having passed the quality-control tests, is certified as a Class-A member of the species. The question is who owns this valuable product. Presumably ownership is fifty-fifty between Mrs. Whitehead and Mr. Stern. Mr. Stern's case is that Mrs. Whitehead had agreed to sell her share of the baby for $10,000 and then reneged on the deal. A Solomonic decision may be required, except Solomon's proposed solution would likely be found unconstitutional. Mary Beth is perplexed by the ownership conundrum. The following is from a taped telephone conversation admitted in evidence: "WHITEHEAD: I gave her life. I did. I had the right during the whole pregnancy to terminate it, didn't I? STERN: It was your body. WHITEHEAD: That's right. It was my body and now you're telling me that I have no right. STERN: Because you made an agreement... you signed an agreement." It is not that nothing is sacred anymore. It is simply that the sacred has been relocated, away from realities such as life and motherhood and placed in a contract signed and sealed by money. Some simplistic types who have not kept up with the demands of cultural change find this repugnant. For example, William Pierce, president of the National Committee for Adoption, flatly says: "If you regulate surrogate motherhood, that is making a public statement that it's all right. We decided a hundred years ago we didn't want people bought and sold in this country."

That is not the question, says the judge in the Baby M case. The question, the only question, is what is "in the best interest" of Baby M. In other words, who can offer Baby M the better prospect for the good things in life, the Whiteheads or the Sterns? Here, although the word is never used, the question of class takes center stage in the courtroom drama. The relative stability of American society is due in part to our kindly veiling of class distinctions and hostilities. People making $20,000 and people making $100,000 or more have tacitly agreed to say they are middle class. In fact, some are rich and some are not rich and some are poor. In terms of income, the Sterns are upper-middle or upper class, the Whiteheads are low-low-middle class and have at times been poor. Perhaps more important than the criterion of income, the Sterns and their allies in the New Jersey courtroom represent the new knowledge class. The disputes are over symbolic knowledge; that is to say, over how to establish the "meaning" of ideas such as parenthood, love, stability, life opportunity, and psychological well-being. In the symbolic knowledge showdown, Mary Beth Whitehead is pitifully outgunned. She has never even heard of the transvaluation of values, which is what the Baby M trial is all about.

CLASS STRUGGLE

It is not simply that the Sterns can hire a battery of lawyers, detectives, psychological experts and social workers, while Mary Beth must get along with a lawyer three years out of school whose main experience has been in liability cases. No, the greater disparity is that the Sterns, their hired experts, the judge, and almost everyone else involved represents the new class arrayed against the world of the Whiteheads who represent the bottom side of the working class. In the class war being waged in the courtroom, the chief weapon of the new class is contempt for the world of their cultural inferiors, a world so blatantly represented by the Whiteheads. Mrs. Whitehead must be criticized for her decision to enter into the agreement in the first place. But that is not a criticism employed in the courtroom to discredit Mrs. Whitehead, for it might reflect unfavorably on the other party to the agreement, even suggesting that perhaps Mr. Stern took advantage.

Rather, Mary Beth Whitehead is to be discredited and declared an unfit mother because the world of which she is part is unfit for Mr. Stern's baby, or at least not nearly so fit as the world of the Sterns. So extensive evidence is presented that the Whiteheads have had a hard time of it financially, even living in a house trailer for a time. More than that, Mrs. Whitehead received welfare payments for a few months and her husband underwent a bout with alcoholism some years ago. The mandatory new class attitude under usual circumstances is that there is absolutely no stigma whatsoever attached to welfare or alcoholism. But that is under usual circumstances. In the class war being fought in the New Jersey courtroom such things are sure evidence of moral turpitude and the Whiteheads' "unsuitability" as parents for the 50 percent wellborn Baby M. In addition, a team of mental health experts has testified that Mrs. Whitehead shows definite signs of "distress," and one psychiatrist bluntly says she is suffering from "mixed personality disorder." That presumed illness is defined as "traits from several personality disorders but not all the criteria of any one disorder." It is a kind of catchall category in which,

one fears, most human beings might be caught. Yet another psychiatrist in the new class alliance attempts to come up with harder evidence. Dr. Judith Brown Greif said that Mrs. Whitehead "often is unable to separate out her own needs from the needs of the baby." Well, there you have it. Mary Beth, in her pathetic ignorance, probably thought that was a sign of being a good mother. Little does she know about the need-fulfilling autonomy of the psychologically mature.

In order to get empirical support for their class biases, a group of mental health and child development experts visited "for several hours" in the Whitehead and Stern homes to observe first-hand how Baby M "related" to the respective parties. At the Whiteheads, Baby M seemed very happy, but their other two children, ages eleven and twelve, were vying for her attention and Mrs. Whitehead exhibited "an inflated sense of self." This, according to Dr. Marshall Schechter, psychiatrist at the University of Pennsylvania, was revealed in her making "an assumption that because she is the mother that the child, Baby M, belongs to her. This gives no credence to or value to the genetic contribution of the birth father." Things were different at the quiet and spacious Stern home. There were no other children to interrupt and, as Dr. and Mr. Stern sat on the living room floor chatting with their mental health visitors, Baby M gave every sign of relating very well to Mr. Stern. Of Mr. Stern one psychiatrist reported, "He is a thoughtful, sensitive man with a deep sense of responsibility and a respect for privacy." He did not need to add that none of those nice things could be said of Mrs. Whitehead.

Another expert (the one who contributed the distinction between renting the woman and renting the uterus), unequivocally declared that the Sterns are "far and away more capable of meeting the baby's needs than the Whiteheads." This includes of course his professional evaluation of Dr. Elizabeth, the wife. She is also, the experts told the court, very good at relating. In Dr. Stern's extensive court testimony, according to the *Times*, "she spoke of her delights at home with the baby and her disdain for Mrs. Whitehead." Often, she testified, she takes the baby shopping. "She's the cutest thing around. She's always pulling at the clothes in Bloomingdale's, trying to get them off the rack." At Bloomies, of course. You can bet that Mary Beth Whitehead probably doesn't even know where it is.

We Americans have a way of declaring something outrageous, repugnant, odious, and beyond the pale—and then concluding that we should regulate it. Surrogate motherhood should not be regulated, it should be outlawed. Some think the buying and selling of human beings was outlawed with the abolition of slavery, and the renting of women with laws against prostitution. But those big questions are bypassed if one agrees with the court, that the only question is, "What is in the best interest of the child?" Then enters the ugly factor of naked class advantage. If "interest" is defined by material well-being, life opportunities, professionally certified mental and emotional health, and a "lifestyle" approved by the new knowledge class, then clearly the baby must go to the Sterns. By the criteria which Mary Beth Whitehead is declared an unsuitable mother, millions of (dare we use the term?) lower-class women are unsuitable mothers. (One waits to see whether the court would take her other two children into custody.) By the criteria by which the Sterns are found to be "far, and away more capable of meeting the baby's needs," people of recognized achievement and approved attitudes have a right to the best babies that money can buy.

POSTSCRIPT

Should Surrogate Parenting Be Permitted?

The legal, ethical, religious, and social questions raised by surrogate parenting are profound—both for our culture and the people directly involved. The issue might seem to be a simple legal matter, but emotions and personal attachment come into the picture after the child is born. Years ago, a pregnant teen who delivered had the option of offering her child up for adoption; in the last 20 years, there has been a distinct trend among pregnant teens who carry to term to keep the child. Perhaps a similar dynamic occurs for some surrogate mothers, causing them to think twice about "selling their children." The issue of a legal contract may be a moot point in some jurisdictions if the natural mother protests the giving up of "her" child.

What are the marital dynamics for a couple that finds it necessary to contract someone to bear their child? Will one partner feel so unfulfilled without parenthood that he or she will seek an annulment of the marriage or a divorce? Perhaps having children is so strong an issue that the marriage would break up if the members could not fulfill their reproductive desires. Or perhaps the woman and man are sufficiently committed to each other so that test-tube conception would have less impact on their psyches than the ultimate achievement of the parenthood role.

Neuhaus makes a strong case for the outlawing of surrogate motherhood because of its purported bias against lower-class individuals. He assumes that middle- and upper-class persons will always take advantage of and triumph over those from the lower echelons because of superior access to resources. Morris, on the other hand, views surrogate parenthood with awe and feels that it has value for many individuals. But she cautions that left unregulated, surrogate parenthood can pose problems not only in the domain of parenthood but in the larger world of science.

SUGGESTED READINGS

L. Andrews, *Between Strangers: Surrogate Mothers, Expectant Fathers and Brave New Babies* (Harper & Row, 1988).

B. K. Rothman, *Recreating Motherhood: Ideology and Technology in a Patriarchal Society* (W. W. Norton, 1990).

W. Wadlington, "United States: The Continuing Debate About Surrogate Parenthood," *Journal of Family Law,* 27 (1988–1989): 321–328.

V. A. Zelizer, "From Baby Farms to Baby M," *Society* (March 1988).

ISSUE 13

Should Pregnant Teens Marry the Fathers of Their Babies?

YES: P. Lindsay Chase-Lansdale and Maris A. Vinovskis, from "Should We Discourage Teenage Marriage?" *The Public Interest* (Spring 1987)

NO: Naomi Farber, from "The Significance of Race and Class in Marital Decisions Among Unmarried Adolescent Mothers," *Social Problems* (February 1990)

ISSUE SUMMARY

YES: P. Lindsay Chase-Lansdale, a fellow of developmental and family research at the Chapin Hall Center for Children, and professor of history Maris A. Vinovskis accuse public policy proponents of overlooking the benefits of marriage for pregnant adolescents. They call for a reexamination of research findings and current policies that cast doubt on the benefits of having adolescent mothers and fathers rear their own children together.

NO: Human services educator and family researcher Naomi Farber argues that although adolescent mothers—regardless of race or class—value marriage, they express legitimate concerns about rushing into marriage solely because they are pregnant.

Adolescent pregnancy is a topic that has periodically aroused the public interest over the last two decades. Though the number of births among teenagers has decreased since the 1970s, enough adolescent women become pregnant each year that there is great concern for the economic and social costs of teenage parenthood.

In an article in *Family Relations* (1989), Gina Adams, Sharon Adams-Taylor, and Karen Pittman explain that one aspect of teenage pregnancy that has remained relatively constant is the statistical profile of adolescent mothers: The great majority of adolescent births is to white mothers. However, black teens, who make up 15 percent of the adolescent population, give birth to at least 30 percent of the babies. Close to 70 percent of teen births are to nonpoor families and about the same percentage of births are to teens who live outside of urban areas. So the common belief that adolescent parenthood is primarily a minority problem among poor youth who live in large cities is a myth.

Despite persistent negative stereotypes, some recent research shows that the young fathers of these children do not always victimize the mothers. Some fathers do provide various types of monetary and emotional support for the mothers and their children, but such support typically comes through informal means rather than through marriage and the establishment of legal paternity.

One reason why people are so concerned about teenage pregnancy is that children born to young, single mothers are at greater risk of being poor. Even though most births are to nonpoor adolescents, all single teenage mothers and their children are more likely to have financial difficulties and end up in poverty. High numbers of adolescent mothers drop out of school and are then unable to find well-paying jobs. As a result, they are less able to provide adequate support for their babies.

In past generations, young men generally married the adolescent mothers of their babies. Today, the marriage rate of this population has dropped to less than 30 percent. P. Lindsay Chase-Lansdale and Maris A. Vinovskis contend that this trend is due to current beliefs that marriage between young people decreases the likelihood that the affected adolescents will finish their schooling and that most of these early marriages will eventually end in divorce. They propose that there is no real evidence supporting such beliefs and that recent research studies suggest that there are potential benefits to having young fathers marry the adolescent mothers of their children.

Naomi Farber contends that to understand more fully adolescent pregnancy, it is necessary to look at differences by race and class. She reports that, upon interviewing various unwed adolescent mothers, many legitimate reasons for not marrying the fathers came to light, including family influences, unreadiness for marriage, and low regard for the fathers themselves.

YES

P. Lindsay Chase-Lansdale
and Maris A. Vinovskis

SHOULD WE DISCOURAGE TEENAGE MARRIAGE?

Adolescent sexual activity, pregnancy, and childbearing have received an extraordinary amount of public and scholarly attention during the past decade. The enormous interest in the topic stems from concern about the negative consequences to the mother, to her children, and to society as a whole. Public concern has been further galvanized by the dramatic increase in the number of out-of-wedlock births. Indeed, it is estimated that half of the federal expenditures for Aid to Families with Dependent Children (AFDC) in 1975 went to families where the woman had had her first child as a teenager. Many observers, however, seem to accept the irreversibility of the growing tendency for teen mothers not to marry. Indeed, some would even discourage pregnant teenagers from marrying because they believe that an early marriage would curtail the adolescent's education and lead to an early divorce. Although there seems to be a near-consensus among social scientists that teenage marriages are impermanent and disadvantageous to the mother and her child, no one has recently reviewed the scientific basis for these ideas nor analyzed the implications for past and future policy when we discourage teenagers from marrying.

PROLONGED MAIDENHOOD

Any discussion of policy toward teenagers must begin by acknowledging that adolescent behavior has undergone a great deal of change over the last two decades. The life course of adolescents is, of course, much affected by general trends in American society. The age at which men and women first marry is one example. Americans in the decade after World War II married at much earlier ages than ever before in the twentieth century. But recently, this trend toward early first marriage has been reversed. . . .

As it happens, this new marriage pattern is really a return to the more traditional marriage pattern dating back to the nineteenth century. But if the timing of marriages among today's youth resembles that of their counterparts in the nineteenth century, the current pattern of sexual activity is

From P. Lindsay Chase-Lansdale and Maris A. Vinovskis, "Should We Discourage Teenage Marriage?" *The Public Interest,* no. 87 (Spring 1987), pp. 23–37. Copyright © 1987 by National Affairs, Inc. Reprinted by permission of *The Public Interest* and the author.

quite different. While there have been considerable fluctuations in premarital sexual activity in our nation's past, the extent of sexual activity among contemporary teenagers seems unprecedented.... American teenagers during the 1970s were increasingly apt to engage in premarital sexual activity at the same time that they postponed marriage until their early or mid-twenties. Beatrice and John Whiting, in their book *Adolescents in a Changing World*, refer to this phenomenon as "prolonged maidenhood."

These changes in adolescent sexual behavior have been accompanied by a greater use of contraception among teens. Some maintain that the increased availability of contraception to teens beginning in the 1970s has failed to reduce the number of adolescent pregnancies, both because few teens are likely to use contraception effectively, and because the very availability of contraception has actually legitimized premarital sexual relations. On the contrary, although contraceptive availability may have contributed to a more permissive sexual climate in the past decade, there is little direct evidence that it alone has played a major role in promoting early sexual activity.

Furthermore, contraceptive use among unmarried sexually active female adolescents has increased steadily during the 1970s and 1980s.... Nevertheless, a sizable proportion of sexually active teens still do not use any contraceptives, use them intermittently, or rely upon ineffective methods. This fact may account for why many commentators speak of an ongoing unprecedented "epidemic" of adolescent childbearing. In actuality, the adolescent birth rate peaked in the late 1950s.... [B]y the time they turn twenty years old, 19 percent of white females and 41 percent of black females have be-

come mothers. Although the proportion of childbearing for blacks is twice that of whites, the absolute numbers of white teen births is more than double that of blacks: 320,953 versus 134,392.

While the number of actual births to teens is high, the number of pregnancies is significantly higher.... This recent increase in teenage pregnancies, however, has *not* led to a sizable increase in adolescent childbearing because of the greater use of legal abortions to terminate pregnancies....

One might conclude that since the rate of adolescent childbearing has decreased as well as the total number of children born to teenagers, public concern and interest in this issue would diminish. But in fact concern has grown, in part because the proportion of out-of-wedlock births among all teen births has increased dramatically, from 15.4 percent in 1960 to 56.3 percent in 1984.... In other words, more than four out of ten births to white teenagers and nearly nine out of ten births to black teenagers are out-of-wedlock. One could conclude from these statistics that attitudes toward teenage sexual behavior have indeed been changing.

ATTITUDES TOWARD MARRIAGE

But perhaps what has undergone an even greater change has been the general attitude toward marriage. Even as Americans in the past postponed marrying until their twenties, few questioned the importance and centrality of marriage as an institution. The family was considered by our ancestors as the cornerstone of society both in theory and practice. Although attitudes toward premarital sex varied over time, there was, until recently, a general consensus among Americans that out-of-wedlock childbearing was immoral and a serious threat to the economic well-being of the community. There was great social and legal pressure for the father of the child to marry the mother. As a result, the practice of marrying after conception was widely accepted and played a key role in keeping the number of out-of-wedlock births to a minimum. In 1955, for example, only 14.9 percent of births to adolescent girls were out-of-wedlock (6.6 percent for whites and 41.9 percent for nonwhites). In addition, pregnant adolescents comprised 25 percent of first marriages. What, then, happened to the notion of teen marriage in the intervening years?

To begin with, the moral stigma attached to out-of-wedlock births seemed to diminish considerably during the 1960s and 1970s. Unwed adolescent mothers were no longer forced to drop out of public schools and the term "illegitimate birth" was gradually replaced by the more neutral designation of "out-of-wedlock birth." At the same time, the expansion of federal, state, and local assistance to unwed mothers and their children made it more feasible economically for single mothers to raise children. While the increase in welfare assistance does not appear to have caused adolescents to initiate sexual activity earlier, it may have helped those who became pregnant to raise their children by themselves rather than marrying the father, having an abortion, or putting the child up for adoption. In addition, the growing recognition that young mothers needed to finish their own education in order to be self-supporting weakened the attractiveness of an early marriage where the teen mother would drop out of school in order to care for her child and husband. Furthermore, the growing

unemployment among young men, especially among young blacks, meant that the financial ability of the father to support the adolescent mother and her child appeared greatly diminished, making marriage seem a less feasible life-course option. These patterns may have been reinforced as the emphasis, during the 1960s and 1970s, shifted from the responsibilities of individuals for their actions to their rights to choose and pursue freely their own particular life styles.

Despite these changes, almost fifteen years passed before the federal government reacted to them. When federal action finally came in the 1970s, it was fueled by a combination of increased media attention, vociferous and organized advocates, emerging scholarly findings on the negative consequences to the teen mother's educational and occupational attainment, growing concern regarding the heightened levels of teen sexual activity, the changing proportion of out-of-wedlock births, the increase in teens choosing to keep their babies rather than give them up for adoption, and the rising cost of existing federal assistance programs. The primary focus of the congressional hearings, the proposed and enacted programs, and the scholarly testimony in the 1970s was not the numbers of unmarried adolescent parents, but rather the plight of the teenage mother herself and to a lesser extent, her children. Surprisingly little effort was made to consider the role of the father or the advantages and disadvantages of having pregnant adolescents marry.

The few scholars who considered the role of fathers downplayed their importance to the economic or emotional well-being of the young mother and her child. . . .

Throughout the extensive congressional hearings on adolescent pregnancy and childbearing in the 1970s and 1980s, virtually all of the participating members of Congress and social scientists accepted the trend in out-of-wedlock births and were more concerned with the stigma associated with out-of-wedlock births and the practices of schools in previous years of requiring pregnant teens to drop out. They did not challenge the view that pregnant adolescents should be discouraged from marrying.... While the discouragement of early marriages by social scientists was not a primary cause of the rise in out-of-wedlock births, it contributed to an atmosphere which minimized the responsibility of the father.

A ROLE FOR THE FATHER

... The change in administrations in 1981 brought greater interest in adolescent pregnancy and childbearing from a broader family perspective and a renewed focus on out-of-wedlock births. In 1984, the Office of Adolescent Pregnancy Programs under the Reagan administration solicited social science research on "The Characteristics and Family Involvement of Fathers of Adolescent Premaritally Conceived Births." This request sought information about the fathers, their interactions with the mother and young child, and the "social, economic, health and developmental consequences of the fathers' involvement in the lives of their partners and their out-of-wedlock children." The Reagan administration... also called for research to analyze both the negative and positive impacts of adolescent marriages on the teenage mother, her partner, and young child. It remains to be seen, however, how the current administration will incorporate this research into policies that pursue the issue of teenage marriage and out-of-wedlock births.

SURPRISING STABILITY

This new interest in teenage marriage for the parents of out-of-wedlock children marks an important change in policy emphasis. Although the recommendations of social scientists to policymakers in the 1970s regarding teen marriage were based on scientific studies at the time, we would argue that there has been too much emphasis on the inevitability of divorce. Even though the rate of marital stability is lower among teens than among older women, the *stability* of teenage marriage should be underscored. Those who argue against early marriages point to the likelihood of these unions to dissolve. Yet the rates of marital disruption are very high today for all couples, but few would suggest that we abandon marriage as an institution altogether. What is needed, though, is a closer look at the characteristics of those teens who do marry and those teen marriages that do survive.

In his classic study of low-income black teens in Baltimore, Frank Furstenberg concluded that the chances of the successful continuation of the marriages occurring in the years following the birth of a child were "minuscule." Yet half of the marriages of adolescent mothers in the Baltimore sample were intact after four years. In a follow-up study by Furstenberg and Brooks-Gunn of the teen mothers seventeen years later, almost one-third of all first marriages had survived. Similarly, Sheppard Kellam and his associates in their 1982 study found that approximately 35 percent of married teen mothers in Woodlawn, a Chicago community, remained married over a ten-year period. While the Baltimore and Woodlawn studies do illustrate higher rates of marital instability among low-income black teen mothers than their older counterparts, it is important to recognize the stability that does exist and to examine more closely the reasons for this.

Two new studies based on national data also provide evidence that teen marriages are more durable than previously believed. Using data from the Current Population Surveys of the Census Bureau in 1980 and 1982, Martin O'Connell and Carolyn Rogers of the Population Division of the Bureau of the Census found that although teenage marriages were twice as likely as adult marriages to be disrupted within the first five years, 76 percent of women who married between ages 15–17 and 85 percent of women who married between ages 18–19 were still married five years later....

In sum, although the sexual activity, pregnancy, and childbearing of adolescents have received an extraordinary amount of public and scholarly attention, teen marriages—especially those precipitated by pregnancy or childbirth—have been understudied by researchers and neglected by policymakers. Recent studies, it is true, have supported the perspective of scientists and policymakers in the 1970s—namely that rates of marital dissolution are higher among teen marriages than those of their older peers. But what has been ignored is that these same studies also reveal the resiliency of some teen marriages in the face of difficult circumstances.

THE BENEFITS OF MARRIAGE

But even if some teen marriages have endured, what advantages or disadvantages have they provided for the indi-viduals and their children? The negative impact of early childbearing on the educational attainment of the young mother is well documented. Although some female adolescents already had dropped out of school prior to their pregnancy or probably would have done so anyway, the additional stress and responsibility associated with early parenting reduces the likelihood of remaining in school. Young black mothers are more likely to continue their education than their white counterparts as their educational careers seem to be relatively less affected by an unintended birth.

The disruption of schooling is a serious problem since it is likely to place limits upon the job opportunities for a young woman throughout her lifetime. It also makes her a more probable candidate for welfare assistance and thereby increases the societal costs of early childbearing. Yet if there is general agreement upon the negative consequences of early childbearing on the educational and economic development of the young mother, there is still considerable uncertainty about the effects of early marriage on her educational and economic success. Again, most social scientists have argued that pregnant adolescents are better advised not to marry the putative father since this so often results in the termination of the young mother's education. Instead, they argue, the pregnant teenager should continue to live with her own parents, who will provide child care and economic support, thereby enabling the teen to complete her education and enhance her future economic well-being.

Few studies have looked specifically at the question of whether marriage helps or hinders a pregnant teenager's ability to continue her education and improve her long-term economic situation. ... [A] study by [Steven] McLaughlin and his associates [at the Battelle Human Affairs Research Center]... found that early marriage had negative effects on black mothers, but not on white mothers. Overall, the high school enrollment rate of black teen mothers, whether married or not, was higher than that of white teen mothers. For black mothers, a marriage either before or after the birth had a significant adverse impact on school enrollment. For white mothers marriage had only a minor impact compared to that of parenthood.

These findings reinforce the growing impression that early marriages following an adolescent pregnancy may damage the teenage mother's educational prospects. Yet this conclusion needs to be tempered by new research that finds that the long-term economic prospects for the young mother may be *adversely* affected by staying with her own parents rather than marrying the father. Furstenberg and Brooks-Gunn found in their seventeen-year follow-up of the Baltimore study that while staying with one's parents for the first year or two promoted school attendance, those teens who remained with their parents for three or more years seemed to become too dependent and were *the least likely* to be economically self-sufficient as thirty-five-year-old adults. In addition, those women who were married at the time of the five-year follow-up were much more likely to have succeeded economically, presumably because of their husbands' income, than those who had never married. Indeed, the small proportion of teens in the Baltimore study who remained married for twenty years were in families most likely to achieve middle-class status. What these statistics tell us is that

although a stable marriage for pregnant adolescents is difficult to attain, it offers tangible economic benefits for those who are able to achieve it.

In promoting a policy that argues that pregnant teens should stay with their own parents rather than marry, one must also question the effects of such a strategy upon the family of origin itself. Since teenage pregnancy and childbearing are disproportionately concentrated among low-income families, does the added financial responsibility upon grandparents in helping to raise their new grandchildren bring additional hardship to the household? Moreover, given the increasing proportion of women of all ages in the labor force, is it realistic to expect that many grandmothers will be available during the day to teen mothers and their babies? ...

WHAT ABOUT THE CHILDREN?

Missing in this discussion so far is an emphasis on the children of teen mothers. The predominant viewpoint has been that the advantages for children of teen marriages are few because the putative fathers are poor providers, prone to divorce, and uninterested and incompetent in parenting. Marriage, this argument continues, would fail to alleviate economic disadvantage, would promote husband-wife conflict, and expose the child to inept fathering, all of which are related to poor cognitive and emotional development in children.

In light of the virtual absence of research on the economic potential and parenting abilities of young fathers and on the quality of teen marriages, we believe that these three concerns remain open questions. Moreover, while some studies have documented demographic characteristics of teen marriages, e.g., rates of stability and divorce, virtually no one has examined the ways in which teen mothers and their spouses interact, nor the impact of the quality of their relationship on their children's well-being. We know from a substantial body of psychological research on older families that in good marriages, a father's emotional support to his wife and vice versa and a father's involvement with his children are important to healthy child development. Why, then, when so little is actually known about the psychological strengths and weaknesses of young families, do social scientists and politicians persist in discouraging teen marriages?

Similarly, remarkably little research has been devoted to the parenting abilities of teen mothers, and only one study, by Michael Lamb and Arthur Elster of the University of Utah, has actually observed the parenting behaviors of young fathers (young fathers are typically not teens themselves; the majority are in their twenties). Lamb and Elster's results tentatively suggest that these men behave toward their six-month-old infants in ways that are typical of older fathers. When we turn to how the children of teen marriages fare, studies suggest that they do indeed benefit from their parents' marriage. According to Furstenburg's study, children whose teen mothers had married the father performed better at age five on assessments of cognitive and social development. Kellam's study found that these children were rated higher in school adjustment by their first grade teachers than those children whose teen mothers lived alone. Furstenberg also found high cognitive performance for preschool children who had regular contact with their absent fathers. In his follow-up study with Brooks-Gunn, those mothers who were economically independent by age thirty-five due to employment or marriage (to the child's father or someone else) had adolescents who performed better in school and reported lower rates of deviance.

While we do not have sufficient research to disentangle the relative importance of economic advantage, emotional assistance from adults, and the unique impact of the father, the effects of economic well-being seem clear. The Baltimore study suggests that within groups of teenage mothers, those who are the most economically disadvantaged have children who do the least well. Although some Baltimore teen mothers successfully lifted themselves out of poverty in later adulthood, as a group their children, in their own adolescence, showed much higher rates of school drop-out, grade retention, and behavior problems than adolescents of older parents. The question emerges: Why must the majority of teen mothers in this country struggle to improve their economic status without financial assistance from the fathers?

Young fathers are believed to be incapable of providing financial support to their families. In fact, little is known about the eventual earning power of young fathers, and work in progress by Robert Lerman of Brandeis University on data from the 1979–1982 National Longitudinal Survey of Labor Force Behavior suggests that young fathers have greater economic potential than previously believed....

Furstenberg... found a low rate of child support payment by never or previously married fathers; not surprisingly, at the five-year follow-up, married fathers were continuing to support their children.

Thus, while it is clear that the vast majority of young absent never-married fathers are not contributing to their children's financial security, we cannot conclude at this time that most young fathers are potentially or even currently incapable of economic assistance. In the context of the poor economic standing of many teen mothers, any level of assistance would be helpful. And what is being required by the federal government as current court-ordered child support is not exorbitant....

Although child-support enforcement has received considerable attention lately, the focus of recent reform has been on middle-class fathers, the vast majority of whom have not come under the system's purview. While this represents an important shift in child-support policy, an equally indifferent group—absent young fathers—has not received enough attention....

A CALL FOR REEXAMINATION

In the 1970s teenage pregnancy and child-bearing became a matter of pressing concern to policymakers and social scientists. As out-of-wedlock births were beginning to soar, lawmakers and experts chose to focus on the teen mother herself, the stigma of adolescent pregnancy, and the detrimental impact of early childbearing on educational and oc-cupational advancement. Marriage as a life course option for adolescent mothers was actively discouraged and considera-tion of the role of the father was practi-cally nonexistent.

In the 1980s, as out-of-wedlock births have reached unprecedented levels, it is necessary to reexamine policies and research related to adolescent parenthood and marriage. New research findings indicate that some teen marriages are more resilient than previously believed. Recommendations that adolescent mothers remain with their own parents in order to maximize educational attainment are being brought into question by recent evidence suggesting adverse long-term outcomes of such an arrangement. Policies that promote single parenthood for teen mothers seem to prevail in the face of very little systematic information about the young fathers and their potential as providers, husbands, or parents. Government policies should be redirected toward helping young couples stay together rather than focusing almost exclusively on the young mother and her child. Furthermore, in a society that claims that children are the future, one must question why a young man's financial responsibility toward his children is open to debate. These and many other issues need to be raised and addressed before we conclude that pregnant teenagers should be discouraged from marrying.

NO

Naomi Farber

THE SIGNIFICANCE OF RACE AND CLASS IN MARITAL DECISIONS AMONG UNMARRIED ADOLESCENT MOTHERS

Overall fertility rates among American adolescents have decreased since 1970. Yet researchers, policy-developers, service providers, and members of the American public alike continue to express deep concern over adolescent childbearing. This concern arises partly from the fact that, while teen birth rates have declined, the proportion of births to teenagers who are unmarried is rising steadily.... Young unmarried mothers and their offspring are at high risk of experiencing long-term poverty and associated disadvantages (Garfinkel and McLanahan 1986).

While marriage has declined sharply among all teens, differences in rates of out of wedlock births by race remain sizeable. In 1985, 45 percent of births to white teens were out of wedlock in contrast to about 90 percent of births to black teens (Hayes 1987). Black adolescents also have a higher rate of childbearing. In 1985 the adolescent birthrates were 42.8 births per 1000 white adolescents aged 15–19, compared to 97.4 births per 1000 black adolescents (Pittman and Adams 1988). Therefore, although black teenagers do not account numerically for the majority of illegitimate births to adolescents, they are much more likely than white teens to become young single mothers.

These differences in rates of illegitimate childbearing by race, coupled with the association between race and class in American society, set up the complex question of how race and class influence out of wedlock births....

In 1985–86 I conducted in-depth interviews with 28 unmarried adolescent mothers aged 15–20 years in the Chicago area. The sample included six subgroups including black and white teenagers from middle-, working-, and lower-class families. Participants' race was self-defined as either black or white....

Young mothers were classified as middle-class if their parent(s) had steadily held white-collar/managerial or highly skilled work. The working-class subgroup was composed of teens whose parent(s) worked at semi-skilled or clerical jobs. The lower-class group includes those whose parent(s) had been significantly unemployed or worked at low-skill or unskilled labor....

From Naomi Farber, "The Significance of Race and Class in Marital Decisions Among Unmarried Adolescent Mothers," *Social Problems*, vol. 37, no. 1 (February 1990), pp. 51–63. Copyright © 1990 by The Society for the Study of Social Problems. Reprinted by permission. Notes omitted.

I asked the young mothers questions that elicited descriptions of their attitudes toward men in general and as potential partners and husbands, the hopes and expectations regarding marriage and single motherhood that they remembered having as children, the hopes that they held at present and for the future, the history of their relationship with their baby's father and subsequent boyfriends, and their perceptions of their families' attitudes toward marriage and single motherhood....

THE VALUE OF MARRIAGE AS AN IDEAL

Nearly all of the teens, regardless of their class or race, view marriage and marital childbearing as an ideal type of family....

Most teens expressed ... attitudes suggesting that, for them, being a single mother does not reflect changed values about how families should be formed. This ideal is also evident in their childhood memories of how they imagined their adult lives would be....

Like the middle-class and working-class teens, the black lower-class mothers had childhood dreams of living in the ideal American family....

The young mothers from all backgrounds described ideal visions that are congruent with traditional values about family formation. These childhood reflections suggest that their present judgments about the undesirability of out of wedlock childbearing are not simply responses to the stress of single motherhood. Most of these teen mothers grew up valuing a way of life from which they have deviated. They were unable to or chose not to act in accordance with these ideals. In the balance of the paper I discuss the factors these young mothers cited in their decisions to deviate from their stated ideals about marriage and remain single.

WHY TEENS DID NOT MARRY: VARIATIONS BY CLASS AND RACE

The young mothers expressed a variety of reasons for remaining unmarried. No teen stated only one specific factor that she believed was responsible for her remaining unmarried. Each teen offered a scenario that usually included the influence of her family, the baby's father, subsequent boyfriends, and her own beliefs, goals, and desires that led to her not marrying to legitimize the birth. Similarities in reasons given among black and white teens from middle-class and working-class backgrounds stand in contrast to the reasons given by lower-class mothers....

Postponing Marriage: Perceptions of Middle- and Working-Class Mothers
Fathers unwilling or not ready. Whether a young woman, pregnant or not, marries depends partly upon the existence of concrete opportunities for marriage. The decision obviously is not hers alone. Among the twenty black and white middle-class and working-class teen mothers, only four of their babies' fathers offered to marry the young women when the women became pregnant.

Those teens whose babies' fathers were not willing to marry them described many kinds of involvement by those young men in their lives. These range from the white middle-class mother whose baby's father not only offered no help to her, but threatened to trip her going downstairs to induce a miscarriage, and eventually threw a volleyball hard at her stomach during a gym class at school, to those few young men who now spend time with and/or money on their children on a regular basis. Typically the young father did not want the young woman to carry the pregnancy to term or to keep the child. They told the pregnant girls that they felt unprepared for fatherhood in all respects.

Patterns of father involvement are an important issue in the study of adolescent parenthood. However, in terms of decisions about marriage, what is especially significant here is that, as far as the young women know, beyond the young men's own personal desires for involvement, the fathers did not receive any pressure from adults—parents or others —or peers to assume parental responsibility, let alone to marry the pregnant girl. In fact, there is little evidence that any young woman, except for one white middle-class teen whose family sent her to a home for unwed mothers, felt the weight of familial or community expectations to marry to legitimize the child's birth. In addition, in only one instance did the parents of a young man intervene by promising the pregnant girl that he would help pay for her medical expenses and provide child support. This is the only teen mother who now receives any regular financial support from the baby's father.

Mothers themselves not ready for marriage. Regardless of the young fathers' intentions, only one black teen from a working-class family expressed disappointment over not marrying her baby's father. While several young mothers wished the father had at least taken some paternal responsibility, they did not regret not having married the father. The decision not to marry in most instances was described by the girls as being mutual. Certainly one

must consider the possibility that this expression of mutuality is a rationalization of rejection by the young fathers. However, nearly all non-poor teens have had subsequent boyfriends, most of whom have proposed marriage, but no teen has yet chosen to marry, suggesting that, for the girls, opportunity alone is not sufficient reason to marry.

A consistent theme expressed by the black and white middle-class and working-class teen mothers is that both they and their families believed that regardless of an unplanned—and nearly universally unwanted—pregnancy, the girls were too young to become wives as well as mothers. That is, both the teenagers and their parents believed that marriage was not appropriate for teenagers, even in the face of their impending motherhood. As one white working-class teen's mother remarked, marriage for her 16-year-old daughter would only be "adding one mistake on top of another."

Some teens and their families believed that in principle a "shotgun" marriage was ill-advised especially among adolescents. One 16-year-old black middle-class mother described her mother's, her grandmother's, and her own views about marriage to legitimize her unplanned pregnancy:

My mother feels that you shouldn't marry because of a baby. It doesn't work, it creates hatred. Basically, that's how I felt, because when my grandmother found out I was pregnant, she was like, "Make him marry her, make him marry her." I'm like, "I don't want to marry him." And my mother was like, "No, she's 16. Seriously, what's she going to do married?"

Other families were in complete agreement in their opposition to early marriage, as described by this 15-year-old black working-class teen:

My father wouldn't let me get married because he doesn't think I'm old enough. He thinks you have to be mature—physical, mental, and financial ways to have a family.... They [parents] want us to be sure that's the person we love, because they're against divorce.

One 18-year-old white working-class mother was forbidden by her parents to marry the father of her child. She and her parents agreed on this matter, though for different reasons: "My parents don't think marriage is the answer for being pregnant ... [and] I was young and wanted space. I seen all my girlfriends were still going out and new boyfriends every month, and I wanted to go out." Indeed, this young white mother has a new boyfriend who wants to marry her and has offered to support her until then, but she still feels too young to give up her remaining freedom. Some middle-class and working-class teens and their families, then, did not consider an unplanned pregnancy to be an adequate basis for marriage among teenagers.

For others marriage was a poor choice because it might interfere with the teen's education and career preparations. The desire to finish their education before marriage was mentioned frequently by black and white middle-class and working-class mothers as a major concern. One 17-year-old black middle-class teen stated:

I told [my boyfriend] I didn't want to marry him until after I got out of school because marriage is just an excuse for going to bed with somebody and ... I don't need another kid. I told him that even after we get married, I'm going to stay on the pill for at least a year, if I haven't gotten my career together already.

A 15-year-old black working-class mother expressed her and her mother's concerns: "I would like to be married, but then again I wouldn't because I'm so young.... My mother's like, "You better go to school and get your education—thinking about marriage!" Another black working-class teen, aged 16, said: "I won't get engaged until I get established, get out of high school and figure everything out."

Thus, some parents considered early marriage to be a potential threat to the young woman's future educational and employment achievement. Implicit in this concern is the assumption expressed by all non-poor teens without exception that they plan to be economically self-supporting through employment. Whether this is a preference or necessity is unclear, but the expectation that they will work is evident in the teens' continuing participation in education and job training during and after the pregnancy. Even those young mothers who receive public assistance (nine out of 20) work and/or attend school full time.

These young women do not look to men and marriage to support them and their children. The absence of this expectation is reinforced by the fact that many teens are involved with young men who are not able to support them. Fifteen of the 20 non-poor mothers, in agreement with their parents, judged their baby's father and their current boyfriend as not being an acceptable marriage partner at present because the young men were poor risks financially and/or emotionally, regardless of their desire to marry.

Consider the remarks of one 17-year-old black middle-class mother: "My mother thinks my daughter's father is a low-life, he's not good for anything. So she let him go about his way." ... Two 19-year-old white working-class mothers and their parents had similar reservations about the fathers of their babies. One said,

My mom thinks, well, they're not real happy with my boyfriend. He doesn't work or anything. I'd like to get married, have my baby have a father. We talked about it. ... It would be a flop. Well, you know, he can't work since he hurt his back. So I would be the one working. And he would be sitting around drinking beers with his friends ... trying to take care of the baby, which I don't think he would do.

Another said: "My parents would not allow me to get married. ... They didn't want me to marry [my baby's father] because I was so young, one reason. And because he had never had a job and they looked at him as a real loser." These young women and their families have specific expectations regarding a husband's role as provider for his family. All of the non-poor teens expressed an intention to work even when they married in the future. However, they also expected a husband to be employed and take at least equal financial and emotional responsibility for his family. They preferred single motherhood to marriage to an unsuitable partner.

Family support. Whether the teen and her family were most concerned about the inappropriateness of marriage among teenagers or the prospects of the young man in her life, all teen mothers in this study reported that their families counseled them against marrying precipitously. The teen mothers further described how their families provided considerable material and/or emotional support to help them survive as single mothers while completing their education. Even when parents were angry about the pregnancy and expressed disapproval through refusing to pay for a grandchild's expenses, all parents at least offered a home to the young mother and her child.

Although all non-poor teens received significant aid from their families, there is an interesting difference between black and white teens in the significance they attached to this familial support and the meaning of single motherhood in their families. The white non-poor teens commonly described their parents' help as their rising to the occasion of a family crisis, often to the young women's surprise. Their experiences are typified by one 16-year-old white middle-class teen who was terrified of her parents' reaction to her pregnancy and feared they would ask her to leave home. Instead, she reported: "When I got pregnant all my parents told me about raising Joshua myself was that they were willing to help me as much as they possibly can to do whatever they can until I can do it on my own. Nobody said I need to get married." In all instances, the white teen was the first in her family to bear a child as an adolescent and outside of marriage. ... Among these white middle-class and working-class teens, only one has a mother who was herself a single mother for any length of time, following a divorce, while another's mother was unmarried briefly between a divorce and remarriage. This stands in sharp contrast to the non-poor black teens, most of whom grew up with a single mother for much of their childhood. Several black middle-class and working-class teens described family traditions of women raising families alone, or at least without husbands. This is typified by the experience of one 17-year-old black middle-class mother: "The women in my family, we've had to support ourselves. And thank God I'm getting all this help [from mother and grandmother]. I couldn't stand it without it." This tradition of black women supporting their families seems to be expressed in these adolescents' belief that although marriage is preferable, single motherhood is an acceptable option when necessary. A 19-year-old black middle-class mother who is engaged expressed this view:

> The way I see it is that you don't necessarily have to have the father [of the baby] around all the time...I keep telling everybody—you can make it as long as you got your family with you. You can make it. You don't need him at all. It's not really the father a baby depends on....

[O]ne indication of the complexity of the relationship between the teens' and their own mothers' marital experiences is that, though they grew up with a single mother, the non-poor black teens generally expect that they will marry in the future, as do their white counterparts. Both white and black non-poor teens perceive single motherhood to be a temporary situation until they find the "right" man or until, like the young woman quoted previously, they "figure everything out."

All but two black and white middle-class and working-class teen mothers now have steady boyfriends, either the father of their baby or, more often, a subsequent partner. Five of the teens are presently engaged to be married but want to wait to get married until they graduate from high school or college or until they have a steady job. Significantly, the young men to whom the teens are engaged are all steadily employed and considered by the young women to be stable and mature.... Even those young women who have not yet found a prospective husband believe that marriage is a normal and realistic goal that they expect to achieve.

"Mama's Baby, Papa's Maybe": Single Motherhood Among Lower-Class Mothers

Like the working-class and middle-class teens, the black and white lower-class mothers value marriage as an ideal. Even so, unlike the more affluent young women, they are not as confident that they will actually marry. There are also differences by race among the lower-class teens in terms of their attitudes toward men and marriage, as well as how realistic they perceive the possibility of marriage to be.

Compromised ideals.   Like the non-poor teens, the black and white lower-class teen mothers have specific expectations about what a husband and father should be. In accordance with mainstream values and norms, both black and white lower-class teens expect a husband to be able to provide emotional and financial support to his family. One 16-year-old black lower-class teen stated,

> I'm like, if I can't find [a man] that got a job or that can help me in some way, I don't want him.... I'm very choosy. Because like, I was walking home from school with one of my friends, and she was like, "Why don't you go and talk to that guy?" I said, "He got a job? Do

he keep money?" She said, "No." I said, " 'Bye."

Yet their childhood dreams of ideal family life as described above have been compromised as they witness how family life around them diverges from that ideal. Another 16-year-old black lower-class mother remarked,

> I don't know, we all figured if you got pregnant, whoever you were with, he would help you. We never looked at it like, "Oh, he's not going to be there and I'm going to have to do this for myself." Being young we all had dreams or fantasies that he'd be there.

These teens have grown up and out-grown their "fantasies" at a very young age. Even this young woman's earlier hope of her baby's father "being there" has proved to be unrealistic. Experience has tempered their expectations, for the men in their lives often prove to be unre-liable, or worse....

Only one black and all three white teen mothers are still involved with their babies' fathers. Three of the four couples have discussed the possibility of marriage, but two of the young women feel they have been abused in the course of their relationships and see marriage to these men as a poor risk....

A perception that is more common and explicit among the black lower-class teens is that marriage as actually experienced by the people they know offers no real advantage over single motherhood. A 16-year-old black lower-class mother said:

> Marriage doesn't make any difference. 'Cause my sister, you know, when she had her first child she was alone. Her second child, she was married... but it still was like she was on her own.

Because no one can really help as much as yourself.

Cynicism about men. The black lower-class teen mothers seem to be more cynical than the whites about what it means to be involved with men. They seem almost to expect men not to be responsible for their families. The young black women convey a sense of self-protection about involvement with men. They want men to be more committed to them but anticipate that their hopes will not be fulfilled and so prepare themselves emotionally for disappointment. They learn this attitude of self-defense from their own experience and also from other women in their family.... A 15-year-old black lower-class teen was abandoned by the father of her baby, an experience that confirmed her mother's views about men:

> My mother just told me to be indepen-dent, not to depend on anybody. If your boyfriend backs out, you can go your own way, and I'll always be there to help. She used to say, "You can go hang-ing around those boys all you want, but when you end up pregnant, don't ex-pect him to stay around. They be saying, "Mama's baby, papa's maybe." My ma said if you get married you're a fool.... First he's all right. But then he turns into —well, you'll be doing all the giving. She said you're better off if you just have a man to associate with and don't get mar-ried.... I suppose it's okay to wait 'till you get married to have a baby. Or if you don't, catch as catch can.

An underlying theme expressed by the black lower-class teens is a dis-junction in both attitude and behav-ior between childbearing and marriage. The conceptual separation between mar-riage and childbearing, reinforced by their mothers' warning about the pitfalls of marriage, is associated with a deep distrust of men as marriage partners. A 16-year-old black lower-class mother who had dreamed of marriage and her "own house" doubts she will marry:

> Well, I don't think I will get married, but I'll just have a boyfriend or something, but I just wouldn't get married.... No, most boys don't stick around. All they be doing is talking. I guess most of the boys think that it makes them feel like a man. "Hey, I've got a son" and all this stuff, and one coming and all. Just make them look stupid if they ain't taking care of it. All they doing is talking.

These young mothers think that most men have limited willingness and ability to support a family....

The more typical experience of the young women is expressed by a 16-year-old black lower-class mother: "You know, he's not working now, so, I can't expect too much from him." She expresses the common perception that there is no point in expecting the young men with whom they are involved to offer much help because they cannot provide adequately for themselves.

The number of white lower-class teens interviewed is too small to offer a genuine racial comparison. However, it is interesting to note that all of the three white teens maintain ongoing relationships with the fathers of their babies. Two white lower-class teens have more than one child by their long-term boyfriends. These boyfriends have expressed willingness to marry if the women so desire. Even so, these young white women are rather vague and unsure about their present expectations regarding marriage to these young men. One 17-year-old

white lower-class mother of three children expresses this sense of being unsure of her plans and how marriage fits into her future:

> I want to get married—I told Tony I want to stay with him. [But] I can't imagine what I'm going to be doing ten years from now ... 'cause I know that people change and stuff and I'm only seventeen. I may want to do something else. At the moment I'm really not sure about marriage—maybe after I finish school and everything. I don't know, I think that if I finish school maybe I won't get pregnant no more. And I believe I'll get a job or something. And maybe I'll probably get married by then.

It is significant that of all the lower-class teens, only this white young woman mentioned that her hopes for an education or work might influence marriage or childbearing.

These white lower-class girls and their babies' fathers do suggest a possible difference between them and the black lower-class mothers. The poor white teens' boyfriends are objectively no more attractive than the poor black young men as marriage partners (one is married, one has abused the young woman, and the third cannot make a living wage as a sometime, part-time short-order cook), and these qualities may well largely account for not marrying. Still, the white young women perceive marriage as at least being possible in their future, depending upon how things go with their boyfriends....

Two of their own mothers were single mothers for some time (the third teen became a ward of the state of Illinois and lived in group homes), but unlike their black counterparts, these mothers have not given the younger women messages that denigrate the value of marriage in principle. The white lower-class teens' social environment may not offer many opportunities to meet more eligible men, but that does not seem to be reflected in cynicism about men in general. The white lower-class teens differ significantly from the white middle-class and working-class teens in having fewer opportunities to achieve their marital goals and in not investing their energies in preparation for self-support. But, at the same time, their attitudes do not indicate the degree of hopelessness about marriage that the black lower-class teens display.

DISCUSSION

...Even though they retain traditional conceptions of the ideal family, these young women feel less pressure to conform to that ideal than did women—and men—in past generations. Significantly, this diminution of pressure to marry, both in general and to legitimize a birth, is supported by the young women's families. Moreover, beyond societal changes in norms such as reduced stigma toward single motherhood and "greater freedoms" for women (Burgess 1954), the young women's experiences with men and marriage are associated with their class background and race.

Typically, the black and white middle-class and working-class teens neither hoped nor expected to become single or adolescent mothers. They acted on contemporary norms permitting the separation of sex and marriage, but they still regard childbearing as properly a marital event. Yet, once pregnant and committed to bearing and keeping the child, the young women and their families did not then or subsequently judge that it was either necessary or in their best interests to marry *in order to legitimize the birth....*

In contrast to the middle- and working-class teens, lower-class mothers perceived their prospects for marriage to be less promising. They saw the men in their lives were not acceptable as husbands, and they gave no indication that they expected to meet more eligible men in the future.... Certainly some poor black women maintain stable relationships with men, but the young women interviewed here display an unmistakable doubt about their own chances for a satisfactory and mutual relationship with a man.

The black lower-class teens are distinguished from the other young women in this study by their not even expecting childbirth to occur within the context of marriage.... As economic circumstances and the social environment have deteriorated for many poor urban blacks in the past two decades, adolescent girls in these communities have grown up surrounded by failed marriages and single mothers. They have been raised by women whose own difficult marital and non-marital relationships served as models to be avoided, while their personal experiences with young men provided no reason to believe their own chances for marital stability would be any better than those of their mothers. The poor black teens in this study expressed mainstream, traditional aspirations for marriage (cf. Anderson 1989). However, their opportunities to achieve their aspirations are severely limited....

Until we know more specifically what differences and similarities exist in sociofamilial dynamics among poor and non-poor whites as well as non-poor blacks in a variety of urban and rural community contexts, it will not be possible to specify with any confidence the true significance of race or class in the women's and men's decisions about forming families.

REFERENCES

Anderson, Elijah. 1989. "Sex codes and family life among poor inner-city youths." The Annals of the American Academy of Political and Social Science 501: 59–78.

Burgess, Ernest. 1954. On Community, Family and Delinquency. Chicago: University of Chicago Press.

Garfinkel, Irwin, and Sarah McLanahan. 1986. Single Mothers and their Children: A New American Dilemma. Washington, D.C.: The Urban Institute Press.

Hayes, Cheryl, ed. 1987. Risking the Future: Adolescent Sexuality, Pregnancy, and Childbearing. Washington, D.C.: National Academy Press.

Pittman, Karen, and Gina Adams. 1988. Teenage Pregnancy: An Advocate's Guide to the Numbers. Washington, D.C.: The Children's Defense Fund.

POSTSCRIPT

Should Pregnant Teens Marry the Fathers of Their Babies?

Why don't more adolescent mothers marry the fathers of their children? Many people believe that society has moved beyond the "shotgun wedding" mentality and that it disapproves of forcing fathers and mothers to marry even when they are adolescents. Chase-Lansdale and Vinovskis, however, argue that this modern social norm is of questionable merit for all concerned, and they use recent studies to support their contention. They also ask how the decision not to marry serves the larger community. For example, if a mother lives with and is supported by her parents and becomes overattached and dependent upon them, consequently never learning economic self-sufficiency, how does this affect the family, the child, or society? Chase-Lansdale and Vinovskis argue that there is a need for additional research on families where the father and adolescent mother do marry, especially regarding how the children fare in such unions.

Farber, after interviewing adolescent mothers, concludes that race and class need to be considered before the marital patterns of adolescent mothers can be adequately understood. Though the mothers she interviewed believe in marriage, they argue against marrying the fathers of their babies. Their attitudes seem to be based on the realities of their particular life situations.

Why don't adolescent mothers (even poor ones) seek legal action against the fathers of their children for the provision of financial support? Frank F. Furstenberg, in "As the Pendulum Swings: Teenage Childbearing and Social Concern," *Family Relations*, 40 (1991): 127–138, relates that the typical father of an adolescent's child, a young adult over age 20, usually lives with the mother and child only briefly or not at all. Furstenberg believes that the involvement of these fathers in the lives of their children has been exaggerated by clinicians who base their conclusions on the small number of fathers they see in private practice and by researchers who rely on the responses of small, nonrepresentative samples of such men. "Only a small minority of these children," he contends, "see their fathers regularly by the time they reach adolescence. Fewer still receive substantial financial support from them."

There could be several explanations for not using legal action to gain support: The father may be providing some type of support already; the mother and her family may not consider the father a good role model for the child and thus may try to distance themselves from him; legal action can work two ways—the father may be required to pay support, but the mother could then be required to give him partial custody; the mother may not know how the legal system operates or even that she has certain legal rights to support; to win support, the mother must prove that he really is the father—an expensive, time-consuming, and emotionally wrenching experience; and the father may be unemployed or underemployed.

Other questions to consider with regard to this issue are: Does government have a role in this issue? Has the current emphasis of government on "just say no to sex" proven effective in resolving the issue of adolescent pregnancy? Are there other government programs in place that are effective? What are the consequences to children of growing up in an out-of-wedlock family situation? How does that compare to family situations in which parents marry because of a pregnancy but divorce after a few years? Has the cultural norm for marrying someone "for the sake of the child" and "to preserve the character and well-being of the mother," which prevailed through much of this century, been replaced by another norm? If so, what is that norm?

SUGGESTED READINGS

E. Anderson, "Sex Codes and Family Life Among Poor Inner-City Youths," *The Annals of the American Academy of Political and Social Science,* 501 (1989): 59–78.

L. M. Burton, "Teenage Childbearing as an Alternative Life-Course Strategy in Multigenerational Black Families," *Human Nature,* 1 (1990): 123–143.

K. Christmon, "Parental Responsibility and Self-Image of African-American Fathers," *Families in Society,* 71 (1990): 562–567.

L. Dash, *When Children Want Children: The Urban Crisis in Teenage Childbearing* (William Morrow, 1989).

D. J. Eggebeen, L. J. Crockett, and A. J. Hawkins, "Patterns of Adult Male Coresidence Among Young Children of Adolescent Mothers," *Family Planning Perspectives,* 22 (1990): 219–223.

F. F. Furstenberg, J. Brooks-Gunn, and P. L. Chase-Lansdale, "Teenage Pregnancy and Childbearing," *American Psychologist,* 44 (1989): 313–320.

B. C. Miller and K. A. Moore, "Adolescent Sexual Behavior, Pregnancy, and Parenting," *Journal of Marriage and the Family,* 52 (1990): 1025–1044.

M. N. Wilson, "Child Development in the Context of the Black Extended Family," *American Psychologist,* 44 (1989): 380–391.

Internet: http://www.parentsplace.com/dialog/get/teenparents.html

PART 4

Relational Conflict and Dissolution

Relationships, especially marriage, are difficult to manage. But additional negative factors can put an unprecedented strain on families and society. Date rape is one social concern that has recently come to light. How do we define date rape, and how prevalent is it in society? Domestic violence is a common occurrence that is not new to our society, but the extent to which it may be reciprocal between men and women is still unknown. Statistics show that almost one out of every two marriages will end in divorce. The extent of the effects of divorce, however, remains a controversy among experts. There is disagreement, for example, on whether or not children of divorce are at greater risk than children of intact families of acquiring emotional and developmental problems as a result of their changed family situations. And what responsibilities does the father who loses custody of his children have to support them? Are there any situations in which the father would be justified in refusing to pay child support? The discussions in this section focus on conflicts in relationships and the impact of a dissolved marriage on the family.

- Is There a Date Rape Crisis in Society?

- Is There a Double Standard for Marital Violence?

- Are Children of Divorce at Greater Risk?

- Do Fathers Have Legitimate Reasons for Refusing to Pay Child Support?

ISSUE 14

Is There a Date Rape Crisis in Society?

YES: Robin Warshaw, from *I Never Called It Rape: The* Ms. *Report on Recognizing, Fighting, and Surviving Date and Acquaintance Rape* (Harper & Row, 1988)

NO: Katie Roiphe, from "Date Rape's Other Victim," *The New York Times Magazine* (June 13, 1993)

ISSUE SUMMARY

YES: Freelance journalist Robin Warshaw argues that date rape is a real problem experienced by many women but reported by few. She maintains that cultural stereotypes promote a blame-the-victim mentality that trivializes women, minimizes their experiences, and hides the true extent of date rape.

NO: Author Katie Roiphe asserts that declarations of a date rape crisis are overblown. Date rape, she writes, is an ill-defined, "catch-all" expression that is mostly used to serve the political purposes of some social critics. Roiphe argues that those who portray date rape as a significant social problem are undermining women's efforts for equality.

According to a nationwide survey conducted by *Ms.* magazine, clinical psychiatrist Mary P. Koss, and the National Institute for Mental Health, which is discussed by Robin Warshaw in the selection that follows, the majority of women who are raped are assaulted by someone they know. In most cases, the rapist is an acquaintance, a friend, or someone with whom the woman has grown familiar from previous dates; the fearsome stranger lurking in the bushes or hiding in the shadows accounts for about 20 percent of attacks on women. The contrast between the monstrous sexual aggressor who assaults women and the familiar dating partner is striking, and it may account for the confusion dating partners can experience over exactly what behaviors constitute date rape.

When is sex considered sex, and when is it considered assault? We are told that sexual activity that results in a woman having intercourse against her consent is rape. If a woman says no, sexual penetration is considered rape. There are those, however, who remain uncomfortable with defining unwanted sex between dates, acquaintances, or friends as a type of rape rather than as sex that resulted because of miscommunication or poor judgment.

Traditional ways of thinking about gender roles often surface to confuse the issue of date rape. For example, in a 1993 poll conducted by Yankelovich,

Clancey, and Shulman, 69 percent of men and 54 percent of women answered yes to the question, Do you believe that some women like to be talked into having sex? This response may reflect the influence of the media. For example, didn't Rhett grab Scarlett, kiss her passionately, and carry her up the stairs despite her protests in Margaret Mitchell's *Gone With the Wind*? And isn't that what she really wanted? Don't women in romance novels and on the soaps strenuously resist their partners' first attempts at lovemaking and then melt into their strong, capable arms?

These cultural images of romantic interaction in sexual situations lead to a wealth of questions on the issue. Is it part of the dating ritual for women to initially resist a man's sexual advances? If a woman is drunk and weakly protests a man's advances without success, is it rape? Do women sometimes mean yes when they say no? If a woman is dressed in revealing clothing, is she inviting sex? If she goes to a man's apartment or invites a man to her apartment for a drink and then participates in heavy petting, does that suggest consent? Do men have strong hormonal urges that, through no fault of their own, render them unrestrainable when sexually aroused? Are men entitled to sexual pleasures if they lavish money and attention on a date? Is it up to the woman to make it known in no uncertain terms that she does not want sex?

Is *rape* too strong a term for what some consider to be sexual miscommunication between partners? Has date rape been built into too big an issue —is it really a crisis? Should all sexual misunderstandings be labeled rape, regardless of intent or the degree of harm inflicted?

In the following selections, Robin Warshaw contends that *rape* is exactly the correct term for the type of sexual assault that sometimes occurs on dates. She asserts that date rape goes beyond a simple miscommunication between dating partners: it has nothing to do with romantic notions of mutual sexual intimacy between loving partners—and everything to do with being forcibly violated and emotionally maimed. To minimize its seriousness is detrimental to teenage girls and women and to society. Katie Roiphe, in opposition, argues that women must take some responsibility for what happens sexually on dates. She finds it demeaning to women to propose that they are so easily manipulated that they require special protection under the law where sex is involved. That attitude, she writes, perpetuates the stereotypes of men as violent, intimidating, and powerful, and of women as pure, fragile, and powerless.

YES
Robin Warshaw

THE REALITY OF ACQUAINTANCE RAPE

Women raped by men they know—acquaintance rape—is not an aberrant quirk of male-female relations. If you are a woman, your risk of being raped by someone you know is *four times greater* than your risk of being raped by a stranger.

A recent scientific study of acquaintance rape on 32 college campuses conducted by *Ms.* magazine and psychologist Mary P. Koss showed that significant numbers of women are raped on dates or by acquaintances, although most victims never report their attacks.

Ms. Survey Stats

- 1 in 4 women surveyed were victims of rape or attempted rape.
- 84 percent of those raped knew their attacker.
- 57 percent of the rapes happened on dates.

Those figures make acquaintance rape and date rape more common than left-handedness or heart attacks or alcoholism. These rapes are no recent campus fad or the fantasy of a few jilted females. They are real. And they are happening all around us.

THE EXTENT OF "HIDDEN" RAPE

Most states define rape as sexual assault in which a man uses his penis to commit vaginal penetration of a victim against her will, by force or threats of force or when she is physically or mentally unable to give her consent. Many states now also include unwanted anal and oral intercourse in that definition and some have removed gender-specific language to broaden the applicability of rape laws.

In acquaintance rape, the rapist and victim may know each other casually—having met through a common activity, mutual friend, at a party, as neighbors, as students in the same class, at work, on a blind date, or while traveling. Or they may have a closer relationship—as steady dates or former sexual partners. Although largely a hidden phenomenon because it's the least reported type of rape (and rape, in general, is the most underreported crime against a person), many organizations, counselors, and social researchers agree that acquaintance rape is the most prevalent rape crime today.

Only 90,434 rapes were reported to U.S. law enforcement agencies in 1986, a number that is conservatively believed to represent a minority of the actual rapes of all types taking place. Government estimates find that anywhere from three to ten rapes are committed for every rape reported. And while rapes by strangers are still underreported, rapes by acquaintances are virtually nonreported. Yet, based on intake observations made by staff at various rape-counseling centers (where victims come for treatment, but do not have to file police reports), 70 to 80 percent of all rape crimes are acquaintance rapes.

Those rapes are happening in a social environment in which sexual aggression occurs regularly. Indeed, less than half the college women questioned in the *Ms.* survey reported that they had experienced *no* sexual victimization in their lives thus far (the average age of respondents was 21). Many had experienced more than one episode of unwanted sexual touching, coercion, attempted rape, or rape. Using the data collected in the study... the following profile can be drawn of what happens in just one year of "social life" on America's college campuses:

Ms. Survey Stats

In one year 3,187 women reported suffering:

- 328 rapes (as defined by law)
- 534 attempted rapes (as defined by law)
- 837 episodes of sexual coercion (sexual intercourse obtained through the aggressor's continual arguments or pressure)
- 2,024 experiences of unwanted sexual contact (fondling, kissing, or petting committed against the woman's will)

Over the years, other researchers have documented the phenomenon of acquaintance rape. In 1957, a study conducted by Eugene J. Kanin of Purdue University in West Lafayette, Indiana, showed that 30 percent of women surveyed had suffered attempted or completed forced sexual intercourse while on a high school date. Ten years later, in 1967, while young people donned flowers and beads and talked of love and peace, Kanin found that more than 25 percent of the male college students surveyed had attempted to force sexual intercourse on a woman to the point that she cried or fought back. In 1977, after the blossoming of the women's movement and countless pop-culture attempts to extol the virtues of becoming a "sensitive man," Kanin found that 26 percent of the men he surveyed had tried to force intercourse on a woman and that 25 percent of the women questioned had suffered attempted or completed rape. In other words, two decades had passed since Kanin's first study, yet women were being raped by men they knew as frequently as before.

In 1982, a doctoral student at Auburn University in Auburn, Alabama, found that 25 percent of the undergraduate women surveyed had at least one experience of forced intercourse and that 93 percent of those episodes involved acquaintances. That same year, Auburn psychology professor and acquaintance-rape expert Barry R. Burkhart conducted a study in which 61 percent of the men said they had sexually touched a woman against her will.

Further north, at St. Cloud State University in St. Cloud, Minnesota, research in 1982 showed 29 percent of women surveyed reported being physically or psychologically forced to have sexual intercourse.

In 1984, 20 percent of the female students questioned in a study at the University of South Dakota in Vermillion, South Dakota, said they had been physically forced to have intercourse while on a date. At Brown University in Providence, Rhode Island, 16 percent of the women surveyed reported they were raped by an acquaintance and 11 percent of the men said they had forced sexual intercourse on a woman. And another study coauthored by Auburn's Burkhart showed 15 percent of the male respondents reporting having raped a date.

That same year, the study of acquaintance rape moved beyond the serenity of leafy college quadrangles into the hard reality of the "dangerous" outside world. A random sample survey of 930 women living in San Francisco, conducted by researcher Diana Russell, showed that 44 percent of the women questioned had been victims of rape or attempted rape —and that 88 percent of the rape victims knew their attackers. A Massachusetts Department of Public Health study, released in 1986, showed that two-thirds of the rapes reported at crisis centers were committed by acquaintances.

These numbers stand in stark contrast to what most people think of as rape: that is, a stranger (usually a black, Hispanic, or other minority) jumping out of the bushes at an unsuspecting female, brandishing a weapon, and assaulting her. The truth about rape—that it usually happens between people who know each other and is often committed by "regular" guys—is difficult to accept.

Most people never learn the truth until rape affects them or someone they care about. And many women are so confused by the dichotomy between their acquaintance-rape experience and what they thought rape really was that they are left with an awful new reality: Where once they feared strange men as they were taught to, they now fear strange men *and* all the men they know....

RAPE IS RAPE

Rape that occurs on dates or between people who know each other should not be seen as some sort of misguided sexual adventure: Rape is violence, not seduction. In stranger rape *and* acquaintance rape, the aggressor makes a decision to force his victim to submit to what he wants. The rapist believes he is entitled to force sexual intercourse from a woman and he sees interpersonal violence (be it simply holding the woman down with his body or brandishing a gun) as an acceptable way to achieve his goal.

"All rape is an exercise in power," writes Susan Brownmiller in her landmark book *Against Our Will: Men, Women and Rape.* Specifically, Brownmiller and others argue, rape is an exercise in the imbalance of power that exists between most men and women, a relationship that has forged the social order from ancient times on.

Today, that relationship continues. Many men are socialized to be sexually aggressive—to score, as it were, regardless of how. Many women are socialized to submit to men's wills, especially those men deemed desirable by society at large.

Maintaining such roles helps set the stage for acquaintance rape.

But despite their socialization, most men are not rapists. That is the good news.

The bad news, of course, is that so many are.

Ms. Survey Stat

1 in 12 of the male students surveyed had committed acts that met the legal definitions of rape or attempted rape.

BLAMING THE ACQUAINTANCE-RAPE VICTIM

Without question, many date rapes and acquaintance rapes could have been prevented by the woman—if she hadn't trusted a seemingly nice guy, if she hadn't gotten drunk, if she had acted earlier on the "bad feeling" that many victims later report they felt but ignored because they didn't want to seem rude, unfriendly, or immature. But acknowledging that in some cases the woman might have prevented the rape by making a different decision does not make her responsible for the crime. Says a counselor for an Oregon rape-crisis agency: "We have a saying here: 'Bad judgment is not a rapeable offense.'"

As a society, we don't blame the victims of most crimes as we do acquaintance-rape survivors. A mugging victim is not believed to "deserve it" for wearing a watch or carrying a pocketbook on the street. Likewise, a company is not "asking for it" when its profits are embezzled; a store owner is not to blame for handing over the cash drawer when threatened. These crimes occur because the perpetrator decides to commit them.

Acquaintance rape is no different. There are ways to reduce the odds, but, like all crimes, there is no way to be certain that it will not happen to you.

Yet acquaintance-rape victims are seen as responsible for the attacks, often more responsible than their assailants. "Date rape threatens the assumption that if you're good, good things happen to you. Most of us believe that bad things don't happen out of the blue," says psychologist Koss, chief investigator of the *Ms.* study, now affiliated with the department of psychiatry at the University of Arizona Medical School in Tucson, Arizona. Society, in general, is so disturbed by the idea that a "regular guy" could do such a thing—and, to be sure, many "regular guys" are made uncomfortable by a concept that views their actions as a crime—that they would rather believe that something is wrong with the woman making such an outlandish claim: She is lying, she has emotional problems, she hates men, she is covering up her own promiscuous behavior. In fact, the research in the *Ms.* survey shows that women who have been raped by men they know are not appreciably different in any personal traits or behaviors than women who are not raped.

Should we ask women not to trust men who seem perfectly nice? Should we tell them not to go to parties or on dates? Should we tell them not to drink? Should we tell them not to feel sexual? Certainly not. *It is not the victim who causes the rape.*

But many persist in believing just that. An April 1987 letter to syndicated columnist Ann Landers from a woman who had been raped by two different men she dated reportedly drew heavy negative reader mail after Landers responded supportively to the woman. "Too bad you didn't file charges against those creeps," Landers wrote. "I urge you to go for counseling immediately to rid yourself of the feeling of guilt and rage. You must get it through your head that you were not to blame."

So far, so good, but not for long. Three months later, Landers published a letter from an irate female reader who noted that the victim said she and the first man had "necked up a storm" before he raped her. Perhaps the raped woman hadn't intended to have intercourse, the reader said, "but she certainly must accept responsibility for encouraging the guy and making him think she was a willing partner. The trouble starts when she changes her mind after his passions are out of control. Then it's too late."

Landers bought this specious argument—a variant on the old "men can't help themselves" nonsense. In her reply to the follow-up letter she wrote, "Now I'm convinced that I must rethink my position and go back to telling women, 'If you don't want a complete sexual experience, keep a lively conversation going and his hands off you.'"

In other words, if you get raped, it's your own fault.

DATE RAPE AND ACQUAINTANCE RAPE ON COLLEGE CAMPUSES

Despite philosophical and political changes brought about by the women's movement, dating relationships between men and women are still often marked by passivity on the woman's part and aggression on the man's. Nowhere are these two seen in stronger contrast than among teenagers and young adults who often, out of their own fears, insecurity, and ignorance, adopt the worst sex-role stereotypes. Such an environment fosters a continuum of sexual victimization—

from unwanted sexual touching to psychologically coerced sex to rape—that is tolerated as normal. "Because sexually coercive behavior is so common in our male-female interactions, rape by an acquaintance may not be perceived as rape," says Py Bateman, director of Alternatives to Fear, a Seattle rape-education organization....

Not surprising, then, that the risk of rape is four times higher for women aged 16 to 24, the prime dating age, than for any other population group. Approximately half of all men arrested for rape are also 24 years old or younger. Since 26 percent of all 18- to 24-year-olds in the United States attend college, those institutions have become focal points for studying date rape and acquaintance rape, such as the *Ms.* research.

Ms. Survey Stat

For both men and women, the average age when a rape incident occurred (either as perpetrator or victim) was 18 1/2 years old.

Going to college often means going away from home, out from under parental control and protection and into a world of seemingly unlimited freedoms. The imperative to party and date, although strong in high school, burgeons in this environment. Alcohol is readily available and often used in stultifying amounts, encouraged by a college world that practically demands heavy drinking as proof of having fun. Marijuana, cocaine, LSD, methamphetamines, and other drugs are also often easy to obtain.

Up until the 1970s, colleges adopted a "substitute parent" attitude toward their students, complete with curfews (often more strict for females than males), liquor bans, and stringent disciplinary punishments. In that era, students were punished for violating the three-feet-on-the-floor rules during coed visiting hours in dormitories or for being caught with alcohol on college property. Although those regulations did not prevent acquaintance rape, they undoubtedly kept down the number of incidents by making women's dorms havens of no-men-allowed safety.

Such regulations were swept out of most schools during the Vietnam War era. Today, many campuses have coed dorms, with men and women often housed in alternating rooms on the same floor, with socializing unchecked by curfews or meaningful controls on alcohol and drugs. Yet, say campus crisis counselors, many parents still believe that they have properly prepared their children for college by helping them open local bank accounts and making sure they have enough underwear to last until the first trip home. By ignoring the realities of social pressures at college on male and female students—and the often catastrophic effects of those pressures—parents help perpetuate the awareness vacuum in which date rape and acquaintance rape continue to happen with regularity.

"What's changed for females is the illusion that they have control and they don't," says Claire P. Walsh, program director of the Sexual Assault Recovery Service at the University of Florida in Gainesville. "They know that they can go into chemical engineering or medical school and they've got their whole life planned, they're on a roll. They transfer that feeling of control into social situations and that's the illusion."

When looking at the statistical results of the *Ms.* survey, it's important to remember that many of these young peo-

ple still have years of socializing and dating ahead of them, years in which they may encounter still more acquaintance rape. Students, parents of college students, and college administrators should be concerned. But many are not, lulled by the same myths that pervade our society at large: Rape is not committed by people you know, against "good" girls, in "safe" places like university campuses.

THE OTHER VICTIMS OF ACQUAINTANCE RAPE

Date rape and acquaintance rape aren't confined to the college population, however. Interviews conducted across the country showed that women both younger and older than university students are frequently acquaintance-rape victims as well.

A significant number of teenage girls suffer date rape as their first or nearly first experience of sexual intercourse... and most tell no one about their attacks. Consider Nora, a high school junior, who was raped by a date as they watched TV in his parents' house or Jenny, 16, who was raped after she drank too much at a party. Even before a girl officially begins dating, she may be raped by a schoolmate or friend.

Then there are the older women, the "hidden" population of "hidden" rape victims—women who are over 30 years old when their rapes occur. Most are socially experienced, yet unprepared for their attacks nonetheless. Many are recently divorced and just beginning to try the dating waters again; some are married; others have never married. They include women like Helene, a Colorado woman who was 37 and the mother of a 10-year-old when she was raped by a man on their third date, and Rae, who was 45 when she was raped by a man she knew after inviting him to her Oklahoma home for coffee.

"I NEVER CALLED IT RAPE"

Ms. Survey Stat

Only 27 percent of the women whose sexual assault met the legal definition of rape thought of themselves as rape victims.

Because of her personal relationship with the attacker, however casual, it often takes a woman longer to perceive an action as rape when it involves a man she knows than it does when a stranger assaults her. For her to acknowledge her experience as rape would be to recognize the extent to which her trust was violated and her ability to control her own life destroyed.

Indeed, regardless of their age or background, many women interviewed ... told no one about their rapes, never confronted their attackers, and never named their assaults as rape until months or years later.

NO

Katie Roiphe

DATE RAPE'S OTHER VICTIM

One in four college women has been the victim of rape or attempted rape. One in four. I remember standing outside the dining hall in college, looking at a purple poster with this statistic written in bold letters. It didn't seem right. If sexual assault was really so pervasive, it seemed strange that the intricate gossip networks hadn't picked up more than one or two shadowy instances of rape. If I was really standing in the middle of an "epidemic," a "crisis" —if 25 percent of my women friends were really being raped—wouldn't I know it?

These posters were not presenting facts. They were advertising a mood. Preoccupied with issues like date rape and sexual harassment, campus feminists produce endless images of women as victims—women offended by a professor's dirty joke, women pressured into sex by peers, women trying to say no but not managing to get it across.

This portrait of the delicate female bears a striking resemblance to that 50's ideal my mother and other women of her generation fought so hard to leave behind. They didn't like her passivity, her wide-eyed innocence. They didn't like the fact that she was perpetually offended by sexual innuendo. They didn't like her excessive need for protection. She represented personal, social and intellectual possibilities collapsed, and they worked and marched, shouted and wrote to make her irrelevant for their daughters. But here she is again, with her pure intentions and her wide eyes. Only this time it is the feminists themselves who are breathing new life into her.

* * *

Is there a rape crisis on campus? Measuring rape is not as straightforward as it might seem. Neil Gilbert, a professor of social welfare at the University of California at Berkeley, questions the validity of the one-in-four statistic. Gilbert points out that in a 1985 survey undertaken by Ms. magazine and financed by the National Institute of Mental Health, 73 percent of the women categorized as rape victims did not initially define their experience as rape; it was Mary Koss, the psychologist conducting the study, who did.

One of the questions used to define rape was: "Have you had sexual intercourse when you didn't want to because a man gave you alcohol or drugs?"

From Katie Roiphe, "Date Rape's Other Victim," *The New York Times Magazine* (June 13, 1993). Adapted from Katie Roiphe, *The Morning After: Sex, Fear and Feminism on Campus* (Little, Brown, 1993). Copyright © 1993 by Katie Roiphe. Reprinted by permission of Little, Brown & Company.

The phrasing raises the issue of agency. Why aren't college women responsible for their own intake of alcohol or drugs? A man may give her drugs, but she herself decides to take them. If we assume that women are not all helpless and naïve, then they should be held responsible for their choice to drink or take drugs. If a woman's "judgment is impaired" and she has sex, it isn't necessarily always the man's fault; it isn't necessarily always rape.

As Gilbert delves further into the numbers, he does not necessarily disprove the one-in-four statistic, but he does clarify what it means—the so-called rape epidemic on campuses is more a way of interpreting, a way of seeing, than a physical phenomenon. It is more about a change in sexual politics than a change in sexual behavior. Whether or not one in four college women has been raped, then, is a matter of opinion, not a matter of mathematical fact.

That rape is a fact in some women's lives is not in question. It's hard to watch the solemn faces of young Bosnian girls, their words haltingly translated, as they tell of brutal rapes; or to read accounts of a suburban teen-ager raped and beaten while walking home from a shopping mall. We all agree that rape is a terrible thing, but we no longer agree on what rape is. Today's definition has stretched beyond bruises and knives, threats of death or violence to include emotional pressure and the influence of alcohol. The lines between rape and sex begin to blur. The one-in-four statistic on those purple posters is measuring something elusive. It is measuring her word against his in a realm where words barely exist. There is a gray area in which one person's rape may be another's bad night. Definitions become entangled in passionate ideological battles. There hasn't been a remarkable change in the number of women being raped; just a change in how receptive the political climate is to those numbers.

The next question, then, is who is identifying this epidemic and why. Somebody is "finding" this rape crisis, and finding it for a reason. Asserting the prevalence of rape lends urgency, authority to a broader critique of culture.

In a dramatic description of the rape crisis, Naomi Wolf writes in "The Beauty Myth" that "Cultural representation of glamorized degradation has created a situation among the young in which boys rape and girls get raped *as a normal course of events*." The italics are hers. Whether or not Wolf really believes rape is part of the "normal course of events" these days, she is making a larger point. Wolf's rhetorical excess serves her larger polemic about sexual politics. Her dramatic prose is a call to arms. She is trying to rally the feminist troops. Wolf uses rape as a red flag, an undeniable sign that things are falling apart.

From Susan Brownmiller—who brought the politics of rape into the mainstream with her 1975 best seller, "Against Our Will: Men, Women and Rape"—to Naomi Wolf, feminist prophets of the rape crisis are talking about something more than forced penetration. They are talking about what they define as a "rape culture." Rape is a natural trump card for feminism. Arguments about rape can be used to sequester feminism in the teary province of trauma and crisis. By blocking analysis with its claims to unique pandemic suffering, the rape crisis becomes a powerful source of authority.

Dead serious, eyes wide with concern, a college senior tells me that she believes one in four is too conservative an estimate. This is not the first time I've heard this. She tells me the right statistic is closer to one in two. That means one in two women are raped. It's amazing, she says, amazing that so many of us are sexually assaulted every day.

What is amazing is that this student actually believes that 50 percent of women are raped. This is the true crisis. Some substantial number of young women are walking around with this alarming belief: a hyperbole containing within it a state of perpetual fear.

* * *

"Acquaintance Rape: Is Dating Dangerous?" is a pamphlet commonly found at counseling centers. The cover title rises from the shards of a shattered photograph of a boy and girl dancing. Inside, the pamphlet offers a sample date-rape scenario. She thinks:

"He was really good looking and he had a great smile. . . . We talked and found we had a lot in common. I really liked him. When he asked me over to his place for a drink I thought it would be O.K. He was such a good listener and I wanted him to ask me out again."

She's just looking for a sensitive boy, a good listener with a nice smile, but unfortunately his intentions are not as pure as hers. Beneath that nice smile, he thinks:

"She looked really hot, wearing a sexy dress that showed off her great body. We started talking right away. I knew that she liked me by the way she kept smiling and touching my arm while she was speaking. She seemed pretty relaxed so I asked her back to my place for a drink. . . . When she said 'Yes' I knew that I was going to be lucky!"

These cardboard stereotypes don't just educate freshmen about rape. They also

educate them about "dates" and about sexual desire. With titles like "Friends Raping Friends: Could It Happen to You?" date-rape pamphlets call into question all relationships between men and women. Beyond warning students about rape, the rape-crisis movement produces its own images of sexual behavior, in which men exert pressure and women resist. By defining the dangerous date in these terms—with this type of male and this type of female, and their different expectations —these pamphlets promote their own perspective on how men and women feel about sex: men are lascivious, women are innocent.

The sleek images of pressure and resistance projected in rape education movies, videotapes, pamphlets and speeches create a model of acceptable sexual behavior. The don'ts imply their own set of do's. The movement against rape, then, not only dictates the way sex *shouldn't be* but also the way it *should be*. Sex should be gentle, it should not be aggressive; it should be absolutely equal, it should not involve domination and submission; it should be tender, not ambivalent; it should communicate respect, it shouldn't communicate consuming desire.

In "Real Rape," Susan Estrich, a professor of law at the University of Southern California Law Center, slips her ideas about the nature of sexual encounters into her legal analysis of the problem of rape. She writes: "Many feminists would argue that so long as women are powerless relative to men, viewing a 'yes' as a sign of true consent is misguided. . . . Many women who say yes to men they know, whether on dates or on the job, would say no if they could. . . . Women's silence sometimes is the product not of passion and desire but of pressure and fear."

Like Estrich, most rape-crisis feminists claim they are not talking about sex; they're talking about violence. But, like Estrich, they are also talking about sex. With their advice, their scenarios, their sample aggressive male, the message projects a clear comment on the nature of sexuality: women are often unwilling participants. They say yes because they feel they have to, because they are intimidated by male power.

The idea of "consent" has been redefined beyond the simple assertion that "no means no." Politically correct sex involves a yes, and a specific yes at that. According to the premise of "active consent," we can no longer afford ambiguity. We can no longer afford the dangers of unspoken consent. A former director of Columbia's date-rape education program told New York magazine, "Stone silence throughout an entire physical encounter with someone is not explicit consent."

This apparently practical, apparently clinical proscription cloaks retrograde assumptions about the way men and women experience sex. The idea that only an explicit yes means yes proposes that, like children, women have trouble communicating what they want. Beyond its dubious premise about the limits of female communication, the idea of active consent bolsters stereotypes of men just out to "get some" and women who don't really want any.

Rape-crisis feminists express nostalgia for the days of greater social control, when the university acted in loco parentis and women were protected from the insatiable force of male desire. The rhetoric of feminists and conservatives blurs and overlaps in this desire to keep our youth safe and pure.

By viewing rape as encompassing more than the use or threat of physical violence to coerce someone into sex, rape-crisis feminists reinforce traditional views about the fragility of the female body and will. According to common definitions of date rape, even "verbal coercion" or "manipulation" constitute rape. Verbal coercion is defined as "a woman's consenting to unwanted sexual activity because of a man's verbal arguments not including verbal threats of force." The belief that "verbal coercion" is rape pervades workshops, counseling sessions and student opinion pieces. The suggestion lurking beneath this definition of rape is that men are not just physically but also intellectually and emotionally more powerful than women.

Imagine men sitting around in a circle talking about how she called him impotent and how she manipulated him into sex, how violated and dirty he felt afterward, how coercive she was, how she got him drunk first, how he hated his body and he couldn't eat for three weeks afterward. Imagine him calling this rape. Everyone feels the weight of emotional pressure at one time or another. The question is not whether people pressure each other but how our minds and our culture transform that pressure into full-blown assault. There would never be a rule or a law or even a pamphlet or peer counseling group for men who claimed to have been emotionally raped or verbally pressured into sex. And for the same reasons—assumption of basic competence, free will and strength of character—there should be no such rules or groups or pamphlets about women.

In discussing rape, campus feminists often slip into an outdated sexist vocabulary. But we have to be careful about using rape as metaphor. The sheer physical fact of rape has always been loaded with cultural meaning. Throughout history, women's bodies have been seen as property, as chaste objects, as virtuous vessels to be "dishonored," "ruined," "defiled." Their purity or lack of purity has been a measure of value for the men to whom they belonged.

"Politically, I call it rape whenever a woman has sex and feels violated," writes Catharine MacKinnon, a law professor and feminist legal scholar best known for her crusade against pornography. The language of virtue and violation reinforces retrograde stereotypes. It backs women into old corners. Younger feminists share MacKinnon's vocabulary and the accompanying assumptions about women's bodies. In one student's account of date rape in the Rag, a feminist magazine at Harvard, she talks about the anguish of being "defiled." Another writes, "I long to be innocent again." With such anachronistic constructions of the female body, with all their assumptions about female purity, these young women frame their experience of rape in archaic, sexist terms. Of course, sophisticated modern-day feminists don't use words like honor or virtue anymore. They know better than to say date-rape victims have been "defiled." Instead, they call it "post-traumatic stress syndrome." They tell the victim she should not feel "shame," she should feel "traumatized." Within their overtly political psychology, forced penetration takes on a level of metaphysical significance: date rape resonates through a woman's entire life.

Combating myths about rape is one of the central missions of the rape-crisis movement. They spend money and energy trying to break down myths like "She asked for it." But with all their noise about rape myths, rape-crisis feminists are generating their own. The plays, the poems, the pamphlets, the Take Back the Night speakouts, are propelled by the myth of innocence lost. . . .

As long as we're taking back the night, we might as well take back our own purity. Sure, we were all kind of innocent, playing in the sandbox with bright red shovels—boys, too. We can all look back through the tumultuous tunnel of adolescence on a honey-glazed childhood, with simple rules and early bedtimes. We don't have to look at parents fighting, at sibling struggles, at casting out one best friend for another in the Darwinian playground. This is not the innocence lost; this is the innocence we never had.

The idea of a fall from childhood grace, pinned on one particular moment, a moment over which we had no control, much lamented, gives our lives a compelling narrative structure. It's easy to see why the 17-year-old likes it; it's easy to see why the rape-crisis feminist likes it. It's a natural human impulse put to political purpose. But in generating and perpetuating such myths, we should keep in mind that myths about innocence have been used to keep women inside and behind veils. They have been used to keep them out of work and in labor. . . .

* * *

People have asked me if I have ever been date-raped. And thinking back on complicated nights, on too many glasses of wine, on strange and familiar beds, I would have to say yes. With such a sweeping definition of rape, I wonder how many people there are, male or female, who haven't been date-raped at one point or another. People pressure and manipulate and cajole each other into all sorts of things all of the time. As Susan Sontag wrote, "Since Christianity upped the ante and concentrated on sexual behavior as the root of virtue, everything pertaining to sex has been a 'special case' in our culture, evoking peculiarly inconsistent attitudes." No human interactions are free from pressure, and the idea that sex is, or can be, makes it what Sontag calls a "special case," vulnerable to the inconsistent expectations of double standard.

With their expansive version of rape, rape-crisis feminists are inventing a kinder, gentler sexuality. Beneath the broad definition of rape, these feminists are endorsing their own utopian vision of sexual relations: sex without struggle, sex without power, sex without persuasion, sex without pursuit. If verbal coercion constitutes rape, then the word rape itself expands to include any kind of sex a woman experiences as negative.

When Martin Amis spoke at Princeton, he included a controversial joke: "As far as I'm concerned, you can change your mind before, even during, but just not after sex." The reason this joke is funny, and the reason it's also too serious to be funny, is that in the current atmosphere you can change your mind afterward. Regret can signify rape. A night that was a blur, a night you wish hadn't happened, can be rape. Since "verbal coercion" and "manipulation" are ambiguous, it's easy to decide afterwards that he manipulated you. You can realize it weeks or even years later. This is a movement that deals in retrospective trauma.

Rape has become a catchall expression, a word used to define everything that is unpleasant and disturbing about relations between the sexes. Students say things like "I realize that sexual harassment is a kind of rape." If we refer to a whole range of behavior from emotional pressure to sexual harassment as "rape," then the idea itself gets diluted. It ceases to be powerful as either description or accusation.

Some feminists actually collapse the distinction between rape and sex. Catharine MacKinnon writes: "Compare victims' reports of rape with women's reports of sex. They look a lot alike.... In this light, the major distinction between intercourse (normal) and rape (abnormal) is that the normal happens so often that one cannot get anyone to see anything wrong with it."

There are a few feminists involved in rape education who object to the current expanding definitions of sexual assault. Gillian Greensite, founder of the rape prevention education program at the University of California at Santa Cruz, writes that the seriousness of the crime "is being undermined by the growing tendency of some feminists to label all heterosexual miscommunication and insensitivity as acquaintance rape." From within the rape-crisis movement, Greensite's dissent makes an important point. If we are going to maintain an *idea* of rape, then we need to reserve it for instances of physical violence, or the threat of physical violence.

But some people want the melodrama. They want the absolute value placed on experience by absolute words. Words like "rape" and "verbal coercion" channel the confusing flow of experience into something easy to understand. The idea of date rape comes at us fast and coherent. It comes at us when we've just left home and haven't yet figured out where to put our new futons or how to organize our new social lives. The rhetoric about date rape defines the terms, gives names to nameless confusions and sorts through mixed feelings with a sort of insistent consistency. In the first rush of sexual experience, the fear of date rape offers a tangible framework to locate fears that are essentially abstract.

When my 55-year-old mother was young, navigating her way through dates, there was a definite social compass. There were places not to let him put his hands. There were invisible lines. The pill wasn't available. Abortion wasn't legal. And sex was just wrong. Her mother gave her "mad money" to take out on dates in case her date got drunk and she needed to escape. She had to go far enough to hold his interest and not far enough to endanger her reputation.

Now the rape-crisis feminists are offering new rules. They are giving a new political weight to the same old no. My mother's mother told her to drink sloe gin fizzes so she wouldn't drink too much and get too drunk and go too far. Now the date rape pamphlets tell us: "Avoid excessive use of alcohol and drugs. Alcohol and drugs interfere with clear thinking and effective communication." My mother's mother told her to stay away from empty rooms and dimly lighted streets. In "I Never Called It Rape," Robin Warshaw writes, "Especially with recent acquaintances, women should insist on going only to public places such as restaurants and movie theaters."

There is a danger in these new rules. We shouldn't need to be reminded that the rigidly conformist 50's were not the heyday of women's power. Barbara Ehrenreich writes of "re-making love," but there is a danger in re-making love

in its old image. The terms may have changed, but attitudes about sex and women's bodies have not. Rape-crisis feminists threaten the progress that's been made. They are chasing the same stereotypes our mothers spent so much energy escaping.

One day I was looking through my mother's bookshelves and I found her old battered copy of Germaine Greer's feminist classic, "The Female Eunuch." The pages were dogeared and whole passages marked with penciled notes. It was 1971 when Germaine Greer fanned the fires with "The Female Eunuch" and it was 1971 when my mother read it, brand new, explosive, a tough and sexy terrorism for the early stirrings of the feminist movement.

Today's rape-crisis feminists threaten to create their own version of the desexualized woman Greer complained of 20 years ago. Her comments need to be recycled for present-day feminism. "It is often falsely assumed," Greer writes, "even by feminists, that sexuality is the enemy of the female who really wants to develop these aspects of her personality.... It was not the insistence upon her sex that weakened the American women student's desire to make something of her education, but the insistence upon a *passive* sexual *role* [Greer's italics]. In fact, the chief instrument in the deflection and perversion of female energy is the denial of female sexuality for the substitution of femininity or sexlessness."

It is the passive sexual role that threatens us still, and it is the denial of female sexual agency that threatens to propel us backward.

POSTSCRIPT

Is There a Date Rape Crisis in Society?

In our society there are those who continue to believe that it is logical for men to expect sex in certain situations. For example, a woman may be perceived as "asking for it" if she wears a low-cut tank top and no bra; or goes to a bar alone; or invites a man into her apartment after a date; or consents to a wide range of heavy petting but turns down actual penetration; or has a reputation for sleeping around; or initially says yes to sex, then changes her mind.

There seems to be a societal consensus that rape is less likely to be considered "real" if there are no bruises, cuts, scratches, or torn clothing, and if the sexual assault is perpetrated by an acquaintance, friend, or dating partner rather than by a knife-wielding stranger. Rape is also less likely to be believed if a woman does not file charges immediately. If she waits two weeks or longer, not many people are likely to consider her account credible.

This debate has many extremes. In Lakewood, California, a group of high school boys, who called themselves the Spur Posse, gave the word *scoring* a whole new meaning. The members of the group would compete to see who could persuade the greatest number of girls to have sexual intercourse. Achieving orgasm with a fresh partner resulted in a point on the Posse scoreboard. Their sexual conquests have been discussed and debated on talk shows and highlighted on news magazine programs, prompting much public dialogue. At the time the story hit the front pages, the young man with the highest score had accumulated 66 points.

When interviewed in *Time* magazine (April 5, 1993), the mother of one of the teenage boys said, "Those girls are trash." About her son, she confided, "What can you do? It's a testosterone thing." Under what conditions would the sexual exploits of these young men qualify as date rape? Does the mother's attitude fit with current cultural attitudes toward gender and sexuality? In a previous article in *Time* (June 3, 1991), Claire Walsh, a consultant with expertise in sexual assault, described prevailing attitudes toward male sexual aggression this way: "Real men don't take no for an answer."

At Antioch College in Ohio, students have voted in a lengthy Sexual Offense Policy, which describes in detail how to proceed in a sexual relationship. With each step of increasing sexual intimacy, partners must confirm their willingness to participate—"May I kiss you?" "May I unbutton your shirt?" "Is it okay if I stroke your thigh?" According to a recent *Newsweek* article (October 25, 1993), the purpose of the policy "is to empower these students to become equal partners when it comes time to mate."

Do you think we have been too quick to label all nonconsensual sex as rape, as Roiphe reports? Or do you believe, as Warshaw insists, that date rape is a real concern that has only recently received the public attention that it deserves?

SUGGESTED READINGS

F. S. Christopher and M. Frandsen, "Strategies of Influence in Sex and Dating," *Journal of Social and Personal Relationships,* 7 (1991): 89–105.

F. S. Christopher, L. A. Owens, and H. Stecker, "Exploring the Darkside of Courtship: A Test of a Model Premarital Sexual Aggressiveness," *Journal of Marriage and the Family,* 55 (1993): 469–479.

R. E. Dobash and R. P. Dobash, *Women, Violence, and Social Change* (Routledge, 1992).

L. A. Fairstein, *Sexual Violence* (William Morrow, 1993).

S. A. Lloyd, "The Darkside of Courtship: Violence and Sexual Exploitation," *Family Relations,* 40 (1991): 14–20.

M. A. Pirog-Good and J. E. Stets, eds., *Violence in Dating Relationships: Emerging Social Issues* (Prager, 1989).

G. W. Russell, ed., *Violence in Intimate Relationships* (PMA, 1988).

A. Vachss, *Sex Crimes* (Random House, 1993).

ISSUE 15

Is There a Double Standard for Marital Violence?

YES: Armin A. Brott, from "Battered Men: The Full Story," An Essay on the World Wide Web (October 18, 1994)

NO: Russell P. Dobash et al., from "The Myth of Sexual Symmetry in Marital Violence," *Social Problems* (February 1992)

ISSUE SUMMARY

YES: Armin A. Brott, a freelance writer and lecturer on fatherhood and parenting issues, argues that there is a double standard for domestic violence, with men being defined by masculine stereotypes and ignored as real victims of spousal battering.

NO: Professor Russell P. Dobash and his colleagues protest that the notion that women and men are equally victimized by marital violence is greatly exaggerated and is based on a misreading of the evidence.

One of the most frequently debated issues among those who study or witness spousal battering is whether or not both partners are equally responsible for the initiation and use of verbal and physical aggression in marital relationships. Is husband battering real? Is society culturally predisposed to discount any incident of spousal battering when it applies to the male partner as victim? Is it considered politically incorrect to suggest that women might reciprocate or initiate marital violence? Is control and domination solely the domain of men in relationships? These are a few of the questions currently being discussed in the realm of domestic violence.

Many men, upset by their portrayal as chronic abusers of women, are beginning to call for fairness in reporting and research. They describe marital violence as a two-way street and ask that women begin to take responsibility for their participation in marital violence. Male advocates argue that women in violent relationships are envisioned as passive and helpless and are given protection and access to social services while men in similar circumstances are ignored. They call the current debate on marital violence one-sided and label it "male bashing."

Some social analysts, distressed by the lack of understanding and community support for battered women, point out that the batterer is almost always male. They cite studies to show that violence by men is more likely to result in serious physical injury than violence by women. Advocates for women point out that if women strike back it is typically in self-defense. They feel that acceptance of coresponsibility and coaccountability ignores the reality of how and why violence occurs in relationships. Individuals on this side of the argument characterize the current dialogue as an attempt to distract the public from the detrimental consequences of wife battering and the necessity of taking social action.

Evidence that marital violence is mutual is based mainly on information gathered from one instrument—the Conflict Tactics Scale (CTS). National surveys using this scale indicate that women are as likely as men to say that they have initiated at least *one* of the behaviors listed—push, shove, slap, choke, kick, hit, beat up, or threaten with a knife or gun—at least *one* time in their current relationship.

In the following selections, Armin A. Brott argues that because husband battering can have severe physical and psychological consequences for the men involved and can lead to regular and more severe violence over time, it deserves attention. He reasons that any violence between spouses, regardless of who initiates it, should not be considered inconsequential. Brott states that accepting some spousal violence as "right" and other types as "wrong" supports the negative cultural stereotype that aggression is sometimes an acceptable way to resolve conflict or to gain control of a person or a situation and that it promotes a double standard of marital violence.

Russell P. Dobash and his colleagues assert that although the CTS measures a few specific acts of battering, it does not gather information on what actions preceded the battering or whether or not any of the responses were in self-defense. Among other criticisms, these researchers say that the CTS also fails to report injuries or to ask whether actions occurred in one violent episode or happened repeatedly over several months or years. Because husband battering is rare and usually occurs in instances in which wives are trying to protect themselves, and because it typically does not lead to severe injury, Dobash et al. question whether it should be considered a serious social concern when compared to wife battering.

YES

Armin A. Brott

BATTERED MEN: THE FULL STORY

" ... she started pawing and ripping at him with her fingers, scratching his back and face ..."

—From Dec. 12, 1990 police report detailing
the beating of Stanley G. by his wife

" ... multiple bruises, abrasions and lacerations ... chest wall contusion ... psychological trauma ..."

—From the hospital injury report of the same incident

Billboards, radio and TV ads across the country proclaim that "every fifteen seconds a woman is beaten by a man." Violence against women is clearly a problem of national importance, but has anyone ever asked how often men are beaten by women? The unfortunate fact is that men are the victims of domestic violence at least as often as women. While the very idea of men being beaten by their wives runs contrary to many of our deeply ingrained beliefs about men and women, female violence against men is a well-documented phenomenon almost completely ignored by both the media and society.

Consider recent studies on family violence. In 1975, and again in 1985, researchers Murray A. Straus, Ph.D., and Richard J. Gelles, Ph.D., et al., conducted the National Family Violence Survey, one of the largest and most respected studies of family violence ever done in this country. The Survey showed that men are just as likely to be the victims of domestic violence as women. In addition, Straus and Gelles found that between 1975 and 1985, the overall rate of domestic violence by men against women decreased, while women's violence against men actually increased. In 1991, to avoid accusations of gender bias, Straus recomputed the assault rates based solely on the responses of the 2,947 women in the 1985 Survey. The new results confirmed that even according to women, men are the ones more likely to be assaulted by their partners.

Violence takes various forms. There is no question that since men are, on average, bigger and stronger than women, they can do more damage in a fistfight. However, according to Professors R. L. McNeely and Coramae

Richey Mann, "the average man's size and strength are neutralized by guns and knives, boiling water, bricks, fireplace pokers and baseball bats." In fact, a 1984 study of 6,200 cases of reported domestic assault found that 86% of female-on-male violence involved weapons, while only 25% of male-on-female violence did.

But not all men are bigger than their wives. On one occasion, Stanley G., whose wife weighed over two hundred pounds, locked himself in his car to keep her from attacking him. She managed to get in anyway. Once inside, she shoved him face-first into the passenger side of the seat and jumped on him, putting her knees in his back. Stanley reached for the cellular phone to call for help but his wife wrestled it away from him and hit him with it several times on the side of the head.

According to many women's rights advocates, female violence against men—if it exists at all—is purely a self-defense response to male violence. Several studies, however, show that women initiate about one quarter of all domestic assaults, men initiate another quarter, and the remaining half are classified as "mutual." Other researchers, attempting to discredit the findings on men as victims, claim that since women are physically weaker and do less damage, only "severe assaults" should be compared. The results of that analysis show men are only slightly more likely (35% by men, 30% by women) to initiate the violence. Overall, Dr. Straus found that whether the analysis is based on all assaults, or is focused exclusively on dangerous assaults, "about as many women as men attack a spouse who has not hit them during a one year period." Clearly, then, the claim that women's violence is purely "self-defense" doesn't hold water.

But if female-on-male domestic violence is so widespread, why haven't we heard about it before? For several reasons. First, men, in general, are extremely reluctant to report that they have been the victims of any assault. After all, men are supposed to be tough, able to take care of themselves, right? What would people think...? "Men are trained not to ask for help, and a man's not being able to solve his own problems is seen as a sign of weakness," says Dr. Alvin Baraff, a psychotherapist and the founder of MenCenter, a Washington, D.C. counseling and research group focusing on men. It's hardly a surprise, then, that men report all types of violent victimization 32% less frequently than women, according to the 1990 Department of Justice Survey of Criminal Victimization.

But confessing to being knocked around by another man is a piece of cake compared to admitting being victimized by a woman. Why? Most likely, men fear—quite justifiably—society's traditional reaction. In 18th- and 19th-century France, a husband who had been pushed around by his wife would be forced by the community to wear women's clothing and to ride through the village, sitting backwards on a donkey, holding its tail. If he tried to avoid the punishment, the crowd would instead punish the man's closest neighbor—for having allowed such a travesty to occur so close to his own home. This humiliating practice, called the charivari, was also common in other parts of Europe. In Brittany, villagers strapped wife-beaten husbands to carts and "paraded them ignominiously through a booing populace."

Modern versions of the charivari persist today. Take Skip W., who participated in a program on domestic violence aired on the short-lived Jesse Jackson Show in 1991. Skip related how his wife repeatedly hit him and attacked him with knives and scissors. The audience's reaction was exactly what male victims who go public fear most: laughter, and constant, derisive snickering. Even when they are severely injured, men will go to great lengths to avoid telling anyone what they've been through. Dr. Ronn Berrol, an emergency-room physician at Mercy Hospital in San Diego, sees a lot of men with hot-water burns on the face, deep cuts on the hands, and other injuries consistent with being on the receiving end of domestic violence. But when Berrol asks how they were injured, most of these victims are evasive and claim they somehow "did it themselves or that their kids accidentally dropped something on them."

A few men, though, are willing to swallow their pride and call the police when they've been abused by their wives. While each of the police officers I spoke with very carefully claimed that "domestic violence calls are all handled the same way—regardless of the gender of the victim," male victims tell a very different story. Tracy T., for example, a 36-year old professional from near San Francisco, was regularly attacked by his wife and, just as regularly, called the police. "But every time they'd show up, they'd just laugh it off and tell me not to take it so seriously."

One evening, after his wife had hit him with a shoe and thrown a phone at him, Tracy says he finally decided enough was enough. When she came at him again, he slapped her. "She immediately stopped hitting me and called the police." When they arrived a few minutes later, Tracy tried to explain what had happened. "There I was, cuts and bruises all over my arms, but when I told the cops I'd only slapped her in self-defense, they told me I was under arrest for beating my wife." For Skip W., things weren't much better. After he reported his wife's violence, he was ordered to attend a program for abusive men, while his wife was put into a program for battered women.

But besides the police, the mental health community has also been in deep denial when it comes to acknowledging men's victimization. Because most therapists rarely see battered men or abusive women, many of them ignore subtle (or not so subtle) clues that their male patients may be abused, or that their female patients may be violent. For example, when a man admits he loses his temper, most therapists, in an attempt to find out whether he might be physically abusive, will ask a few questions. The most common ones would probably be, "How do you express your anger when you lose your temper? Do you throw things? Do you hit people?" On the other hand, female patients who admit they lose their tempers are rarely asked these questions.

But if the right questions aren't asked, the truth just won't come out. Dr. John G. Macchietto, a counseling psychologist and Director of the Student Counseling Center at Tarleton State University in Texas, recently began doing what he calls "role reversals" with his patients. A woman patient who wanted a better relationship with her boyfriend, complained she was often angry at how insensitive he was. When Macchietto pressed her to explain how she expressed her anger, the woman replied that she "hit him—sometimes with heavy objects—during arguments" and that it was always she who struck him, never the reverse.

Unfortunately, most therapists seem uninterested in confronting their own stereotypes about domestic violence. One man, Dean C. had an experience that in many ways sums up the mental health community's attitude towards the problem. Dean and his then-girlfriend went to see a therapist to discuss, among other things, her violence towards him. During one session, Dean told the therapist about an occasion when he had fallen asleep on the couch while watching TV. About 2 a.m., he was awakened by his girlfriend, pounding on the front door. After Dean opened the door to tell her to go home, she suddenly clobbered him over the head with a glass seltzer bottle. After hearing of this incident, the therapist looked at Dean and asked: "Do you often fall asleep in front of the TV?"

Another aspect of female violence the mental-health professionals usually overlook is lesbian partner abuse. Victims of female-against-female domestic violence—a widespread yet completely unacknowledged issue in the lesbian community—are frequently viewed as crazy. Susan L. Morrow, one of the authors of a 1989 article in the Journal of Counseling and Development, witnessed a therapist refer to a lesbian who had been abused by her partner as "borderline" and "paranoid." The fact that the patient was a victim was completely ignored. Morrow and co-author Donna M. Hawxhurst found that several myths—that women are less aggressive than men and therefore don't batter, and that women are incapable of inflicting serious harm—"have contributed to the secrecy surrounding the issue" of lesbian partner abuse.

When it comes to domestic violence, society seems to have one set of rules for men and another for women. Perhaps it's because we have been socialized to view women's violence as somehow less "real" (and consequently more acceptable) than men's violence. A 1989 study published

in the Journal of Interpersonal Violence found that "both men and women evaluated female violence less negatively than male violence." When it came to domestic violence, the researchers found that "[p]hysical violence of any kind was perceived less negatively when the female in the arguing couple was the aggressor." The double standard for violence apparently extends as far as murder. A recent survey of 60,000 people over 18, conducted by the Department of Justice, found that people rated a husband's stabbing his wife to death 40% worse than a wife's stabbing her husband to death.

There are several very serious effects of society's reluctance to acknowledge the female potential for violence. First, women are subtly encouraged to be more violent. Dr. Straus found that "a large number of girls have been told by their mothers 'If he gets fresh, slap him.'" Images of women kicking, punching, and slapping men with complete impunity are not only widespread in movies, TV, and books, but the viewer/reader's reaction is usually "good for her." Second, while it is possible to argue that a slap is unlikely to do any severe damage, not recognizing that a slap is still violence sets a rather dangerous precedent. Arresting a man who slaps a woman, while dismissing a woman who slaps a man as "nothing to worry about," both condones violence and reinforces a double standard that historically has been used to oppress women in the name of "protection."

Men's victimization is a fact. Nevertheless, a few nagging questions remain: First, if men are so much bigger and stronger, why don't they protect themselves? The answer, when you think about it, makes perfect sense. First of all, at the same time little girls are being taught it's OK to slap, little boys are being told "Never hit a girl." And when these little boys grow up, they are told that any man who hits a woman is a bully. But if a woman hits him, he's supposed to "take it like a man." James B., for example, is a battered husband who was repeatedly told by his therapists that his wife's violence was something he'd "just have to put up with." Second, according to Professor Suzanne Steinmetz, Director of the Family Research Institute at Indiana University-Purdue University at Indianapolis (IUPUI), men recognize the severe damage they are capable of doing and therefore consciously try to limit it.

These reasons explain why most abused men, no matter how capable they are of doing so, offer little or no resistance to their partners' physical violence. And many women, well aware of these fears, may actually continue their abuse, knowing they can get away with it. One man interviewed by Dr. Steinmetz recounted the single time he retaliated against his wife's physical abuse, hitting her in the mouth. "She went flying across the room...." After that, because he realized how badly he could hurt her, he continued to take her physical abuse without retaliation.

Some men, though, are simply unable to offer any resistance to their partner's violence. James B., who now helps other men by doing volunteer peer-counseling, told me about one of his clients, a blind man who was regularly abused by his girlfriend. "She'd just turn the TV up real loud," he said. "So he could never tell when she was coming at him."

Not fighting back is one thing, but why would any sane person stay in an abusive relationship? It may surprise some people to learn that men's reasons differ little from women's: economics and con-

cern for the children. Although the average male victim of domestic abuse has more financial resources available than his average female counterpart, this is changing fast. As more and more women enter the workforce, it's getting harder and harder to find a traditional "man-is-the-sole-breadwinner" family any more. In addition, more men than women lost their jobs in the recent depression, leaving them completely dependent on their wives' income and unable to support themselves alone.

Many abused women fear that if they leave their husbands, the violence they have experienced may be directed against their children. But abused men too—despite widespread stereotypes to the contrary—are just as concerned for their children as women are. Dean C. (the guy who falls asleep in front of the TV) for example, delayed breaking up with his abusive girlfriend because he thought he could better protect the children by staying. His girlfriend repeatedly beat her daughter (from a previous relationship) and often screamed viciously at their infant son. Moreover, since women still get physical custody of children in over 85% of all divorce cases, many men are hesitant to leave, realizing that if they do, the courts will severely limit their access to their children.

For a man, deciding to leave an abusive relationship is only half the battle. The other half is, "Where do I go?" For women, shelters and support groups exist, although still scarce and pathetically under-funded. But where are the facilities for men? Over a dozen calls to battered women's shelters, parental stress hotlines, and men's groups in the San Francisco Bay Area produced not a single resource or shelter for battered men. However, comments like these were common: "Men's victimization is statistically irrelevant," and "Any violence women may do is purely the result of living in a violent patriarchy." After his wife knocked him over, splitting his head open on a bathtub, James B. tried to get help from a local battered women's shelter, but was rudely turned away. The only shelter for battered men in the entire state of California is run by Community United Against Violence (CUAV) in San Francisco, an organization dealing exclusively with gay men. Even straight men who are brave enough to risk the stigma of admitting victimization are unlikely to turn to a group of gay men for support.

In some other states, attempts are being made to help abused men. In St. Paul, Minnesota, George Gilliland, Sr., the director of the Domestic Rights Coalition, has been trying to set up a shelter for battered men for quite a while, although without much success. Gilliland, whose wife hit him in the head with a board with a nail in it, missing his eye by a fraction of an inch, attributes part of the delay to efforts by battered women's groups and other women's organizations to block the project. In San Luis Obispo, California, David Gross is organizing the Allen Wells Memorial Fund for Battered Husbands. Mr. Wells was a battered man who could find no help and finally committed suicide after losing his children to his violent wife in a custody battle.

While battered men find few facilities or support, there are a variety of programs (many of which are run by feminist men's groups) to help abusive men deal more effectively with their violence. But for violent women—strangely enough—no comparable treatment programs exist. This fact further illustrates a serious problem: society is simply unwilling—or unable—to acknowledge and deal with vio-

lent women. Dr. Suzanne Steinmetz says there are plenty of women who have been violent to their husbands or who are feeling out of control and are afraid they will hurt someone. But these women have no place to turn. When they call women's shelters or support groups, they are often told that they "can't do any real damage anyway, that their violent feelings are nothing to worry about."

Despite all the evidence about female-on-male violence, many groups actively try to suppress coverage of the issue. Dr. Steinmetz told me that she received verbal threats and anonymous phone calls from radical women's groups threatening to harm her children after she published "The Battered Husband Syndrome" in 1978. In addition, all of her female colleagues were contacted and told to "do everything possible to deny" Steinmetz tenure. And when the ACLU invited her to speak on domestic violence, it received a bomb threat. Steinmetz finds it ironic that the same people who claim that women-initiated violence is purely self-defense are so quick to threaten violence against people who do nothing more than publish a scientific study.

Unfortunately, Steinmetz's story is not unique. Ten years later, R. L. McNeely, Ph.D., a professor at the School of Social Welfare at the University of Wisconsin-Milwaukee, and Gloria Robinson-Simpson, EdD., published "The Truth About Domestic Violence: A Falsely Framed Issue." The article examined various studies on domestic violence and concluded that society must recognize that men are victims "or we will be addressing only a part of the phenomenon." Shortly thereafter, McNeely received letters from a Pennsylvania women's organization threatening to use its influence in Washington to pull his research funding. He also suffered many other "character assassinations." Professor Robinson-Simpson, who uncovered some of the most important data, received relatively little abuse because, according to McNeely, "she, a young assistant professor, was assumed to have been 'duped' by the more senior male professor."

But existence of female-against-male attacks is not the only aspect of women's capacity for violence that has been suppressed. Morrow and Hawxhurst found that many feminists also refuse to acknowledge battered lesbians, because it would "endanger a feminist gender-specific analysis . . . that viewed battering as a consequence of male privilege and power in society."

And in the rare instances when female-against-male violence is publicly acknowledged, the woman's responsibility is frequently mitigated. In the recent CBS movie, "Men Don't Tell" (which told the story of a physically abused man), for example, the abusive woman was clearly mentally ill—a fact that made the viewer feel somewhat sympathetic toward her.

The victims and the perpetrators of domestic violence—women and men—have been suffering for too long. As the sharp distinctions between traditional men's and women's roles continue to blur, women are more frequently behaving in ways once thought (often erroneously) to be the exclusive province of men. Many experts feel that the problem of female-initiated violence must be exposed, "legitimized," and addressed by the media, the mental health and law-enforcement communities, and the Legislature.

Resources and facilities to combat domestic violence are, unfortunately, in short supply due to cutbacks in almost all social services. Perhaps some battered women's groups fear that if society recognizes that men are victims too, what little money is available will be diverted. But acknowledging men's victimization in no way involves denying that women are victims. Women's groups that help battered women could also help battered men, while men's groups that counsel abusive men could make their expertise available to violent women as well.

Continuing to portray spousal violence solely as a women's issue is not only wrong—it's also counterproductive. And encouraging such unnecessary fragmentation and divisiveness will ultimately do more harm than good. No one has (or should have) a monopoly on pain and suffering. But until society as a whole confronts its deeply ingrained stereotypes and recognizes all the victims of domestic violence, we will never be able to solve the problem. Domestic violence is neither a male or a female issue—it's simply a human issue.

NO
Russell P. Dobash et al.

THE MYTH OF SEXUAL SYMMETRY IN MARITAL VIOLENCE

Long denied, legitimized, and made light of, wife-beating is at last the object of widespread public concern and condemnation. Extensive survey research and intensive interpretive investigations tell a common story. Violence against wives... is often persistent and severe, occurs in the context of continuous intimidation and coercion, and is inextricably linked to attempts to dominate and control women. Historical and contemporary investigations further reveal that this violence has been explicitly decriminalized, ignored, or treated in an ineffectual manner by criminal justice systems, by medical and social service institutions, and by communities. Increased attention to these failures has inspired increased efforts to redress them, and in many places legislative amendments have mandated arrest and made assault a crime whether the offender is married to the victim or not.

A number of researchers and commentators have suggested that assaults upon men by their wives constitute a social problem comparable in nature and magnitude to that of wife-beating. Two main bodies of evidence have been offered in support of these authors' claims that husbands and wives are similarly victimized: (1) self-reports of violent acts perpetrated and suffered by survey respondents, especially those in two U.S. national probability samples (Straus and Gelles 1986); and (2) U.S. homicide data. Unlike the case of violence against wives, however, the victimization of husbands allegedly continues to be denied and trivialized. "Violence by wives has not been an object of public concern," note Straus and Gelles (1986:472). "There has been no publicity, and no funds have been invested in ameliorating this problem because it has not been defined as a problem."

We shall argue that claims of sexual symmetry in marital violence are exaggerated, and that wives' and husbands' uses of violence differ greatly.... We shall further argue that there is no reason to expect the sexes to be alike in this domain, and that efforts to avoid sexism by lumping male and female data and by the use of gender-neutral terms such as "spouse-beating" are misguided. If violence is gendered, as it assuredly is, explicit characterization

From Russell P. Dobash, R. Emerson Dobash, Margo Wilson, and Martin Daly, "The Myth of Sexual Symmetry in Marital Violence," *Social Problems*, vol. 39, no. 1 (February 1992), pp. 71–76, 78–83, 85–90. Copyright © 1992 by The Society for the Study of Social Problems. Reprinted by permission of Russell Dobash and Rebecca Dobash, University of Manchester, and Martin Daly and Margo Wilson, McMaster University. Some references omitted.

of gender's relevance to violence is essential. The alleged similarity of women and men in their use of violence in intimate relationships stands in marked contrast to men's virtual monopoly on the use of violence in other social contexts.…

THE CLAIM OF SEXUALLY SYMMETRICAL MARITAL VIOLENCE

Authoritative claims about the prevalence and sexual symmetry of spousal violence in America began with a 1975 U.S. national survey in which 2,143 married or cohabiting persons were interviewed in person about their actions in the preceding year. Straus (1977/78) announced that the survey results showed that the "marriage license is a hitting licence," and moreover that the rates of perpetrating spousal violence, including severe violence, were higher for wives than for husbands. He concluded:

Violence between husband and wife is far from a one way street. The old cartoons of the wife chasing the husband with a rolling pin or throwing pots and pans are closer to reality than most (and especially those with feminist sympathies) realize (Straus 1977/78:447–448).

In 1985, the survey was repeated by telephone with a new national probability sample including 3,520 husband-wife households, and with similar results. In each survey, the researchers interviewed either the wife or the husband (but not both) in each contacted household about how the couple settled their differences when they had a disagreement. The individual who was interviewed was presented with a list of eighteen "acts" ranging from "dis-cussed an issue calmly" and "cried" to "threw something at him/her/you" and "beat him/her/you up," with the addition of "choked him/her/you" in 1985 (Straus 1990a:33). These acts constituted the Conflict Tactics Scales (CTS) and were intended to measure three constructs: "Reasoning," "Verbal Aggression," and "Physical Aggression" or "Violence," which was further subdivided into "Minor Violence" and "Severe Violence" according to a presumed potential for injury (Straus 1979, Straus and Gelles 1990a). Respondents were asked how frequently they had perpetrated each act in the course of "conflicts or disagreements" with their spouses (and with one randomly selected child) within the past year, and how frequently they had been on the receiving end. Each respondent's self-reports of victimization and perpetration contributed to estimates of rates of violence by both husbands and wives.

According to both surveys, rates of violence by husbands and wives were strikingly similar (Straus and Gelles 1986, 1990b, Straus et al. 1980). The authors estimated that in the year prior to the 1975 survey 11.6 percent of U.S. husbands were victims of physical violence perpetrated by their wives, while 12.1 percent of wives were victims of their husbands' violence. In 1985, these percentages had scarcely changed, but husbands seemed more vulnerable: 12.1 percent of husbands and 11.3 percent of wives were victims. In both surveys, husbands were more likely to be victims of acts of "severe violence": in 1975, 4.6 percent of husbands were such victims versus 3.8 percent of wives, and in 1985, 4.4 percent of husbands versus 3.0 percent of wives were victims.In reporting their results, the surveys' authors stressed the surprising assaultiveness of wives:

> The repeated finding that the rate of assault by women is similar to the rate by their male partners is an important and distressing aspect of violence in American families. It contrasts markedly to the behavior of women outside the family. It shows that within the family or in dating and cohabiting relationships, women are about as violent as men (Straus and Gelles 1990b:104).

Others have endorsed and publicized these conclusions. For example, a recent review of marital violence concludes, with heavy reliance on Straus and Gelles's survey results, that "(a) women are more prone than men to engage in severely violent acts, (b) each year more men than women are victimized by their intimates" (McNeely and Mann 1990:130). One of Straus and Gelles's collaborators in the 1975 survey, Steinmetz (1977/78), used the same survey evidence to proclaim the existence of "battered husbands" and a "battered husband syndrome." She has remained one of the leading defenders of the claim that violence between men and women in the family is symmetrical (Steinmetz 1981, 1986, Steinmetz and Lucca 1988, Straus et al. 1980). Steinmetz and her collaborators maintain that the problem is not wife-beating perpetrated by violent men, but "violent couples" and "violent people." Men may be stronger on average, argues Steinmetz, but weaponry equalizes matters, as is allegedly shown by the nearly equivalent numbers of U.S. husbands and wives who are killed by their partners. The reason why battered husbands are inconspicuous and seemingly rare is supposedly that shame prevents them from seeking help.

Straus and his collaborators have sometimes qualified their claims that their surveys demonstrate sexual symmetry in marital violence, noting, for example, that men are usually larger and stronger than women and thus able to inflict more damage and that women are more likely to use violence in self-defense or retaliation (e.g. Stets and Straus 1990, Straus 1980, 1990b, Straus and Gelles 1986, Straus et al. 1980). However, the survey results indicate a symmetry not just in the perpetration of violence but in its initiation as well, and from this further symmetry, Stets and Straus (1990; 154–155) conclude that the equal assaultiveness of husbands and wives cannot be attributed to the wives acting in self-defense, after all.

Other surveys using the CTS in the United States and in other countries have replicated the finding that wives are about as violent as husbands....

Some authors maintain not only that wives initiate violence at rates comparable to husbands, but that they rival them in the damage they inflict as well. McNeely and Robinson-Simpson (1987), for example, argue that research shows that the "truth about domestic violence" is that "women are as violent, if not more violent than men," in their inclinations, in their actions, and in the damage they inflict. The most dramatic evidence invoked in this context is again the fact that wives kill: spousal homicides—for which detection should be minimally or not at all biased because homicides are nearly always discovered and recorded —produce much more nearly equivalent numbers of male and female victims in the United States than do sublethal assault data, which are subject to sampling biases when obtained from police, shelters and hospitals. According to McNeely and Mann (1990:130), "the average man's size and strength are neutralized by guns and knives, boiling water, bricks, fireplace pokers, and baseball bats."

A corollary of the notion that the sexes are alike in their use of violence is that satisfactory causal accounts of violence will be gender-blind. Discussion thus focuses, for example, on the role of one's prior experiences with violence as a child, social stresses, frustration, inability to control anger, impoverished social skills, and so forth, without reference to gender. This presumption that the sexes are alike not merely in action but in the reasons for that action is occasionally explicit, such as when Shupe et al. (1987:56) write: "Everything we have found points to parallel processes that lead women and men to become violent.... Women may be more likely than men to use kitchen utensils or sewing scissors when they commit assault, but their frustrations, motives and lack of control over these feelings predictably resemble men's."

In sum, the existence of an invisible legion of assaulted husbands is an inference which strikes many family violence researchers as reasonable. Two lines of evidence—homicide data and the CTS survey results—suggest to those supporting the sexual-symmetry-of-violence thesis that large numbers of men are trapped in violent relationships. These men are allegedly being denied medical, social welfare, and criminal justice services because of an unwillingness to accept the evidence from homicide statistics and the CTS surveys (Gelles 1982, Steinmetz 1986).

VIOLENCE AGAINST WIVES

Any argument that marital violence is sexually symmetrical must either dis-

miss or ignore a large body of contradictory evidence indicating that wives greatly outnumber husbands as victims. While CTS researchers were discovering and publicizing the mutual violence of wives and husbands, other researchers —using evidence from courts, police, and women's shelters—were finding that wives were much more likely than husbands to be victims. After an extensive review of extant research, Lystad (1975) expressed the consensus: "The occurrence of adult violence in the home usually involves males as aggressors towards females." This conclusion was subsequently supported by numerous further studies of divorce records, emergency room patients treated for nonaccidental injuries, police assault records, and spouses seeking assistance and refuge. Analyses of police and court records in North America and Europe have persistently indicated that women constitute ninety to ninety-five percent of the victims of those assaults in the home reported to the criminal justice system.

Defenders of the sexual-symmetry-of-violence thesis do not deny these results, but they question their representativeness: these studies could be biased because samples of victims were self-selected. However, criminal victimization surveys using national probability samples similarly indicate that wives are much more often victimized than husbands. Such surveys in the United States, Canada and Great Britain have been replicated in various years, with essentially the same results....

The national crime surveys also indicate that women are much more likely than men to suffer injury as a result of assaults in the home. After analyzing the results of the U.S. National Crime Surveys, Schwartz (1987:67) concludes, "there are still more than 13 times as many women seeking medical care from a private physician for injuries received in a spousal assault." This result again replicates the typical findings of studies of police or hospital records. For example, women constituted 94 percent of the injury victims in an analysis of the spousal assault cases among 262 domestic disturbance calls to police in Santa Barbara County, California (Berk et al. 1983); moreover, the women's injuries were more serious than the men's. Berk et al. (1983:207) conclude that "when injuries are used as the outcome of interest, a marriage license is a hitting license *but for men only*." Brush (1990) reports that a U.S. national probability sample survey of over 13,000 respondents in 1987–1988 replicated the evident symmetry of marital violence when CTS-like questions about acts were posed, but also revealed that women were much more often injured than men (and that men downplayed women's injuries).

In response, defenders of the sexual-symmetry-of-violence thesis contend that data from police, courts, hospitals, and social service agencies are suspect because men are reluctant to report physical violence by their wives. For example, Steinmetz (1977/78) asserts that husband-beating is a camouflaged social problem because men must overcome extraordinary stigma in order to report that their wives have beaten them. Similarly, Shupe et al. (1987) maintain that men are unwilling to report their wives because "it would be unmanly or unchivalrous to go to the police for protection from a woman" (52). However, the limited available evidence does not support these authors' presumption that men are less likely to report assaults by their spouses than are women. Schwartz's (1987) analysis of the 1973–1982 U.S. National Crime Survey data found that 67.2 percent of men and 56.8 percent of women called the police after being assaulted by their spouses. One may protest that these high percentages imply that only a tiny proportion of the most severe spousal assaults were acknowledged as assaults by respondents to these crime surveys, but the results are nonetheless contrary to the notion that assaulted men are especially reticent. Moreover, Rouse et al. (1988), using "act" definitions of assaults which inspired much higher proportions to acknowledge victimization, similarly report that men were likelier than women to call the police after assaults by intimate partners, both among married couples and among those dating. In addition, a sample of 337 cases of domestic violence drawn from family court cases in Ontario showed that men were more likely than women to press charges against their spouses: there were 17 times as many female victims as male victims, but only 22 percent of women laid charges in contrast to 40 percent of the men, and men were less likely to drop the charges, too (Kincaid 1982:91). What those who argue that men are reluctant or ashamed to report their wives' assaults overlook is that women have their own reasons to be reticent, fearing both the loss of a jailed or alienated husband's economic support and his vengeance. Whereas the claim that husbands underreport because of shame or chivalry is largely speculative, there is considerable evidence that women report very little of the violence perpetrated by their male partners (e.g., Dobash and Dobash 1979, Kantor and Straus 1990, Solicitor General of Canada 1985, Schwartz 1987).

The CTS survey data indicating equivalent violence by wives and husbands thus stand in contradiction to injury data, to police incident reports, to help-seeking statistics, and even to other, larger, national probability sample survey of self-reported victimization (e.g., ... Dobash and Dobash 1992)....

DO CTS DATA REFLECT THE REALITY OF MARITAL VIOLENCE?

The CTS instrument has been much used and much criticized. Critics have complained that its exclusive focus on "acts" ignores the actors' interpretations, motivations, and intentions; that physical violence is arbitrarily delimited, excluding, for example, sexual assault and rape; that retrospective reports of the past year's events are unlikely to be accurate; that researchers' attributions of "violence" (with resultant claims about its statistical prevalence) are based on respondents' admitting to acts described in such an impoverished manner as to conflate severe assaults with trivial gestures; that the formulaic distinction between "minor" and "severe violence" (whereby, for example, "tried to hit with something" is definitionally "severe" and "slapped" is definitionally "minor") constitutes a poor operationalization of severity; that the responses of aggressors and victims have been given identical evidentiary status in deriving incidence estimates, while their inconsistencies have been ignored; that the CTS omits the contexts of violence, the events precipitating it, and the sequences of events by which it progresses; and that it fails to connect outcomes, especially injury, with the acts producing them....

Problems With the Interpretation of CTS Responses

... Respondents are asked whether they have "pushed" their partners, have "slapped" them, and so forth, rather than whether they have "assaulted" them or behaved "violently." This focus on "acts" is intended to reduce problems of self-serving and biased definitional criteria on the part of the respondents. However, any gain in objectivity has been undermined by the way that CTS survey data have then been analyzed and interpreted. Any respondent who acknowledges a single instance of having "pushed," "grabbed," "shoved," "slapped" *or* "hit or tried to hit" another person is deemed a perpetrator of "violence" by the researchers, regardless of the act's context, consequences, or meaning to the parties involved. Similarly, a single instance of having "kicked," "bit," "hit or tried to hit with an object," "beat up," "choked," "threatened with a knife or gun," or "used a knife or fired a gun" makes one a perpetrator of "severe violence."

Affirmation of any one of the "violence" items provides the basis for estimates such as Straus and Gelles's (1990b:97) claim that 6.8 million U.S. husbands and 6.25 million U.S. wives were spousal assault victims in 1985. Similarly, estimates of large numbers of "beaten" or "battered" wives and husbands have been based on affirmation of any one of the "severe violence" items. For example, Steinmetz (1986:734) and Straus and Gelles (1987:638) claim on this basis that 1.8 million U.S. women are "beaten" by their husbands annually. But note that any man who once threw an "object" at his wife, regardless of its nature and regardless of whether the throw missed, qualifies has having "beaten" her; some unknown proportion of the women and men who are alleged to have been "beaten," on the basis of their survey responses, never claimed to have been struck at all. Thus, the "objective" scoring of the CTS not only fails to explore the meanings and intentions associated with the acts but has in practice entailed interpretive transformations that guarantee exaggeration, misinterpretation, and ultimately trivialization of the genuine problems of violence.

Consider a "slap." The word encompasses anything from a slap on the hand chastizing a dinner companion for reaching for a bite of one's dessert to a tooth-loosening assault intended to punish, humiliate, and terrorize. These are not trivial distinctions; indeed, they constitute the essense of definitional issues concerning violence....

Research focusing on specific violent events shows that women almost always employ violence in defense of self and children in response to cues of imminent assault in the past and in retaliation for previous physical abuse (e.g., Browne 1987, Campbell 1992, Dobash and Dobash 1979, 1984, Jones 1980, Pagelow 1984, Polk and Ranson 1991, Saunders 1986). Proponents of the sexual-symmetry-of-violence thesis have made much of the fact that CTS surveys indicate that women "initiate" the violence about as often as men, but a case in which a woman struck the first blow is unlikely to be the mirror image of one in which her husband "initiated." A noteworthy feature of the literature proclaiming the existence of battered husbands and battering wives is how little the meager case descriptions resemble those of battered wives and battering husbands. Especially lacking in the alleged male victim cases is any indication of the sort of chronic intimidation characteristic of prototypical woman battering cases....

HOMICIDES

The second line of evidence that has been invoked in support of the claim that marital violence is more or less sexually symmetrical is the number of lethal outcomes:

> Data on homicide between spouses suggest that an almost equal number of wives kill their husbands as husbands kill their wives (Wolfgang 1958). Thus is appears that men and women might have equal potential for violent marital interaction; initiate similar acts of violence; and when differences of physical strength are equalized by weapons, commit similar amounts of spousal homicide (Steinmetz and Lucca 1988:241).

McNeely and Robinson-Simpson (1987: 485) elevated the latter hypothesis about the relevance of weapons to the status of a fact: "Steinmetz observed that when weapons neutralize differences in physical strength, about as many men as women are victims of homicide."

Steinmetz and Lucca's citation of Wolfgang refers to his finding that 53 Philadelphia men killed their wives between 1948 and 1952, while 47 women killed their husbands. This is a slender basis for such generalization, but fuller information does indeed bear Steinmetz out as regards the near equivalence of body counts in the United States: Maxfield (1989) reported that there were 10,529 wives and 7,888 husbands killed by their mates in the entire country between 1976 and 1985, a 1.3:1 ratio of female to male victims.

Husbands are indeed almost as often slain as are wives in the United States, then. However, there remain several problems with Steinmetz and Lucca's (as well as McNeely and Robinson-

Simpson's) interpretation of this fact. Studies of actual cases (Campbell 1992, Daly and Wilson 1988b, Goetting 1989, Lundsgaarde 1977) lend no support to the facile claim that homicidal husbands and wives "initiate similar acts of violence." Men often kill wives after lengthy periods of prolonged physical violence accompanied by other forms of abuse and coercion; the roles in such cases are seldom if ever reversed. Men perpetrate familicidal massacres, killing spouse and children together; women do not. Men commonly hunt down and kill wives who have left them; women hardly ever behave similarly. Men kill wives as part of planned murder-suicides; analogous acts by women are almost unheard of. Men kill in response to revelations of wifely infidelity; women almost never respond similarly, though their mates are more often adulterous. The evidence is overwhelming that a large proportion of the spouse-killings perpetrated by wives, but almost none of those perpetrated by husbands, are acts of self-defense. Unlike men, women kill male partners after years of suffering physical violence, after they have exhausted all available sources of assistance, when they feel trapped, and because they fear for their own lives....

Even among lethal acts, it is essential to discriminate among different victim-killer relationships, because motives, risk factors, and conflict typologies are relationship-specific (Daly and Wilson 1988b). Steinmetz (1977/78, Steinmetz and Lucca 1988) has invoked the occurrence of maternally perpetrated infanticides as evidence of women's violence, imagining that the fact that some women commit infanticide somehow bolsters the claim that they batter their husbands, too. But maternal infanticides are more often motivated by desperation than by hostile aggression and are often effected by acts of neglect or abandonment rather than by assault. To conflate such acts with aggressive attacks is to misunderstand their utterly distinct motives, forms, and perpetrator profiles, and the distinct social and material circumstances in which they occur.

HOW TO GAIN A VALID ACCOUNT OF MARITAL VIOLENCE?

How ought researchers to conceive of "violence"? People differ in their views about whether a particular act was a violent one and about who was responsible. Assessments of intention and justifiability are no less relevant to the labelling of an event as "violent" than are more directly observable considerations like the force exerted or the damage inflicted. Presumably, it is this problem of subjectivity that has inspired efforts to objectify the study of family violence by the counting of "acts," as in the Conflict Tactics Scales....

Enormous differences in meaning and consequence exist between a woman pummelling her laughing husband in an attempt to convey strong feelings and a man pummelling his weeping wife in an attempt to punish her for coming home late. It is not enough to acknowledge such contrasts (as CTS researchers have sometimes done), if such acknowledgements neither inform further research nor alter such conclusions as "within the family or in dating and cohabiting relationships, women are about as violent as men" (Straus and Gelles 1990b:104). What is needed are forms of analysis that will lead to a comprehensive description of the violence itself as well as an explanation of it. In order to do this, it is, at the very least, necessary to analyze the violent event in a holistic manner, with attention to the entire sequences of distinct acts as well as associated motives, intentions, and consequences, all of which must in turn be situated within the wider context of the relationship.

REFERENCES

Berk, Richard A., Sarah F. Berk, Donileen R. Loseke, and D. Rauma. 1983. "Mutual combat and other family violence myths." In The Dark Side of Families, ed. David Finkelhor, Richard J. Gelles, Gerald T. Hotaling, and Murray A. Straus, 197–212. Beverly Hills, Calif.: Sage.

Browne, Angela. 1987. When Battered Women Kill. New York: Free Press.

Brush, Lisa D. 1990. "Violent acts and injurious outcomes in married couples: Methodological issues in the National Survey of Families and Households." Gender and Society 4:56–67.

Campbell, Jacqueline C. 1992. "If I can't have you, no one can: Issues of power and control in homicide of female partners." In Femicide: The Politics of Woman Killing, ed. Jill Radford and Diana E. H. Russell. New York: Twayne.

Daly, Martin, and Margo Wilson. 1988b. Homicide. Hawthorne, N.Y.: Aldine de Gruyter.

Dobash, R. Emerson, and Russell P. Dobash. 1979. Violence against Wives: A Case against the Patriarchy. New York: Free Press.

———. 1984. "The nature and antecedents of violent events." British Journal of Criminology 24:269–288.

———. 1992. Women, Violence and Social Change. London: Routledge.

Gelles, Richard J. 1982. "Domestic criminal violence." In Criminal Violence, Ed. Marvin E. Wolfgang and Neil A. Weiner, 201–235. Beverly Hills, Calif.: Sage.

Goetting, Ann. 1988. "When females kill one another." Criminal Justice and Behavior 15:179–189.

———. 1989. "Patterns of marital homicide: A comparison of husbands and wives." Journal of Comparative Family Studies 20:341–354.

Jones, Ann. 1980. Women Who Kill. New York: Holt, Rinehart and Winston.

Kantor, Glenda K., and Murray A. Straus. 1990. "Response of victims and the police to assaults on wives." In Physical Violence in American Families, ed. Murray A. Straus and Richard J. Gelles, 473–487. New Brunswick N.J.: Transaction Publishers.

Kincaid, Pat J. 1982. The Omitted Reality: Husband-Wife Violence in Ontario and Policy Implications for Education. Maple, Ontario: Learners Press.

Lundsgaarde, Henry P. 1977. Murder in Space City. New York: Oxford University Press.

Lystad, Mary H. 1975. "Violence at home: A review of literature." American Journal of Orthopsychiatry 45:328–345.

Maxfield, Michael G. 1989. "Circumstances in Supplementary Homicide Reports: Variety and validity." Criminology 27:671–695.

McNeely, R. L., and CoraMae Richey Mann. 1990. "Domestic violence is a human issue." Journal of Interpersonal Violence 5:129–132.

McNeely, R. L., and Gloria Robinson-Simpson. 1987. "The truth about domestic violence: A falsely framed issue." Social Work 32:485–490.

Pagelow, Mildred D. 1984. Family Violence. New York: Praeger.

Polk, Kenneth, and David Ranson. 1991. "The role of gender in intimate violence." Australia and New Zealand Journal of Criminology 24:15–24.

Rouse, Linda P., Richard Breen, and Marilyn Howell. 1988. "Abuse in intimate relationships. A comparison of married and dating college students." Journal of Interpersonal Violence 3:414–429.

Saunders, Daniel G. 1986. "When battered women use violence: Husband-abuse or self-defense?" Violence and Victims 1:47–60.

Schwartz, Martin D. 1987. "Gender and injury in spousal assault." Sociological Focus 20:61–75.

Shupe, Anson, William A. Stacey, and Lonnie R. Hazelwood. 1987. Violent Men, Violent Couples: The Dynamics of Domestic Violence. Lexington Mass.: Lexington Books.

Solicitor General of Canada. 1985. Female Victims of Crime. Canadian Urban Victimization Survey Bulletin No. 4. Ottawa: Programs Branch/Research and Statistics Group.

Steinmetz, Suzanne K. 1977/78. "The battered husband syndrome." Victimology 2:499–509.

———. 1981. "A cross-cultural comparison of marital abuse." Journal of Sociology and Social Welfare 8:404–414.

———. 1986. "Family violence. Past, present, and future." In Handbook of Marriage and the Family, ed. Marvin B. Sussman and Suzanne K. Steinmetz, 725–765. New York: Plenum.

Steinmetz, Suzanne K., and Joseph S. Lucca. 1988. "Husband battering." In Handbook of Family Violence ed. Vincent B. Van Hasselt, R. L. Morrison, A. S. Bellack and M. Hersen, 233–246. New York: Plenum Press.

Stets, Jan. E., and Murray A. Straus. 1990. "Gender differences in reporting marital violence and its medical and psychological consequences." In Physical Violence in American Families, ed.

Murray A. Straus and Richard J. Gelles, 151–165. New Brunswick, N.J.: Transaction Publishers.

Straus, Murray A. 1977/78. "Wife-beating: How common and why?" Victimology 2:443–458.

———. 1979. "Measuring intrafamily conflict and violence: The Conflict Tactics (CT) Scales." Journal of Marriage and the Family 51:75–88.

———. 1980. "The marriage license as a hitting license: Evidence from popular culture, law, and social science." In The Social Causes of Husband-Wife Violence, ed. Murray A. Straus and Gerald T. Hotaling, 39–50. Minneapolis, Minn.: University of Minnesota Press.

———. 1990a. "Measuring intrafamily conflict and violence: The Conflict Tactics (CT) Scales." In Physical Violence in American Families, ed., Murray A. Straus and Richard J. Gelles, 29–47. New Brunswick, N.J.: Transaction Publishers.

———. 1990b. "The Conflict Tactics Scales and its critics: An evaluation and new data on validity and reliability." In Physical Violence in American Families, ed. Murray A. Straus and Richard J. Gelles, 49–73. New Brunswick, N.J.: Transaction Publishers.

Straus, Murray A., and Richard J. Gelles, eds. 1990a. Physical Violence in American Families. New Brunswick, N.J.: Transaction Publishers.

Straus, Murray A., and Richard J. Gelles. 1986. "Societal change and change in family violence from 1975 to 1985 as revealed by two national surveys." Journal of Marriage and the Family 48:465–480.

———. 1990b. "How violent are American families? Estimates from the National Family Violence Resurvey and other studies." In Physical Violence in American Families, ed. Murray A. Straus and Richard J. Gelles, 95–112. New Brunswick, N.J.: Transaction Publishers.

Straus, Murray A., Richard J. Gelles, and Suzanne K. Steinmetz. 1980. Behind Closed Doors: Violence in the American Family. New York: Doubleday/Anchor.

Wolfgang, Marvin E. 1958. Patterns in Criminal Homicide. Philadelphia: University of Pennsylvania Press.

POSTSCRIPT

Is There a Double Standard for Marital Violence?

Brott insists that wives can be violent, that some husbands are physically and psychologically battered by wives, and that husbands (like wives) may stay in violent relationships to protect their families. He contends that society continues to ignore husband battering because men continue to be stereotyped as more privileged and powerful than women and consequently less deserving of help. Brott urges us to view marital violence as a human issue rather than a male or female issue.

Dobash et al. contend that research studies that report on husband battering typically rely on the Conflict Tactics Scale (CTS), which they feel distorts and misrepresents women's acts of physical violence and mislabels such behaviors as violence against men. They claim that the CTS does not take into account that most of the violence reported by women is self-protective in nature. The CTS fails to consider the context within which marital violence occurs, such as the motivation for the violence, what is said and done during and immediately after violent episodes, and what emotions are stirred throughout each incident. Until researchers know more about the context, Dobash et al. conclude, it is wrong to give much attention to husband battering as a social concern.

Do you think that *husband battering* is the correct term for the actions women take in instances of marital violence? Does husband battering deserve to be treated as a serious social problem requiring publicity, research funding, public policy attention, and intervention programs equal to those recommended for battered women? Do you think that publicity devoted to husband battering will divert attention away from battered women?

SUGGESTED READINGS

R. Gelles and D. Loseke, eds., *Current Controversies in Family Violence* (Sage Publications, 1993).

A. Jones, *Next Time She'll Be Dead: Battering and How to Stop It* (Beacon Press, 1994).

A. R. Roberts, *Helping Battered Women* (Oxford University Press, 1996).

M. N. Russell, *Confronting Abusive Beliefs: Group Treatment for Abusive Men* (Sage Publications, 1995).

A. M. Stan, *Debating Sexual Correctness* (Dell, 1995).

Internet: http://www.cybergrrl.com/dv.html

Internet: http://www.vix.com/men/battery/battery.html

ISSUE 16

Are Children of Divorce at Greater Risk?

YES: Judith S. Wallerstein, from "Children of Divorce: The Dilemma of a Decade," in Elam W. Nunnally, Catherine S. Chilman, and Fred M. Cox, eds., *Troubled Relationships* (Sage Publications, 1988)

NO: David H. Demo and Alan C. Acock, from "The Impact of Divorce on Children," *Journal of Marriage and the Family* (August 1988)

ISSUE SUMMARY

YES: Clinician and researcher Judith S. Wallerstein contends that children whose parents divorce are at greater risk of mental and physical health problems than are children whose families are intact.

NO: Sociologists David H. Demo and Alan C. Acock argue that much of the research on children of divorce is theoretically or methodologically flawed and that, consequently, the findings cannot be trusted.

Despite a stabilization of divorce rates in the 1980s, it has been estimated that at the present rate well over half of the current first marriages in the United States will end in divorce. Over the past two decades the number of children involved in divorce has more than tripled. Current literature suggests that over 60 percent of children will experience life in a single-parent family before they reach age 18. The rates are even higher for black children.

Because divorce significantly changes the lives of parents and their children, many people have expressed great concern for the well-being of children of divorce. Some even predict that significant numbers of children of divorce may remain dysfunctional for much of their adolescence and young adulthood. Although the majority of children of divorce do experience periods of extreme anxiety and stress, some family researchers maintain that the effects of divorce may be less harmful for children than the effects of living in a conflict-ridden home environment. Other researchers point out that much of the research on these children is flawed, either because it is based on clinical studies or because it has theoretical and methodological problems that render it unreliable.

Clinical research is usually developed and implemented by family professionals in applied fields of study (counselors or therapists, family life educators, and clergy, for example), who tend to focus on providing assistance to families with particular problems. Thus, much of the available data are based on studies of children with the most severe reactions to divorce because such children and their parents make up the researchers' clientele. Although this research is often useful to other clinicians and helping professionals, it does not advance knowledge about the majority of children of divorce, who often have less severe problems. Much of the clinical research concentrates on the problems and failures of the research participants and spends little time on the more positive ways in which children and their families adapt or cope with the problems of divorce. On the plus side, clinical research usually focuses more strongly on the long-term developmental changes that affect children of divorce.

Another problem with research in the area of children and divorce is that there has been a tendency for researchers to use a "deficit-family" framework to explain their findings. This means that researchers compare children of divorce to children in intact families (where the two biological parents are present), with the expectation that deviations from the intact family will result in major problems for the children. Such a problem-oriented approach to research narrows the focus of studies and prevents identification of the diversity of factors that affect children after divorce.

Other limitations of the literature on children of divorce include using nonrepresentative samples and then generalizing the findings to all children. Researchers often fail to study income level or social class as factors that affect children's coping abilities and ignore the developmental nature of children's reactions to the divorce process.

In the following selections, Judith S. Wallerstein, while acknowledging certain limitations with the accumulated research on children of divorce, contends that these children are at great risk of developing physical and emotional health problems. She argues that increased attention to education, treatment, and prevention programs is needed for this special population of children. David H. Demo and Alan C. Acock discuss various limitations in the way children of divorce are usually studied, summarize the conclusions from studies they feel are more reliable, and call for future research that pays more attention to the current theoretical and methodological problems of past studies.

YES
Judith S. Wallerstein

CHILDREN OF DIVORCE:
THE DILEMMA OF A DECADE

It is now estimated that 45% of all children born in 1983 will experience their parents' divorce, 35% will experience a remarriage, and 20% will experience a second divorce (A. J. Norton, Assistant Chief, Population Bureau, United States Bureau of the Census, personal communication, 1983)....

Although the incidence of divorce has increased across all age groups, the most dramatic rise has occurred among young adults (Norton, 1980). As a result, children in divorcing families are younger than in previous years and include more preschool children....

Although many children weather the stress of marital discord and family breakup without psychopathological sequelae, a significant number falter along the way. Children of divorce are significantly overrepresented in outpatient psychiatric, family agency, and private practice populations compared with children in the general population (Gardner, 1976; Kalter, 1977; Tessman, 1977; Tooley, 1976). The best predictors of mental health referrals for school-aged children are parental divorce or parental loss as a result of death (Felner, Stolberg, & Cowen, 1975). A national survey of adolescents whose parents had separated and divorced by the time the children were seven years old found that 30% of these children had received psychiatric or psychological therapy by the time they reached adolescence compared with 10% of adolescents in intact families (Zill, 1983).

A longitudinal study in northern California followed 131 children who were age 3 to 18 at the decisive separation. At the 5-year mark, the investigators found that more than one-third were suffering with moderate to severe depression (Wallerstein & Kelly, 1980a). These findings are especially striking because the children were drawn from a nonclinical population and were accepted into the study only if they had never been identified before the divorce as needing psychological treatment and only if they were performing at age-appropriate levels in school. Therefore, the deterioration observed in these children's adjustment occurred largely following the family breakup....

Divorce is a long, drawn-out process of radically changing family relationships that has several stages, beginning with the marital rupture and its immediate aftermath, continuing over several years of disequilibrium, and finally coming to rest with the stabilization of a new postdivorce or remarried family unit. A complex chain of changes, many of them unanticipated and unforeseeable, are set into motion by the marital rupture and are likely to occupy a significant portion of the child or adolescent's growing years. As the author and her colleague have reported elsewhere, women in the California Children of Divorce study required three to three-and-one-half years following the decisive separation before they achieved a sense of order and predictability in their lives (Wallerstein & Kelly, 1980a). This figure probably underestimates the actual time trajectory of the child's experience of divorce. A prospective study reported that parent–child relationships began to deteriorate many years prior to the divorce decision and that the adjustment of many children in these families began to fail long before the decisive separation (Morrison, 1982). This view of the divorcing process as long lasting accords with the perspective of a group of young people who reported at a 10-year follow-up that their entire childhood or adolescence had been dominated by the family crisis and its extended aftermath (Wallerstein, 1978).

Stages in the Process

The three broad, successive stages in the divorcing process, while they overlap, are nevertheless clinically distinguishable. *The acute phase* is precipitated by the decisive separation and the decision to divorce. This stage is often marked by steeply escalating conflict between the adults, physical violence, severe distress, depression accompanied by suicidal ideation, and a range of behaviors reflecting a spilling of aggressive and sexual impulses. The adults frequently react with severe ego regression and not unusually behave at odds with their more customary demeanor. Sharp disagreement in the wish to end the marriage is very common, and the narcissistic injury to the person who feels rejected sets the stage for rage, sexual jealousy, and depression. Children are generally not shielded from this parental conflict or distress. Confronted by a marked discrepancy in images of their parents, children do not have the assurance that the bizarre or depressed behaviors and moods will subside. As a result, they are likely to be terrified by the very figures they usually rely on for nurturance and protection.

As the acute phase comes to a close, usually within the first 2 years of the divorce decision, the marital partners gradually disengage from each other and pick up the new tasks of reestablishing their separate lives. *The transitional phase* is characterized by ventures into new, more committed relationships; new work, school, and friendship groups; and sometimes new settings, new lifestyles, and new geographical locations. This phase is marked by alternating success and failure, encouragement and discouragement, and it may also last for several years. Children observe and participate in the many changes of this period. They share the trials and errors and the fluctuations in mood. For several years life may be unstable, and home may be unsettled.

Finally, *the postdivorce phase* ensues with the establishment of a fairly stable single-parent or remarried household. Eventually three out of four divorced women and four out of five divorced men reenter wedlock (Cherlin, 1981). Unfortunately, though, remarriage does not bring immediate tranquility into the lives of the family members. The early years of the remarriage are often encumbered by ghostly presences from the earlier failed marriages and by the actual presences of children and visiting parents from the prior marriage or marriages. Several studies suggest widespread upset among children and adolescents following remarriage (Crohn, Brown, Walker, & Beir, 1981; Goldstein, 1974; Kalter, 1977). A large-scale investigation that is still in process reports longlasting friction around visitation (Jacobson, 1983).

Changes in Parent–Child Relationships

Parents experience a diminished capacity to parent their children during the acute phase of the divorcing process and often during the transitional phase as well (Wallerstein & Kelly, 1980a). This phenomenon is widespread and can be considered an expectable, divorce-specific change in parent–child relationships. At its simplest level this diminished parenting capacity appears in the household disorder that prevails in the aftermath of divorce, in the rising tempers of custodial parent and child, in reduced competence and a greater sense of helplessness in the custodial parent, and in lower expectations of the child for appropriate social behavior (Hetherington, Cox, & Cox, 1978; 1982). Diminished parenting also entails a sharp decline in emotional sensitivity and support for the child; decreased pleasure in the parent–child relationship; decreased attentiveness to the child's needs and wishes; less talk, play, and interaction with the child; and a steep escalation in inappropriate expression of anger. One not uncommon component of the parent–child relationship coincident with the marital breakup is the adult's

conscious or unconscious wish to abandon the child and thus to erase the unhappy marriage in its entirety. Child neglect can be a serious hazard.

In counterpoint to the temporary emotional withdrawal from the child, the parent may develop a dependent, sometimes passionate, attachment to the child or adolescent, beginning with the breakup and lasting throughout the lonely postseparation years (Wallerstein, 1985). Parents are likely to lean on the child and turn to the child for help, placing the child in a wide range of roles such as confidante, advisor, mentor, sibling, parent, caretaker, lover, concubine, extended conscience or ego control, ally within the marital conflict, or pivotal supportive presence in staving off depression or even suicide. This expectation that children should not only take much greater responsibility for themselves but also should provide psychological and social support for the distressed parent is sufficiently widespread to be considered a divorce-specific response along with that of diminished parenting. Such relationships frequently develop with an only child or with a very young, even a preschool, child. Not accidentally, issues of custody and visitation often arise with regard to the younger children. While such disputes, of course, reflect the generally unresolved anger of the marriage and the divorce, they may also reflect the intense emotional need of one or both parents for the young child's constant presence (Wallerstein, 1985).

Parents may also lean more appropriately on the older child or adolescent. Many youngsters become proud helpers, confidantes, and allies in facing the difficult postdivorce period (Weiss, 1979b). Other youngsters draw away from close involvement out of their fears of engulfment, and they move precipitously out of the family orbit, sometimes before they are developmentally ready. . . .

CHILDREN'S REACTIONS TO DIVORCE

Initial Responses

Children and adolescents experience separation and its aftermath as the most stressful period of their lives. The family rupture evokes an acute sense of shock, intense anxiety, and profound sorrow. Many children are relatively content and even well-parented in families where one or both parents are unhappy. Few youngsters experience any relief with the divorce decision, and those who do are usually older and have witnessed physical violence or open conflict between their parents. The child's early responses are governed neither by an understanding of issues leading to the divorce nor by the fact that divorce has a high incidence in the community. To the child, divorce signifies the collapse of the structure that provides support and protection. The child reacts as to the cutting of his or her lifeline.

The initial suffering of children and adolescents in response to a marital separation is compounded by realistic fears and fantasies about catastrophes that the divorce will bring in its wake. Children suffer with a pervasive sense of vulnerability because they feel that the protective and nurturant function of the family has given way. They grieve over the loss of the noncustodial parent, over the loss of the intact family, and often over the multiple losses of neighborhood, friends, and school. Children also worry about their distressed parents. They are concerned about who will take care of

the parent who has left and whether the custodial parent will be able to manage alone. They experience intense anger toward one or both parents whom they hold responsible for disrupting the family. Some of their anger is reactive and defends them against their own feelings of powerlessness, their concern about being lost in the shuffle, and their fear that their needs will be disregarded as the parents give priority to their own wishes and needs. Some children, especially young children, suffer with guilt over fantasied misdeeds that they feel may have contributed to the family quarrels and led to the divorce. Others feel that it is their responsibility to mend the broken marriage (Wallerstein & Kelly, 1980a).

The responses of the child also must be considered within the social context of the divorce and in particular within the loneliness and social isolation that so many children experience. Children face the tensions and sorrows of divorce with little help from anybody else. Fewer than 10% of the children in the California Children of Divorce study had any help at the time of the crisis from adults outside the family although many people, including neighbors, pediatricians, ministers, rabbis, and family friends, knew the family and the children (Wallerstein & Kelly, 1980a). Thus, another striking feature of divorce as a childhood stress is that it occurs in the absence of or falling away of customary support.

Developmental factors are critical to the responses of children and adolescents at the time of the marital rupture. Despite significant individual differences in the child, in the family, and in parent–child relations, the child's age and developmental stage appear to be the most important factors governing the initial response. The child's dominant needs, his or her capacity to perceive and understand family events, the central psychological preoccupation and conflict, the available repertoire of defense and coping strategies, and the dominant patterning of relationships and expectations all reflect the child's age and developmental stage.

A major finding in divorce research has been the common patterns of response within different age groups (Wallerstein & Kelly, 1980a). The age groups that share significant commonalities in perceptions, responses, underlying fantasies, and behaviors are the preschool ages 3 to 5, early school age or early latency ages $5^1/_2$ to 8, later school age or latency ages 8 to 11, and, finally, adolescent ages 12 to 18 (Kelly & Wallerstein, 1976; Wallerstein, 1977; Wallerstein & Kelly, 1974; 1975; 1980a). These responses, falling as they do into age-related groupings, may reflect children's responses to acute stress generally, not only their responses to marital rupture.

Observations about preschool children derived from longitudinal studies in two widely different regions, namely, Virginia and northern California, are remarkably similar in their findings (Hetherington, 1979; Hetherington et al., 1978; 1982; Wallerstein & Kelly, 1975, 1980a). Preschool children are likely to show regression following one parent's departure from the household, and the regression usually occurs in the most recent developmental achievement of the child. Intensified fears are frequent and are evoked by routine separations from the custodial parent during the day and at bedtime. Sleep disturbances are also frequent, with preoccupying fantasies of many of the little children being fear of abandonment by both parents. Yearning for the departed parent is intense. Young children are likely to become irritable and demanding and to behave aggressively with parents, with younger siblings, and with peers.

Children in the 5- to 8-year-old group are likely to show open grieving and are preoccupied with feelings of concern and longing for the departed parent. Many share the terrifying fantasy of replacement. "Will my daddy get a new dog, a new mommy, a new little boy?" were the comments of several boys in this age group. Little girls wove elaborate Madame Butterfly fantasies, asserting that the departed father would some day return to them, that he loved them "the best." Many of the children in this age group could not believe that the divorce would endure. About half suffered a precipitous decline in their school work (Kelly & Wallerstein, 1979).

In the 9- to 12-year-old group the central response often seems to be intense anger at one or both parents for causing the divorce. In addition, these children suffer with grief over the loss of the intact family and with anxiety, loneliness, and the humiliating sense of their own powerlessness. Youngsters in this age group often see one parent as the "good" parent and the other as "bad," and they appear especially vulnerable to the blandishments of one or the other parent to engage in marital battles. Children in later latency also have a high potential for assuming a helpful and empathic role in the care of a needy parent. School performances and peer relationships suffered a decline in approximately one-half of these children (Wallerstein & Kelly, 1974).

Adolescents are very vulnerable to their parents' divorce. The precipitation of acute depression, accompanied by suicidal preoccupation and acting out, is frequent enough to be alarming. Anger can be intense. Several instances have been reported of direct violent attacks on custodial parents by young adolescents who had not previously shown such behavior (Springer & Wallerstein, 1983). Preoccupied with issues of morality, adolescents may judge the parents' conduct during the marriage and the divorce, and they may identify with one parent and do battle against the other. Many become anxious about their own future entry into adulthood, concerned that they may experience marital failure like their parents (Wallerstein & Kelly, 1974). By way of contrast, however, researchers have also called attention to the adolescent's impressive capacity to grow in maturity and independence as they respond to the family crisis and the parents' need for help (Weiss, 1979a)....

Long-Range Outcomes

The child's initial response to divorce should be distinguished from his or her long-range development and psychological adjustment. No single theme appears among all of those children who enhance, consolidate, or continue their good development after the divorce crisis has finally ended. Nor is there a single theme that appears among all of those who deteriorate either moderately or markedly. Instead, the author and her colleague (Wallerstein & Kelly, 1980a) have found a set of complex configurations in which the relevant components appear to include (a) the extent to which the parent has been able to resolve and put aside conflict and anger and to make use of the relief from conflict provided by the divorce (Emery, 1982; Jacobson, 1978 a, b, c); (b) the course of the custodial parent's handling of the child and the resumption or improvement of parenting within the home (Hess & Ca-

mara, 1979); (c) the extent to which the child does not feel rejected by the noncustodial or visiting parent and the extent to which this relationship has continued regularly and kept pace with the child's growth; (d) the extent to which the divorce has helped to attenuate or dilute a psychopathological parent–child relationship; (e) the range of personality assets and deficits that the child brought to the divorce, including both the child's history in the predivorce family and his or her capacities in the present, particularly intelligence, the capacity for fantasy, social maturity, and the ability to turn to peers and adults; (f) the availability to the child of a supportive human network (Tessman, 1977); (g) the absence in the child of continued anger and depression; and (h) the sex and age of the child....

FUTURE DIRECTIONS

Despite the accumulating reports of the difficulties that many children in divorced families experience, society has on the whole been reluctant to regard children of divorce as a special group at risk. Notwithstanding the magnitude of the population affected and the widespread implications for public policy and law, community attention has been very limited; research has been poorly supported; and appropriate social, psychological, economic, or preventive measures have hardly begun to develop. Recently the alarm has been sounded in the national press about the tragically unprotected and foreshortened childhoods of children of divorce and their subsequent difficulties in reaching maturity (Winn, 1983). Perhaps this reflects a long-overdue awakening of community concern.

The agenda for research on marital breakdown, separation, divorce, and remarriage and the roads that families travel between each of these way stations [are] long and [have] been cited repeatedly in this [article]. The knowledge that we have acquired is considerable but the knowledge that we still lack is critical. More knowledge is essential in order to provide responsible advice to parents; to consult effectively with the wide range of other professionals whose daily work brings them in contact with these families; to design and mount education, treatment, or prevention programs; and to provide guidelines for informed social policy.

AUTHOR'S NOTE

The Center for the Family in Transition, of which the author is the Executive Director, is supported by a grant from the San Francisco Foundation. The Zellerback Family Fund supported the author's research in the California Children of Divorce Project, one of the sources for this [article]. A slightly different version of this paper has been published in *Psychiatry Update: The American Psychiatric Association Annual Review, Vol. III.* L. Grinspoon (Ed.), pp. 144–158, 1984.

REFERENCES

Cherlin, A. J. (1981). *Marriage, divorce, remarriage.* Cambridge, MA: Harvard University Press.

Crohn, H., Brown, H., Walker, L., & Beir, J. (1981). Understanding and treating the child in the remarried family. In I. R. Stuart & L. E. Abt (Eds.), *Children of separation and divorce: Management and treatment.* New York: Van Nostrand Reinhold.

Emery, R. E. (1982). Interparental conflict and children of discord and divorce. *Psychological Bulletin, 92,* 310–330.

Felner, R. D., Stolberg, A. L., & Cowen, E. L. (1975). Crisis events and school mental health referral

patterns of young children. *Journal of Consulting and Clinical Psychology, 43,* 303–310.

Gardner, R. A. (1976). *Psychotherapy and children of divorce.* New York: Jason Aronson.

Goldstein, H. S. (1974). Reconstructed families: The second marriage and its children. *Psychiatric Quarterly, 48,* 433–440.

Hess, R. D., & Camara, K. A. (1979). Postdivorce relationships as mediating factors in the consequences of divorce for children. *Journal of Social Issues, 35,* 79–96.

Hetherington, E. (1979). Divorce: A child's perspective. *American Psychology, 34,* 79–96.

Hetherington, E., Cox, M., & Cox, R. (1978). The aftermath of divorce. In H. Stevens & M. Mathews (Eds.), *Mother–child relations.* Washington, DC: National Association for the Education of Young Children.

Hetherington, E. M., Cox, M., & Cox, R. (1982). Effects of divorce on parents and children. In M. E. Lamb (Ed.), *Nontraditional families: Parenting and child development.* Hillsdale, NJ: Lawrence Erlbaum Associates.

Jacobson, D. (1978a). The impact of marital separation/divorce on children: I. Parent–child separation and child adjustment. *Journal of Divorce, 1,* 341–360.

Jacobson, D. (1978b). The impact of marital separation/divorce on children: II. Interparent hostility and child adjustment. *Journal of Divorce, 2,* 3–20.

Jacobson, D. (1978c). The impact of marital separation/divorce on children: III. Parent–child communication and child adjustment, and regression analysis of findings from overall study. *Journal of Divorce, 2,* 175–194.

Jacobson, D. S. (1983). *Conflict, visiting and child adjustment in the stepfamily: A linked family system.* Paper presented at annual meeting of the American Orthopsychiatric Association, Boston.

Kalter, N. (1977). Children of divorce in an outpatient psychiatric population. *American Journal of Orthopsychiatry, 47,* 40–51.

Kelly, J. B., & Wallerstein, J. S. (1976). The effects of parental divorce: Experiences of the child in early latency. *American Journal of Orthopsychiatry, 46,* 20–32.

Kelly, J. B., & Wallerstein, J. S. (1979). The divorced child in the school. *National Principal, 59,* 51–58.

Morrison, A. L. (1982). *A prospective study of divorce: Its relation to children's development and parental functioning.* Unpublished dissertation, University of California at Berkeley.

Norton, A. J. (1980). The influence of divorce on traditional life cycle measures. *Journal of Marriage and the Family, 42,* 63–69.

Springer, C., & Wallerstein, J. S. (1983). Young adolescents' responses to their parents' divorces.

In L. A. Kurdek (Ed.), *Children and divorce*. San Francisco: Jossey-Bass.

Tessman, L. H. (1977). *Children of parting parents*. New York: Jason Aronson.

Tooley, K. (1976). Antisocial behavior and social alienation post divorce: The "man of the house" and his mother. *American Journal of Orthopsychiatry, 46*, 33–42.

Wallerstein, J. S. (1977). Responses of the preschool child to divorce: Those who cope. In M. F. McMillan & S. Henao (Eds.), *Child psychiatry: Treatment and research*. New York: Brunner/Mazel.

Wallerstein, J. S. (1978). Children of divorce: Preliminary report of a ten-year follow-up. In J. Anthony & C. Chilland (Eds.), *The child in his family* (Vol. 5). New York: Wiley.

Wallerstein, J. S. (1985). Parent–child relationships following divorce. In E. J. Anthony & G. Pollock (Eds.), *Parental influences in health and disease* (pp. 317–348). Boston: Little, Brown.

Wallerstein, J. S., & Kelly, J. B. (1974). The effects of parental divorce: The adolescent experience. In J. Anthony & C. Koupernik (Eds.), *The child in his family: Children at psychiatric risk* (Vol. 3). New York: Wiley.

Wallerstein, J. S., & Kelly, J. B. (1975). The effects of parental divorce: The experiences of the preschool child. *American Journal of Orthopsychiatry, 46*, 256–269.

Wallerstein, J. S., & Kelly, J. B. (1980a). *Surviving the breakup: How children and parents cope with divorce*. New York: Basic Books.

Weiss, R. S. (1979a). *Going it alone: The family life and social situation of the single parent*. New York: Basic Books.

Weiss, R. S. (1979b). Growing up a little faster. *Journal of Social Issues, 35*, 97–111.

Winn, M. (8 May 1983). The loss of childhood. *The New York Times Magazine*.

Zill, N. (22 March 1983). *Divorce, marital conflict, and children's mental health: Research findings and policy recommendations*. Testimony before Subcommittee on Family and Human Services, United States Senate Subcommittee on Labor and Human Resources.

NO

David H. Demo and
Alan C. Acock

THE IMPACT OF DIVORCE
ON CHILDREN

The purpose of this article is to review and assess recent empirical evidence on the impact of divorce on children, concentrating on studies of nonclinical populations published in the last decade. We also direct attention to a number of important theoretical and methodological considerations in the study of family structure and youthful well-being. . . .

It logically follows that departures from the nuclear family norm are problematic for the child's development, especially for adolescents, inasmuch as this represents a crucial stage in the developmental process. Accordingly, a large body of research literature deals with father absence, the effects of institutionalization, and a host of "deficiencies" in maturation, such as those having to do with cognitive development, achievement, moral learning, and conformity. This focus has pointed to the crucial importance of both parents' presence but also has suggested that certain causes for parental absence may accentuate any negative effects. . . .

EXISTING RESEARCH

A substantial amount of research has examined the effects of family structure on children's social and psychological well-being. Many studies document negative consequences for children whose parents divorce and for those living in single-parent families. But most studies have been concerned with limited dimensions of a quite complex problem. Specifically, the research to date has typically (a) examined the effects of divorce or father absence on children, ignoring the effects on adolescents; (b) examined only selected dimensions of children's well-being; (c) compared intact units and single-parent families but not recognized important variations (e.g., levels of marital instability and conflict) within these structures; and (d) relied on cross-sectional designs to assess developmental processes.

Social and psychological well-being includes aspects of personal adjustment, self-concept, interpersonal relationships, antisocial behavior, and cognitive functioning. . . .

From David H. Demo and Alan C. Acock, "The Impact of Divorce on Children," *Journal of Marriage and the Family*, vol. 50, no. 3 (August 1988), pp. 619–648. Copyright © 1988 by The National Council on Family Relations, 3989 Central Avenue, NE, Suite 550, Minneapolis, MN 55421. Reprinted by permission. Notes omitted.

Personal Adjustment

Personal adjustment... includes such variables as self-control, leadership, responsibility, independence, achievement orientation, aggressiveness, and gender-role orientation.... [T]he overall pattern of empirical findings suggests temporary deleterious effects of parental divorce on children's adjustment, with these effects most common among young children (Desimone-Luis, O'Mahoney, and Hunt, 1979; Hetherington, Cox, and Cox, 1979; Kurdek, Blisk, and Siesky, 1981; Wallerstein and Kelly, 1975, 1980a). Kurdek and Siesky (1980b; c) suggest that older children adjust more readily because they are more likely to discuss the situation with friends (many of whom have had similar experiences), to understand that they are not personally responsible, to recognize the finality of the situation, to appreciate both parents for their positive qualities, and to recognize beneficial consequences such as the end of parental fighting and improved relations with parents.

On the basis of her review of research conducted between 1970 and 1980, Cashion (1984: 483) concludes: "The evidence is overwhelming that after the initial trauma of divorce, the children are as emotionally well-adjusted in these [female-headed] families as in two-parent families." Investigations of long-term effects (Acock and Kiecolt, 1988; Kulka and Weingarten, 1979) suggest that, when socioeconomic status is controlled, adolescents who have experienced a parental divorce or separation have only slightly lower levels of adult adjustment....

While their findings are not definitive, Kinard and Reinherz speculate that either "the effects of parental divorce on children diminish over time; or that the impact of marital disruption is less severe for preschool-age children than for school-age children" (1986: 291). Children's age at the time of disruption may also mediate the impact of these events on other dimensions of their well-being (e.g., self-esteem or gender-role orientation) and thus will be discussed in greater detail below.... But two variables that critically affect children's adjustment to divorce are marital discord and children's gender.

Marital discord.... [E]xtensive data on children who had experienced their parents' divorce indicated that, although learning of the divorce and adjusting to the loss of the noncustodial parent were painful, children indicated that these adjustments were preferable to living in conflict. Many studies report that children's adjustment to divorce is facilitated under conditions of low parental conflict—both prior to *and* subsequent to the divorce (Guidubaldi, Cleminshaw, Perry, Nastasi, and Lightel, 1986; Jacobson, 1978; Lowenstein and Koopman, 1978; Porter and O'Leary, 1980; Raschke and Raschke, 1979; Rosen, 1979).

Children's gender. Children's gender may be especially important in mediating the effects of family disruption, as most of the evidence suggests that adjustment problems are more severe and last for longer periods of time among boys (Hess and Camara, 1979; Hetherington, 1979; Hetherington, Cox, and Cox, 1978, 1979, 1982; Wallerstein, 1984; Wallerstein and Kelly, 1980b). Guidubaldi and Perry (1985) found, controlling for social class, that boys in divorced families manifested significantly more maladaptive symptoms and behavior problems than boys in intact families. Girls differed only on the dimension of locus of control; girls in divorced households scored significantly higher than their counterparts in intact households....

While custodial mothers provide girls with same-sex role models, most boys have to adjust to living without same-sex parents. In examining boys and girls living in intact families and in different custodial arrangements, Santrock and Warshak (1979) found that few effects could be attributed to family structure per se, but that children living with opposite-sex parents (mother-custody boys and father-custody girls) were not as well adjusted on measures of competent social behavior....

Along related lines, a number of researchers have examined gender-role orientation and, specifically, the relation of father absence to boys' personality development. Most of the evidence indicates that boys without adult male role models demonstrate more feminine behavior (Biller, 1976; Herzog and Sudia, 1973; Lamb, 1977a), except in lower-class families (Biller, 1981b). A variety of studies have shown that fathers influence children's gender role development to be more traditional because, compared to mothers, they more routinely differentiate between masculine and feminine behaviors and encourage greater conformity to conventional gender roles (Biller, 1981a; Biller and Davids, 1973; Bronfenbrenner, 1961; Heilbrun, 1965; Lamb, 1977b; Noller, 1978).... But it should be reiterated that these effects have been attributed to father absence and thus would be expected to occur among boys in all female-headed families, not simply those that have experienced divorce....

[M]ost of the research on boys' adjustment fails to consider the quality or quantity of father-child contact or the availability of alternative male role models (e.g., foster father, grand-

father, big brother, other male relatives, coach, friend, etc.), which makes it difficult to assess the impact of changing family structure on boys' behavior. There are also limitations imposed by conceptualizing and measuring masculinity-femininity as a bipolar construct (Bem, 1974; Constantinople, 1973; Worell, 1978), and there is evidence that boys and girls in father-absent families are better described as androgynous (Kurdek and Siesky, 1980a).

Positive outcomes of divorce.... [T]he tendency of children in single-parent families to display more androgynous behavior may be interpreted as a beneficial effect. Because of father absence, children in female-headed families are not pressured as strongly as their counterparts in two-parent families to conform to traditional gender roles. These children frequently assume a variety of domestic responsibilities to compensate for the absent parent (Weiss, 1979), thereby broadening their skills and competencies and their definitions of gender-appropriate behavior. Divorced parents also must broaden their behavioral patterns to meet increased parenting responsibilities, thereby providing more androgynous role models. Kurdek and Siesky (1980a: 250) give the illustration that custodial mothers often "find themselves needing to acquire and demonstrate a greater degree of dominance, assertiveness, and independence while custodial fathers may find themselves in situations eliciting high degrees of warmth, nurturance, and tenderness."

Aside from becoming more androgynous, adolescents living in single-parent families are characterized by greater maturity, feelings of efficacy, and an internal locus of control (Guidubaldi and Perry, 1985; Kalter, Alpern, Spence, and Plunkett, 1984; Wallerstein and Kelly, 1974; Weiss, 1979). For adolescent girls this maturity stems partly from the status and responsibilities they acquire in peer and confidant relationships with custodial mothers....

There is evidence (Kurdek et al., 1981) that children and adolescents with an internal locus of control and a high level of interpersonal reasoning adjust more easily to their parents' divorce and that children's divorce adjustment is related to their more global personal adjustment.

Self-Concept...

Marital discord.... [F]amily structure is unrelated to children's self-esteem (Feldman and Feldman, 1975; Kinard and Reinherz, 1984; Parish, 1981; Parish, Dostal, and Parish, 1981), but parental discord is negatively related (Amato, 1986; Berg and Kelly, 1979; Cooper, Holman, and Braithwaite, 1983; Long, 1986; Raschke and Raschke, 1979; Slater and Haber, 1984). Because this conclusion is based on diverse samples of boys and girls of different ages in different living arrangements, the failure to obtain effects of family structure suggests either that family composition really does not matter for children's self-concept or that family structure alone is an insufficient index of familial relations. Further, these studies suggest that divorce per se does not adversely affect children's self-concept. Cashion's (1984) review of the literature indicates that children living in single-parent families suffer no losses to self-esteem, except in situations where the child's family situation is stigmatized (Rosenberg, 1979)....

Cognitive Functioning

... Many... studies find that family conflict and disruption are associated with inhibited cognitive functioning (Blanchard and Biller, 1971; Feldman and Feldman, 1975; Hess and Camara, 1979; Kinard and Reinherz, 1986; Kurdek, 1981; Radin, 1981).... In this section we summarize the differential effects of family disruption on academic performance by gender and social class and offer some insights as to the mechanisms by which these effects occur.

Children's gender. Some studies suggest that negative effects of family disruption on academic performance are stronger for boys than for girls (Chapman, 1977; Werner and Smith, 1982), but most of the evidence suggests similar effects by gender (Hess and Camara, 1979; Kinard and Reinherz, 1986; Shinn, 1978). While females traditionally outscore males on standardized tests of verbal skills and males outperform females on mathematical skills, males who have experienced family disruption generally score higher on verbal aptitude (Radin, 1981). Thus, the absence of a father may result in a "feminine" orientation toward education (Fowler and Richards, 1978; Herzog and Sudia, 1973). But an important and unresolved question is whether this pattern results from boys acquiring greater verbal skills in mother-headed families or from deficiencies in mathematical skills attributable to father absence. The latter explanation is supported by evidence showing that father-absent girls are disadvantaged in mathematics (Radin, 1981).

Children's race.... [M]ost studies show academic achievement among black children to be unaffected by family structure (Hunt and Hunt, 1975, 1977; Shinn, 1978; Solomon, Hirsch, Scheinfeld, and Jackson, 1972). Svanum, Bringle, and McLaughlin (1982) found, controlling for social class, that there are no significant effects of father absence on cognitive performance for white or black children. Again, these investigations focus on family composition and demonstrate that the effects of family structure on academic performance do not vary as much by race as by social class, but race differences in the impact of divorce remain largely unexplored....

Family socioeconomic status.... When social class is controlled, children in female-headed families fare no worse than children from two-parent families on measures of intelligence (Bachman, 1970; Kopf, 1970), academic achievement (Shinn, 1978; Svanum et al., 1982), and educational attainment (Bachman, O'Malley, and Johnston, 1978).... In order to disentangle the intricate effects of family structure and SES [socioeconomic status] on children's cognitive performance, family researchers need to examine the socioeconomic history of intact families and those in which disruption occurs, to examine the economic resources available to children at various stages of cognitive development, and to assess changes in economic resources and family relationships that accompany marital disruption.

Family processes.... First, family disruption alters daily routines and work schedules and imposes additional demands on adults and children living in single-parent families (Amato, 1987; Furstenberg and Nord, 1985; Hetherington et al., 1983; Weiss, 1979). Most adolescents must assume extra domestic and child care responsibilities, and financial conditions require some to work part-time. These burdens result in greater absenteeism, tardiness, and truancy among children in single-parent households (Hetherington et al., 1983). Second, children in recently disrupted families are prone to experi-

ence emotional and behavioral problems such as aggression, distractibility, dependency, anxiety, and withdrawal (Hess and Camara, 1979; Kinard and Reinherz, 1984), factors that may help to explain problems in school conduct and the propensity of teachers to label and stereotype children from broken families (Hess and Camara, 1979; Hetherington et al., 1979, 1983). Third, emotional problems may interfere with study patterns, while demanding schedules reduce the time available for single parents to help with homework....

Interpersonal Relationships...

Peer relations. Studies of preschool children (Hetherington et al., 1979) and preadolescents (Santrock, 1975; Wyman, Cowen, Hightower, and Pedro-Carroll, 1985) suggest that children in disrupted families are less sociable: they have fewer close friends, spend less time with friends, and participate in fewer shared activities. Stolberg and Anker (1983) observe that children in families disrupted by divorce exhibit psychopathology in interpersonal relations, often behaving in unusual and inappropriate ways. Other studies suggest that the effects are temporary. Kinard and Reinherz (1984) found no differences in peer relations among children in intact and disrupted families, but those in recently disrupted families displayed greater hostility. Kurdek et al. (1981) conducted a two-year follow-up of children whose parents had divorced and showed that relationships with peers improved after the divorce and that personal adjustment was facilitated by opportunities to discuss experiences with peers, some of whom had similar experiences....

Dating patterns. Hetherington (1972) reported that adolescent girls whose fathers were absent prior to age 5 had difficulties in heterosexual relations, but Hainline and Feig's (1978) analyses of female college students indicated that early and later father-absent women could not be distinguished on measures of romanticism and heterosexual attitudes.

An examination of dating and sexual behavior among female college students found that women with divorced parents began dating slightly later than those in intact families, but women in both groups were socially active (Kalter, Riemer, Brickman, and Chen, 1985). Booth, Brinkerhoff, and White (1984) reported that, compared to college students with intact families, those whose parents were divorced or permanently separated exhibited higher levels of dating activity, and this activity increased further if parental or parent-child conflict persisted during and after the divorce....Regarding adolescent sexual behavior, the findings consistently demonstrate that males and females not living with both biological parents initiate coitus earlier than their counterparts in intact families (Hogan and Kitagawa, 1985; Newcomer and Udry, 1987). But Newcomer and Udry propose that, because parental marital status is also associated with a broad range of deviant behaviors, these effects may stem from general loss of parental control rather than simply loss of control over sexual behavior. Studies of antisocial behavior support this interpretation.

Antisocial Behavior

Many studies over the years have linked juvenile delinquency, deviancy, and antisocial behavior to children living in broken homes (Bandura and Walters, 1959; Glueck and Glueck, 1962; Hoffman, 1971; McCord, McCord, and Thurber, 1962; Santrock, 1975; Stolberg and Anker, 1983; Tooley, 1976; Tuckman and Regan, 1966). Unfortunately, these studies either relied on clinical samples or failed to control for social class and other factors related to delinquency. However,... a number of studies involving large representative samples and controlling for social class provide similar findings (Dornbusch, Carlsmith, Bushwall, Ritter, Leiderman, Hastorf, and Gross, 1985; Kalter et al., 1985; Peterson and Zill, 1986; Rickel and Langner, 1985). Kalter et al. (1985) studied 522 teenage girls and found that girls in divorced families committed more delinquent acts (e.g., drug use, larceny, skipping school) than their counterparts in intact families. Dornbusch et al. (1985) examined a representative national sample of male and female youth aged 12–17 and found that adolescents in mother-only households were more likely than their counterparts in intact families to engage in deviant acts, partly because of their tendency to make decisions independent of parental input. The presence of an additional adult (a grandparent, an uncle, a lover, a friend) in mother-only households increased control over adolescent behavior and lowered rates of deviant behavior, which suggests that "there are functional equivalents of two-parent families—nontraditional groupings that can do the job of parenting" (1985: 340)....

A tentative conclusion based on the evidence reviewed here is that antisocial behavior is less likely to occur in families where two adults are present, whether as biological parents, stepparents, or some combination of biological parents and other adults. Short-term increases in antisocial behavior may occur during periods of disruption, however, as children adjust to restructured relationships and parents struggle to maintain consistency in disciplining (Rickel and Langner, 1985).... Peterson and Zill (1986) demonstrated that, when social class was controlled, behavior problems were as likely to occur among adolescents living in intact families characterized by persistent conflict as among those living in disrupted families.... Peterson and Zill found that "poor parent-child relationships lead to more negative child behavior, yet maintaining good relationships with parents can go some way in reducing the effects of conflict and disruption" (1986: 306). Hess and Camara's (1979) analyses of a much smaller sample yielded a similar conclusion: aggressive behavior in children was unrelated to family type but was more common in situations characterized by infrequent or low-quality parent-child interaction and parental discord....

LIMITATIONS OF PRIOR RESEARCH

In this section we discuss some of the principal limitations of research assessing the impact of divorce on children....

Nonrepresentative Samples
Sampling is a virtually universal dilemma for researchers....

Among the most problematic nonrepresentative samples are those that rely on clinical populations. While these studies are crucial to our understanding of children and adolescents who are most severely influenced by divorce, they tell us little or nothing about the typical experience following divorce. Since most children whose parents divorce do not receive professional help, such studies can be very misleading about the consequences of divorce for the majority of youth.

While nonrepresentative samples have shortcomings, national surveys typically involve reanalysis of data collected for other purposes and for which the effects of divorce are not a central concern. Because these surveys are not designed to investigate the consequences of divorce, many theoretically important variables are either excluded or poorly operationalized and important control variables are often absent.

What Family Structures Are Being Compared?
Generally, investigations of family structure rely on classification schemes, such as father absence, in which the types derive from different events. For example, many military families are classified as father-absent, but the absence is temporary, the father's income is available to the family, and no social stigma is attached. Alternatively, a single-parent household may consist of a 25-year-old never-married woman and her five children. Other families are father-absent as the result of death, permanent separation, or divorce. A central problem in identifying the effects of family structure is that all of these families are frequently classified as one monolithic family form called "father-absent."...

Failure to Control for Income or Social Class
... With very few exceptions... studies rely on samples of children in one socioeconomic category, usually the middle class, for whom the economic consequences of divorce are dissimilar to those of children in lower socioeconomic categories. As a result, it is impossible to distinguish the effects of divorce and family structure from those of socioeconomic conditions....

Economic factors are important considerations in explicating causal processes for several reasons (see Greenberg and Wolf, 1982; Hill and Duncan, 1987; Kinard and Reinherz, 1984; McLanahan, 1985). First, low-income, single-parent mothers are more likely to work and, as a result, may provide inadequate supervision (Colletta, 1979). Children's behavioral problems associated with "mother-absence" (Hill, Augustyniak, and Ponza, 1986) may therefore be attributable to low income and the need for maternal employment rather than being the result of single-parent family structure per se. Second, the effects of marital disruption on children may be indirect, operating through the economic and emotional impact of divorce on custodial mothers (Longfellow, 1979; Shinn, 1978). As mothers adjust to divorce, single-parenthood, and lower economic status, their anxiety and emotional distress may induce anxiety and stress in children, which in turn may hinder children's academic performance (Kinard and Reinherz, 1986). Failure to examine socioeconomic variation in single-parent families thus obscures the specific processes through which marital disruption affects children. Third, children in single-parent households are more likely to assume adult roles at an early age—for example, working full-time and being responsible for younger siblings, responsibilities that require many adolescents to leave school (Kelly and Wallerstein, 1979; Weiss, 1979). The effects (both positive and negative) of these accelerated life course transitions are consequences of economic deprivation....

Single-parent families precipitated by divorce may be poor as a result of a sudden loss of income. Dramatic changes in lifestyle, financial instability, and loss of status may affect children indirectly through custodial parents' loss of control and altered childrearing practices. Increased labor force participation or increased transfer payments may help, but the net effect is still a dramatic loss of income (Cherlin, 1981; Hoffman, 1977; Weitzman, 1985).

While many families lose a stable middle-class environment and encounter stigmatization and financial instability, other families experience relatively minor changes. Santrock and Warshak (1979) report that postdivorce income losses were severe for mother-custody families but not for father-custody families. Further, the source of income is an important consideration, in that welfare dollars may stigmatize the poor and child support payments are unreliable (Bould, 1977)....

The long-term positive effect of divorce on the earning power of women needs to be recognized and may explain why most of the adverse effects of divorce diminish over time. Employed single mothers may provide stronger role models than dependent mothers in intact families, fostering egalitarian sex role attitudes among both women and men whose parents divorced (Kiecolt and Acock, 1988).

Failure to Examine Contextual Factors
A number of contextual factors that distinguish the living conditions of children in intact and disrupted families may be linked to behavioral differences between the two groups. Glenn and Supancic (1984) note that divorced persons participate less in church activities than married persons.... If children living in single-parent households are systematically less likely to be exposed to other children who are active in a church, this

may have a substantial impact on their adjustment....

Another contextual variable is urban residence. Single-parent households are far more common in urban areas. Urban areas provide a different environment for children than do suburbs, rural areas, or small towns. The quality of the educational system and the exposure to deviant subcultures are two correlates of residential patterns that may affect children who live in a female-headed household.... Other contextual factors that influence children include the number of fatherless children in their school, neighborhood SES, presence of a gang subculture, presence of peer groups using drugs (Blechman, Berberian, and Thompson, 1977), and the geographic mobility of peers....

Lack of Longitudinal Designs

Among the hundreds of studies on children of divorce, there are only a pair of widely cited longitudinal studies (Hetherington et al., 1978, 1979; Wallerstein and Kelly, 1980b), and even these studies have serious methodological limitations (Blechman, 1982, Cherlin, 1981). Yet adjustment to changes in family structure is a developmental process.... [T]ypical cross-sectional comparisons of children living in disrupted families with children in intact families provide very little, if any, information on the socioeconomic history of these families, level of family conflict, parent-child relations, and so on. If, for example, children from single-parent households were formerly in two-parent households that were poor and conflict-ridden, any problems the children now have may be scars from long ago rather than a direct consequence of the divorce....

CONCLUSIONS

... It is simplistic and inaccurate to think of divorce as having uniform consequences for children. The consequences of divorce vary along different dimensions of well-being, characteristics of children (e.g., predivorce adjustment, age at the time of disruption) and characteristics of families (e.g., socioeconomic history, pre- and postdivorce level of conflict, parent-child relationships, and maternal employment). Most of the evidence reviewed here suggests that some sociodemographic characteristics of children, such as race and gender, are not as important as characteristics of families in mediating the effects of divorce. Many studies report boys to be at a greater disadvantage, but these differences usually disappear when other relevant variables are controlled. At present, there are too few methodologically adequate studies comparing white and black children to conclude that one group is more damaged by family disruption than the other.

Characteristics of families, on the other hand, are critical to youthful well-being. Family conflict contributes to many problems in social development, emotional stability, and cognitive skills (Edwards, 1987; Kurdek, 1981), and these effects continue long after the divorce is finalized. Slater and Haber (1984) report that ongoing high levels of conflict, whether in intact or divorced homes, produce lower self-esteem, increased anxiety, and a loss of self-control.... Rosen (1979) concludes that parental separation is more beneficial for children than continued conflict.... Such conflict and hostility may account for adolescent adjustment problems whether the family in question goes through divorce or remains intact (Hoffman, 1971)....

Maternal employment is another variable mediating the consequences of divorce for children. Divorced women often find the dual responsibilities of provider and parent to be stressful (Bronfenbrenner, 1976). But studies indicate that women who work prior to the divorce do not find continued employment problematic (Kinard and Reinherz, 1984); the problem occurs for women who enter the labor force after the divorce and who view the loss of time with their children as another detriment to the children that is caused by the divorce (Kinard and Reinherz, 1984). As a practical matter, the alternative to employment for single-parent mothers is likely to be poverty or, at best, economic dependency....

Other bases of social support for single-parent mothers and their children must also be examined. The presence of strong social networks may ease the parents' and, presumably, the child's adjustment after a divorce (Milardo, 1987; Savage et al., 1978).... Kinship ties are usually strained, as both biological parents and parents-in-law are more critical of the divorce than friends are (Spanier and Thompson, 1984)....

Methodologically, research in support of the family composition hypothesis has been flawed in a number of respects (Blechman, 1982). As described above, most studies (*a*) rely on simplistic classifications of family structure; (*b*) overlook potentially confounding factors such as income and social class; (*c*) use nonrepresentative samples; (*d*) examine limited dimensions of social and psychological well-being; (*e*) fail to assess possible beneficial effects deriving from different family structures; and (*f*) rely on nonlongitudinal designs to detect developmental processes.

REFERENCES

Acock, Alan C., and K. Jill Kiecolt. 1988. "Is it family structure or socioeconomic status: Effects of family structure during adolescence on adult adjustment." Paper presented at the annual meetings of the American Sociological Association, Atlanta.

Amato, Paul R. 1986. "Marital conflict, the parent-child relationship, and child self-esteem." Family Relations 35: 403–410.

Amato, Paul R. 1987. "Family processes in one-parent, stepparent, and intact families: The child's point of view." Journal of Marriage and the Family 49: 327–337.

Bachman, Jerald G. 1970. Youth in Transition, Vol. 2: The Impact of Family Background and Intelligence on Tenth Grade Boys. Ann Arbor, MI: Survey Research Center, Institute for Social Research.

Bachman, Jerald G., Patrick M. O'Malley, and Jerome J. Johnston. 1978. Youth in Transition, Vol. 6: Adolescence to Adulthood: A Study of Change and Stability in the Lives of Young Men. Ann Arbor, MI: Survey Research Center, Institute for Social Research.

Bandura, Albert, and Richard H. Walters. 1959. Adolescent Aggression. New York: Ronald Press.

Bem, Sandra L. 1974. "The measurement of psychological androgyny." Journal of Consulting and Clinical Psychology 42: 155–162.

Berg, Berthold, and Robert Kelly. 1979. "The measured self-esteem of children from broken, rejected, and accepted families." Journal of Divorce 2: 363–369.

Biller, Henry B. 1976. "The father and personality development: Paternal deprivation and sex-role development." Pp. 89–156 in Michael E. Lamb (ed.), The Role of the Father in Child Development. New York: Wiley.

Biller, Henry B. 1981a. "The father and sex role development." Pp. 319–358 in Michael E. lamb (ed.), The Role of the Father in Child Development (2nd ed.). New York: Wiley.

Biller, Henry B. 1981b. "Father absence, divorce, and personality development." Pp. 489–552 in Michael E. Lamb (ed.), The Role of the Father in Child Development (2nd ed.). New York: Wiley.

Biller, Henry B., and Anthony Davids. 1973. "Parent-child relations, personality development and psychopathology." Pp. 48–77 in Anthony Davids (ed.), Issues in Abnormal Child Psychology. Monterey, CA: Wadsworth.

Blanchard, Robert W., and Henry B. Biller. 1971. "Father availability and academic performance among third-grade boys." Developmental Psychology 4: 301–305.

Blechman, Elaine A. 1982. "Are children with one parent at psychological risk? A methodological review." Journal of Marriage and the Family 44: 179–195.

Blechman, Elaine A., Rosalie M. Berberian, and W. Douglas Thompson. 1977. "How well does number of parents explain unique variance in self-reported drug use?" Journal of Consulting and Clinical Psychology 45: 1182–1183.

Booth, Alan, David B. Brinkerhoff, and Lynn K. White. 1984. "The impact of parental divorce on courtship." Journal of Marriage and the Family 46: 85–94.

Bould, Sally. 1977. "Female-headed families: Personal fate control and provider role." Journal of Marriage and the Family 39: 339–349.

Bronfenbrenner, Urie. 1961. "The changing American child: A speculative analysis." Journal of Social Issues 17: 6–18.

Bronfenbrenner, Urie. 1976. "Who cares for America's children?" Pp. 3–32 in Victor C. Vaugh and T. Berry Brazelton (eds.), The Family—Can It Be Saved? Chicago: Yearbook Medical Publishers.

Cashion, Barbara G. 1984. "Female-headed families: Effects on children and clinical implications." Pp. 481–489 in David H. Olson and Brent C. Miller (eds.), Family Studies Review Yearbook. Beverly Hills, CA: Sage.

Chapman, Michael. 1977. "Father absence, stepfathers, and the cognitive performance of college students." Child Development 48: 1155–1158.

Cherlin, Andrew J. 1981. Marriage, Divorce, Remarriage. Cambridge, MA: Harvard University Press.

Colletta, Nancy D. 1979. "The impact of divorce: Father absence or poverty?" Journal of Divorce 3: 27–35.

Constantinople, Anne. 1973. "Masculinity-femininity: An exception to a famous dictum?" Psychological Bulletin 80: 389–407.

Cooper, Judith E., Jacqueline Holman, and Valerie A. Braithwaite. 1983. "Self-esteem and family cohesion: The child's perspective and adjustment." Journal of Marriage and the Family 45: 153–159.

DeSimone-Luis, Judith, Katherine O'Mahoney, and Dennis Hunt. 1979. "Children of separation and divorce: Factors influencing adjustment." Journal of Divorce 3: 37–42.

Dornbusch, Sanford M., J. Merrill Carlsmith, Steven J. Bushwall, Philip L. Ritter, Herbert Leiderman, Albert H. Hastorf, and Ruth T. Gross. 1985. "Single parents, extended households, and the control of adolescents." Child Development 56: 326–341.

Edwards, John N. 1987. "Changing family structure and youthful well-being: Assessing the future." Journal of Family Issues 8: 355–372.

Feldman, Harold, and Margaret Feldman. 1975. "The effects of father absence on adolescents." Family Perspective 10: 3–16.

Fowler, Patrick D., and Herbert C. Richards. 1978. "Father absence, educational preparedness, and academic achievement: A test of the confluence model." Journal of Educational Psychology 70: 595–601.

Furstenberg, Frank F., Jr., and Christine Winquist Nord. 1985. "Parenting apart: Patterns of childrearing after marital disruption." Journal of Marriage and the Family 47: 893–904. Glenn, Norval, and Michael Supancic. 1984. "The social and demographic correlates of divorce and separation in the United States: An update and reconsideration." Journal of Marriage and the Family 46: 563–576.

Glueck, Sheldon, and Eleanor Glueck. 1962. Family Environment and Delinquency. Boston: Houghton Mifflin.

Greenberg, David, and Douglas Wolf. 1982. "The economic consequences of experiencing parental marital disruption." Child and Youth Services Review 4: 141–162.

Guidubaldi, John, Helen K. Cleminshaw, Joseph D. Perry, Bonnie K. Nastasi, and Jeanine Lightel. 1986. "The role of selected family environment factors in children's post-divorce adjustment." Family Relations 35: 141–151.

Guidubaldi, John, and Joseph D. Perry. 1985. "Divorce and mental health sequelae for children: A two-year follow-up of a nationwide sample." Journal of the American Academy of Child Psychiatry 24: 531–537.

Hainline, Louise, and Ellen Feig. 1978. "The correlates of childhood father absence in college-aged women." Child Development 49:37–42.

Heilbrun, A. B. 1965. "An empirical test of the modeling theory of sex-role learning." Child Development 36: 789–799.

Herzog, Elizabeth, and Cecilia E. Sudia. 1973. "Children in fatherless families." Pp. 141–232 in B. M. Caldwell and N. H. Riccuiti (eds.), Review of Child Development Research (Vol. 3). Chicago: University of Chicago Press.

Hess, Robert D., and Kathleen A. Camara. 1979. "Post-divorce family relationships as mediating factors in the consequences of divorce for children." Journal of Social Issues 35: 79–96.

Hetherington, E. Mavis. 1972. "Effects of father absence on personality development in adolescent daughters." Developmental Psychology 7: 313–326.

Hetherington, E. Mavis. 1979. "Divorce: A child's perspective." American Psychologist 34: 851–858.

Hetherington, E. Mavis, Kathleen A. Camara, and David L. Featherman. 1983. "Achievement and intellectual functioning of children in one-parent households." Pp. 205–284 in Janet T. Spence (ed.), Achievement and Achievement Motives:

Psychological and Sociological Approaches. San Francisco: Freeman.

Hetherington, E. Mavis, Martha Cox, and Roger Cox. 1978. "The aftermath of divorce." In J. H. Stevens, Jr., and M. Mathews (eds.), Mother-Child, Father-Child Relations. Washington, DC: National Association for the Education of Young Children.

Hetherington, E. Mavis, Martha Cox, and Roger Cox. 1979. "Play and social interaction in children following divorce." Journal of Social Issues 35: 26–49.

Hetherington, E. Mavis, Martha Cox, and Roger Cox. 1982. "Effects of divorce on parents and young children." In M. Lamb (ed.), Nontraditional Families: Parenting and Child Development. Hillsdale, NJ: Erlbaum.

Hill, Martha S., Sue Augustyniak, and Michael Ponza. 1986. "Adolescent years with parents divorced or separated: Effects on the social and economic attainments of children as adults." Paper presented at the meetings of the Population Association of America, Detroit.

Hill, Martha S., and Greg J. Duncan. 1987. "Parental family income and the socioeconomic attainment of children." Social Science Research 16:39–73.

Hoffman, Martin L. 1971. "Father absence and conscience development." Developmental Psychology 4: 400–406.

Hoffman, Saul. 1977. "Marital instability and the economic status of women." Demography 14: 67–76.

Hogan, Dennis P., and Evelyn M. Kitagawa. 1985. "The impact of social status, family structure, and neighborhood on the fertility of black adolescents." American Journal of Sociology 90: 825–855.

Hunt, Janet G., and Larry L. Hunt. 1977. "Race, daughters, and father-loss: Does absence make the girl grow stronger?" Social Problems 25: 90–102.

Hunt, Larry L., and Janet G. Hunt. 1975. "Race and the father-son connection: The conditional relevance of father absence for the orientations and identities of adolescent boys." Social Problems 23: 35–52.

Jacobson, Doris S. 1978. "The impact of marital separation/divorce on children: II. Interparent hostility and child adjustment." Journal of Divorce 2: 3–19.

Kalter, Neil, Dana Alpern, Rebecca Spence, and James W. Plunkett. 1984. "Locus of control in children of divorce." Journal of Personality Assessment 48: 410–414.

Kalter, Neil, Barbara Riemer, Arthur Brickman, and Jade Woo Chen. 1985. "Implications of parental divorce for female development." Journal of the American Academy of Child Psychiatry 24: 538–544.

Kelly, Joan B., and Judith Wallerstein. 1979. "Children of divorce." National Elementary Principal 59: 51–58.

Kiecolt, K. Jill, and Alan C. Acock. 1988. "The long-term effects of family structure on gender-role attitudes." Journal of Marriage and the Family 50: 709–717.

Kinard, E. Milling, and Helen Reinherz. 1984. "Marital disruption: Effects of behavioral and emotional functioning in children." Journal of Family Issues 5: 90–115.

Kinard, E. Milling, and Helen Reinherz. 1986. "Effects of marital disruption on children's school aptitude and achievement." Journal of Marriage and the Family 48: 285–293.

Kopf, Kathryn E. 1970. "Family variables and school adjustment of eighth grade father-absent boys." Family Coordinator 19: 145–151.

Kulka, Richard A., and Helen Weingarten. 1979. "The long-term effects of parental divorce in childhood on adult adjustment." Journal of Social Issues 35: 50–78.

Kurdek, Lawrence A. 1981. "An integrative perspective on children's divorce adjustment." American Psychologist 36: 856–866.

Kurdek, Lawrence A., Darlene Blisk, and Albert E. Siesky, Jr. 1981. "Correlates of children's long-term adjustment to their parents' divorce." Developmental Psychology 17: 565–579.

Kurdek, Lawrence A., and Albert E. Siesky, Jr. 1980a. "Sex role self-concepts of single divorced parents and their children." Journal of Divorce 3: 249–261.

Kurdek, Lawrence A., and Albert E. Siesky, Jr. 1980b. "Children's perceptions of their parents' divorce." Journal of Divorce 3: 339–378.

Kurdek, Lawrence A., and Albert E. Siesky, Jr. 1980c. "Effects of divorce on children: The relationship between parent and child perspectives." Journal of Divorce 4: 85–99.

Lamb, Michael E. 1977a. "The effects of divorce on children's personality development." Journal of Divorce 1: 163–174.

Lamb, Michael E. 1977b. "The development of mother- and father-infant attachments in the second year of life." Developmental Psychology 13: 637–648.

Long, Barbara H. 1986. "Parental discord vs. family structure: Effects of divorce on the self-esteem of daughters." Journal of Youth and Adolescence 15: 19–27.

Longfellow, Cynthia. 1979. "Divorce in context: Its impact on children." Pp. 287–306 in George K. Levinger and Oliver C. Moles (eds.), Divorce and Separation: Context, Causes, and Consequences. New York: Basic Books.

Lowenstein, Joyce S., and Elizabeth J. Koopman. 1978. "A comparison of the self-esteem between boys living with single-parent mothers and single-parent fathers." Journal of Divorce 2: 195–208.

McCord, Joan, William McCord, and Emily Thurber. 1962. "Some effects of parental absence on male children." Journal of Abnormal and Social Psychology 64: 361–369.

McLanahan, Sara S. 1985. "Family structure and the reproduction of poverty." American Journal of Sociology 90: 873–901.

Milardo, Robert M. 1987. "Changes in social networks of women and men following divorce: A review." Journal of Family Issues 8: 78–96.

Newcomer, Susan, and J. Richard Udry. 1987. "Parental marital status effects on adolescent sexual behavior." Journal of Marriage and the Family 49: 235–240.

Noller, Patricia. 1978. "Sex differences in the socialization of affectionate expression." Developmental Psychology 14: 317–319.

Parish, Thomas S. 1981. "The Impact of divorce on the family." Adolescence 16 (63): 577–580.

Parish, Thomas S., Judy W. Dostal, and Jocelyn G. Parish. 1981. "Evaluations of self and parents as a function of intactness of family and family happiness." Adolescence 16 (61): 203–210.

Peterson, James L., and Nicholas Zill. 1986. "Marital disruption, parent-child relationships, and behavior problems in children." Journal of Marriage and the Family 48: 295–307.

Porter, Beatrice, and K. Daniel O'Leary. 1980. "Marital discord and childhood behavior problems." Journal of Abnormal Child Psychology 8: 287–295.

Radin, Norma. 1981. "The role of the father in cognitive, academic, and intellectual development." Pp. 379–427 in Michael E. Lamb (ed.), The Role of the Father in Child Development (2nd ed.). New York: Wiley.

Raschke, Helen J., and Vernon J. Raschke. 1979. "Family conflict and the children's self-concepts." Journal of Marriage and the Family 41: 367–374.

Rickel, Annette U., and Thomas S. Langner. 1985. "Short-term and long-term effects of marital disruption on children." American Journal of Community Psychology 13: 599–611.

Rosen, Rhona. 1979. "Some crucial issues concerning children of divorce." Journal of Divorce 3: 19–25.

Rosenberg, Morris. 1979. Conceiving the Self. New York: Basic Books.

Santrock, John W. 1975. "Father absence, perceived maternal behavior, and moral development in boys." Child Development 46: 753–757.

Santrock, John W., and Richard A. Warshak. 1979. "Father custody and social development in boys and girls." Journal of Social Issues 35: 112–125.

Savage, James E., Jr., Alvis V. Adair, and Phillip Friedman. 1978. "Community-social variables related to black parent-absent families." Journal of Marriage and the Family 40: 779–785.

Shinn, Marybeth. 1978. "Father absence and children's cognitive development." Psychological Bulletin 85: 295–324.

Slater, Elisa J., and Joel D. Haber. 1984. "Adolescent adjustment following divorce as a function of familial conflict." Journal of Consulting and Clinical Psychology 52: 920–921.

Solomon, Daniel, Jay O. Hirsch, Daniel R. Scheinfeld, and John C. Jackson. 1972. "Family characteristics and elementary school achievement in an urban ghetto." Journal of Consulting and Clinical Psychology 39: 462–466.

Spanier, Graham B., and Linda Thompson. 1984. Parting: The Aftermath of Separation and Divorce. Beverly Hills, CA: Sage.

Stolberg, Arnold L., and James M. Anker. 1983. "Cognitive and behavioral changes in children resulting from parental divorce and consequent environmental changes." Journal of Divorce 7: 23–41.

Svanum, Soren, Robert G. Bringle, and Joan E. McLaughlin. 1982. "Father absence and cognitive performance in a large sample of six- to eleven-year-old children." Child Development 53: 136–143.

Tooley, Kay. 1976. "Antisocial behavior and social alienation post divorce: The 'man of the house' and his mother." American Journal of Orthopsychiatry 46: 33–42.

Tuckman, J., and R. A. Regan. 1966. "Intactness of the home and behavioral problems in children." Journal of Child Psychology and Psychiatry 7: 225–233.

Wallerstein, Judith S. 1984. "Children of divorce: Preliminary report of a ten-year follow-up of young children." American Journal of Orthopsychiatry 54: 444–458.

Wallerstein, Judith S., and Joan B. Kelly. 1974. "The effects of parental divorce: The adolescent experience." In E. James Anthony and Cyrille Koupernik (eds.), The Child in His Family, (Vol 3). New York: Wiley.

Wallerstein, Judith S., and Joan B. Kelly. 1975. "The effects of parental divorce. The experiences of the preschool child." Journal of the American Academy of Child Psychiatry 14: 600–616.

Wallerstein, Judith S., and Joan B. Kelly. 1980a. "Children and divorce: A review." Social Work 24: 468–475.

Wallerstein, Judith S., and Joan B. Kelly. 1980b. Surviving the Breakup: How Children and Parents Cope with Divorce. Basic Books: New York.

Weiss, Robert S. 1979. "Growing up a little faster: The experience of growing up in a single-parent household." Journal of Social Issues 35: 97–111.

Weitzman, Lenore. 1985. The Divorce Revolution: The Unexpected Social and Economic Consequences for Women and Children in America. New York: Free Press.

Werner, Emmy E., and Ruth S. Smith. 1982. Vulnerable but Not Invincible: A Study of Resilient Children. New York: McGraw-Hill.

Worell, J. 1978. "Sex roles and psychological well-being: Perspectives on methodology." Journal of Consulting and Clinical Psychology 46: 777–791.

Wyman, Peter A., Emory L. Cowen, A. Dirk Hightower, and JoAnne L. Pedro-Carroll. 1985. "Perceived competence, self-esteem, and anxiety in latency-aged children of divorce." Journal of Clinical Child Psychology 14: 20–26.

POSTSCRIPT

Are Children of Divorce at Greater Risk?

Divorce is typically a painful experience for children. The question is, do children become debilitated for long periods of their lives or do they gradually adapt to their changed family situations? Wallerstein contends that divorce leads to long-lasting social and psychological problems for many children, but other scholars argue that the most troublesome symptoms diminish within about two years as parents settle into a routine and as family members learn to cope with the realities of their new life situations.

Demo and Acock maintain that it is inaccurate and simplistic to think that divorce has identical effects on all children. They caution that factors such as the child's age, how she or he reacts to the divorce from the time it is announced or the parents separate through the actual divorce, the family's income before the divorce, the mother's income after the divorce (if the mother becomes the main caregiver), the amount of conflict between the parents before and after the divorce, and the relationship between the child and each parent before and after the divorce should all be considered. They claim that most studies to date have been flawed because they relied on non-representative samples, examined only a few of the many factors that affect adjustment to divorce, overlooked any beneficial aspects of divorce on children, and failed to perform follow-up research on the children after the initial study.

If Wallerstein's conclusions about children of divorce are more accurate, should educational and treatment programs be established and social policies that would help such children be promoted? Or should more reliable information be sought, as Demo and Acock suggest, to counter the prevailing attitude that single-parent families, as compared to dual-parent families, are less able to rear healthy children?

In an interview with Jane E. Brody in the *New York Times* (June 23, 1991), Wallerstein discussed her review of several longitudinal studies on children of divorce that appeared in the May 1991 issue of the *Journal of the American Academy of Child and Adolescent Psychiatry*. After reading the research, she concluded that although many children "do manage to pull their lives together... for about half the children of divorce, the unhappy baggage of their parents' battles remain a lasting legacy." She also asserts that "we are allowing our children to bear the psychological, economic and moral brunt of divorce."

In the June 1991 issue of *Science*, P. Lindsay Chase-Lansdale and Andrew Cherlin caution against making hasty judgments. Their report is based on a sample of over 17,000 British children, age 7, and a follow-up study of

239 of these children whose parents had divorced within four years of the initial interview (the children were then age 11). They found that many of the adverse effects perceived in the children that were previously attributed to divorce actually were present before the divorce. Chase-Lansdale and Cherlin claim that strain caused by marital conflict before the divorce or other *unrelated* problems affecting the children at the time were apparently misinterpreted by other researchers as strictly the result of divorce.

One problem to consider is whether the alleviation of children's negative reactions to divorce is a societal problem or one that is better solved by the parents themselves. How should parents help their children successfully adapt to divorce?

SUGGESTED READINGS

T M. Cooney and P. Uhlenberg, "The Role of Divorce in Men's Relations With Their Adult Children After Midlife," *Journal of Marriage and the Family*, 52 (1990): 677–688.

R. E. Emery, *Marriage, Divorce, and Children's Adjustment* (Sage Publications, 1988).

E. M. Hetherington, "Coping With Family Transitions: Winners, Losers, and Survivors," *Child Development*, 60 (1989): 1–14.

E. M. Hetherington and J. Arasteh, eds., *The Impact of Divorce, Single Parenting and Stepparenting on Children* (Lawrence Erlbaum, 1988).

S. McLanahan and K. Booth, "Mother-Only Families: Problems, Prospects, and Politics," *Journal of Marriage and the Family*, 51 (1989): 557–580.

J. S. Wallerstein and S. Blakeslee, *Second Chances: Men, Women and Children a Decade After Divorce* (Ticknor & Fields, 1989).

S. A. Wolchik and P. Karoly, eds., *Children of Divorce: Empirical Perspectives on Divorce* (Gardner, 1988).

Internet: http://www.psych.med.umich.edu/web/aacap/factsfam/divorce.htm

Internet: http://www-leland.stanford.edu/~rmahony/Divorce.html

ISSUE 17

Do Fathers Have Legitimate Reasons for Refusing to Pay Child Support?

YES: Joyce A. Arditti, from "Child Support Noncompliance and Divorced Fathers: Rethinking the Role of Paternal Involvement," *Journal of Divorce and Remarriage* (vol. 14, nos. 3 and 4, 1991)

NO: Steven Waldman, from "Deadbeat Dads," *Newsweek* (May 4, 1992)

ISSUE SUMMARY

YES: Assistant professor Joyce A. Arditti asserts that there are legitimate reasons for some noncustodial fathers to refuse to provide financial support for their children after divorce.

NO: Journalist Steven Waldman argues that fathers should not abandon their financial responsibilities to their children following divorce, regardless of the kind of relationship that is maintained between them.

Twenty-five percent of all American families with children are single-parent families. Of those, 84 percent are headed by mothers and 16 percent are headed by fathers. Currently, there are 1.2 million single-father families; 75 percent result from divorce and the remaining 25 percent are comprised of single fathers who have never married or are widowed. Since 1925 the legal guideline used in custody decisions has been the "best interest of the child," but the norm has been for mothers to have sole custody: 88 percent of children continue to live with their mothers after divorce.

Increasing numbers of noncustodial fathers are being accused of abandoning their parental roles after divorce. On the average, such fathers pay child support for less than two years and then gradually become estranged from their children as their visits drop off. Should the father remarry, his relationship with his children suffers further. One of the hallmarks of absentee fatherhood is the dearth of time spent with biological children. The National Survey of Families and Households reveals that 25 percent of noncustodial fathers have direct contact with their children less than once per month, while 20 percent have not seen their children at all in the previous 12 months. Only 25 percent of noncustodial fathers see their children once a week.

It is not uncommon for single-mother families to suffer severe economic hardships, partly because fathers pay less than the agreed-upon amount of child support or pay no support at all. Recent legislation has been implemented to enforce more rigorous collection of child-support payments. The purpose of such legislation is to improve the quality of children's lives by increasing the money available for their care. Preliminary reports indicate that this strategy seems to be having limited success. Fathers who regularly pay child support have been found to maintain more frequent child visitation schedules. When fathers stay economically and socially connected, children adapt better to single-parent family status.

Some social commentators have expressed their dissatisfaction with "deadbeat" fathers in the form of outrage. In "The Teflon Father," *Ms.* (1990), for example, Letty Cottin Pogrebin writes,

> Millions of men are little more than sperm donors in their children's lives. They leave their children with mothers who are trapped in poverty and despair and cannot possibly provide for them adequately. These men are deserters. When a man deserts the army, he is court-martialed, stigmatized, despised. When a father deserts his own flesh and blood, all we do is (sometimes) track him down to pay the freight, but otherwise he's off the hook.

As men begin to come forward in their own defense, many describe situations that, for them, justify the nonpayment of child support. These justifications raise a number of questions: Does a conflictual relationship with an ex-wife justify a father's refusal to pay child support? If a father is not allowed to see his children on a regular basis or must bend to meet visitation terms he finds unsuitable, is he right to withdraw support payments? If a father loses his job, is it okay for him to pay less than the agreed-upon amount of child support? In other words, should paying child support be contingent upon situational events, used as a means of forcing changes in relationships between ex-spouses, or considered ammunition to force alteration in visitation agreements?

To date, family scientists have no consistent empirical documentation on the degree of emotional support that children of divorce need from their fathers nor are they sure what kind of fatherly involvement most affects children's well-being. However, they are beginning to understand the economic and educational consequences for children when fathers do not pay child support.

In the following selections, Joyce A. Arditti contends that there has been an overemphasis in the divorce literature on the economic consequences of fathers' failure to pay child support. She believes that more attention should be paid to the social, emotional, and interpersonal reasons fathers resist paying. She further argues that fathers suffer for withdrawing physically and emotionally from their children and that this makes an even stronger case for father involvement after divorce. Steven Waldman acknowledges that absentee fathers suffer emotionally and that some have seemingly compelling reasons for nonpayment. But he argues that none of these reasons justifies the abandonment of parental responsibilities.

YES

Joyce A. Arditti

CHILD SUPPORT NONCOMPLIANCE AND DIVORCED FATHERS: RETHINKING THE ROLE OF PATERNAL INVOLVEMENT

Concern about the divorce experience often revolves around the financial adequacy of custodial mothers and their children. Figures vary with regard to how many children actually receive child support, and as to what the financial situations of their custodial mothers and noncustodial fathers may be. Weitzman (1985) reports that 71% of custodial mothers experience a downward financial spiral after divorce while 43% of divorced fathers experience an improved financial situation. An investigation sponsored by the Office of Child Support Enforcement reports that of the 8.7 million single mothers living with children under the age of 21, 58% were awarded or had an agreement to receive child support payments and 46% were due payments in 1983. Of those due payments, one-half received the full amount due, one-quarter received partial payment, and one-quarter received no payments (U.S. Bureau of the Census, 1985). Another report indicated that in 1985, approximately half of the women with ordered support awards received the full payment (U.S. Bureau of the Census, 1986). Clearly, for many women following divorce, the high noncompliance rate contributes to an insecure and unstable financial situation (Buehler 1989).

The problem of child support noncompliance has become so serious in terms of its economic implications for custodial mothers and children that Congress has passed Child Support Enforcement Amendments which require states to institute programs to deduct support from fathers' paychecks and tax returns. The underlying argument for enforcement legislation is that lax child support enforcement is the root cause of fathers' nonpayment and that implementing stronger enforcement procedures is the only way to insure that men will fulfill their support obligations (Weitzman, 1988). This perspective, while receiving support among some researchers and policymakers, ignores underlying social, emotional, and interpersonal factors that may contribute to men's resistance to pay child support.

Chambers (1983), in contrast to Weitzman's perspective, believes that an absence of financial responsibility on the part of many divorced fathers is

From Joyce A. Arditti, "Child Support Noncompliance and Divorced Fathers: Rethinking the Role of Paternal Involvement," *Journal of Divorce and Remarriage*, vol. 14, nos. 3 and 4 (1991). Copyright © 1991 by The Haworth Press, Inc. All rights reserved. Reprinted by permission. For copies of the complete work, contact Marianne Arnold at The Haworth Document Delivery Service (Telephone 1-800-3-HAWORTH; 10 Alice Street, Binghamton, NY 13904). For other questions concerning rights and permissions, contact Wanda Latour at the above address.

rooted in the typically devitalized or distant relations between noncustodial fathers and their children, rather than in weak enforcement policies. He asserts that a sense of responsibility grows from a sense of attachment and that attachment is nurtured by quality interaction. Generally it is very difficult for noncustodial fathers to develop and sustain vital relationships with children and they begin to feel less and less a part of their children's lives. Subsequently, child support orders are often experienced as a form of "taxation without representation" for many divorced fathers (Chambers, 1983, p. 287).

In a similar vein, Haskins (1988) comments that the popular view of all noncustodial fathers as "brazen" and "unconcerned" is too simplistic. He found that in his sample of fathers only two reasons—unemployment and mother's failure to spend money on children—were cited as justification for not paying support (1988). In a study on single fathers, Grief (1985) explores the issue of child support noncompliance noting a number of reasons fathers give for not paying support (p. 124): (a) Harsh economic conditions and unemployment; (b) Fathers believe the judge has been biased toward the mother and has set an unreasonably high amount to be paid—especially when the ex-wife works and is making a decent salary; and (c) Fathers frequently claim they are not paying child support because their visitation rights have been withheld or made difficult to arrange.

In sum then, despite the wide citation of the number of children not receiving child support, not enough is known about the characteristics and conditions that might be related to fathers' child support payments. This gap in the literature can partially be attributed to an overemphasis on the financial or economic aspects of child support and a relative absence of psychosocial analysis....

The purpose of this discussion is to explore the issue of child support compliance within the context of the fathers' divorce experience by considering the broader issue of post-divorce paternal involvement. A more comprehensive explanation of why many noncustodial fathers fail to pay support may lie in a broader pattern of distancing and increasing noninvolvement.... Koch & Lowery (1984), summarizing the available research on noncustodial fathers, state that many fathers withdraw from their families physically, emotionally, and financially, often at considerable emotional cost to most men.

In considering explanations other than poor enforcement for many men's failure to pay child support, it is important to acknowledge evidence that a discrepancy may exist between mothers' reports of fathers' involvement and fathers' own report of their activities. Weitzman (1985) found that in her sample, the median report by fathers was that they saw their children weekly, whereas mothers reported those same fathers as seeing their children less than monthly. Another study by Goldsmith (1981) found that fathers reported significantly more involvement with their children than custodial mothers corroborated. This included the overall frequency of reported contact and paternal involvement with various activities. Some of the research suggests that child support payment may also be underestimated in some cases due to the heavy reliance on mothers' reports. Fathers tended to report paying more child support than mothers reported receiving. For example, 79% of the men surveyed in Tropf's (1980) study reported never missing one payment of support. Wright and Price (1986) also report a parallel discrepancy between ex-spouses' reports of child support payment. Seventy-two percent of the fathers they surveyed reported that they always paid their child support on time, while less than half of the mothers (41%) reported that they received their support on time.

The above discrepancies are important because nearly all the Census Bureau statistics on divorce and child support are based on interviews with mothers (Haskins et al., 1987, unpublished manuscript). Subsequently, most of the statistics used by researchers, policymakers, and the media may be inaccurate or at least reinforce a particularly dim picture of child support compliance and visitation patterns. It is possible that divorced fathers are more involved than previously believed based on the the heavy reliance on mothers' reports and the absence of information about divorced fathers' participation in parenting. . . .

VISITATION

Information regarding visitation may be the most important link to understanding the dynamics of child support compliance. It is relatively well known that fathers tend to decrease the frequency and duration of their visits over time (Furstenburg et al., 1983; Hetherington, Cox, & Cox, 1976; Wallerstein and Kelly, 1980). Moreover, contact with the noncustodial parent is crucial for children's psychological adjustment and emotional well-being (Hetherington et al., 1976; Wallerstein and Kelly, 1980; Emery, Hetherington, & Dilalla, 1984). What remains relatively unexplored is the relationship between visitation and children's economic well-being. . . . There is some evidence that suggests a link between frequent or satisfying visitation patterns and child support payment (Chambers, 1979; Furstenburg et al., 1983). The direction of influence is unclear—that is it is unknown as to whether fathers who support their children financially feel more obligated to attend to their "investment" or whether fathers who have more frequent contact with their children somehow are "reminded" to financially support them. Wallerstein and Huntington (1983) emphasize the importance of visitation with respect to child support compliance. . . . They found that over time, the link between visitation and child support payment becomes more profound. Furthermore, the frequency was discovered to be less important than the pattern and duration of each visit—child support was found to be highly correlated with weekend and overnight visits. However, it should be recognized that frequent or regular visitation may not necessarily reflect a loving or concerned father. It is possible that the impact of visitation on child support may be mitigated by the quality of the father-child relationship. Wallerstein and Huntington note that the significant link between a loving father-child relationship and good child support over the years was striking. Thus it may be that visitation—to the extent that it is associated with loving father-child relations—is related to good support.

COPARENTAL RELATIONSHIP

Much of the concern regarding noncustodial fathers' involvement centers on the quality of the relationship between former spouses and this has bearing on the issue of child support compliance.

Koch and Lowery (1984) suggest that the coparental relationship between ex-spouses is a key determinant in the level of overall postdivorce paternal involvement. Wright and Price (1986) offer some evidence supporting a direct link between good relations between ex-spouses and child support compliance. They examined the relation of attachment between former spouses, the quality of their coparental communication, and compliance with court-ordered payment of child support. Results suggested that divorced persons who continue to have some level of attachment to their former spouse and who view their current relationship with the ex-spouse as being of good quality, reflect a family pattern in which the father has a stronger desire to fulfill his responsibility to maintain financial support of his children even if he does not have custody.

... Other research points to the fact that coparental relations have an important role in determining visitation patterns and fathers' feelings of warmth for their children. ... In general, hostile relations between ex-spouses and little discussion regarding childrearing are negatively associated with father involvement and contact with children (Ahrons, 1983; Hetherington, Cox, & Cox, 1986; Lund, 1987). Furstenburg (1988) however, found that the quality of relations between former spouses had only a modest effect on the level of participation by the noncustodial parent. In fact, he attributes situational factors such as geographical distance between fathers' residence and children's residence as being more important in determining the level of postdivorce involvement between fathers and children.

It may be then that coparental relations (as mitigated by situational factors such as geographic distance) are important in two ways. First, fathers may directly associate payment with what they are feeling for their ex-spouses. For although it is "child support" it is paid to the mother —the former spouse—and negative feelings could arouse a resistance to pay that spouse and an inability to separate children's needs from personal animosity. Conversely, positive or cooperative sentiments would arouse no such hostility or resistance to pay a former spouse and perhaps serve as an incentive to continue to provide support. Second, coparental relations may be important to the extent they facilitate or restrict visitation....

CUSTODY

Another variable which may have significance in terms of child support compliance and to paternal involvement in general is legal custody status and subsequent satisfaction with that status. Although an increasing number of fathers are awarded joint-legal custody and a small number of fathers are awarded sole custody, in the overwhelming majority of cases custody of children is awarded to the mother (Buehler, 1989; Furstenburg, 1988; Grief, 1979). This may contribute to stressful postdivorce relationships and a lack of incentives for fathers to pay child support. Salkind (1983) notes a paradox with respect to modern expectations about fathering. There is a conflict between the encouragement and social pressure for fathers to participate fully in childrearing and yet the "denial" of equal parenting in the event of marital dissolution. He sees an arrangement that gives one parent (usually the mother) total control over visitation as placing the custodial parent in a position of control and power. This places the other parent (usually the father) in a position of powerlessness leading to stress and emotional withdrawal. Salkind emphasizes that it is important to remember that father absence for the child is also child absence for the father. Current custody practices tend to be insensitive to this notion of "child absence" and the emotional well-being of fathers—especially those fathers who were active and involved in parenting before the divorce. Salkind believes that if fathers are emotionally supported following divorce, it is more likely they will provide financial support.

There is some evidence that joint custody status can be positively and significantly related to overall paternal involvement (Bowman, 1983; Grief 1979; D'Andrea, 1983). Generally, joint custody is an arrangement whereby both parents are vested with equal legal authority for making important decisions pertaining to the welfare of their child(ren) and stipulates greater parity with regard to child care than sole custody. Sole custody restricts the noncustodial parent's legal right of child access to that visitation set out by the court (Hyde, 1984; Roman and Haddad, 1978). Overall, joint custody fathers tend to be more satisfied with their custody status than noncustodial/visitation fathers and more frequent contact with children is found to be associated with satisfaction of custody status (D'Andrea, 1983; Grief, 1979). Furthermore, joint custody fathers report greater perceptions of being close with and having greater influence on their children than visitation fathers (D'Andrea, 1983; Grief, 1979). However, it is important to recognize that when joint custody is entered into under duress, satisfaction levels may be even lower than for sole-custody families (Felner and Terre, 1987).

It seems then, that a different kind of psychological involvement may grow out of the opportunity to take care of or parent one's children rather than "visiting" them. Recall that Wallerstein and Huntington (1983) note the significance of the emotional quality of the father-child relationship in terms of contact and financial support. Greater psychological involvement stemming out of joint custody arrangements may facilitate emotional closeness between divorced fathers and their children and thus more frequent and compliant child support payments.

CONCLUSIONS AND POLICY IMPLICATIONS

It is clear that we need to learn more about the conditions and situational factors that may facilitate different facets of postdivorce paternal involvement. More research is needed which examines the divorce experience from the perspective of the father in order to better understand the dynamics of postdivorce paternal involvement and further explore the linkages between custody, the coparental relationship, visitation, and child support compliance....

It is possible that a more positive approach (and one that will be more welcomed on the part of divorced men) would be to legally facilitate father-child contact through more explicitly liberal visitation policies or varied custodial arrangements. There is evidence that suggests divorced men are generally unsatisfied with their visitation schedule, would like to see their children more frequently, and often believe that their visitation is interfered with by their ex-spouses (Haskins et al., 1987). If child support from fathers is in part contingent on the quality of the postdivorce relationship they have with their children, to advise anything other than a policy that facilitates father-child contact would be self-defeating and destructive to the postdivorce adjustment for all members of the family.

Joint custody may be an effective policy for insuring that child support payments are made. Although there is some controversy as to the appropriateness of this kind of arrangement and its impact on the psychological adjustment of children, there are several studies that seem to support the viability of joint custody awards.... For many families, joint custody is an arrangement that will facilitate the healthy development of children without sacrificing the integrity of the noncustodial parent. It also allows both parents to seek a fuller life outside of parenting because major childrearing responsibilities (including financial) would be shared.

... In many cases, the adversary system may promote or exacerbate conflict and hostility between parents.... Divorce mediation has emerged as the major alternative to either litigation or out-of-court negotiation between attorneys (Scott & Emery, 1987). In divorce mediation, divorcing parties meet with an impartial third party to identify, discuss, and hopefully settle the disputes that result from marital dissolution.... Divorce mediation reduces the adversarial nature of the divorce process, encourages cooperativeness, and promotes the subsequent exploration of options other than traditional custody and visitation arrangements. Bahr (1980) found that the use of divorce mediation as opposed to litigation led to more satisfaction with respect to custody arrangements, financial settlement and the decision to divorce in general.

... In terms of the private cost of mediation, the overall expense is not much different from the cost of litigation (Bahr, 1981b). However in terms of whether mediation is effective in reducing public costs, evidence does suggest that divorce mediation can successfully divert a large percentage of cases from the more expensive custody hearing. Furthermore, agreements are reached more quickly in mediation and mediated agreements tend to last longer (McIsaac, 1982). Fiscal analyses of several court-based programs project that mediation reduces costs (as a function of court time) by 10%–50% (Bahr, 1981a).

Facilitating and encouraging parental involvement on the part of divorced fathers may be an easier, more effective approach to insuring that children receive their child support than enforcement. Enforcement may actually have a negative effect in terms of further alienating fathers from their children. Perhaps the place of enforcement should be a last ditch effort for those divorced fathers who do not respond to other types of legislation. Of course, this kind of philosophy is in contrast to the underlying argument of universal enforcement whereby all noncustodial parents who are ordered to pay child support automatically have that amount of money deducted from their paycheck—similar to the Social-Security system. However, such a system, while perhaps benefiting those children whose fathers would not pay child support otherwise, overlooks those fathers who voluntarily comply and poses risks for individual privacy. Furthermore, universal enforcement does not address the problem of psychological disengagement over time of most divorced fathers from their children.

... Rather than simply focusing on financial responsibility, it is important to recognize that father involvement is multifaceted—financial (child support), physical (visitation), and emotional (feelings of closeness with children)—and that these different aspects of involvement are most likely interrelated. Policies and interventions promoting more liberal visitation rights, divorce mediation, and joint custody may be instrumental in fostering father involvement, represent viable alternatives to the majority of current postdivorce arrangements, and challenge the underlying philosophy of enforcement policy.

REFERENCES

Ahrons, C. (1983). Predictors of paternal involvement postdivorce: Mothers' & fathers' perceptions. *Journal of Divorce, 6,* 55–69.

Bahr, S. J. (1980). *Divorce Mediation: An evaluation of an alternative divorce policy.* Unpublished manuscript, University of Utah.

Bahr, S. J. (1981a). An evaluation of court mediation: A comparison in divorce cases with children. *Journal of Family Issues, 2,* 39–60.

Bahr, S. J. (1981b). Mediation is the answer. *Family Advocate,* 32–35.

Bowman, M. (1983). Parenting after divorce: A comparative study of mother custody and joint custody families. *Dissertation Abstracts International, 44,* 578A.

Buehler, C. (1989). Influential factors and equity issues in divorce settlements. *Family Relations, 38,* 76–82.

Chambers, D. (1979). *Making Fathers Pay: The enforcement of child support.* Chicago: University of Chicago Press.

Chambers, D. (1983). Child support in the twenty-first century. In J. Cassetty (Ed.), *The Parental Child-Support Obligation* (pp. 283–298). Lexington, MA: Lexington Books.

D'Andrea, Ann (1983). Joint custody as related to paternal involvement and paternal self-esteem. *Conciliation Courts Review, 21,* 81–87.

Emery, R., Hetherington, M., and Dilalla, L. (1984). Divorce, children, and social policy. In H. Stevenson and A. Siegal (Eds.), *Child Development Research and Social Policy* (pp. 189–266). Chicago: University of Chicago Press.

Felner, R. D., & Terre, Lisa (1987). Child custody dispositions and children's adaptation following divorce. In Lois Weithorn, (Ed.), *Psychology and Child Custody Determinations.* University of Nebraska Press: Lincoln.

Furstenburg, F. F., J. L. Peterson, C. W. Nord, and Zill, N. (1983). The life course of children of divorce: Marital disruption and parental contact. *American Sociological Review, 48,* 656–658.

Furstenburg, F. (1988). Marital disruptions, child custody, and visitation. In S. Kamerman & A. Kahn (Eds.), *Child Support: From Debt Collection to Social Policy* (pp. 277–305). Beverly Hills: Sage.

Goldsmith, Jean (1980). Relationships between former spouses: Descriptive findings. *Journal of Divorce, 4,* 1–20.

Grief, G. (1985). *Single Fathers.* Lexington, MA: Lexington Books.

Grief, Judith (1979). Fathers, children, and joint custody. *American Journal of Orthopsychiatry, 49,* 311–319.

Haskins, R. (1988). Child Support: A father's view. In S. Kamerman & A. Kahn (Eds.), *Child Support: From Debt Collection to Social Policy* (pp. 306–327). Beverly Hills: Sage.

Haskins, R., Richey, T., Wicker, F. (1987). *Paying and visiting: Child support enforcement and fathering from afar.* Unpublished Manuscript.

Hetherington, M., Cox, M., & Cox, R. (1976). Divorced Fathers. *The Family Coordinator, 25,* 417–428.

Hyde, L. (1984). Child custody in divorce. *Juvenile and Family Court Journal, 35*(1).

Koch, M. & Lowery, C. (1984). Visitation & the noncustodial father. *Journal of Divorce, 8,* 47–65.

Lund, M. (1987). The noncustodial father: Common challenges in parenting after divorce. In C. Lewis & M. O'Brien (Eds.), *Reassessing Fatherhood* (pp. 212–224). Beverly Hills: Sage.

McIsaac, H. (1982). Court-connected mediation. *Conciliation Courts Review, 21,* 49–56.

Roman, M., & Haddad, W. (1978). *The disposable parent.* New York: Holt, Rinehart and Winston.

Salkind, N. J. (1983). The father-child postdivorce relationship and child support. In J. Cassetty (Ed.), *The Parental Child-Support Obligation* (pp. 173–192). Lexington, MA: Lexington Books.

Scott, E. S. & Emery, R. E. (1987). Child custody dispute resolution: The adversarial system and divorce mediation. In Lois Weithorn (Ed.), *Psychology and Child Custody Determinations* (pp. 23–56). University of Nebraska Press: Lincoln.

Tropf, W. D. (1980). The nature of relationships divorced men maintain with their first families. (Doctoral Dissertation, University of Florida, 1980). *Dissertation Abstracts International, 42,* 875A.

U.S. Bureau of the Census (1985). Child Support & Alimony: 1983. *Current Population Reports, Special Studies, Series P. 23, No. 141.* Washington, D.C.: U.S. Government Printing Office.

U.S. Bureau of the Census (1986). Child support and alimony; 1985. *Current Population Reports, Series P. 23, No. 152.* Washington D.C.: U.S. Government Printing Office.

Wallerstein, J. S. & Huntington, D. S. (1983). Bread and roses: Nonfinancial issues related to fathers' economic support of their children following divorce. In J. Cassetty (Ed.), *The Parental Child-Support Obligation* (pp. 135–155). Lexington, MA: Lexington Books.

Wallerstein, J. S. & Kelly, J. (1980). *Surviving the breakup: How children and parents cope with divorce.* New York: Basic Books.

Weitzman, L. (1985). *The divorce revolution: The Unexpected Social and Economic Consequences for Women and Children in America,* New York: Free Press.

Weitzman, L. (1988). Child support myths and reality. In S. Kamerman & A. Kahn (Eds.) *Child Support: From Debt Collection to Social Policy* (pp. 251–276). Beverly Hills: Sage.

Wright, David, & Price, Sharon (1986). Court-ordered child support payment: The effect of the former spouse relationship on compliance. *Journal of Marriage & The Family, 48,* 869–874.

NO

Steven Waldman

DEADBEAT DADS

John Lock goes to court in Chicago next week to explain why he owes back child support, but his ex-wife Esther isn't expecting much. They have, after all, been through more than 100 court hearings about child support and their divorce over the past 19 years. And, according to the state of Illinois, he still owes more than $160,000 for his four children. She's feeling needy now because she lost her job as a social worker 17 months ago, but she remembers more desperate times, like February 1977. "Our electricity was being turned off," she recalls. "We were lighting the house with candles. We were on what we called the 'white diet'—a lot of rice and cereal. No medical coverage, no dental." Her ex-husband, then a dentist, was living in the affluent suburb of Highland Park with his new family. "I knew he didn't want the kids so I figured I'd use it as a scare tactic," says Esther. She gave their two teenage sons overnight packs and dropped them off in front of their father's house in subzero weather. He called the police. "He told the Highland Park police that there were two boys outside trespassing," she says. "I'm not proud of it, but I was desperate."

John Lock admits he called the police but says he had to because one of his sons was on the verge of "kicking the door down." He concedes he didn't pay the $1,100 monthly child support for nine years, and admits he fled to Costa Rica for three years because he was "physically, emotionally, financially devastated." But he says he had paid regularly prior to 1977, owes "significantly less" than the state claims and thinks that his ex-wife and the state of Illinois are obsessed with trying to put him in jail. He no longer practices dentistry and works part time delivering flowers in Ida, Mich. "The kids were my world," he wrote in a recent letter to NEWSWEEK. "I did my best to give them a nice life." In an interview, he added, "This has gone on to a point where there's no hope." His oldest son, Byron, now 32, agrees. He says he still can't comprehend his father's behavior. "We were his *children*, " he says. "Why would he want to hurt us? That's what was so confusing about the whole deal—why would a father turn his back on a child?"

In battles like these, nobody ever comes out a winner. Fierce struggles over child support pit parent against parent and inevitably spray the children with emotional shrapnel. Increasingly, the private family traumas are spilling into public view. Posters of most-wanted deadbeat dads began peppering subways and bulletin boards in Massachusetts this month, and police quickly arrested five of the fathers. They also hauled in Frederick Grimaldi, who owes $22,144 and was working in Florida as, of all things, a deputy sheriff, according to Massachusetts officials. Grimaldi has pleaded not guilty to charges of criminal nonpayment, and his lawyer says he owes just $19,000, some of which accumulated while Grimaldi was unemployed. Next month an association of state child-support enforcement agencies will release its second annual national Wanted list, which will include a Louisiana attorney who owes $123,000 and a Tennessee man who owes his quadriplegic daughter $21,500. These small steps reflect a growing awareness on the part of public officials of just how potent an issue this has become. Consultants for former Louisiana governor Buddy Roemer were surprised to discover that in focus groups during the 1991 campaign, middle-class voters spontaneously mentioned child support as one of their most important concerns. Bill Clinton, in campaign speeches, regularly urges tougher enforcement.

It's easy to understand why: of the 5 million women who are supposed to receive child support, only half reported receiving full payment, according to a 1990 U.S. Census Bureau study. One quarter of the women got partial payment, and one quarter got nothing. An additional 2.7 million women said they wanted support but were never able to obtain an award. Deadbeatedness cuts across income groups: college graduates are about as likely to have a negligent ex-spouse or ex-boyfriend as high-school grads. It even spans gender lines. Fifteen percent

of custodial parents are now men, and mothers in those cases have an equally dismal record of supporting their children. The consequences of nonpayment are staggering. On average, the family income of the mother retaining custody drops 23 percent after divorce or separation—a disparity that could be wiped out for many families if full child-support payments were made. Families headed by a mother alone are six times as likely to be poor as those with two parents.

These dreary statistics have recently led social-policy thinkers of many ideological stripes to the same conclusion: child support is key both to fighting poverty and to sustaining middle-class families. The government's role in child support has already undergone a little-noticed revolution. In 1984, Congress passed one of the most sweeping pieces of social legislation in decades, requiring local governments to help any custodial parent—not just the poor—to collect child support. Since then, nonwelfare mothers have flooded government offices asking for help in collecting money. These agencies have garnished paychecks, seized tax returns and devised innovative solutions to enforcement problems. Despite the increased vigor, though, the government seems to be running in place. In 1990, state agencies reported they were collecting money in only 17.9 percent of the 12 million cases they were then handling.

But while society moves to confront the child-support problem, one question has received relatively little attention: who are these deadbeat dads, and why would they refuse to support the human beings they helped create? It's hard to look at such behavior as anything but simple irresponsibility. But a closer look reveals a group of men with a wide range of emotionally complex motives.

* * *

For a father, child support often becomes not a helping hand to a child, but a lethal weapon in the battle against his ex-wife. Kenneth Marcelles of Schiller Park, Ill., fell about $6,000 behind on paying support to the two children he had with Donna Caliendo. Partly because of that, she says, the family went on welfare and their daughter had to get eyeglasses donated by the Lions Club. She wasn't shy about telling the kids the source of the deprivation. "In the summer," she says, "I'd say, 'If your father would send money maybe we could go to Kiddieland or buy a new bathing suit'." Marcelles offers several explanations for not paying. "I don't know what she does with the money," he says. "I had a chance meeting with her in the grocery store and my daughter was wearing some raggedy-looking Levi jacket and [Donna's] got a brand new coat on." Caliendo denies that claim, and in any event, such complaints have a logical flaw: if the kids suffer from poverty, cutting off child support will only make it worse. It's when Marcelles talks about his fractured relationship with his children that his explanations strike a deeper chord. "When you get into a situation where you don't see them and they blatantly slam the door in your face, it becomes an emotional thing," he says. "I know that [withholding payment] was not quite the thing to do, but... I reacted in an emotional way." He says that he's paid more than $17,000 over the years, mostly fell behind due to financial hardship and now has child support deducted from his paycheck regularly. But finally, he adds a simple comment about his ex-wife that cuts to the heart of many child-support battles. Withholding money, he says, "was the only way I could hurt her."

How does a father come to see withholding child support in terms of what it does to the former spouse instead of what it does to the children? Several studies have shown that fathers who retain close contact with their children are more likely to pay child support. Some fathers' rights groups cite these data in arguing that most child-support problems stem from mothers cutting off access to the children. That definitely does happen. But fathers are quite capable of becoming alienated from children without help from mothers. "Fathers tend to see their relationships with their children as being mediated by the wife," says Frank Furstenberg, a sociologist at the University of Pennsylvania and author of "Divided Families." "[It's] a package deal. When the relationship is damaged, it severs the direct connection between fathers and their children." In a survey conducted in central Pennsylvania, close to half the children from broken families had not even seen their fathers in the previous year. Many nonpaying dads ask, in essence, "What's in it for me?" —a statement that is strikingly crass on one level but quite poignant on another. If they have grown distant from their children, fathers come to view child support like making payments on a car they no longer own. Child support becomes a debt competing with all others. "My bills, my car payments were taking all that money up," said Walter Forde, an unemployed father in Riverdale, Md., explaining in court in January why he had fallen $8,500 behind. Joel Worshtil, the hearing officer at the Prince Georges County circuit court, responded: "If the child had been living with you, you would have found a way to find the $500 to clothe the child." "What if your wife and kids just leave you?" Forde asked. "I can't speak to the equity of the relationship," Worshtil replied, with sympathy. "But we certainly know the child wasn't at fault."

Clearly, the failure to pay often sprouts from the initial rupture in the relationship. Fathers who felt humiliated by the breakup may be particularly eager to cut ties with the family. Deanna Willis moved her family to Eugene, Ore., in 1979 while her husband, Drew Itschner, was in the Marines in Okinawa, because she believed he was neglecting them. Itschner paid hardly any child support over the next 12 years and didn't visit his children at all. He says that the state of Oregon treated him unfairly and that the money wouldn't have gone to the kids anyway because she was "going out partying." But Willis has another explanation. "I think in the beginning he was just hurt because I left him," Willis says. "He didn't want to go back into it and bring back up that hurt." Despite his long absence, Itschner carried his kids' pictures in his wallet for more than a decade and on a few occasions drove by their house or to a nearby park and watched them from a distance. His daughter Jewel, who has for several years kept Itschner's service medals in a box by her night stand, recently started a correspondence with him. During a recent interview he pulled out photographs of the girls at the ages of 4 and 2. "You look at those pictures," Itschner says. His eyes well up. "And you look at these," he points to pictures of them at 13 and 15. "How much have they gone through? How much have I missed? How much have they missed from not being with me? All three of us have lost out on the deal, and now we're trying to get it back."

*　*　*

In truth, some men never really develop any relationship with their children, so not paying child support doesn't arouse guilty feelings. Roger Hollenbeck of Des Plaines, Ill., met Rose Brown at a pig roast in Louisville, Ky., in 1980. He describes the relationship as a brief fling (she says they lived together seven months) and was furious to learn she was pregnant because she had told him that a medical condition made that impossible. He left town a few months later and over the next 10 years missed $21,000 in payments. Hollenbeck's explanation for why he didn't pay: he didn't realize he owed any child support. (This seems unlikely, since the IRS in 1985 intercepted his tax refund for nonpayment of child support.) Under threat of a jail sentence, Hollenbeck recently paid $10,000 of back support and spoke with his son. " 'Do you hate my mother?' " the boy asked, according to Hollenbeck. "I said, 'No. We were friends, and I moved away'." But asked later what kind of relationship he expects he will have with his son, Hollenbeck says, "absolutely nothing. I know that sounds cold to say, but facts are facts."

Some fathers make so little money that their child-support payments feel like an enormous burden. Since payments are usually based on a percentage of parental income, however, even wealthy fathers can feel the pinch. Washington, D.C., lawyer Grier Raclin currently pays $4,150 per month to his ex-wife Victoria Reggie, a well-paid Washington lawyer who is about to marry Sen. Edward M. Kennedy. Despite their lucrative jobs, the parents regularly bickered over child support, according to correspondence filed in court. Raclin tried to get reimbursed for camping gear he had bought for a trip with his son. "I absolutely refuse," Reggie replied in October 1990. "I have already paid $100 for Cub Scouts—an activity for which you said you would be responsible—and I will not pay for the gear you decided you need to take Curran camping... If you try to deduct anything from the support payments you are contractually obligated to pay, I will not hesitate to take you to court for contempt." Last Friday, Raclin asked the court to eliminate his child-support payments because both of their financial situations have changed and he says he's spending, roughly, equal time with his son....

* * *

Knowing why absent parents don't want to pay child support does not, of course, excuse their behavior. It also leaves an essential question unanswered: how do they get away with not paying? Ultimately, many parents do not pay because no one makes them. A parent who is having trouble collecting child support has two main choices. She can hire a private lawyer who will try to bring the husband into court. But any real conflict will quickly push the legal fees into the thousands of dollars, outstripping the amount of support the custodial parent is seeking. Or, the mother can turn to the local government for free—and enter a surreal world where social workers juggle 1,000 cases at a time, a prosecutor might handle 100 cases a week and fathers evade pursuit for years by merely moving a few miles away across state lines.

... Knowing who the father is doesn't mean knowing where he is, how much he earns or how to collect from him. Roughly one third of all child-support cases involve parents living in different states—and women in such cases were twice as likely to get nothing as those with the father nearby, according to a 1990 General Accounting Office study.

* * *

... Despite the many examples of governmental foul-ups, the system works much better than it did 10 years ago. Although the average support award is just $57.59 per week, most courts have increased payment levels because Congress in 1984 required states to write specific child-support guidelines. As the issue has become politically hot, it has even seeped into electoral politics, in sometimes troubling ways. A fathers'-rights group in Las Vegas is running a slate of candidates in the elections for family-court judges, backing only those who, the group thinks, will lean more toward fathers in custody and support cases.

Reforming child-support policy may prevent a few families from entering into the war zone inhabited by people like John Chappell of Port St. Lucie, Fla., and his ex-wife Linda Place of Springfield, Va. She says he owes his three children more than $20,000 in child support and reimbursement of medical expenses. Eleven-year-old Matthew spends weeks at a time in a hospital with a serious immune disorder; Place has so far been unable to afford specialized treatment at Duke University. Chappell used to earn $26,000 a year as a medical-bill collector, but he was, until last Friday, unemployed. Place believes he was intentionally not working to avoid paying the $540 a month and medical expenses. "There's nothing *wrong* with him that he could not maintain a job," says Place, who works 32 hours a week as a nurse and often sleeps in a cot by Matthew's bed. "He's removed himself from the situation so it's not real anymore. He doesn't go to the hospital every day and see Matthew with IVs and needles."

Chappell complains bitterly that his ex-wife is pursuing him out of "raw hate" and turning the children against him. He says his new job in a convenience store will enable him to pay more. "To me, this is a battle between her and me—not the kids," he says. He's right that the parents are the combatants, but he shouldn't delude himself about the names of the casualties. Matthew is growing up thinking that his debilitating illness might be better treated if only his father would pay more in child support. Chappell's oldest son, Chris, speaks in more emotional terms. "Not getting stuff hurts," says 14-year-old Chris, "but thinking that Dad doesn't care enough to support you—that really hurts. I don't think I'm ever going to forgive him. It's just too hard." Chris visited his father in Florida just last summer, and Chappell brought him on a special afternoon outing—to court. There, Chris got to watch the judge chastise his father for failure to pay child support, put him in handcuffs and lead him off to jail.

POSTSCRIPT

Do Fathers Have Legitimate Reasons for Refusing to Pay Child Support?

The personal reflections of the parents and children in Waldman's selection on "deadbeat dads" are poignant. Waldman raises a number of questions: How can fathers abandon their children? Don't fathers realize that in punishing their ex-wives they are also inflicting pain on their children? Aren't fathers aware that their actions have lifelong economic and emotional consequences for children? Don't they understand that children find it difficult to forgive such behavior?

Noncustodial fathers voice a multitude of motives for their behavior, but Waldman asks, Should these reasons excuse their negligent actions? He describes the complex and overloaded government-operated system for collecting from fathers who evade support payments. He points out that hiring a private lawyer and bringing the father to court is time-consuming and costly, both economically and psychologically. Children who are forced to endure these procedures may also be further traumatized.

Arditti makes a plea for additional research from the father's perspective. She maintains that most studies on fathers after divorce are based on data provided by mothers and are likely to be biased against fathers. She believes that fathers would provide greater financial support for their children if they had more say in visitation arrangements, were allowed joint custody of their children, and had better relationships with their former spouses.

Arditti argues against government enforcement of child-support payments because she believes that such enforcement is unfair to those fathers who voluntarily comply with court rulings. To her, enforcement is a threat to individual privacy. A better method of encouraging fathers to pay child support, says Arditti, would be to facilitate and encourage fathers' involvement in parenting responsibilities through the process of divorce mediation.

What do you think? Is there ample evidence to support the contention that a primary reason for the poverty of many mother-headed families is the nonsupport of divorced fathers? Are there legitimate reasons for fathers to withhold child support, and if so, for how long? Because most divorced mothers and their children count on support money for daily living expenses, how do you suggest they make up the difference? Should more government resources be invested in tracking down nonpaying fathers, or are there other ways of convincing fathers of the importance of their involvement—financial and otherwise—to their children's overall well-being?

SUGGESTED READINGS

S. Braver, P. Fitzpatrick, and R. Bay, "Noncustodial Parent's Report of Child Support Payments," *Family Relations*, 40 (1991): 180–185.

V. R. Fuchs and D. M. Reklis, "America's Children: Economic Perspectives and Policy Options," *Science*, 255 (1992): 41–46.

J. M. Healy, J. E. Malley, and A. J. Stewart, "Children and Their Fathers After Parental Separation," *American Journal of Orthopsychiatry*, 60 (1990): 531–543.

S. McLanahan and K. Booth, "Mother-Only Families: Problems, Prospects, and Politics," *Journal of Marriage and the Family*, 51 (1989): 557–580.

D. R. Meyer and S. Garasky, "Custodial Fathers: Myths, Realities, and Child Support Policy," *Journal of Marriage and the Family*, 55 (1993): 73–89.

K. Rettig, D. H. Christensen, and C. M. Dahl, "Impact of Child Support Guidelines on the Economic Well-Being of Children," *Family Relations*, 40 (1991): 167–175.

J. A. Seltzer, "Legal Custody Arrangements and Children's Economic Welfare," *American Journal of Sociology*, 96 (1991): 895–929.

J. A. Seltzer, "Relationships Between Fathers and Children Who Live Apart: The Father's Role After Separation," *Journal of Marriage and the Family*, 53 (1991): 79–101.

Internet: `http://www.parentsplace.com/dialog/get/custody/html`

CONTRIBUTORS
TO THIS VOLUME

EDITORS

GLORIA W. BIRD is an associate professor of family studies in the Department of Family and Child Development at Virginia Polytechnic Institute and State University in Blacksburg, Virginia. An active member of the National Council on Family Relations and the International Society for the Study of Personal Relationships, her work has appeared in such journals as *Family Relations, Journal of Marriage and the Family,* and *Journal of Social and Personal Relationships.* She received a B.S. and an M.S. from Kansas State University and a Ph.D. in family and consumer environmental studies from Oklahoma State University. She is coauthor, with Keith Melville, of *Families and Intimate Relationships* (McGraw-Hill, 1994), a text on family studies.

MICHAEL J. SPORAKOWSKI is a professor of family studies and family therapy and interim head of the Department of Family and Child Development at Virginia Polytechnic Institute and State University in Blacksburg, Virginia, where he has been on the faculty since 1970. He is also the 1996–1997 president of the National Council on Family Relations. A life member of the American Association for Marriage and Family Therapy, he also maintains memberships in several other professional organizations, including the American Psychological Association and the National Council on Family Relations. A licensed professional counselor, he holds certification as a family life educator through the National Council on Family Relations. He received a B.S. and an M.Ed. from Pennsylvania State University and a Ph.D. in the Interdivisional Program in Marriage and Family Living from Florida State University.

STAFF

David Dean   List Manager
David Brackley   Developmental Editor
Tammy Ward   Administrative Assistant
Brenda S. Filley   Production Manager
Libra Ann Cusack   Typesetting Supervisor
Juliana Arbo   Typesetter
Diane Barker   Proofreader
Lara Johnson   Graphics
Richard Tietjen   Systems Manager

AUTHORS

ALAN C. ACOCK is a professor in and chair of the Department of Human Development and Family Sciences at Oregon State University in Corvallis, Oregon. He is coauthor, with David H. Demo, of *Family Diversity and Well-Being* (Sage Publications, 1994).

JOYCE A. ARDITTI is an assistant professor in the Department of Family and Child Development at the Virginia Polytechnic Institute and State University in Blacksburg, Virginia.

DAVID BLANKENHORN is chair of the National Fatherhood Initiative and president of the Institute of American Values.

ROBERT BLY is a leader of workshops on men's issues and the author of *Iron John: A Book About Men.*

ARMIN A. BROTT is a freelance writer and lecturer who focuses mainly on parenting and fatherhood. He is the author of *The New Father: A Dad's Guide to the First Three Years* (Abbeville Press, 1997). He also writes regularly for the *Washington Post*, the *Knight-Ridder*, and dozens of other national publications.

P. LINDSAY CHASE-LANSDALE is an assistant professor in the Irving B. Harris Graduate School of Public Policy Studies at the University of Chicago in Chicago, Illinois, and a fellow of developmental and family research in the university's Chapin Hall Center for Children. She is also chair of the Society for Research on Adolescence Committee on Social Policy.

MARY CRAWFORD is a professor of psychology and women's studies at West Chester University of Pennsylvania.

DAVID H. DEMO is a professor at the University of Missouri. His research focuses on the influences of family structure and family relations on parents and children. He is coauthor, with Alan C. Acock, of *Family Diversity and Well-Being* (Sage Publications, 1994).

RUSSELL P. DOBASH is a professor in the Department of Social Policy and Social Work at the University of Manchester in Great Britain. He has coauthored with R. Emerson Dobash *Women, Violence and Social Change* (Routledge, 1992).

BARBARA EHRENREICH is vice chair of the Democratic Socialists of America. Her articles have been featured in several publications, including *The New York Times Magazine, The New Republic, Esquire,* and the *Wall Street Journal.* She has authored or coauthored numerous books, including *The Snarling Citizen* (Farrar, Straus & Giroux, 1995).

DEIRDRE ENGLISH is a freelance writer and lecturer. A feminist and a former executive editor of *Mother Jones* magazine, she has collaborated with Barbara Ehrenreich on several books, including *For Her Own Good: One Hundred Fifty Years of the Experts' Advice to Women* (Doubleday, 1978).

PAULA L. ETTELBRICK is legislative counsel for the Empire State Pride Agenda in New York City, where she directs statewide lobbying, legislative, and policy efforts on behalf of the New York State lesbian and gay community. She is former director of public policy for the National Center for Lesbian Rights.

NAOMI FARBER is a member of the faculty of the Doctoral Program at Bryn Mawr College in Bryn Mawr, Pennsylvania. She specializes in adolescent sexuality, pregnancy, and parenthood.

WARREN FARRELL is a leader of workshops on men's issues and the author of many articles on men's lives. He is also the author of *The Liberated Man* (Berkley, 1993).

JEFF GRABMEIER is managing editor of research news at Ohio State Unviersity in Columbus, Ohio.

SUSAN JOHNSON is an associate professor of clinical psychology and psychiatry at Ottawa University and director of the Marital and Family Clinic at Ottawa Civic Hospital. She is coeditor of *Emotion in Marriage and Marital Therapy* (Bruner Mazel, 1994).

LAWRENCE A. KURDEK is a psychologist at Wright State University in Dayton, Ohio.

HARA ESTROFF MARANO is the editor of *Psychology Today*.

BRENT A. McBRIDE is director of the Child Development Laboratory and assistant professor of human development and family studies at the University of Illinois at Urbana/Champaign.

MONICA B. MORRIS is an independent sociologist and a former professor of sociology at California State University, Los Angeles, whose current research focuses on love relationships in later life. She is the author of *Last-Chance Children: Growing Up With Older Parents* (Columbia University Press, 1988).

RICHARD JOHN NEUHAUS has been director of the Rockford Institute Center on Religion and Society since 1984. He is editor in chief of *This Word* and editor of *Forum Letter* and *The Religion and Society Report*. His publications include *America*

Against Itself: Moral Vision and the Public Order (University of Notre Dame Press, 1992).

KATHLEEN O'NEIL is vice president of Roper Starch Worldwide, Inc., in New York City, which conducts public opinion polling, political polling, and market research for governments, businesses, and nonprofit organizations worldwide. She was the project director of the Roper Organization's 1990 Virginia Slims Opinion Poll.

GERALDINE K. PIORKOWSKI is a clinical associate professor of psychology and director of the Counseling Center at the University of Illinois at Chicago. She is the author of *Too Close for Comfort* (Plenum Press, 1994).

JOSEPH H. PLECK is a member of the American Psychological Association and the National Council on Family Relations. He has also held the position of Luce Professor of Families, Change, and Society at Wheaton College in Norton, Massachusetts. His publications include *Working Wives, Working Husbands* (Sage Publications, 1985).

DAVID POPENOE is a professor of sociology and an associate dean for the social sciences at Rutgers–The State University in New Brunswick, New Jersey. He is the author of *Disturbing the Nest* (Aldine de Gruyter, 1988).

KATIE ROIPHE is the author of *The Morning After: Sex, Fear and Feminism on Campus* (Little, Brown, 1993).

DENISE SCHIPANI is a New York City–based writer and editor. She writes frequently about children's health and development and about family and women's issues. She received a B.A. in English from Vassar College.

FELICE N. SCHWARTZ (1925–1996) was president and founder of Catalyst, a nonprofit research and advisory organization that works with corporations to foster the career and leadership development of women. She retired in 1993.

ARLENE S. SKOLNICK is a research psychologist for the Institute of Human Development at the University of California, Berkeley.

JUNE STEPHENSON received a B.A. in economics and a Ph.D. in psychology from Stanford University in Stanford, California. In addition to numerous articles, her publications include *Humanity's Search for the Meaning of Life*, 3rd ed. (Diemer, Smith, 1990).

HAYA STIER is a sociologist at the University of Haifa, Israel.

ANDREW SULLIVAN is a former editor of *The New Republic* magazine. He received an M.A. in public administration and a Ph.D. in political science from Harvard University in 1986 and 1990, respectively. His articles have been published in the *New York Times*, the *Wall Street Journal*, *Esquire*, *The Public Interest*, and the *Times* of London.

DEBORAH TANNEN is a professor of sociolinguistics at Georgetown University in Washington, D.C. She is the author of *You Just Don't Understand: Women and Men in Conversation.*

MARTA TIENDA is a sociologist at the University of Chicago in Chicago, Illinois.

BICKLEY TOWNSEND, a former vice president of the Roper Organization in New York City, currently works for the American Statistical Association. She is also a member of the Caucus for Women in Statistics.

MARIS A. VINOVSKIS is a professor in and chair of the Department of History and a research scientist in the Institute for Social Research at the University of Michigan in Ann Arbor, Michigan. His publications include *Religion, Family, and the Life Course* (University of Michigan Press, 1992), coauthored with Gerald F. Moran.

STEVEN WALDMAN is a reporter for the Washington, D.C., bureau of *Newsweek.*

JUDITH S. WALLERSTEIN is an internationally recognized authority on the effects of divorce on children and their parents. She has been executive director of the Center for the Family in Transition and a senior lecturer in the School of Social Welfare at the University of California, Berkeley. She is coauthor, with Sandra Blakeslee, of *Second Chances* (Ticknor & Fields, 1989).

ROBIN WARSHAW is a freelance journalist based in Pennsauken, New Jersey, and the author of *I Never Called It Rape: The Ms. Report on Recognizing, Fighting, and Surviving Date and Acquaintance Rape* (Harper & Row, 1988).

BARBARA DAFOE WHITEHEAD is a research associate at the Institute for American Values in New York City, a nonpartisan research organization devoted to issues of family and civic well-being.

INDEX